Donated by
Ian Thomson

THE EVOLUTION OF MONETARY POLICY STRATEGIES IN EUROPE

FINANCIAL AND MONETARY POLICY STUDIES

Volume 34

The titles published in this series are listed at the end of this volume.

The Evolution of Monetary Policy Strategies in Europe

by

Aerdt C.F.J. Houben

De Nederlandsche Bank,
Amsterdam, The Netherlands

KLUWER ACADEMIC PUBLISHERS
BOSTON / DORDRECHT / LONDON

A C.I.P. Catalogue record for this book is available from the Library of Congress.

ISBN 0-7923-7869-5

Published by Kluwer Academic Publishers,
P.O. Box 17, 3300 AA Dordrecht, The Netherlands.

Sold and distributed in North, Central and South America
by Kluwer Academic Publishers,
101 Philip Drive, Norwell, MA 02061, U.S.A.

In all other countries, sold and distributed
by Kluwer Academic Publishers,
P.O. Box 322, 3300 AH Dordrecht, The Netherlands.

Printed on acid-free paper

Printed in the Netherlands.

CONTENTS

Tables

Charts

Foreword

Europe has a rich monetary history. Until recently, its many central banks assigned divergent priorities and pursued policy objectives via different routes. As a result, Europe's past provides fertile ground for those seeking practical guidance to the art of central banking. The importance of this past gained a new dimension with the prospect of Economic and Monetary Union in 1999, as the participating countries were faced with the challenge of bridging their differences and forging a common monetary policy strategy that would apply throughout the new currency area. At the same time, these countries sought to build forth on the theretofore most successful central bank strategies, thereby maintaining a certain degree of policy continuity.

Monetary policy strategy is at the core of central banking. This strategy determines how incoming information on economic developments is translated into monetary policy actions and how these policy actions are communicated to the public at large. In other words, the strategy fulfils the dual role of imposing a structure on the internal policy-making process and of providing a vehicle for the external communication of this process. The design of a monetary policy strategy thus brings together key elements – such as consistency and transparency – that together determine the effectiveness and credibility of monetary policy.

That is what this book is all about. It spells out the intricacies of alternative monetary policy strategies, analyses how these strategies have been implemented in Europe in the recent past, and draws lessons from the continent's happy, and at times less happy, monetary policy experiences. Knowledge of these experiences is indeed crucial to an adequate understanding of our monetary past. But it is also essential for full insight into the current monetary policy strategy of the euro area, as this strategy is deeply rooted in Europe's separate monetary traditions. This book is therefore of interest not only to monetary economists and economic historians in general, but also specifically to those seeking insight into the policy design of the European Central Bank. In a sense this is like one of the basic elements of driving a car: make sure you have a rear view mirror and look into it every so often.

Willem F. Duisenberg
President of the European Central Bank

Acknowledgements

Fresh from university, I joined the Dutch central bank and was quickly imbued with the virtues of exchange rate targeting. It was the late 1980s and Europe was entering its golden age of exchange rate stability. Just as this experience was taking root, I switched to the IMF staff to work on adjustment programs. This impressed upon me the benefits of credit targeting and the potency of the exchange rate as a policy instrument, rather than as an immobile policy anchor. Subsequently, I returned to Europe and became involved in the discussions between the EU national central banks on monetary strategy alternatives for the prospective European Central Bank. As the focus narrowed on the options of money targeting and direct inflation targeting, my remaining convictions became footloose. The logical way out of this conundrum was to try to write down why it made sense to do different things in different times under different circumstances. Besides this, the different national viewpoints on monetary policy strategy had made me highly curious about the experiences that lay behind the convictions of others.

Numerous people have contributed to the writing of this book. Right from the start, Lex Hoogduin gave expert and to-the-point advice. He also brought on board Jakob De Haan, who enlightened me with his vast knowledge of monetary and institutional economics. Together, they provided a complementary balance of practical and academic insights. Age Bakker and Nout Wellink prodded me to take this project up, Henk Brouwer fuelled my enthusiasm along the way, and my colleagues in the front office of the Monetary and Economic Affairs Department, and especially Peter van Bergeijk and Coen Voormeulen, helped create scope to bring the book to a close. Economists in this Department, and particularly those in its Monetary Analysis Division, provided a dependable source of knowledge and inspiration. Jan-Marc Berk and Simon Kuipers perused their way through the final draft and pointed out rough edges in need of smoothing. In a practical sense, Martin Admiraal, René Bierdrager, Cees De Boer and Kasper van Veen kindly assisted with the statistical hurdles, Anna Geerts expeditiously compiled the Subject Index, and Diana Deira, Jacqueline Hanssens, Wilke van de Kamp and Rodetta Noordwijk gave patient secretarial assistance.

The Tables in the Appendices summarising the evolution of monetary strategies in the individual European countries are the factual backbone of this book. These Tables have been compiled on the basis of a myriad of sources and, without exception, have been reviewed and extensively commented on by the respective national central banks. In this context I thank, without implication, Peter Charleton, Heinz Herrmann, Karolina

Holmberg, Pierre Jaillet, Hugo Frey Jensen, Ana Leal, David Maude, Peter Mooslechner, Vincent Périlleux, Penti Pikkarainen, Daniele Terlizzese, José Viñals, and Hercules Voridis. Most of them were congenial colleagues during the preparatory work on monetary policy strategy under the aegis of the European Monetary Institute and are now much the same in the Monetary Policy Committee of the European System of Central Banks. In compiling these appendices, excellent assistance was provided by Arjan Brouwer, who processed the countless nuances on the evolution of central bank strategies in the member states with diligence and good humour.

Last but first, I owe an immeasurable debt of gratitude to Els without whose support this book, and so much else, would never have come about. And to my daughters Zoë, Nadine and Yannicke who happily often persisted in providing distraction. To the extent you feel you have seen too little of me in the recent past, I will now do my best to let you know what it's like when you see too much of me.

1 INTRODUCTION

1.1 Background

The essence of monetary policy, it seems, used to be much more straightforward. During the Bretton Woods era of pegged exchange rates, as well as under the previous Gold Standard, monetary policy had a clear-cut, predetermined nominal anchor. The main challenge for monetary policy-makers lay in using available margins for domestic purposes, while at the same time ensuring that the prime objectives of exchange rate stability and gold convertibility would not be unduly strained. Given restrictions on capital mobility and other sources of financial markets segmentation, these margins, although diminishing, were significant. This all changed when the system of pegged exchange rates collapsed. By lifting the external constraint that had previously dominated domestic policy choices, the definite end of the Bretton Woods regime in March 1973 ushered in a new era. National authorities were faced with the quintessential question of what compass to choose for their monetary policy-making and how to maximise the stabilising effects of this choice, including through interaction with the public. The choice was particularly pertinent in Europe, where different and varying monetary strategies have attempted to do justice to the interwoven nature of the economies and the common goal of more effective regional integration, on the one hand, and to the diverse views on the functioning of the economy and policy objectives, on the other.

This study analyses the evolution of monetary policy strategies in Europe. It is written primarily from a policy-maker's perspective. The central question posed is: what are the considerations that determine the monetary strategy choice and how have these considerations featured in, and been influenced by, recent European monetary history? In contrast with the voluminous recent literature on monetary strategies, written from a forward-looking angle and focused on the challenges facing monetary policy in the new-born euro area, this study is backward-looking and seeks to establish what we have learnt (or should have learnt) and how we learnt it. Put differently, this book maps out the diverse monetary traditions that now flow together in Frankfurt under the aegis of the European System of Central Banks and thereby provides insight into a prime influence on the system's decision-making – that is, the countries' past experiences.

1.2 What is a monetary policy strategy?

Monetary policy strategy is a wide-ranging concept that seems to mean different things to different people. In this study, monetary policy strategy is considered to consist of the specification of the intended monetary reaction function to economic developments as well as the communication of this reaction function and of actual policy decisions to the outside world. As regards the first of these two elements, monetary policy strategy comprises the key factors that determine the monetary reaction function, including the end objective that is set for the central bank, the (intermediate) policy target that is pursued towards that end objective, and the institutional framework that is adopted for monetary policy decision-making. As regards the second element, monetary policy strategy encompasses all aspects related to the external presentation of this reaction function, in particular the precommitment to policy targets and the transparency of the policy-making process, which together aim to condition public expectations on the desired monetary policy outcome.

The principal elements of monetary policy strategy are depicted in Chart 1. As will be clear, many of the key components of this strategy relate directly to the monetary transmission mechanism. For instance, the central question of the monetary strategy choice is on which element of the transmission mechanism policy-makers should focus. This depends on how the operational and intermediate targets are impacted by adjustments in the monetary policy instruments and, in turn, how changes in these targets affect the final objectives of monetary policy. In this respect, there is a well-known trade-off between controllability, which is stronger at the early stages of the transmission process, and relevance for the final objectives, which is greater towards the end of the transmission process. This explains why the monetary policy strategy choice also depends on the exogenous influences affecting the economy and the transmission process, as these influences determine the strength of the central bank's control over its policy target and the tightness of the relationship between the policy target and the final objectives.

The structural characteristics of the economy have a direct bearing on the choice of monetary policy strategy, since these characteristics determine the extent to which exogenous disturbances are absorbed before they impact the targets and objectives of monetary policy. In a similar vein, the institutional structure and credibility of the central bank are also essential to the optimal strategic thrust of monetary policy. This is because these elements determine whether monetary policy can be firmly directed at its targets and objectives and whether – thanks to consistent expectations – the behaviour of economic agents conforms with these targets and objectives. In this context, the monetary authority may actively seek to steer expectations by clearly communicating its views and by enhancing transparency about how monetary policy is conducted towards its objectives. Such transparency will also shed light on the extent to which policy success or failure is attributable to factors that are under central bank control. In this way, transparency has an implicit impact on the reputation of the monetary authority that complements the explicit accountability incorporated in the institutional structure of the central bank.

Chart 1: Principal elements of monetary policy strategy and transmission mechanism

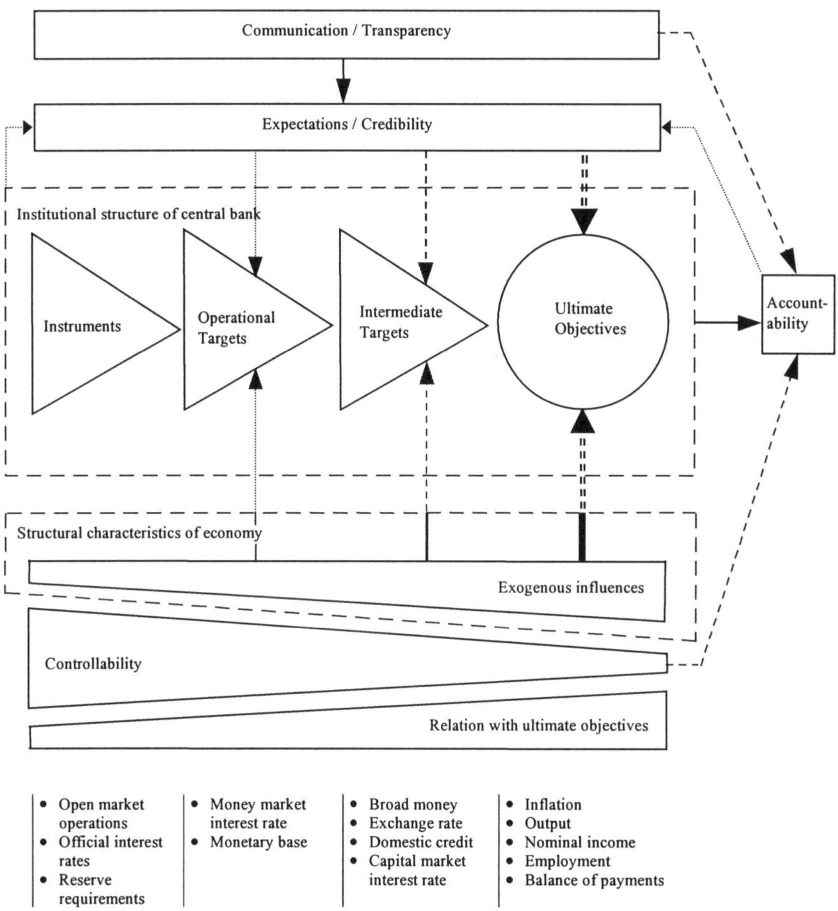

This study does not elaborate on technical operational aspects of monetary policy which, although linked to the strategy choice, are not part of its defining features. Monetary policy strategy, it is argued, boils down

to 'doing the right thing', whereas the operational techniques of monetary policy are a question of 'doing the thing right'. This approach is supported by empirical evidence indicating that monetary instruments and operational procedures are of no apparent relevance to the monetary strategy choice.[1]

1.3 Outline

To provide structure, this book is split into two parts. First, the monetary strategy choice is assessed from a conceptual and normative viewpoint. This part serves to highlight the complexity, ambiguity and uncertainty inherent in the monetary strategy choice and spells out the unavoidable trade-offs dominating the various targeting options for monetary policy. Subsequently, the second part reviews the practical experience with alternative monetary policy strategies in Europe. This part analyses how these strategies have actually evolved, seeking to explain why the individual European countries have adopted such different and varying strategies in the past. It culminates in a discussion of the monetary policy strategy adopted by the European System of Central Banks at the outset of Economic and Monetary Union (EMU) in 1999, highlighting the evident links between this strategy and the earlier experiences of the individual European countries.

The first part is organised as follows. In *Chapter 2*, the main theoretical considerations underlying the monetary strategy choice are set out. A qualitative analysis is presented of how the superior monetary strategy is determined by the susceptibility to different types of economic disturbances (specified in terms of type, origin, degree of symmetry, and duration), the structural characteristics of the economy (such as differences in wage and price flexibility, labour mobility, openness, capital restrictions, production diversity, budgetary stabilisers, and financial structure), the prioritisation of economic objectives (stabilising output versus stabilising prices), and political economy considerations (establishing credibility and incentives for financial discipline, including through transparency and accountability). This creates a broad conceptual framework for the assessment of monetary strategy alternatives, with building blocks provided by the literature on optimal monetary targets, alternative exchange regimes, optimal currency areas, time consistency and central bank independence.

Using this conceptual framework, *Chapter 3* discusses the trade-offs for the main monetary policy strategies. Following a discussion of what targeting actually means and why it makes sense to do so, the benefits and drawbacks of seven targeting options for monetary policy are successively appraised: money targeting, domestic credit targeting, interest rate targeting, exchange rate pegging, nominal income targeting, direct inflation targeting, and adoption of a combined approach. These appraisals focus on elements such as the controllability of the target alternatives, their stabilising properties relative to the end objectives of monetary policy and, specifically, their provision of a nominal anchor to economic developments. Aspects such as the visibility and communicability of the different targeting options are likewise assessed, as well as practical issues such as the timeliness, frequency and reliability of necessary data. The evaluations of the strategic alternatives also take into account political economy considerations such as the contribution that specific targets can make to precommitting monetary policy and enhancing the autonomy of the central bank.

The theoretical and normative analysis in the first part of this book provides the background for a review of the driving factors behind the actual monetary strategy preferences in the second part – the core of the study. The review covers each of the 15 current member states of the EU. While a number of these countries only joined the Union relatively recently, their monetary authorities have participated from the start in the discussions on the design of the European Central Bank's monetary strategy. These countries' experiences have thus also fed directly into the monetary policy strategy selected for EMU. Moreover, the monetary history of these 'latecomers' is generally inexorably intertwined with that of the earlier member states. This is the case in for instance Austria, where monetary policy was tightly anchored on Germany long before it became a member of the Union, and in Sweden where history seems to have contained similar elements of parallelism, as illustrated by its membership of the European snake arrangement for over four years in the 1970s and its unilateral exchange rate ECU-peg in the early 1990s.

Following a succinct discussion of the relevant historical setting in *Chapter 4*, the survey of practical central banking takes 1975 as a point of departure. This is the first year after the demise of the Bretton Woods system that a new coherent monetary strategy was introduced in Europe: the adoption of a money supply target by Germany. The study covers the quarter of a century until 1999, thus ending with the European Central Bank, in which the different monetary track records of Europe come together. Within this time frame, the experiences of the different countries are dissected, in broad chronological order, along the lines of the three principal strategies pursued: money targeting (*Chapter 5*), exchange rate targeting (*Chapter 6*) and inflation targeting (*Chapter 7*). At a general level, the rise of each strategy is discussed in terms of the motives that prompted its adoption in individual countries. Hereafter, the targeting experiences are placed in a comparative historical perspective, with the aim of bringing out the common elements and, especially, the common learning curve. At a more technical level, money and inflation oriented strategies are analysed in terms of the different choices underlying the diversity of the targeting frameworks. In particular, why have countries preferred to target a broad rather than a narrow money measure, or a headline rather than a core inflation measure? What considerations have driven countries to adopt a ceiling rather than a range or point target? Why has a specific time horizon been selected? To what extent has the strategy been underpinned by changes in the institutional setting or external communication? Since exchange rate targeting has generally been moulded according to the requirements of a common framework, the experiences under this strategy are appraised from the vantage point of both the regional system and the individual countries. For each of these different strategies, a subsection spells out the lessons that can be drawn from the European experiences.

Finally, *Chapter 8* discusses the monetary policy strategy adopted by the nascent Eurosystem, relating this choice to the specific circumstances at the start of EMU and to the diverse previous experiences of the EU member states. In this latter respect, the strategy choice powerfully illustrates the considerable progress that has been made in European monetary thinking over the past quarter of a century. This chapter further evaluates the Eurosystem's strategy on the basis of selected key principles and an international comparison. Moreover, it places the monetary policy strategy in the broader context of macroeconomic policy setting within the euro area. While the generally high speed of monetary strategy changes in Europe suggests this is a risky exercise, the book ends with a tentative look at the future of the Eurosystem's strategy.

The *Appendices* to this book provide a tabular summary, for each of the current European Union members, of the pre-announced monetary policy targets and outcomes for every year since 1975 (unofficial targets are presented in italics). To the extent practical, this overview includes detailed information on the nature and precise timing of these targets. Besides perhaps evoking nostalgia for the days in which all of these European countries still had their own monetary policy targets – and the liberty to deviate from these targets on their own accord – this overview may serve as a useful reference work in its own right.

NOTES

[1] Using a case study method for six major industrial countries, Bernanke and Mishkin (1992) find the outcomes of monetary policy to be independent of the choice of instruments and operating procedures. Similarly, in a specific survey of central bank adjustments following the adoption of inflation targets, Almeida and Goodhart (1998) do not establish a significant shift in operational behaviour. More broadly, in a review of monetary policy in 21 OECD countries, Swank and Van Velden (1997) find no clear relationship between a central bank's monetary strategy, on the one hand, and its instruments and operating procedures, on the other. Nonetheless, there may be a link to the monetary strategy choice,

for instance in the case of exchange rate targeting countries that adapt their instruments to those in the anchor country – as occurred in several European countries in the 1980s and 1990s – in order to be able to signal and to adjust the policy stance in unison. Similarly, money targeting may be supported by reserve requirements that are not remunerated at market rates; however, such reserve requirements are not a prerequisite for this strategy.

PART ONE

CONCEPTUAL ISSUES

2 KEY CONSIDERATIONS GOVERNING THE CHOICE OF MONETARY POLICY STRATEGY

2.1 Introduction

At an abstract level, the choice of monetary policy strategy is determined first by the relationships underlying the economy and second by the desired reaction function of the central bank to economic developments. The former is a function of the structural characteristics of the economy and of the nature of disturbances to which the economy is likely to be subjected. The latter depends on the authorities' prioritisation of economic objectives in the face of different transitory disturbances. And the interrelation between the two is driven by political economy variables, which *inter alia* determine the credibility of the authorities' monetary policy commitments. This chapter elaborates on these general considerations determining the monetary strategy choice, drawing on the large body of related theoretical literature. The objective is to provide a normative backdrop against which to evaluate the development of European monetary strategies in practice.

2.2 The nature of shocks

Against the background of increasing evidence that the global system of stable exchange rates would not hold together, the early 1970s spawned a literature on the criteria for assessing an optimal monetary policy target and for choosing between alternative monetary policy regimes. Following a seminal article by Poole (1970), the initial focus was on the choice between a price (that is, an interest or exchange rate) or quantity (money supply) target to guide monetary policy setting.[1] The contribution of this analysis has not so much been to shed light on the effects of certain monetary policy actions under differing circumstances, but rather to identify the economic consequences of pursuing a specific policy target – in current terminology to determine key advantages and disadvantages of adopting a specific monetary policy strategy. In line with the original framework and in order to maintain clarity of exposition, this section concentrates on the two opposites in monetary policy targeting – money and exchange rate rules – thereby leaving the characteristics of other strategies, and of different specifications within a given strategy type, to subsequent sections.

2.2.1 Monetary and expenditure shocks

The crux of the initial analysis, which has lost none of its relevance, is that the superior monetary target depends on the nature of shocks that affect the economy. The standard hypothesis runs as follows. To the extent that shocks are primarily of a monetary nature, such as disturbances to money demand, an interest or exchange rate target will better insulate the economy. With monetary instruments aimed at an interest or exchange rate target, the money supply becomes endogenous and adjusts to the shock. More specifically, the change in money demand is reflected in a change in the domestic sources of money supply or, to the extent it is absorbed through the balance of payments, in a different level of international reserves. The shock is thus fully accommodated, leaving both real output and the price level unaffected. By contrast, if monetary policy is centred on the money supply, a monetary shock elicits a policy reaction to keep money growth in line with the predetermined target for money expansion. This involves a change in interest rates, thereby negatively impacting the stability of both output growth and prices.

If, on the other hand, the economy is primarily exposed to real disturbances, in particular expenditure shocks, a money target will be more effective in dampening price and output growth fluctuations. In this case, disturbances in expenditure influence money demand and, given a fixed money supply target, prompt a change in interest rates. For instance, under a money supply rule a positive domestic demand impulse necessitates a tightening of interest rate policy. This dampens the expenditure pressure, thus partly offsetting the impact of the initial shock on the real economy and prices. Part of the compensating mechanism may also lie in an accompanying exchange rate appreciation, which adjusts the level of external spending on domestic goods and domestic spending on external goods. By comparison, under an interest rate or exchange rate rule, the expenditure shock does not elicit a compensating interest rate rise, but prompts an increased money supply, thereby magnifying the original fluctuation in output and prices.

This analytical framework has been considerably broadened.[2] As in the standard analysis, these extensions aim to identify the preferred policy target under different economic circumstances. In these analyses, the magnitude of the differences between the target choices importantly reflects the prior assumptions, in particular regarding the interest rate elasticities underlying money demand as well as investment and savings. This underscores the essentially empirical character of the monetary target choice. But these are only differences in degree. Under normal circumstances (e.g., barring full wage indexation and binding capital restrictions) the standard framework does allow normative conclusions to be drawn.[3] This is shown graphically in the context of a straightforward IS/LM framework in Chart 2. The income consequences of adhering to a money target (thus keeping the LM curve unchanged) in the face of an adverse expenditure shock (shifting the IS schedule towards the origin) are much smaller when money demand is relatively interest inelastic (i.e., BA < CA). But in both these cases the outcome is better than if an interest rate rule (r*) were to be pursued (when the income loss would amount to DA).

Chart 2: Impact of adverse expenditure shock under different money demand elasticities

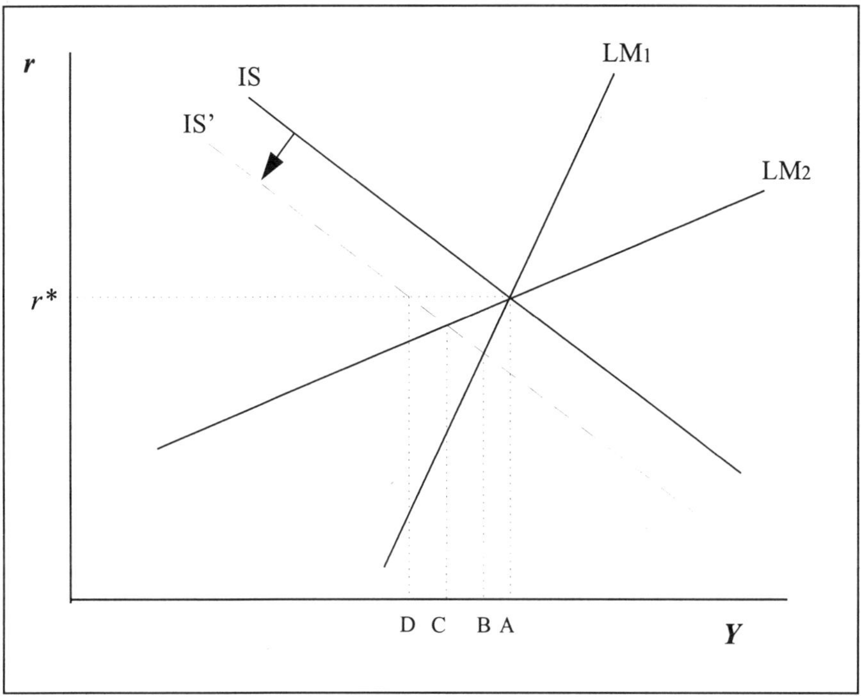

2.2.2 Supply side and external shocks

One extension is to look not only at shocks stemming from the demand (expenditure) side, but also at those originating in the supply side, such as abrupt productivity changes. The preferred policy rule is now ambiguous. Given the divergent impact of supply changes on output and inflation – and thus the uncertain impact of maintaining a fixed money target on interest rates – the superior policy regime is not clear-cut. At this point, it is necessary to specify the definition of optimality in the face of random disturbances.

Should the focus be on maximising the stability of real output or the stability of prices, or some weighted average of both?[4] For money and real expenditure shocks the outcome is straightforward: in the case of the former, the stability of both output and prices is better preserved under an interest rate or exchange rate rule, and in the case of the latter the same is true under a money rule. With supply side shocks, however, there is an opposite impact on the two objectives: a negative supply shock will depress output (suggesting monetary policy should be loosened) and fuel inflation (suggesting monetary policy should be tightened). The superior regime thus depends on the magnitude of the price effect in relation to the output effect (if the former is larger, a monetary target would be more constraining than an interest rate target, and vice versa), on the prioritisation of economic objectives (in particular regarding the stability of output against that of inflation), and on the extent to which other instruments (such as fiscal and incomes policy) can be activated to pursue these objectives.[5]

Another extension of the standard framework is to investigate how each regime insulates the domestic economy from disturbances originating abroad. One clear-cut example, emphasised in the monetarist school and highlighted in the debate on flexible versus fixed exchange rates, considers the optimal policy regime when nominal shocks occur abroad.[6] In particular, if the foreign price level fluctuates, domestic output and prices can best be stabilised by adopting a money rule, as this provides scope to implement offsetting nominal exchange rate adjustments. More generally, a flexible, money oriented approach is arguably likely to be superior in stabilising output under most external shocks since it allows the exchange rate to be used as an instrument to add or withdraw foreign demand.[7] When viewed from a more dynamic perspective, however, it needs to be recognised that the effect of an external shock will also depend on the foreign policy reaction to this shock. Indeed, a foreign disturbance is usually not limited to one aggregate – money demand, expenditure or supply – but has an interrelated impact on foreign demand, foreign prices, and possibly foreign interest rates. As these variables may have opposing influences on the domestic economy, nothing conclusive can be said about the superior regime under foreign shocks.[8]

2.2.3 The symmetry and duration of shocks

There is, however, one case in which the assumption that a flexible exchange rate system is superior under foreign shocks will clearly not hold: when shocks are symmetric (i.e., not country specific). As highlighted in the optimal currency area literature, if two countries suffer the same shock *and* their economic structures are not dissimilar, policies could be adjusted while their exchange rate may be best left unchanged. More specifically, with a symmetric money shock, both the exchange rate and the interest rate in the two countries may best remain unchanged. In the case of a symmetric demand shock, the exchange rate may also be kept stable, although interest rates would need to be adjusted commensurately in both countries. And in the case of a symmetric supply shock, the exchange rate between the two countries may also be kept fixed, even if the preferable interest rate path (in both countries) is ambiguous.

The framework can be elaborated further still, by distinguishing between temporary and permanent expenditure shocks, and by taking time lags in the transmission of policy changes into account. Here, the conclusion is that the more likely a disturbance is temporary (i.e., self-reversing) and the longer the time lag before a policy change is felt in the real economy, the stronger the case – within limits – to accommodate the shock (i.e., to keep the interest rate and the exchange rate unchanged). Conversely, the more likely a shock is permanent and the quicker the pass-through of policy changes, the stronger the case for an interest/exchange rate adjustment.

2.2.4 Conclusions

These stylised cases (summarised in Table 1) serve to illustrate that, at a conceptual level, the choice of monetary policy target determines the extent to which an economy is insulated from different types of shocks. Money targets are preferable to the extent an economy is primarily affected by shocks in domestic demand or external prices, interest/exchange rate targets are superior when shocks are mostly monetary or temporary in nature, and an exchange rate target may by itself be appropriate when shocks are generally symmetric. With supply side shocks and all other types of external shocks, the outcome is *a priori* ambiguous.

At a more practical level, however, it is clear that each economy is regularly – and at times simultaneously – affected by shocks stemming from the monetary, demand, and supply side of the economy, as well as from external sources, and that it is difficult to distinguish between these shocks at the moment they occur. Indeed, the preceding analysis suggests that the accurate identification of disturbances requires the following information: (i) does the shock stem from the monetary, expenditure or supply side of the economy; (ii) is the shock of domestic or foreign origin; (iii) is the shock symmetric; (iv) is the shock temporary or permanent? It is clear that distilling this information is no mean task.

Table 1: Optimal monetary policy target under different types of shocks

Type of shock	***Monetary policy target and objective***			
	Price target (Interest rate or Exchange rate)		***Quantity target*** (Money supply)	
	Stability of Output	Stability of Prices	Stability of Output	Stability of Prices
Domestic monetary shock	+	+	-	-
Domestic real demand shock	-	-	+	+
Domestic real supply shock	? + / -	? - / +	? - / +	? + / -
External nominal shock	-	-	+	+
External symmetric shock	(outcome according to same domestic shock type, but with stable exchange rate)			
Other external shock	?	?	?	?
Temporary shock	+	+	-	-

Legend: with given type of shock, pursuing stated monetary policy target enhances (+) respectively undermines (–) fulfilment of stated policy objective; a question mark (?) indicates that the superior monetary policy target is unclear.

Of course, the nature, origin, symmetry and duration of any shock may often be evident *ex post*. But delaying policy reactions until this information is available will generally be costly. A further complication is that in choosing a monetary policy target, it is not the nature of past or present shocks that counts, but that of future ones. This makes the selection of a monetary strategy on the basis of the proneness to certain shocks even more precarious. In addition, it makes clear that uncertainty is intrinsic to the choice of strategic setting for monetary policy.

Overall, there would seem to be a case to take broad account of the likely characteristics of future disturbances when tailoring the monetary strategy, but also to preclude an overly active (or 'fine-tuning') approach to the strategic framework, since this framework should not in itself become a contributing factor to economic uncertainty and public confusion. At the same time, however, this uncertainty stresses the importance of viewing the monetary strategy choice as an ongoing process and of providing scope for a strategy switch in the event of large unanticipated disturbances.

2.3 Structural characteristics of the economy

The preferred monetary strategy depends not only on the type of potential shocks, but also on the structural characteristics of the economy, as these determine the ability to absorb such shocks. Foremost among the structural aspects that have a bearing on the monetary strategy choice are: the extent of wage rigidity (especially the presence of indexation practices) and labour mobility, the openness of the economy, the degree of capital mobility, the diversity of the economic production base, the prevalence of budgetary stabilisers, and the differences between countries' financial structures.

2.3.1 Wage flexibility

Clearly, the degree of wage flexibility is an important consideration in the choice of monetary strategy, particularly regarding the degree of exchange rate flexibility. At one extreme, if there is no real wage flexibility, the exchange regime choice is of no consequence. In this case, wages are fully indexed and any nominal exchange rate adjustment is fully offset by opposite nominal wage changes, such that real wages remain unaffected. Under these circumstances, the exchange rate would be a totally ineffective instrument to stabilise output in reaction to economic disturbances.[9] Given the practical inefficiencies inherent in exchange rate changes and concurrent commensurate wage adjustments, the case for a flexible exchange regime would be unclear and another policy instrument would need to be used to address any emerging imbalance. At the other extreme, if there is full real wage flexibility, both monetary regimes – other things being equal – function equally well and the need for exchange rate flexibility is similarly unclear.

The difference between the exchange regimes arises when the degree of real wage flexibility is limited by nominal wage rigidity, such as when downward nominal wage adjustments are resisted and when nominal wage agreements cover a longer time span. In this case, a downward real wage correction through exchange rate depreciation circumvents the nominal rigidity and involves lower output costs than when the exchange rate is fixed (and when the adjustment would require a period of deflation). In short, downward nominal wage rigidity increases the attractiveness of a flexible exchange regime in stabilising output, but this appeal disappears to the extent nominal wages are indexed.

At a deeper level, it may be argued that the factor of importance is not the degree of nominal wage rigidity *per se*, but the underlying institutional framework of labour markets. In a centralised system of wage bargaining, labour unions may take appropriate account of the inflationary effects of their wage demands when supply shocks occur. Similarly, in a very decentralised system, wage claims may adequately reflect firm-specific output prospects and thus rapidly adjust to supply shocks. Problems may then arise with half-way systems: labour unions representing only a small share of the employed will experience a free rider incentive to disregard the marginal impact of their decision on inflation and to postpone the adjustment of their wages to adverse supply shocks.[10] Put differently, since the price elasticity of demand will be higher for an individual firm than for a whole industry, wage setting at the industry level will tend to be more demanding. Thus, an intermediate system with union bargaining at the industry level could lead to an equilibrium with a relatively higher average wage claim and a greater need for offsetting exchange rate adjustment. In this sense, the preferred exchange regime may in part become a function of the labour market system.

Two comments can be made to put this conclusion in perspective. First, it is doubtful whether countries with an intermediate system will find themselves in a stable equilibrium, since wage demands are bound to vary between the different small scale labour unions. Any union with above average wage claims (these would not be fully compensated by exchange rate adjustment) would experience a loss of competitiveness, thus eventually bleakening employment prospects for its members. Second, although the trade-off with equity objectives may pose limitations, adequate wage flexibility is desirable on grounds of efficiency. By implication, priorities may be skewed if the exchange regime is adjusted to the structure of labour institutions, and not vice versa. In this regard, it seems the decision on monetary strategy – and thus on exchange regime – should be made first, without attaching undue weight to the organisational structure of labour. Subsequently, if unions place too much emphasis on improving real wages and too little on the welfare loss implied by higher inflation and lower employment, this may be expected to elicit changes towards a more centralised or a more decentralised wage bargaining structure, thereby making the inadequate labour structure a transitory problem.[11]

2.3.2 Labour mobility

The arguments on nominal wage flexibility apply in broadly the same manner for labour mobility. This is the point originally highlighted by Mundell (1961) in his pathbreaking article: the lower the labour mobility, the greater the need for exchange rate changes to promote adjustment in the face of economic disturbances. It is no small irony that while Mundell's optimal currency area hypothesis has been put to the test primarily in the context of introducing exchange rate fixity between the culturally and linguistically diverse countries of Europe, he initially argued his case on the basis of the immobility of labour and of the need for exchange rate flexibility *within* Canada. In this context it may also be argued that labour mobility is a function of the degree of economic uncertainty facing an individual: the higher the uncertainty about prospective income abroad, the lower the labour mobility. But this does not provide an unambiguous preference for a certain exchange regime or monetary target: the outcome depends on the relative stability of prospective income (which, in turn, depends on the types of shocks affecting the economies), but also, perhaps, on the stability of the exchange rate development itself (to the extent the individual may look forward to reconverting part of his or her foreign earnings into national currency).[12]

When viewed from a broader perspective, however, labour mobility cannot be seen as a panacea against adverse shocks – particularly not labour mobility in a cross-border context such as that prevailing in Europe. If labour market adjustments were to take place on a significant scale through cross-border movements, this could lead to massive international transfers of human capital and related asset stocks, and could exacerbate differences in national welfare.[13] More practically, recent studies have confirmed the relative immobility of the European labour force, including the lack of a significant improvement in the degree of European labour market integration in recent decades.[14] In itself this strengthens the case against strategies of exchange rate targeting. But, if output and unemployment fluctuations are to be minimised in the face of country-specific disturbances, a relatively immobile labour force will also place a larger adjustment burden on other mechanisms such as the flexibility of real wages and budgetary policy. To the extent these mechanisms provide adequate compensatory resilience, labour immobility may well be compatible with exchange rate fixity.

2.3.3 Budgetary stabilisation

Indeed, another instrument providing insulation in the face of economic disturbances, and thus affecting the monetary strategy choice, is the budget.[15] In particular, insofar as the levying of taxes and the provision of income transfers soften the impact of both expansionary and deflationary impulses, the budgetary instrument acts as a shock-absorber. As a result, budgetary policy may mitigate one of the main costs of a fixed exchange regime – the loss of the monetary instrument for stabilisation purposes in the event of asymmetric shocks. And this stabilising role need not require discretionary policy-making, as long as automatic stabilisers in budgets are allowed to do their work.

The stabilising properties of fiscal flows will be strongest in the case of a supranational budget. Conceptually, when countries experience different and varying shocks but form part of a common budgetary framework, the common budgetary framework acts as a stabiliser, since funds will be transferred from countries beneficially to countries adversely affected. In absence of supranational budgetary transfers, national budgets can take on a similar stabilising role, as opposite changes in national budgetary positions can smoothen differences in economic developments. However, to the extent that Ricardian equivalence prevails, stabilisation at the national level may not be as effective.[16]

Specifically, if a rational private sector anticipates changes in future tax payments on the basis of developments in the public debt, any adjustment in net national budgetary outlays for stabilisation purposes will lead to offsetting changes in private sector expenditures. This offset will be larger when fiscal stabilisation takes place at the national than at the supranational level, since in the former case the private sector will anticipate having to shoulder all rather than just part of the increased debt build-up. At the same time, since differing cycles across countries will tend to compensate each other, supranational budgetary stabilisation will generally involve less changes in future tax liabilities – and hence less Ricardian effects – than national budgetary stabilisation. Furthermore, with respect to active budgetary stabilisation, the effectiveness of measures at the national level may also be smaller on account of the mobility of the tax base, as this may limit the extent to which taxes can be raised above levels in other countries to repay debts incurred during a cyclical downturn.

From a practical perspective, however, Europe's continuous quest for greater exchange rate stability has clearly not been complemented by increasing supranational budgetary integration nor, in a substantive way, by greater stabilisation at the national level.[17] As regards the former, the EEC's Structural and Regional funds, although substantial, have been targeted at reducing differences in the *levels* of development, and not at limiting differences in the stability of output growth. Thus, international fiscal transfers have not become a significant instrument to smooth out economic disturbances. As regards national fiscal policies, during the past quarter century the use of the budget as a stabilising tool has also been limited in practice, mainly for two reasons. First, countries initially took an overly activist attitude to fiscal stabilisation. Owing to difficulties in finding the correct timing for actions and in reversing discretionary measures once private demand picked up, these policies all too often proved to be pro-cyclical and generally led to sharp rises in government debt.[18] Second, and ensuing from the latter development, the need to consolidate underlying fiscal positions has subsequently constrained countries in their ability to implement a countercyclical budgetary policy. As a result of these factors, the issue of the budgetary instrument as a stabilisation instrument, whether international or national, seems to have only influenced the monetary strategy choice of the European countries in a negatory sense: in general it does not appear to have offered much of an alternative to the use of the exchange (interest) rate instrument.

However, in 1991, with the adoption of the Maastricht Treaty on European Union and of its well-defined budgetary criteria, there was a shift to a common rules-based approach aimed at avoiding excessive budgetary imbalances that burden monetary policy. Moreover, after the EMS crises of 1992-93 had underscored the importance of cushioning cyclical divergences amongst countries pursuing a mutually aligned monetary policy, budgetary stabilisation was explicitly incorporated into the institutional design of EMU. This occurred in the context of the Stability and Growth Pact finalised at the European Summit in Amsterdam in June 1997. According to the Pact, member states are expressly committed to strive for budgets that are in balance (or in surplus) across the cycle, such that automatic stabilisers can be fully accommodated during any normal conjunctural downturn.

2.3.4 Openness

Another structural characteristic with a bearing on the superior monetary regime is the degree of openness of an economy. This factor influences the monetary strategy choice in several ways. To start with, the more open the economy (that is, the larger the share of the traded goods sector), the greater the potential cost savings from a reduction in the frequency of exchange rate adjustments – this is the efficiency argument. Moreover, with openness, the exchange rate can become the single most important factor determining relative prices in the economy and exchange rate stability tends to be a prerequisite for domestic price stability. In addition, when monetary policy targets the exchange rate, greater openness facilitates the accommodation of monetary shocks through the balance of payments. There are, however, also considerations that argue against exchange rate fixity. For example, greater openness increases the vulnerability to external shocks, thereby possibly increasing the need for exchange rate adjustment. Furthermore, other things being equal, openness increases the effectiveness of the exchange rate instrument in stabilising output when domestic demand or external disturbances occur. This latter principle assumes, however, that domestic wages and prices are not closely linked to exchange rate movements, which may not be the case in a very open economy. To the extent that wages and prices are actually influenced by developments in the foreign exchange market, the effectiveness of the exchange rate instrument will be commensurately smaller.

As a result of these partly opposing considerations, the influence of the degree of openness on the monetary strategy choice is to some degree ambiguous.[19] However, the majority view is that, on balance, openness favours a monetary policy strategy aimed at exchange rate stability.[20] The empirical evidence also lends some support to this position. Viewed from the European experience, the smaller countries (which are usually more open) have been more focused on exchange rate anchors, whereas the larger countries have more frequently emphasised money anchors. In this context, Chart 3 tentatively shows how the EU countries with more open economies have generally experienced somewhat less bilateral exchange rate depreciation vis-à-vis the Deutsche mark, the anchor currency of the European exchange rate systems, in the past 25 years. (While this relationship is similarly significant when Luxembourg is excluded from the sample, it also partly reflects the tightness of bilateral trade links with Germany.) In addition, there is evidence that, as trade links between two countries intensify, the bilateral correlation of business cycle activity increases and economic disturbances become more symmetric.[21] Thus, trade integration leads to more similar economic developments in the

Chart 3: Openness and exchange rate stability

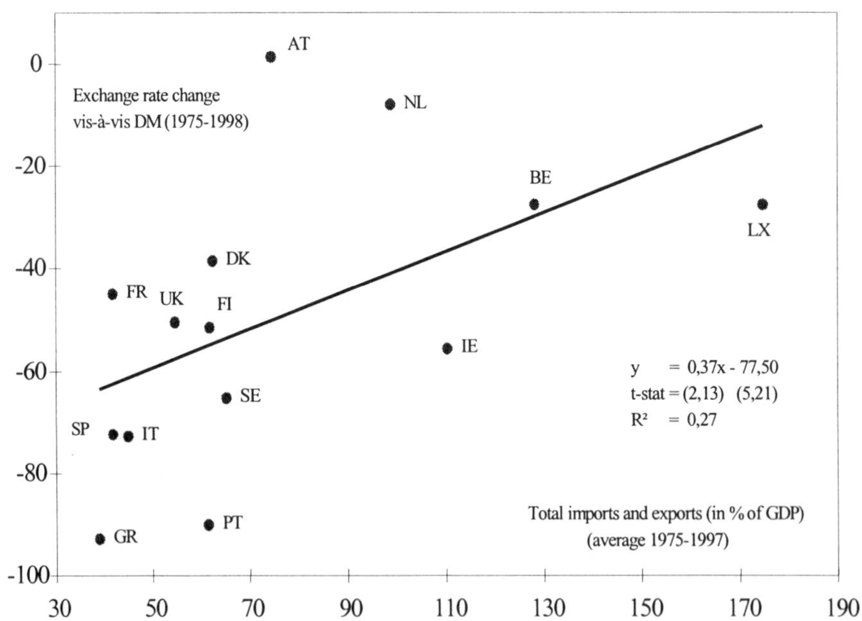

respective countries, thereby reducing the need for monetary policy autonomy and making a monetary strategy aimed at exchange rate stability more appropriate (or less inappropriate as the case may be).

Against this background, Table 2 illustrates three points with a bearing on the preferred monetary strategy: EU-economies are characterised by a relatively high degree of openness, they have become increasingly open during the past decades, and this increasing openness is primarily attributable to growth in intra-EU trade. (The upward trend in openness is masked between 1985 and 1995 by the reversal of the dollar overvaluation in the wake of the Plaza Agreement and by the effects of the German unification on both trade and GDP.) This leads to one important conclusion regarding monetary strategy. Since the expansion of intra-European trade over the past quarter of a century has generally been more rapid than that of output, then by implication, on the basis of this variable, the superior monetary strategy in Europe has shifted in the direction of greater exchange rate fixity.

Table 2: Openness of EU economies and intra-EU trade, 1975 - 1995

Country	***Total imports and exports (in % of gdp)***			***Intra-EU trade (in share of total trade)***		
	1975	**1985**	**1995**	**1975**	**1985**	**1995**
Austria	63	81	76	60	62	69
Belgium [1]	106	150	140	74	73	74
Denmark	61	73	65	65	63	64
Germany [2]	47	62	46	57	58	57
Greece	36	44	44	51	53	65
Finland	54	58	67	56	51	57
France	37	47	45	56	58	64
Ireland	87	112	134	78	71	65
Italy	41	46	51	50	52	63
Luxembourg [1]	177	208	174	..	..	..
Netherlands	93	117	100	69	70	67
Portugal	48	72	73	54	57	79
Spain	31	44	47	43	46	68
Sweden	56	69	75	59	59	60
United Kingdom	54	57	57	44	54	56
EU	50	61	57	57	59	63
USA	16	18	24	..	..	..
Japan	26	26	17	..	..	..

Source: European Economy, No. 63, various tables.
[1] Belgium data on intra-EU trade include Luxembourg.
[2] 1975 and 1985 relate to West Germany.

2.3.5 Capital mobility

While openness is usually considered in terms of the relative size of the tradables sector (recorded in the current account of the balance of payments), it can also be viewed in terms of the financial sector (the capital and financial account). Indeed, the degree of integration between domestic and external financial markets is a structural characteristic with far-reaching consequences for the relative importance of different types of domestic and external shocks, as well as for the linkages between different macroeconomic policy instruments. As a result, the extent of capital liberalisation and financial integration is a key consideration in the monetary strategy choice.

Specifically, the absence of capital controls facilitates the channelling abroad of monetary shocks, but also makes a country more vulnerable to foreign disturbances, particularly adjustments to international interest rates. At the same time, a liberalised capital regime diminishes the scope to tailor policies to domestic considerations, notably by reducing the extent to which monetary policy and exchange rate policy can be treated as separate instruments. This is the well-known incompatible triangle of unrestricted capital flows, monetary policy autonomy and exchange rate stability; of these three objectives, only two can be fully met at any point in time.[22]

In deciding on this tri-dimensional trade-off, policy-makers in Europe have by-and-large assigned priority to the first objective, without, however, wishing to abandon either of the other two.[23] The erratic but successful drive towards full capital liberalisation has reflected benefits at both the microeconomic and macroeconomic level. Prominent among the former are the efficiency-enhancing effects of economies of scale, increased technology transfers and greater competition in financial markets. Examples of the latter are the improved allocation of savings and heightened policy discipline that come with capital mobility. And in first instance when capital mobility is still relatively modest (as it initially was), the consequences of capital liberalisation for monetary policy choices may remain limited. In practice, the freeing of capital flows then first erodes the effectiveness of policy instruments such as direct credit controls, which require capital restrictions to preclude the delocation of credit demand abroad. As capital becomes mobile and financial portfolio's become internationally easily adjustable, the instrument of foreign exchange intervention also loses its potency.[24] Ultimately, when capital markets become deeply integrated and capital flows overshadow transactions in the current account, it becomes well-nigh impossible to combine an exchange rate commitment (in terms of a peg or a narrow band) with a monetary policy at times oriented at, or expected to be oriented at, domestic objectives. Any deviation, or anticipation of deviation, of domestic monetary policy from that of the exchange rate anchor will prompt capital flows that either lead to an adjustment in the domestic policy stance or cause the exchange rate link to founder.

Besides this, capital liberalisation may spur portfolio adjustments that destabilise given monetary aggregates, thereby undermining their reliability as a guide for monetary policy-making. This may be a predominantly transitional difficulty, stemming from the liberalisation process and disappearing once financial behaviour settles down to the new regulatory environment. However, since greater capital mobility implies increased substitutability of domestic and international financial assets, and by implication broader scope for financial innovation, it may also permanently raise the volatility of money demand.

All told, capital mobility has a direct impact on the monetary strategy choice. On the one hand, exchange rate targeting is made less attractive, since this mobility ties monetary policy more rigidly to the external objective.[25] In particular, capital liberalisation makes the exchange rate development more susceptible to market sentiments, including, at the extreme, the risk of self-fulfilling attacks.[26] Thus, while capital flows may be a stabilising factor in the case of fully credible fixed exchange rate systems, these flows lose their stabilising properties when this credibility is at all questionable. This will notably be the case when exchange rates are fixed but ultimately adjustable, as market participants will be keen on pre-empting any adjustments.[27] In effect, capital mobility reduces the scope for 'in between'-solutions that combine a more-or-less fixed exchange rate with some monetary flexibility geared to domestic policy concerns. In this respect, capital mobility raises the costs of pursuing an exchange rate based strategy, since the policy requirements become more demanding and, when they are not met, the adverse effects are heavier. On the other hand, capital liberalisation also tarnishes the gleam of money targeting strategies, as the relationship between given monetary aggregates and monetary policy's final objectives may become less predictable. This risk is particularly grave during the transitional deregulation process, but may also be present thereafter. Taken together, these considerations suggest that the factor of increased capital mobility, such as occurred in Europe over the past quarter of a century, favours by-passing intermediate targets such as money or the exchange rate and focusing directly on end-objectives such as inflation or nominal income.

2.3.6 Diversity and cross-border similarity of the production base

While the structural characteristics determine the extent to which an economy may be affected by shocks, they also influence the likelihood of such disturbances occurring in the first place. In particular, if the production base of an economy is well-diversified and similar to that of trading partners, substantive shocks are less likely to occur, and if they do, are more likely to be symmetric.[28] In essence, with a high degree of industry or product diversity, the destabilising effects of industry or product specific supply shocks will be smaller and specific demand shifts will have a less pronounced impact on output and prices. Other things equal, this would influence the monetary strategy choice by implying a reduced need for exchange rate flexibility to cope with adverse shocks.

In practice, European countries have traditionally had well-diversified economic structures, in which the share of production of primary commodities (including agriculture, energy, and mining) is relatively small, while that of manufactures and services is very high. This diversification was already well-advanced in 1975, but increased further over the years. As is evident from Table 3 the share of primary commodities was above 10 per cent in the majority of European countries at the beginning of this period, but had declined to well beneath this level in most countries by 1995. At the same time, the share of manufacturing and construction also fell from a range of generally 35-50 per cent in 1975 to 25-40 in 1995. The difference was, of course, captured by a marked increase in the share of services to between one-half and two-thirds of the total by 1995.

A similar picture emerges from the composition of exports (see Table 4), where the share of agricultural and energy exports – which are notoriously vulnerable to terms-of-trade shocks – fell from 20 per cent in 1975 to about 15 per cent in 1995. In this context, it is also remarkable that the differences in export composition (as measured by the standard deviation of the different shares in the EU countries) have become significantly smaller within the Union. Although the level of aggregation in these Tables does not allow firm conclusions to be drawn, they do provide an indication of high and increasing diversification. Besides this, product market integration in the European countries is generally intra-industry (rather than inter-industry), especially in the manufacturing sector. In particular, it has been estimated that the share of intra-industry trade amounted to 62 per cent of total intra-EU trade in 1994, having increased by about 5 percentage points over the previous seven year period. In this context, it is noteworthy that the increase was especially marked in the relative newcomers to the community, Spain and Portugal (12 and 9 percentage points respectively).[29]

Table 3: Diversity of production base (shares in per cent of total[1])

Country	Agricultural, energy and mining [2]		Manufacturing and construction		Services [3]	
	1975	1995	1975	1995	1975	1995
Austria	10.5	5.8	46.1	33.9	43.4	60.3
Belgium	7.9	6.9	39.8	29.3	52.4	63.8
Denmark	9.1	8.8	35.8	32.0	55.0	59.2
Finland	16.0	9.0	43.0	40.2	40.9	50.8
France	9.3	6.5	42.4	30.2	48.2	63.3
Germany	7.7	4.9	48.8	36.5	43.4	58.6
Greece	23.8	21.0	29.8	24.0	46.4	55.1
Ireland	25.0	9.7	36.8	42.3	38.3	47.9
Italy [4]	13.0	10.0	41.1	30.0	45.9	59.9
Luxembourg	7.7	3.1	41.7	25.0	50.5	71.9
Netherlands	13.2	8.7	35.4	26.8	51.3	64.5
Portugal	20.6	10.2	45.6	34.2	33.8	55.6
Spain	15.2	7.2	39.0	33.6	45.8	59.2
Sweden	9.9	7.0	46.8	34.7	43.3	58.2
United Kingdom	8.8	7.6	42.3	29.0	49.0	63.4
EU	10.4	7.1	43.1	32.4	46.5	60.6
United States	10.0	6.8	31.8	24.4	58.2	68.8
Japan	8.6	5.3	42.6	37.3	48.8	57.4
EU (st. dev.)	5.6	3.9	4.9	5.0	5.4	5.6

Source: National Accounts Vol. II, Edition 1982, 1989 and 1997.
Quarterly National Accounts, No. 2, 1997, OECD.

[1] Total is sum of agriculture, energy and mining, manufacturing and construction, and services. Based on GDP by kind of activity at current prices.

[2] Agriculture, hunting, forestry and fishing; mining and quarrying; electricity, gas and water.

[3] Wholesale and retail trade, restaurants and hotels; transport storage and communication; finance, insurance, real estate and business services; community, social and personal services.

[4] For Italy, mining and quarrying is included in manufacturing.

Taken together, this relatively high and increasing degree of diversification, as well as of mutual intra-industry dependence, suggests that adverse shocks are less likely to have a major impact on the European economies and, if they do, that the effect is more likely to be symmetric. This is borne out by empirical studies suggesting that the European

Table 4: Shares of exports by commodity categories (in per cent)

Country	Agricultural products [1]		Energy products [2]		Other [3]	
	1975	1995	1975	1995	1975	1995
Austria	11.1	7.8	2.1	1.0	86.8	91.2
Belgium-Luxembourg	12.8	12.6	4.9	2.6	82.3	84.7
Denmark	39.7	29.0	2.9	3.3	56.9	68.1
Finland	19.5	11.3	0.4	1.9	80.1	86.8
France	19.5	16.7	2.4	2.3	77.8	81.0
Germany	6.8	6.9	3.1	1.0	90.1	92.2
Greece	41.2	36.3	11.0	6.6	47.8	57.1
Ireland	51.6	21.4	1.3	0.4	47.0	78.1
Italy	10.0	7.5	5.7	1.2	84.2	91.2
Netherlands	27.2	24.8	17.0	7.1	55.8	68.1
Portugal	27.3	13.9	2.0	0.4	70.7	85.7
Spain	25.2	18.1	3.3	2.2	71.5	79.8
Sweden	18.4	10.0	1.6	1.9	80.0	88.1
United Kingdom	10.0	8.4	4.1	4.3	85.9	87.3
EU	15.0	12.4	4.9	2.4	80.0	85.2
United States	25.9	15.7	4.2	1.9	69.8	82.4
Japan	2.9	1.2	0.4	0.6	96.7	98.2
EU (st. dev.)	13.0	8.6	4.3	2.0	14.3	10.0

Source: 1975: Historical Statistics of Foreign Trade 1965-80, OECD.
1995: Foreign Trade by Commodities 1995, OECD.

[1] Food and live animals; beverages and tobacco; crude materials, inedible, except fuels; animal and vegetables oils, fats and waxes (SITC 0+1+2+4).
[2] Mineral fuels, lubricants and related materials (SITC 3).
[3] SITC 5 to 9.

economies are relatively well-diversified and are characterised by a considerable overlap of industry-specific employment.[30] To put this in perspective (although it is debatable whether this is the correct yardstick for a comparison), these studies find that the EU economies are more alike and tend to develop more in unison than the US regions.[31]

The strategic implication for monetary policy is that the degree of diversification and intra-industry integration do not, by themselves, seem to have formed a major obstacle for greater exchange rate fixity. While this may have been the case for some of the southern European countries (in particular Greece and Portugal) in 1975, the subsequent broadening of their economic production base, as well as the deeper integration of their industries with the rest of the EU, has reduced the costs of relinquishing the exchange rate as an instrument to mitigate the adverse effects of country-specific shocks.

2.3.7 Differences in financial structure

An issue overlooked in much of the literature on optimal currency areas and on the optimal monetary target, but of potentially great practical importance to monetary authorities deciding on their policy strategy, is the extent to which the monetary policy transmission mechanism varies across countries as a result of differences in financial structure.[32] This oversight may reflect the limited understanding of the way monetary policy actions are actually transmitted to the real economy and of the extent to which this feed-through is influenced by financial arrangements. But even if the monetary transmission process is in many ways still comparable to a 'black box', differences in its effects may have a crucial bearing on the monetary strategy choice.[33]

After all, the nature of shocks and the economy's previously mentioned structural characteristics only provide a partial view of how output and prices can best be stabilised in the face of disturbances. The influence of different financial structures on how the economy reacts to policy changes clearly also needs to be taken into account. For example, the adoption of an exchange rate peg target may *a priori* seem advantageous for countries with substantial bilateral trade and not dissimilar production structures, since these countries would be less likely to be struck by asymmetric disturbances. But if, as a result of dissimilar financial structures, an identical monetary policy reaction to a symmetric shock is transmitted differently (in terms of magnitude or timing) to each country's real economy, it may be desirable to pursue independent policies in the first place, thereby implying a preference for exchange rate flexibility.

Cross-country differences in monetary policy transmission may primarily reflect dissimilar private sector financial arrangements such as differences in the degree of net sectoral indebtedness, the maturity profile of debts, the share of fixed versus variable interest rate financing, and the relative importance of bank credit versus other forms of financing (including equity). In effect, the structure of these arrangements determines the composition of balance sheets and the overall sensitivity to changes in short-term interest rates. Similarly, these differences may be attributable to factors within the banking system itself, such as this sector's financial health and the regulations and practices governing its activities. For example, the strength of the collateral channel depends mainly on the prevalence of collateral in debt contracts and on the sensitivity of the collateral value to changes in interest rates. However, dissimilar financial structures are not the only causes of differences in monetary policy transmission, since this transmission is also influenced by other factors such as institutional characteristics (including elements that determine nominal rigidity, such as wage indexation practices), varying degrees of openness (the exchange rate channel of monetary policy changes will be stronger, *ceteris paribus*, in a more open economy) and, more broadly, the credibility of monetary policy (since this will impact the feed-through of changes in short-term interest rates into long-term rates).

Empirical research has indeed found substantive differences between European countries in the response of output and inflation to adjustments in monetary policy; these differences relate to both the magnitude and the timing of the policy effects. To some degree the diversity of these effects can be traced to the differences in the financial structure of countries. For instance, the total amount of credit outstanding, the prevalence of short-term and variable rate debt contracts, as well as the share of loans backed by real estate collateral, are known to be relatively higher in the United Kingdom than in other European countries.[34] Such characteristics, particularly in the context of fragile balance sheets, by themselves reduce the attractiveness of pursuing an exchange rate oriented monetary strategy, since interest rate adjustments to defend the external commitment will have stronger and more immediate domestic cash-flow and income implications.[35] More broadly, this illustrates that a country's financial structure has a bearing on the degree of activism to be pursued when conducting monetary policy.

But, in practice, the various elements of the monetary transmission process may have partly offsetting influences – the end-result being determined by the cumulative impact of the traditional money channel, the interest rate channel, the credit channel of bank behaviour, the exchange rate channel, other asset price channels, the effects of adjusted expectations (for example on the term structure of interest rates), and the nominal rigidities governing the link between output and inflation. These intricacies preclude a conclusive judgement on the monetary transmission process, all the more as this process is likely to vary markedly over the course of time. Indeed, a further consideration is that harmonisation efforts in other policy fields (for example in the fiscal treatment of mortgages) may contribute to a greater similarity in financing methods and therefore, in due course, in monetary policy transmission. This complexity seems to be borne out by the findings of many cross-EU country studies: these establish the unique nature of each economy's monetary transmission process, identifying distinct differences in the response to interest rate changes, but also memorising that these differences may narrow following the adoption of an aligned monetary policy.[36]

2.3.8 Endogeneity in the monetary strategy choice

A more subtle issue relates to the question of whether the adopted monetary strategy will itself impact the structural and behavioural characteristics of the economy, thus introducing an element of endogeneity in the monetary strategy choice. In essence, the selection of a monetary strategy is subject to the well-known 'Lucas Critique', whereby a policy decision based on certain relationships in the past, gives rise to changes in these relationships and thereby removes the basis for the initial policy decision. The most notable example lies in the field of money targeting, where according to Goodhart's Law (rooted in the United Kingdom's experience with money targeting) any statistical stability between a monetary aggregate and nominal income is likely to disappear once this aggregate becomes the focal point for policy implementation.[37] But this view can be parried by claiming the counterfactual: the statistical stability will tend to be inferior when policy is not aimed at stabilising the aggregate. Indeed, there is some empirical evidence suggesting the stabilising impact of a policy focus on money aggregates may dominate the destabilising impact.[38]

Moreover, such circularity may also apply to other strategy options, notably exchange rate targeting. For instance, while the costs of exchange rate fixity are higher in case of significant labour market rigidities, the incentives to implement labour market reforms and to moderate wages will be larger once such exchange rate fixity has been adopted.[39] Besides this, a strategy of exchange rate targeting potentially increases transparency and the efficiency of the international allocation of production resources; this may in turn influence elements of the economic structure such as the diversity of the production base or the degree of openness. As regards the issue of whether greater exchange rate stability in fact changes the extent of national economic diversity, this depends on whether the impact on regional specialisation dominates over the impact on intra-industry trade. The available evidence is ambiguous.[40] On the issue of openness, the many empirical studies of the impact of exchange rate variability on trade have generally been unable to establish a robust relationship; in those few studies where such an effect was identified, it was generally found to be marginal and decreasing over the years.[41] By contrast, with respect to openness in terms of capital flows, there is evidence that greater exchange rate stability has promoted international capital mobility and may have resulted in lower savings-investment correlation in Europe.[42] Hence, capital mobility will allow greater external imbalances which may, within limits, substitute for labour mobility or other adjustments in accommodating demand shifts or other income shocks. In turn, this may contribute to making an exchange rate strategy more sustainable. At the same time, however, the heightened capital mobility will further limit the scope for pursuing other monetary policy objectives than the exchange rate anchor.

Another factor where endogeneity influences a strategy of exchange rate targeting, is in the process of monetary policy transmission. As previously set out, the similarity of this transmission process between two countries will influence the degree in which a mutual exchange rate link is likely to contribute to the stability of both countries' output and price developments. However, even if their transmission processes are *a priori* characterised by significant differences, these differences may fade once a credible exchange rate commitment is established. This adjustment will, of course, be gradual, as the behaviour of private agents is likely to be determined by considerable inertia and as the establishment of credibility typically requires perseverance and the passage of time.[43] One transmission channel that adapts strongly to actual policy implementation and that is sensitive to the credibility effects of monetary policy, is the term structure of interest rates. In particular, once an exchange rate link is established and is made credible, changes in central bank rates in the respective countries will tend to have a similar impact on both short-term and long-term interest rates. This is confirmed by empirical evidence that the impact of monetary policy changes on the term structure of interest rates reflects the extent to which central exchange rate parities have been changed in the past.[44]

In all, endogeneity underscores the complexity of selecting a monetary strategy and, since it is largely unpredictable, increases the uncertainty inherent in the selection process. This uncertainty emphasises the value of constancy in the strategic orientation, but also of vigilance in reviewing the appropriateness of this same orientation.

2.4 Prioritisation of macroeconomic objectives

Identifying the superior monetary strategy is thus, in principle, partly an exercise of objective analysis: what are the types of shocks that an economy is likely to experience and what are the structural characteristics that provide insulation against the detrimental effects of such shocks? But this does not give an unequivocal answer, since alternative strategies involve short-term trade-offs between different policy objectives – particularly those relating to the stability of output growth, inflation and the balance of payments. For example, if a negative supply shock occurs in the domestic market, a monetary loosening and exchange rate depreciation may be desirable from the viewpoint of stabilising output and the balance of payments. At the same time, however, the shock will have increased prices and any monetary easing or exchange rate depreciation would undermine efforts to reduce the incipient inflationary momentum. Thus, given the scope for potential policy conflicts, identifying the preferred monetary strategy also involves a subjective analysis: which policy objectives should generally be granted priority over others? [45] In its barest form, this boils down to taking a position on inevitable short-term trade-offs between the stability of output and prices, and the strength of the external account.

Trade-offs between different monetary policy strategies

Of course, this trade-off will vary from country to country and will depend crucially on whether a certain type of shock dominates and whether the economy's structure can easily absorb such shocks. While there are no unambiguous analytical conclusions, there is some evidence that countries adopting money anchors experience higher and more volatile inflation, but less short-term variability in output and the balance of payments than countries pegging the exchange rate.[46] The generally more favourable inflation performance of countries with fixed exchange regimes is found to be related to a usually lower money supply growth (a discipline effect) and higher money demand growth (a credibility effect). At the same time, the outcome may reflect the fact that countries pursuing a money-oriented framework tend to circumvent other nominal rigidities by using the exchange rate as an adjustment instrument towards greater stability of output growth and the external position. In turn, the higher implied exchange rate variability is likely to translate into more volatile (import) prices. However, further than this, it is difficult to come to normative statements. The extent to which other strategies lead to different trade-offs primarily depends on the scope of the monetary authority to adjust policies in the face of various types of disturbances. Thus, a rigidly pursued direct inflation strategy may in itself be expected to reduce inflation variability, but at the cost of greater output variability in the presence of supply shocks. While this vulnerability can be addressed by prespecifying escape clauses (such as for oil price increases), this dilemma cannot be fully resolved, since it is infeasible to define all such disturbances in advance and it is not always possible to determine the nature of a shock the moment it occurs. Moreover, a multitude of escape clauses is likely to undermine the solidity, clarity and credibility of the targeting framework.

A further consideration is that, in weighing monetary strategy options, countries not only take account of their own policy priorities, but also of those of other countries. This runs parallel to the question of whether or not shocks are likely to be symmetric. Generally speaking, the more similar the prioritisation of policy objectives between countries, and thus the more comparable the desired policy reaction in the face of economic disturbances, the stronger the case for a fixed exchange rate regime, and vice versa. In this respect, adoption of an exchange rate peg and of the concomitant policy discipline may also reflect the desire to bring actual policy implementation closer in line with the policy reaction function exhibited by the anchor country.

Trade-offs within a monetary policy strategy

At a more detailed level, there are alternative designs within each monetary strategy type that also define the authorities' prioritisation of economic objectives. For instance, when considering the implementation of a money-oriented strategy, authorities face the practical question of which specific money aggregate to target. The different characteristics of these aggregates imply certain trade-offs between economic objectives. This point can be illustrated as follows: if the interest elasticity of the demand for M1 is higher than that for M2 and the economy is susceptible to supply shocks, then targeting the narrow monetary aggregate is likely to imply smaller output fluctuations but larger price fluctuations.[47] Similarly, in the case of exchange rate strategies, countries can opt for different degrees of rigidity, ranging from currency board arrangements with full backing of base money by official reserves at one end of the spectrum, to exchange rate commitments within a wide and adjustable band at the other. Since this determines the authorities' margins to accommodate domestic objectives within the confines of the adopted exchange regime, these specifications have direct implications for the trade-offs underlying the exchange rate strategy. As regards direct inflation targeting approaches, the trade-offs are predominantly determined by the degree of flexibility incorporated into the targeting framework. This relates to issues such as whether the policy objective is tightly defined, whether deviations from target are permissible under certain prespecified circumstances, and whether missing the target has far-reaching consequences.

In this sense it is not only the choice of monetary strategy but also its precise specification that determines the extent to which the authorities' (or society's) welfare function is maximised. In fact, given the wide scope for different specifications within each type of monetary strategy, the dividing lines between the alternative strategy types are actually quite fluid. As a result, different monetary strategy types may, in their implementation and trade-offs, actually be very much alike.

The institutional perspective

From an institutional perspective, making a central bank independent in the use of its instruments and attaching this independence to a prime objective in terms of price stability, seems to formalise a preference on how the typical short-term trade-off between inflation and output growth should be decided. Indeed, it has been suggested that because independent central banks are more likely to be strict in the implementation of their monetary policy strategy than institutionally weaker ones, they are also more likely to implement policies that involve higher output variability.[48] However, there are several reasons to doubt whether prioritising monetary policy's price objective over the smoothing of output growth will *per se* end up magnifying the business cycle. First, there is the influence of Friedman's long, variable and unpredictable lags in the transmission of monetary policy, which imply that an active monetary policy aimed primarily at offsetting output fluctuations may in fact exacerbate these fluctuations. Second, the impact of a credible institutional commitment to stable prices may mitigate any adverse output effects of the policies actually needed to maintain this price stability.[49] In particular, with such credibility, the wage formation process and expectations in general may help preserve an environment of price stability. Third, once output-oriented policy activism takes centre stage, monetary measures risk responding to the political (electoral) as well as the business cycle.[50] And fourth, if price stability is interpreted as a medium-term objective, the monetary authority will retain scope to take due account of the output consequences of its anti-inflation policies.[51]

This leaves the answer in the empirical arena, where the evidence convincingly refutes the claim that countries with more independent central banks experience lower output growth or greater output variability. While there may be incidental evidence suggesting such a relationship, it is clearly not apparent in broad-ranging industrial country samples. On the other hand, however, a positive relationship between central bank independence and output growth has not been established either.[52]

The consistency of the policy mix

Finally, it deserves emphasis that the scope to tailor a monetary policy strategy tightly to the authorities' preferred policy objectives assumes, of course, the absence of binding fiscal or balance of payments constraints. In this sense, a monetary policy strategy can only deliver the desired outcome when supported by a consistent policy mix. It goes without saying that once budgetary or external financing issues dominate the policy-making process, any customary trade-off in the monetary policy realm is likely to be overridden by other dynamics. For instance, when the public finances are on an unsustainable course, there is an increasing risk that the central bank will, in the end, be forced to levy the inflation tax. And the impact on monetary policy will be felt well in advance. Indeed, once an excessive budget deficits emerges, the rational public will increasingly anticipate surprise inflation and will augment its inflationary expectations accordingly.[53] This will fuel the inflationary process independent of the monetary strategy being pursued. To make it worse, any monetary tightening aimed at preserving inflation objectives will advance the point at which fiscal policy becomes unsustainable. By the same token, excessive wage increases will create expectations of higher domestic demand, external competitiveness erosion and balance of payments weakening. This will lead to heightened anticipation of currency depreciation and may prompt capital outflows, well before the macroeconomic effects of the wage increases are actually felt.

To a certain extent, the chosen strategy can limit the likelihood of monetary policy-making being dominated by events outside its scope of influence. Strengthening the institutional position of the central bank and increasing the transparency of the inflationary process can serve to raise the pressure to tackle inflationary problems at their roots. In this respect, much also depends on a monetary policy's communicability. However, in the final analysis, if the central bank is not willing to impose unlimited output costs to achieve its inflation objective – which is the case in the real world – then other policy developments will crucially determine the sustainability of a monetary strategy and whether the trade-offs inherent in that strategy are actually achieved.

In Europe, the importance of a consistent policy mix has been powerfully illustrated by the turmoiled history of exchange rate targeting arrangements, where monetary policy commitments have often proven to be untenable once overtaken by stronger forces linked to instability in other areas. This is, of course, the logic underlying the convergence criteria for EMU and the later agreements on budgetary policy under the Stability and Growth Pact. In fact, exchange rate targeting may be considered the most demanding strategy in terms of policy mix considerations, since it implies the tightest limitations on monetary policy for domestic stabilisation purposes. But policy mix considerations have also featured in the implementation of other strategies. In particular, monetary authorities pursuing domestically oriented strategies have at times visibly geared their policy decisions to developments in other fields – for instance, by delaying a monetary easing until consistent wage or fiscal agreements had been reached. By way of exception, inflation targeting central banks have tended to view such other developments as given, often choosing to exclude the impact of indirect taxes from the targeted inflation measure or even to incorporate a broad generic caveat for wage and fiscal developments. In principle, however, a compatible policy mix is equally vital for the medium-term viability of any monetary policy strategy.

2.5 Political economy considerations and the credibility of monetary policy

The efficacy of monetary policy depends crucially on its credibility. This has long been recognised, as illustrated by Keynes' early insight that: "a monetary policy which strikes public opinion as being experimental in character or easily liable to change may fail in its objective of greatly reducing the long-term rate of interest. ... The same policy, on the other hand, may prove easily successful if it appeals to public opinion as being reasonable and practicable and in the public interest, rooted in strong conviction, and promoted by an authority unlikely to be superseded." [54] What factors, then, determine the credibility of monetary policy? Much of the answer lies in the political environment of monetary policy decision-making.

2.5.1 Rules versus discretion

At the heart of the monetary strategy choice lies one of the oldest debates among economists: that on rules versus discretion.[55] Under a rules-based approach to monetary policy-making, there is a predefined reaction function specifying how policy adjusts to developments in specific (intermediate) variables. By contrast, under discretion, policy decisions are essentially *ad hoc*, based on the then prevailing assessment of policy needs. Although the scope for activism is significantly smaller under rules (being limited to prespecified, state contingent policy adjustments), in principle both systems can be activist. The distinguishing feature between the two approaches is whether the monetary authority precommits to how policy will be set in the future.

Proponents of rules, on the one hand, have claimed that discretionary policy-making is likely to be destabilising, because policy-makers have an imperfect knowledge of the economy and their measures will therefore tend to be ill-dosed or ill-timed.[56] When policy-making is discretionary, the public at large will also be less able to predict prospective policies, thereby increasing uncertainty. Moreover, given greater policy freedom, the relevant authorities may prioritise short-term objectives or special interests, to the detriment of overall economic development over the medium term. With respect to monetary policy, the supremacy of rules is thus seen to reflect the limited understanding of the policy transmission process, the role of policy predictability in stabilising expectations, the tendency of the private sector to revert swiftly to equilibrium, and the inappropriate prioritisation that results from the unavoidable incentives to boost short-term economic activity or to increase fiscal (seigniorage) revenues. Hence it is argued that discretion in monetary policy leads to greater economic volatility, increases uncertainty and introduces an inflationary bias.

Advocates of discretion, on the other hand, have pointed at the absence of durably stable relationships in the economy and at the need to retain policy flexibility for dealing with unforeseen developments. Assuming that policy-makers are benevolent and well-informed, it is difficult to deny them broad scope for policy adjustments required by changed circumstances. In principle, monetary authorities then have the advantage of being able to take unfolding developments duly into account when they determine the policy stance towards their medium-term objectives. And, since the authorities will act to offset the destabilising effects of unforeseen shocks, economic agents will actually face less aggregate uncertainty. In other words, the uncertainties stemming from future disturbances are viewed as larger than those created by a less predictable policy course. Most convincingly, proponents of discretion have argued that if pursuance of a rule (for example for money growth) were in practice indeed optimal, nothing stands in the way of authorities from choosing to implement the policies implied by such a rule under a discretionary regime.

The case for rules strengthened over the course of the 1970s as confidence in the efficacy of discretionary activist policies dwindled and, more specifically, belief in a downwards sloping Phillips curve waned, implying no durable trade-off between inflation and unemployment. Evidence mounted that the widespread stagflation in the industrialised countries could not be solely attributed to the adverse impact of the first oil shock of 1973, but that accommodating policies, especially in the monetary realm, were also at fault. With the broad acceptance that monetary policy may at best only temporarily increase output, but at the cost of a sustained higher rate of price increases, the argument for monetary policy rules gained momentum. At the same time, the introduction of rational expectations into economic thought and the implication that activist monetary policy may be impotent in influencing output, even in the shorter term, provided a further theoretical underpinning of the case against discretion.[57] The case for rules was still not clear, however, since the source of the inflationary bias under a discretionary system with benevolent policy-makers remained unidentified.

Dynamic inconsistency

The missing link was provided by Kydland and Prescott (1977) who formally set out how a discretionary regime may lead an economy towards an equilibrium with higher inflation and unchanged output. In effect, the bias stems from the public's expectation that in a discretionary system policy-makers will announce one thing (e.g., to pursue a tight monetary policy) and subsequently, once wages and other nominal contracts are set, do another (ease monetary policy). In a nutshell, the rational monetary authority faces incentives to behave inconsistently over the course of time. Hence, because the public anticipates a policy reversal, it will pre-emptively discount this in its wage and other nominal agreements. A new equilibrium is then reached at a point where the marginal cost to the policy-maker in terms of higher inflation exactly equals the marginal benefit of the higher output it would generate.[58] This equilibrium is determined by the perceived size of the short-term benefits of inflation surprises, by the expected magnitude and duration of the costs of higher inflation, and by the authorities' time discount rate. At this equilibrium, inflation is higher than it would otherwise be and the policy-maker no longer succeeds in systematically generating unexpected inflation. As a result, an economy governed by discretion suffers the costs of higher inflation, but does not reap the benefits of inflation surprises. The experience of most European countries during the past century, where periods governed by discretion have seen significantly higher inflation, leaves open the possibility that elements of dynamic inconsistency have indeed been at play.

The dynamic inconsistency dilemma essentially reflects the inflationary pressures that stem from the continuous desire for lower unemployment, higher economic activity, and better budgetary outcomes. It is centred on the plausible assumption that a rational monetary authority pursuing price stability will make full use of any leeway also to promote output or other objectives, even if this involves backtracking on previous policy intentions.[59] This is where policy rules provide a remedy: the precommitment of future policies provides assurances that actual policy implementation will be time consistent. Thus, by precluding inflation surprises and lowering inflation expectations, a rules-based system will in and of itself generate a lower inflation outcome.

The time consistency arguments claiming the predominance of rules over discretion were further refined by the introduction of reputational considerations.[60] When reputation is taken into account and policy-makers are assumed to attach greater weight to longer-term considerations, the costs of inflation surprises increase, and hence the monetary policy outcome improves. Another approach to counter dynamic inconsistency is by appointing an independent central banker whose dislike for inflation is greater than that of society.[61] Again, the monetary authority will perceive greater costs of inflation surprises and will therefore implement more consistent policies over the course of time. However, such an approach does not contain the guarantee of continuity (since appointments need to be renewed and can be more easily reversed than institutional changes) and will thus be less potent in reducing inflation expectations. Moreover, in terms of inflation the conclusion favouring rules is unchanged: inflation outcomes are better with conservative central bankers concerned about their reputation than under a discretionary system, but are still inferior to rules-based regimes.

Policy inflexibility

Regardless of the validity of these game theoretic arguments, a rules-based system maintains the severe drawback that it creates policy inflexibility. Even a central banker who thinks modestly of his or her ability to improve on economic developments through fine-tuning, will view this inflexibility as a heavy cost in the face of uncertain future shocks. Of course, this disadvantage will be less pronounced in the case of activist (state contingent) rules with prespecified feedback mechanisms that adjust the policy stance to the actual state of the economy.[62] Such mechanisms create scope for monetary policy to adapt to different types of disturbances as they occur. But, in the real world, all contingencies cannot be comprehensively prespecified. And a myriad of escape clauses undermines the effectiveness of any monetary policy rule, which depends at least in part on its being easily communicable, that is, simple and readily understood. Moreover, to the extent that the prespecification of conditional responses needs to be continually adjusted to reflect ongoing structural and other changes, incorporating feedback rules inevitably introduces an element of discretion into the system. As a more straightforward alternative, a mixed strategy involving both rules and discretion can be adopted.[63] Such an approach will not, however, fully resolve the time inconsistency dilemma as there will be room for the monetary policy rule, once adopted, to be interpreted loosely.

To summarise, the advances in the rules versus discretion debate have strengthened the case for rules, but have not resolved the drawback of policy inflexibility. On balance, the debate has made clear that neither binding rules nor pure discretion are likely to constitute optimal monetary policy strategies. While the former imply undue output volatility, the latter introduces an inflationary bias. In fact, overall, the debate does not seem to have contributed to an increase in the popularity of rules-based monetary systems *per se*. Rather, it has served to unmask the importance of, first, monetary policy being consistent over the course of time and, second, there being public confidence in this consistency. In turn, this has highlighted the role that is played by credibility. And this role is key to explaining the evolution of monetary strategies in Europe. On the one hand, credibility is important to clarify the divergent performances of European central banks, on the other hand it has also been a prime factor behind the convergence in Europe of the institutional elements of the monetary strategy choice.

2.5.2 Credibility

In essence, while the adoption of rules can address the problem of the inflationary bias in discretionary policy-making, the benefits of such an approach may not outweigh the costs of policy inflexibility. The root of the problem is not that monetary policy generally tends to deviate from some superior policy rule, but rather that monetary authorities experience incentives to deviate from an optimal policy course (which may not be a rule) and that the public anticipates their doing so. Hence, the solution lies in establishing credibility that such deviations will not take place, which does not necessarily mean adopting a rule.

In first instance, credibility seems to imply nothing more than that the central bank's announced objectives are believed. But in a world with rational expectations this is not enough. In that case, credibility is only sustainable if the monetary authority is explicitly able, and motivated, to deliver on its promises. Thus, three crucial elements are required for a monetary policy strategy to be credible. First, the monetary authority must have the capacity to carry out its stated policy objective. Second, it must be in the genuine interest of this authority consistently to pursue this objective. And, third, the public must be convinced that these two preconditions are indeed met.

The benefits of credibility

Before addressing the question of how to establish and maintain such monetary policy credibility, it is helpful to clarify why this is so important. Indeed, although the issue of monetary policy credibility is rather abstract, its benefits are very concrete. First, when a central bank is credible in the strategy it pursues and thereby contributes to lower inflation expectations, nominal wage demands will be lower. This facilitates the achievement of the inflation objective while also strengthening the balance of payments. Second, credibility directly reduces the level of long-term interest rates which are importantly determined by inflation expectations and inflation risk premia. These factors will not only lower the nominal interest rate level, but also the real level (in *ex post* terms on account of inflation expectations not lying above actual inflation, but also in *ex ante* terms on account of lower risk premia). This more subdued interest rate level will support economic activity and financial sector solidity, while at the same time alleviating debt service obligations in the budget. Third, from the perspective of policy effectiveness, credibility also reduces the sacrifice ratio (that is, the output costs) of disinflation, and increases the real effects, and thus the salutary impact, of stabilisation policies. This is because policy actions would otherwise have to be relatively stronger to offset public scepticism about the policy objectives. Put differently, a credible monetary authority will have greater scope to engage in discretionary policies without raising the suspicion that it is concocting an inflation surprise. In general terms, these benefits of credibility will be greater when an economy is subject to more nominal rigidities and is more open, in particular regarding its capital regime.

The importance of credibility can also be illustrated with reference to alternative monetary policy strategies. For instance, in the case of money targeting, credibility generates greater confidence in a currency as a store of value and thereby contributes to a higher and more stable demand for money. This enhanced stability increases the relevance of money aggregates as intermediate targets for the achievement of an inflation objective and hence makes money targeting more viable. By the same token, in the case of exchange rate targeting, credibility reduces the policy costs of maintaining the external peg, especially in terms of the interest rate spread vis-à-vis the anchor country. With full credibility, market forces will actually serve to buttress rather than undermine the exchange rate commitment. Similarly, the success of direct inflation targeting strategies is conditioned on their credibility, since the inflation target will not be realistically feasible without consistent private sector behaviour, especially regarding the setting of nominal wages.

2.5.3 Establishing credibility through policy precommitment

How then is credibility to be established? In view of the key elements of monetary policy credibility stated above – namely the monetary authority's ability to deliver on its promises, its genuine interest in doing so, as well as the public's confidence therein – the following specific contributing elements can be identified. First, monetary policy should be precommitted to a desired inflation or price stability objective. Second, the central bank should have autonomy durably to implement its policy instruments towards this objective, and other macroeconomic developments should not make this infeasible. Third, the monetary authority's incentive structure should promote policy decision-making that is consistent with the objective. And, fourth, this objective, the precommitment, the instrument independence and the incentive structure should all be effectively communicated to the public. This final element encompasses the first three and is dealt with separately.

Exchange rate anchors for policy precommitment

These first two elements can be achieved in a number of ways. One approach involves precommitting monetary policy to an intermediate nominal anchor and granting the monetary authority operational independence to uphold this anchor. In practice, the only intermediate nominal target capable of fulfilling this credibility boosting role is the exchange rate, because this rate is continuously monitorable, highly visible and subject to ongoing market testing. Given that devaluation is usually perceived as a policy failure, an exchange rate commitment is also politically charged and has a direct disciplinary impact. This stems from the fact that the exchange rate allows a direct comparison of national monetary performance with that of another country, rather than with an abstract variable. By consequence, an exchange rate devaluation is more tangibly embarrassing than, for example, an overrun of a target for money or credit growth.

Under an exchange rate commitment credibility is essentially derived from the strength of another currency (to which the exchange rate is pegged), rather than from that of one's own. Monetary policy is then geared to that of the anchor country, thereby 'tying the hands' of the central bank and reducing the incentives for inflation surprises. In effect, the exchange rate peg imports external discipline on domestic policies and raises the stakes against incompatible policies. More specifically, the exchange rate commitment removes the inflationary bias present when policy is not precommitted by adding to the costs of inflation in several ways: first, inflation between realignments is subject to an extra penalty in terms of a loss of real competitiveness, second, realignments may not fully compensate the real appreciation experienced between realignments, and perhaps most importantly, third, realignments generally involve a political loss of face for the authorities responsible for currencies being devalued.[64]

Institutional approaches to policy precommitment

The exchange rate approach is not, however, universally applicable, since the advantages of increased policy discipline need to be weighed against the drawback of sharply reduced monetary and exchange rate policy autonomy. This harks back to optimal currency area criteria. In fact, if these criteria are insufficiently met, adopting or adhering to an exchange rate commitment may actually reduce credibility.[65] Against this background, there are two other methods of credibility building which are less stringent in terms of policy constraints and which thus have greater normative value. One method is to pursue a 'legislative approach' in which the central bank is made legally independent, is given an explicit price stability objective and is made free to adjust its instruments. Another method is to follow what has become known as a 'contracting approach' in which the central bank is mandated to pursue a prespecified inflation objective and is provided autonomy in its operations towards that objective.[66] Under both these methods, it is the institutional strengthening of the monetary authority rather than the programming of monetary policy that increases the credibility of the policy precommitment. A subtle difference between the two set-ups is that, under the contracting approach, the agreement with the central bank is devised and enforced by the government, and therefore does not fully rule out incentives for time inconsistent behaviour.[67] In addition, the contracting approach may be perceived as less durable, since the target needs to be periodically renewed by the government rather than being rooted in a timeless legal structure. However, although significant, these differences should not be exaggerated. Indeed, given the considerable difficulty of exploiting monetary policy under this approach as well as the explicitness of the inflation objective embedded in the central bank contract, it is doubtful whether its credibility enhancing impact should *a priori* be that much weaker than under the legislative approach. Moreover, inherent in the legislative approach is the risk that the government may, at some later stage, seek to repeal the legal basis for the central bank's independence – even if this would generally be an unduly heavy and politically risky measure to take.[68]

The crucial elements in the institutional approaches to establishing credibility are that monetary policy is precommitted to price stability and that the central bank is, at a minimum, granted independence in the deployment of its instruments. This mainly requires a clear mandate and autonomy in actual monetary policy decision-making.[69] But, for this instrument independence to be effective and for operational decision-making to be essentially free of outside influence, institutional arrangements also need to provide for independence in personnel and financial matters.[70] Thus, establishing credibility also involves ruling out excessive government influence in central bank appointment procedures, in particular by setting sufficiently long terms of office, prespecifying possible dismissal motives, and creating a nomination process that focuses on well-qualified candidates and includes, for instance, consultation of the central bank board. In addition, the central bank needs to be financially independent, especially by ensuring an appropriate level of capital and by prespecifying rules on the transfer of profits and losses such that this level is maintained. Although central banks can function well in a technical sense without capital or even with negative net worth, in practice weak balance sheets lead to reduced control over inflation, financial system repression, or reliance on the fiscal authority for capital infusions.[71] Beyond these factors, the independence and credibility of the monetary authority are importantly determined by less tangible aspects such as the personality and stature of the governor (and perhaps even of his or her advisors). These latter aspects are, however, impossible to capture in institutional or procedural arrangements. Overall, the point is that independence is a broad-ranging concept, comprising much more than just the statutory independence of the monetary authority.

More generally, the key implication of the institutional approaches to credibility building is that monetary policy is divorced from other policies, especially fiscal policy, in order to avoid conflicts of interest that may otherwise jeopardise the inflation objective. This draws a clear dividing line between the monetary authority on the one hand, and the political executive, who is also the fiscal authority, on the other. Although this may complicate co-ordination issues such as the implementation of an optimal policy mix, the advantages of a partition are likely to dominate. In absence of a separation of power, the sources of conflicts of interest are obvious: pressures to provide direct budgetary financing, to increase seigniorage income by otherwise raising the issuance of high-powered money, to increase tax revenue by stimulating economic activity with lower interest and exchange rates, or to erode the real value of a given public debt stock through unexpected inflation.

The dominant argument for an autonomous central bank is that monetary policy can only be expected to be successful in its prime task of achieving price stability if this objective is elevated above others, in particular regarding economic growth or the soundness of the public finances. The underlying justification is that, notwithstanding some short-term trade-offs, there are no long-term trade-offs between these objectives. And if inflation has no durable beneficial effects, but does involve costs, prioritising price stability is welfare-enhancing. In this regard, establishing an institutional structure that prioritises price stability will by itself help reduce inflationary expectations, thereby contributing to this objective without adversely affecting the others.

Moreover, there is evidence that inflation, particularly once it exceeds certain threshold levels, has a strong negative impact on growth and therefore also on the underlying strength of the public finances.[72] In addition, the higher the level of inflation, the greater its volatility, and this volatility independently undermines growth.[73] Finally, even abstracting from any beneficial impact on longer-term growth, price stability is desirable to avoid arbitrary redistribution of wealth and income. These arguments further buttress the case to establish either an independent monetary authority or a monetary authority with operational independence, and to provide this authority with a clear price stability objective. Admittedly, these are neither sufficient nor even strictly necessary conditions for monetary policy success, but they may generally be expected to be key contributing elements.

The motives for institutional strengthening are broadly the same as those favouring policy rules over discretion. In particular, the firm precommitment of monetary policy to a final objective of price stability limits incentives to create inflation surprises through time inconsistent policies, and thus reduces inflationary expectations and uncertainty. However, there is one important distinction with a situation under a policy rule linked to an objectively monitorable (intermediate) target. In particular, since such a rules-based policy system predetermines not only the end objective but also the policy conduct towards that objective, the system's success depends crucially on the stability between the (intermediate) policy targets and the end objective. By contrast, when only the end objective is prespecified and the monetary authority is given autonomy in reaching it, there is discretion to adjust policy instruments to unforeseen shifts in economic relationships. In this way, the option of providing the monetary authority with a clear objective, the right incentive structure, and autonomy limits the inflationary bias while also addressing the issue of policy inflexibility.

The fashion of the institutional approach

In hindsight, it remains puzzling why it took so long for the link between central bank independence and inflation performance to be commonly recognised. While there is abundant evidence of this link throughout European monetary history, it was not until the second half of the 1980s that its importance was widely and duly appreciated. The eventual broad-based awareness of the importance of central bank independence seems to have stemmed directly from the prospects of deepened monetary integration and from the precondition emphasised by the countries with lower inflation that such integration comprise an independent monetary authority. This was reflected in the 1989 report by the Delors Committee for the Study of Economic and Monetary Union (largely comprised of central bankers) which explicitly specified that a future European System of Central Banks "should be independent of instructions from national governments and Community authorities" and that this system "would be committed to the objective of price stability".[74] Similar language was subsequently incorporated in the Maastricht Treaty on European Union adopted in December 1991.

But, while the initiative may have rested with the policy-makers, an essential element in the broad-based support for the concept of central bank independence was the compelling case made by academics. The rules versus discretion debate, and in particular the emphasis on dynamic consistency in monetary policy, spawned a vast literature that provided strong theoretical support for central bank independence. The institutional proposals for an independent European central bank subsequently triggered many empirical studies. In turn, these confirmed that central bank independence did indeed seem to be a 'free lunch', since industrial countries with more independent central banks generally have lower inflation without experiencing lower real growth or, more subtly, higher real growth variability.[75]

2.5.4 Credibility and incentives: the role of accountability

Strengthening the institutional framework governing monetary policy directly raises the issue of accountability. Just as central bank independence seeks to avoid misuse of monetary policy by politicians, so accountability seeks to avoid misuse of monetary policy by central bankers themselves. In this context, accountability can contribute to the credibility of a monetary strategy in two ways. First, it can enhance credibility by creating an incentive structure for the central bank that rewards the achievement of the desired objectives (for example in terms of price stability and countercyclical policy) and penalises any abuse of the scope for discretion. This can help reduce the inflationary bias that may otherwise accompany (instrument) independence. Second, from a viewpoint of democracy, making the central bank accountable for its performance relative to its policy objectives is the logical counterpart of granting it policy autonomy.[76] In this sense, accountability serves to validate institutional independence, implying that these can be made complementary rather than contradictory elements. Indeed, by ensuring that monetary authorities stick to their democratically determined mandate, an appropriate degree of accountability may be expected to augment the longer-term viability of institutional independence.

Monetary policy accountability may be defined as the extent to which a central bank is held answerable for the policies it pursues. The basis for this accountability is provided by the arrangements that enhance the monitoring of central bank policies by members of elected bodies and by the public at large. As regards the former group, these arrangements may include parliamentary hearings and the presence of governmental observers in monetary policy-making bodies. As regards the latter group, these arrangements may comprise the publication of periodic reports on the monetary policy environment, of explanations for monetary policy decisions, of transcripts of monetary policy meetings, and of voting patterns at these meetings. In a broad sense, this also encompasses public appearances by monetary officials, such as speeches and interviews.

But for this monitoring to be effective, accountability must also have teeth. This is because transparency is a necessary, but not a sufficient condition for accountability; it must be complemented by other disciplinary influences. With respect to the monitoring by elected bodies, the accountability arrangements may include an override mechanism allowing the government or the parliament – under certain circumstances – to give instructions to the central bank or to dismiss a central bank governor. In a democracy, such a potential correction mechanism may be viewed as essential to establish the political responsibility of monetary policy, even when this policy has been delegated by the executive power to an independent central bank. In a less immediate sense, re-appointment procedures may similarly be viewed as a disciplinary device in the hands of elected officials. Furthermore, at a fundamental level, there is the risk of having the legislative body reverse a given policy autonomy. Obviously, it is imperative that these disciplinary tools are tightly defined and strictly demarcated, so that accountability does not encroach on the objectives underlying monetary policy independence. Only then will the trade-off between accountability and independence be mitigated and will these elements become complementary. Finally, although more implicit, the general public also has at its disposal an instrument to penalise policy mistakes: downgrading the reputation of the governor.

Besides the issues of what accountability means, why it is important, and how it is to be established, there is also the question of which standard to use when assessing the central bank's performance. Essentially, this standard depends on the mandate of the central bank. In this respect, accountability can hardly be established for a central bank that has goal independence – i.e., for which the end objectives are not clearly legislated. In such cases, central bank independence inevitably creates a democratic deficit. But even in cases where the monetary authority is provided a specific objective such as price stability or a numerical inflation target, the standard for accountability is far from clear-cut. After all, this end objective should not be pursued regardless of the cost in terms of interest rate (and thus output) instability and, anyway, developments under this end objective are not fully controlled by the central bank. Moreover, policy measures only affect this end objective after a considerable time lag, which may be too long a period for effective accountability.

This is where the choice of monetary policy strategy comes in. By selecting an appropriate intermediate target, the monetary authority can specify a variable that gives more timely information on its policies and that is subject to greater control. In this manner, the adoption of an intermediate policy target can provide a supplementary and more practical standard for accountability. The target design may also pre-specify the desired balance between the stability of inflation and that of output. For instance, this trade-off is explicitly internalised in nominal income targets, but may also be incorporated into money targets (when these targets are set on the basis of trend rather than actual output growth) or inflation targets (when these are defined in terms of underlying inflation or when these include caveats for supply shocks).

Announcing an intermediate policy target thus makes it easier to hold the central bank responsible for its policy deeds. This is because the central bank not only says what it strives to achieve, but also how it plans to do this. Nonetheless, even with an intermediate target, the accountability standard is all but straightforward. In first instance, the monetary authority may then be held accountable for keeping the intermediate variable on its precommitted track. As long as it is successful on this score, the central bank need only be able to make the case that the chosen target is consistent with the given end objectives. However, there may be valid reasons for the central bank to accept deviations under the intermediate target. This may occur, for example, when the relationship with the end objective changes unexpectedly or when an unforeseen adverse shock raises the costs of sticking to the predetermined policy course to unacceptable heights. In such instances, accountability implies that the central bank must be able to justify deviations from target on the basis of its end objectives.

In a theoretical context, these accountability issues have been addressed within the principal-agent framework. Specifically, applications of this framework show that an optimal policy outcome can be achieved by providing the central bank governor with a wage contract that is inversely linked to the inflation outcome after correcting for inflation responses to aggregate supply shocks.[77] Of course, these model-based insights focus on salary benefits while, in practice, such benefits probably are unlikely to play a dominant role in the minds of central bank governors. But the framework's approach to institutional design is also broadly applicable to the other variables determining the central banker's incentive structure, including prospects for reappointment, risks of having independence reversed and, especially, reputational considerations. A role for these variables in the incentive structure of the central bank assumes, of course, a sufficient degree of transparency in the monetary policy-making process. However, as will be set out below, transparency is of considerably broader relevance to the success and credibility of a monetary policy strategy.

2.5.5 Credibility and communication: the role of transparency

While a central bank's policy precommitment, instrument independence and incentive structure are important elements in establishing credibility, the degree in which these elements actually contribute to credibility-building depends on their communication to the public at large. In effect, a monetary policy strategy is more than just the decisions of what (intermediate) target to set for monetary policy and what institutional design to adopt for the central bank. It is also the issue of how to communicate this strategy to the general public in an effort to maximise the stabilising effects of monetary policy. This is where the role of transparency comes in.

The benefits of transparency

In the context of monetary policy, transparency can be defined as the public disclosure of information relevant to monetary policy decision-making. Essentially, transparency serves to clarify the links between the instruments, operational targets, intermediate targets, and end objectives of monetary policy. By making these links explicit, including the institutional setting governing them, transparency can advertise the consistency of a given policy framework and can thereby contribute to confidence in policy implementation. Put differently, a reduction in the ambiguity of monetary policy-making effectively limits the scope for central banks to engage in unheeded monetary surprises.[78] In itself, this will instil greater confidence in the monetary authority and lessen any inflationary bias stemming from the perceived risk of time inconsistent policies.

In practice, transparency is mainly established at two levels: (i) transparency about monetary policy objectives, whether intermediate or final; and (ii) transparency about the monetary instruments and policy measures implemented towards these objectives (necessarily framed by an analysis of the economic outlook). Both essentially form part of the communication elements of the monetary strategy, the former being a question of announcement, the latter of explanation.

As regards the first level, transparency involves making the monetary authorities' objectives explicit in a monitorable (i.e., specific and time-bound) manner. In particular, the announcement of objectives strengthens monetary policy in several ways by:

- increasing *policy ambition*: the publicity associated with the announcement of objectives provides the monetary authorities with an (*ex ante*) incentive to adopt appropriately ambitious objectives within a coherent policy strategy;
- increasing *policy discipline*: once authorities have publicly announced their policy objectives, they will have an (*ex post*) incentive to live up to them to preserve their reputation;
- increasing *policy accountability*: announcement provides a yardstick against which the central bank can be held accountable for its actions; this not only reduces incentives for time inconsistent policies, but in a democratic context also broadens public acceptance of the policy framework;
- increasing *policy effectiveness*: announcement signals policy intentions, thereby reducing uncertainty and favourably influencing expectations.

The extent to which this fourth benefit arises depends, however, on the credibility of the announced monetary policy objective. This credibility may be rooted in a firm institutional framework with central bank independence, but needs to be validated at the second level of transparency: that of monetary policy measures. Transparency at this level means providing information on the specifics of monetary policy measures and on the considerations driving these measures. This strengthens monetary policy in a number of further ways by:

- *increasing policy consistency* between measures and objectives: transparency in the monetary decision-making process subjects policy implementation to closer external scrutiny, thereby exerting a disciplinary influence that promotes consistency between policy measures and objectives (this is an *ex ante* effect);
- *increasing public support* for monetary policy measures: when there is support for the end objective of monetary policy, clarifying the monetary transmission process enhances public support for the policy measures necessary to achieve that objective (this effect occurs *during* implementation);
- *reducing policy uncertainty*: transparency on operational motives and measures reduces market uncertainty about the underlying policy course (*during* implementation);

- *accelerating credibility gains*: operational transparency provides insight into the extent to which monetary policy operations and objectives are consistent, thereby accelerating a build-up in credibility (*during* implementation); these gains are especially relevant when there are initial doubts about the authorities' commitment to their target;
- *limiting potential credibility losses*: transparency at the operational level provides justification for the monetary authorities' actions, thereby limiting credibility losses if the policy target turns out to have been missed and if policies are shown in hindsight to have been deficient (this is an *ex post* effect).

The credibility effects at these two levels of transparency may involve an intertemporal trade-off. In particular, the (immediate) credibility bonus of announcing an ambitious policy objective needs to be weighed against the risk of a (later) credibility loss if the objective is not met. In this respect, two further considerations need to be borne in mind when specifying a policy target. First, the announced objective should not be overly tight and demanding, since favourable announcement effects only accrue if the public considers the target to be realistically feasible. Second, there are benefits to making the assumptions underlying the policy target transparent, since this will mitigate the credibility costs of later adjustments to this target if exogenous circumstances change unexpectedly.

All told, transparency fosters more effective monetary policy-making. This is true regardless of the monetary strategy pursued. In this respect, the strength of the monetary policy strategy as a communication device will greatly depend on its perceived relevance for policy adjustments. This underscores the importance of explicitly justifying any policy change on the basis of the chosen (intermediate) monetary policy target.

However, the degree in which transparency actually contributes to policy objectives is not wholly independent of the adopted strategy. Specifically, the need for transparency depends on the opacity of the monetary policy targets. In principle, the less tangible these targets and the less clear their role in the process of monetary transmission, the greater the need for transparency to explain that monetary policy measures are consistent with given end objectives. For instance, direct inflation targeting requires considerable transparency to elucidate the relationship between instruments and objectives. Since the policy target is situated at the end of the monetary transmission process, transparency will need to clarify that any (lack of) policy measures affecting the beginning of this process are consistent with the target. Similarly, in the case of a money-oriented strategy communication with the public may be marred by the abstract character of the policy target. This difficulty can be addressed, to a degree, by being transparent about how the money target has been derived, for example by providing the breakdown of the target. In contrast with these two strategies, exchange rate targeting can be continuously monitored and tested by markets, and thus does not place as heavy requirements on transparency.

The importance of transparency also depends on other factors. As a rule, the more market-determined the financial environment, the greater the potential role for transparency. In effect, transparency can help bring market forces in line with policy intentions, which is crucial once markets form an integral part of monetary policy transmission. This is reflected in European monetary history, where financial deregulation and capital liberalisation have been followed by an increasing emphasis on transparency in the monetary policy process. A further consideration is the initial credibility of the monetary authorities: the lower this is, the greater the potential gains attached to transparency. In the extremes, a fully credible central bank has little need or incentive to be transparent, whereas a central bank lacking all credibility can use transparency to convince markets of its good intentions.

Transparency and the degree of policy ambition

The case for transparency is generally framed in terms of reducing the inflationary bias of monetary policy by precommitting policies and by establishing a basis for accountability. The focus is thus on locking in certain policies, stabilising expectations, and providing a basis for an *ex post* assessment of whether the monetary authorities have lived up to their promises.[79] However, the potential contribution of transparency to policy ambition, that is the *ex ante* assessment of the monetary authorities' own promises, is insufficiently recognised. In essence, this contribution reflects the fact that the requirement to announce a strategic objective will, in itself, tend to elicit an appropriately ambitious target. After all, when asked to declare objectives for an uncertain future, policy-makers will generally seek to confirm their intention of pursuing sound policies. Subsequently, once the target is announced and reputations are at stake, there will be an additional incentive actually to deliver on this intention.

With respect to the hypothesis that the announcement of policy targets creates an incentive for policy ambition, it is noteworthy that monetary policy targets publicised for any given period have mostly been at least as ambitious as the target for the previous period. A comparison of the different EU countries' announcements of money, credit and inflation targets over the past quarter of a century clearly brings this out (see Table 5). Of the announced targets, more than four out of five were at least

Table 5: Ambition of announced monetary policy target [1]

Monetary policy target compared to target in the previous year [2]	Country	Year
More ambitious (65x ; 48%)	France (8x)	1978, 1979, 1983, 1984, 1985, 1990, 1992, 1994
	Germany (9x)	1979[#], 1980, 1981, 1984, 1985, 1991, 1994, 1997, 1998
	Greece (10x)	1979, 1980, 1984, 1987, 1988[#], 1991, 1992[x], 1994, 1995[x], 1996[#]
	Ireland (5x)	1976”, 1979”, 1980”, 1982”, 1983”
	Italy (12x)	1977”, 1979”, 1980”,1981”,1982”,1985, 1986[#], 1987[x], 1991, 1992[x], 1995[x], 1996
	Portugal (2x)	1988[x], 1989[#]
	Spain (10x)	1981, 1982, 1983, 1986, 1987, 1989, 1993, 1994[#], 1997*, 1998*
	United Kingdom 9x)	1978, 1979, 1981, 1983, 1984, 1985, 1988, 1991, 1996*
Equally ambitious (41x ; 30%)	Finland (3x)	1996*, 1997*, 1998*
	France (8x)	1980, 1987, 1988, 1989, 1995, 1996, 1997, 1998
	Germany (9x)	1976, 1977, 1978, 1982, 1983, 1987[#], 1988, 1990[#], 1995
	Greece (3x)	1983, 1993, 1997
	Italy (6x)	1988, 1989, 1990, 1993, 1994, 1997
	Spain (1x)	1990
	Sweden (3x)	1996*, 1997*, 1998*
	United Kingdom (8x)	1977, 1980, 1987, 1989, 1990, 1993*, 1994*, 1995*
Less ambitious (29x ; 21%)	France (3x)	1981, 1982, 1993
	Germany (5x)	1986, 1989[x], 1992, 1993, 1996
	Greece (6x)	1977, 1978, 1981, 1982, 1989, 1990
	Ireland (3x)	1977”, 1978”, 1981”
	Italy (4x)	1976”, 1978”, 1983”, 1998
	Spain (6x)	1979[x], 1980, 1985[x], 1988, 1991[#], 1992[#]
	United Kingdom (2x)	1982, 1997*

Source: Appendix Tables.

[x] : with narrowing of the target range; [#] : with widening of target range;
” : relates to total domestic credit target; * : relates to announced inflation target.

[1] A target is considered ‘more ambitious’ if the point target or midpoint of the target range is lower than the target in the previous year and ‘less ambitious’ in the opposite case. Similarly, a ceiling is considered ‘more ambitious’ than a point target or midpoint of target range, and vice versa. A target is defined as ‘equally ambitious’ if the value of the point target or midpoint of the target range is equal to that in the previous year.

[2] Targets relate to money aggregates unless otherwise indicated. Target years do not always fully coincide with calendar years and have been matched with closest equivalent. Years relating to the introduction of a monetary policy strategy or to a switch to an incomparable aggregate have been excluded: this was the case in Finland (1995*); France (1977, 1986, 1991); Germany (1975); Greece (1976); Ireland (1975); Italy (1976, 1984); Portugal (1987); Spain (1978, 1984, 1996*); Sweden (1995*); and the United Kingdom (1976, 1992*). Years with two targets providing an ambiguous signal have been excluded: this was the case in the United Kingdom (1986) and in Greece (1985, 1986) when one target was loosened and the other was tightened. Not publicly announced targets and monitoring ranges have also been excluded.

as ambitious as the target in the previous period; at the same time, targets exhibiting an increase in ambition were more than twice as common as those indicating a relaxation.[80] Moreover, in several of the cases where the announced (intermediate) target was not as tight as in the previous period, this was explicitly related to stronger, offsetting, factors that implied no weakening of the end-objective. Prime examples are the loosening of the money targets in Germany in 1986 and 1987: given the sought-after appreciation of the Deutsche Mark following the G-5 New York Plaza agreement, higher money growth targets could be announced even with lower implicit inflation targets.[81]

Of course, this tendency to announce at least as ambitious policy targets says nothing about policy outcomes. In this respect, it could be argued that the gradual tightening of policy targets has been a result rather than a cause of the general decline in inflation since the mid-1970s. Moreover, intermediate targets are not always representative of the degree of policy ambition, since exogenous disturbances (such as shocks to oil prices or money velocity) may outweigh the influence of ambition in the setting of policy intentions. On balance, however, the preponderance of unchanged or more stringent targets, and the scarcity of looser ones, provides an indication that monetary authorities indeed strive to announce policy objectives indicating progress, or at least no backtracking, relative to the previous year. In itself, this seems to be a significant, although generally overlooked, reason why transparency contributes to the strength of monetary policy-making.

In this context it is also noteworthy that, in virtually all countries, deviations from intermediate targets (thereby excluding inflation targets) have on average tended to be positive – that is, outcomes have generally been looser than targets. By way of illustration, even in the case of Germany, the money target mid-points have been on average 1 percentage point tighter than the related outcomes. This further suggests that targets contain an element of policy ambition or, if you will, of wishful thinking. Besides this, from a political economy perspective, ambitious intermediate targets may also be used to facilitate sufficiently tight monetary policy operations in the future. For instance, since above target money growth will usually make it easier to gain acceptance for the need for policy tightening, the setting of ambitious money targets in Germany has presumably smoothed the path for timely policy adjustments. Of course, this is contingent on the initial credibility of the targets, which the Bundesbank has gone to great lengths to establish (*inter alia*, by providing a breakdown of the targets' individual components).

Potential costs of transparency

Transparency does not come without potential costs, however. By consequence, the case for open communication with the public is not entirely one-sided. At the level of the intermediate or final targets of a monetary policy strategy, the drawbacks of transparency may be felt on two fronts. First, given ongoing changes in economic structures and continuous susceptibility to unexpected shocks, the central bank may have valid reasons to change the policy course in mid-stream and to depart from predetermined targets. But each departure from a preannounced target will to some extent undermine the credibility of future announcements and, more generally, of the monetary authority. Therefore, the higher the risk of significant departures and the more difficult the communication of their justification, the weaker the case to make targets public. In essence, there is a trade-off between the credibility-strengthening impact of announcing a target and the credibility-weakening impact of later deviating from it. This latter effect is likely to prevail when deviations are generally one-sided and repeatedly involve a loosening vis-à-vis the target.

Second, also at the level of policy targets, too much communication and transparency may actually reduce the strength of policy signals. Indeed, a monetary strategy is likely to be more potent as a communication device when the policy signals are uniform and straightforward. In broad terms, the more simple the strategy, the larger its potential impact on economic expectations.[82] This argues against setting more than one target for specific intermediate objectives, as for example was done in the United Kingdom from February 1982 until March 1987 (with targets set concurrently for two, and at times even three, money definitions), in France in 1987 (for two money definitions), and in Greece from 1983 until 1987 (for two money definitions). It also argues against frequent changes in target definitions and target time horizons, as notably occurred in these first two countries in the 1980s.[83] Furthermore, simplicity suggests not setting multiple targets for different intermediate and final objectives, as has been done by many European countries that have combined exchange rate commitments with money, credit or inflation targets. In such cases, however, the additional target(s) could be seen as confirming the monetary authority's anti-inflationary resolve on domestic grounds and thus as fulfilling a complementary signalling role to the external commitment. Nonetheless, publicising more than one (potentially incompatible) monetary policy target risks sending confusing signals and compromising the credibility of the monetary authority in times of policy conflict between the targets. This basically reflects Tinbergen's rule, according to which the number of policy targets should not exceed the number of policy instruments.

There are similar arguments for limiting transparency at the level of operational policy-making. In general, too much transparency may lead to an information overdose that clouds rather than clarifies the understanding of the germane considerations driving monetary policy. This especially applies to the release of unstructured information. In a similar vein, some forms of openness may actually detract attention from the essential issues at stake. For instance, the publication of individual voting patterns may lead to an excessive public focus on the personalities of the individual policy-makers (is so-and-so a 'hawk' or a 'dove'?), rather than on the substance of the policy decision. Moreover, when the underlying state of the economy is unclear and the preferred policy course is uncertain, the central bank may wish to keep its policy options open. In this situation, publicising the central bank's wavering may heighten public uncertainty and undermine confidence in the monetary authority's proficiency. Indeed, undue transparency may cause confusion.[84] When such factors are at play, there may be a case to restrict the flow of information to the public and to implement policy with a 'hidden hand'. This approach may also be attractive on political grounds when the central bank wishes to attribute a change in the policy stance – especially a monetary tightening – to market-driven developments rather than to a policy-led adjustment. Similarly, there may be specific circumstances when the central bank wishes to augment uncertainty by keeping the public in the dark, for example in a situation of exuberant market conditions.

Besides this, external publicity may have a detrimental impact on the internal decision-making process itself. Although not often recognized as such, in practice this may be the chief consideration determining the setup of the communication arrangements. Specifically, increased transparency of the internal decision-making process may lead to more formal proceedings, may undermine individual policy-makers' readiness to compromise, and may reduce their willingness to discuss issues they feel unsure about. Conversely, a degree of secrecy can be instrumental in avoiding a highly politicised environment surrounding monetary policy decisions. In particular, limited or delayed public disclosure may make it more difficult for specific political interest groups to pressure monetary policy-makers.[85] Finally, from a broader perspective, transparency on the positions of individual members of the policy-making body may, in case of differences of opinion, be interpreted as a weaker overall commitment to a certain policy course.

Striking a balance

In view of the evident benefits as well as the potential costs of monetary policy transparency, a balance needs to be struck. At the level of the objectives of monetary policy, there is a trade-off between a strategy's signalling role, which requires simple and uniform targets, and its explanatory role, which calls for more open and broad-ranging communication. Together, these considerations suggest advertising a single official monetary policy target and explicating the assumptions underlying this target. This enhances the signalling role of the target, while also providing a basis to justify any subsequent deviations from the preannounced target. To the extent other policy objectives or reference points are announced, their motivation must be clear and their priority vis-à-vis the prime policy target must be specified.

At the operational level of monetary policy-making, the recipe for transparency is more complex. Here, the trade-off is primarily between, on the one hand, steering expectations and establishing an adequate basis for accountability and, on the other hand, not unduly constraining the monetary policy decision-making process. In general, this trade-off is dominated by the culture governing monetary policy: the arguments for transparency will be stronger when the monetary authority's initial credibility is frail and its legitimacy is perceived to be weak. Besides this, the specific circumstances may also play a role, since there will be an inclination towards greater transparency when the central bank is more confident about its prospective policy course and when policy uncertainty is not instrumental in limiting market exuberance.

However, the quest for transparency may reach a limit beyond which it impinges on the ensemble of the internal policy-making process. This will be the case when the publicity of internal proceedings creates more partisan decision-making, undermines the candour of policy discussions, and subjects individual central bankers to pressures from specific interest groups. In this context, much depends on the assessment of the precise elements that are needed to make a policy decision transparent. Is a comprehensive explanation of a policy decision sufficient, or does the full discourse leading up to the decision need to be made public? Should there be openness on the degree of support for each decision, and perhaps even on the exact voting pattern? And, if such information is made public, should this be immediate or should there be a time lag? On these issues, again, there is not one size that fits all – much depends on the culture and circumstances governing a policy-making body.

In general, however, it may be beneficial to apply transparency selectively. This may involve, for instance, providing a detailed motivation of final policy decisions, but not granting a verbatim transcript of the unstructured policy debate (or, for that matter, a live broadcast in the media), as this is unlikely to increase insight into the true thrust of monetary policy. Indeed, beyond such a motivation, external openness is likely to infringe upon the internal openness of the policy debate.[86] Whether or not to publicise the weight of the majority or the individual voting pattern may largely be determined by the collective nature of the decisions by the policy-making body and the degree in which its members are liable to outside pressures. To the extent these two factors are deemed relevant, the costs of transparency on voting behaviour are likely to outweigh the benefits of transparency in terms of raising individual accountability. As regards the related issue of whether specific information on voting patterns should be published quickly in order to establish individual accountability, it may also be argued that such publicity should at least await the policy outcome – implying a publication lag that covers the (uncertain) time horizon of the monetary transmission process. Only after such a lag will there be a solid basis on which to hold individual policy-maker accountable.

2.6 Conclusions

A review of the general considerations determining the preferred monetary strategy makes clear that there is no unequivocal answer to the optimal monetary strategy question for any country for any significant length of time. This reflects the complex and changing nature of the many considerations underlying the monetary strategy choice. A first issue to take into account is the type, origin, symmetry and duration of shocks most commonly afflicting an economy. These aspects have a direct bearing on monetary strategy design, which should strive to minimise the disruptive impact of economic disturbances. When distinguishing conceptually between the two opposite regime choices, money targeting is advisable if shocks are primarily in domestic expenditure and foreign prices, exchange rate targeting is preferable if shocks are mainly monetary, temporary and symmetric, and the superior regime is ambiguous if other external and supply side shocks dominate. At this same level of abstraction, a strategy of direct inflation targeting may perform relatively well under more diverse circumstances as it is attuned to a broader set of variables, but it may risk larger output costs when shocks are primarily of the supply side type. In practice, however, it is usually difficult to accurately assess this relevant information on shocks, since shocks commonly have a variety of causes with intertwined effects. Moreover, the appraisal of disturbances needs to be forward-looking, since it is the likelihood of certain types of shocks occurring in the future – and not their probability distribution in the past – that is relevant to the monetary strategy choice.

A second issue determining the optimal monetary strategy is the extent to which the structural characteristics of the economy allow an easy accommodation of economic disturbances, as this reduces the need for a monetary policy reaction. Prominent among the relevant structural characteristics are the degree of wage flexibility, labour mobility, production diversity and openness, as well as the scope for budgetary stabilisation and the similarity of the monetary transmission process with that of partner countries. In normative terms, the more prevalent these characteristics, the lower the net costs of adopting a monetary strategy that limits the scope for domestic policy orientation, such as with an exchange rate-based strategy. At the same time, however, a liberalisation of capital movements raises these costs, notably by increasing the policy demands of an exchange rate commitment. The resulting ambiguity in the assessment of the costs and benefits of adopting a specific monetary strategy increases when second-round influences on the structural and behavioural characteristics of the economy are taken into account, such as Goodhart's Law in the case of monetary targeting and convergence of monetary transmission processes in the case of exchange rate targeting.

A third element driving the monetary strategy choice is the authorities' prioritisation of macroeconomic objectives. Essentially, this reflects the different implications of each monetary policy strategy for short-term trade-offs between the stability of output, prices, and the balance of payments. It is difficult to arrive at normative statements on these trade-offs, as these depend not only on the nature of shocks, the structural characteristics of the economy and the monetary strategy pursued, but also on the rigidity with which this latter is implemented. For instance, unfavourable trade-offs can easily be envisaged in the case of either a tight exchange rate peg with large expenditure shocks, a binding money rule with substantial money demand swings, or a rigid inflation target with sizeable supply side disturbances. To avoid such detrimental rigidity, the operational specifications of monetary strategies generally include elements of flexibility that aim at accommodating given prioritisations of objectives. In this respect, the differences between the various monetary strategy types actually become quite fluid when the alternative operational specifications are taken into account. In practice, however, there is some evidence that, on balance, money anchors may generally be associated with less short-term variability in output and the balance of payments, but higher and more volatile inflation than exchange rate anchors. More generally, it should be underscored that a monetary policy strategy will only be able to deliver a chosen prioritisation of these objectives if it is not overwhelmed by instability in other areas – notably in the realm of fiscal policy and wage developments. While tight exchange rate targeting may be the strategy that places the heaviest demands on other policy fields (given the lack of the monetary and exchange rate instrument for domestic stabilisation purposes), a consistent policy mix is indispensable for the medium-term viability of any monetary policy strategy.

A final set of considerations underlying the monetary strategy choice relates to political economy variables that determine central bank credibility. This credibility generates crucial benefits in terms of lower inflation expectations, moderate wage demands, reduced real interest rates and greater effectiveness of monetary policy, and enhances the stabilising properties of each distinct monetary policy strategy. To establish such credibility, it must be in the monetary authority's genuine interest to consistently pursue appropriate preannounced policy objectives and the public must be convinced that this is indeed the case. In practice, this means the monetary authority should be precommitted to prioritise a price stability objective, that it should be free to implement its instruments towards this objective, that its incentive structure should promote decision-making consistent with this objective, and that these different elements are transparently communicated to the public at large.

A first strategic approach to credibility building involves precommitting monetary policy through adoption of an exchange rate anchor and granting the central bank policy autonomy to uphold this peg. However, this approach is not broadly applicable since the benefits of increased credibility may not outweigh the costs of having less scope to adjust policies to domestic developments. A second, universally applicable, approach entails strengthening the institutional framework governing monetary policy, either by making the central bank independent and giving it an explicit price stability objective, or by contracting the central bank to pursue a prespecified inflation objective and granting it autonomy in its operations.

The credibility-enhancing impact of monetary policy independence may be further strengthened by an appropriate degree of central bank accountability, as this creates incentives for policy success and disincentives for policy abuse. In addition, in a democratic context, accountability may serve to validate a given policy independence and thus to underpin its longer term viability. However, the disciplinary instruments of accountability must be clearly delineated in order to ensure that these do not encroach on the objectives underlying central bank independence. In this context, the standard for accountability is far from straightforward, as developments in terms of the end objectives for price and output stability are not fully under the central bank's control and are subject to lengthy policy transmission lags. While the adoption of intermediate policy targets may establish a supplementary standard with more timely information on the rectitude of the policy course, unforeseen economic shocks may create valid reasons to deviate from such targets. Thus, to a large extent, accountability boils down to the central bank allowing a close external monitoring and being able to justify its (lack of) policy decisions relative to its mandate – at the risk of a policy override, a dismissal/non-reappointment, or a reputation loss if it does not have a convincing case. This makes clear that transparency is a necessary precondition for accountability. However, transparency is of considerably broader relevance.

Indeed, by advertising the consistency of a given policy framework and instilling confidence in the appropriateness of policy implementation, transparency can play a crucial, complementary role in the credibility-building process. In particular, transparency at the level of monetary policy objectives increases policy ambition, policy discipline, policy accountability and, through its impact on expectations, policy effectiveness. Similarly, transparency at the level of monetary policy operations enhances policy consistency, reduces policy uncertainty, accelerates credibility gains, limits credibility losses (in case of policy mistakes) and, more generally, increases public support for monetary policy actions. At the same time, however, a delicate balance needs to be struck in the pursuit for transparency, since too much transparency may limit policy options in the face of unforeseen developments and may reduce the strength of policy signals. Moreover, external publicity may intrude on the internal decision-making process by reducing the candour of the policy discussions, making the individual central bankers more liable to outside pressures, and limiting the flexibility of the positions and proceedings. On balance, a normative prescription for this monetary strategy element would be to adopt a uniform and easily understood monetary policy target, to explicate the assumptions underlying this target, to consistently explain monetary policy operations in the context of this target, and to tailor the amount of such information to the credibility of monetary policy, the uncertainty prevailing in the markets, and the certitude of the central bank's decision-making.

The European context, 1975-1998

All told, the complexity, ambiguity, uncertainty, and endogeneity underlying the monetary strategy choice leaves limited room for clear-cut, uniform policy prescriptions. This is borne out by the European experience, which has been characterised by many different and varying strategy choices. To a certain extent, this reflects the uncertainty inherent in a decision based on a forecast of future shocks, structures, behavioural patterns and preferences. But it is also a result of the ambiguities and trade-offs underlying the general considerations that determine the monetary strategy choice. In practice, alternative assessments, learning effects and changing circumstances have continually called for strategy refinements and in some cases even regime shifts.

Of the various issues governing the monetary strategy choice, three have undergone a particularly pronounced change over the past quarter century. First, the increasingly market-determined financial environment has added to the importance of monetary policy credibility. This has been reflected in a general movement towards greater transparency in monetary policy-making and, more specifically, in the granting of (at least) operational independence to all EU central banks. Second, the European economies have experienced a progressive opening up and have irrefutably become increasingly interwoven. This has broadened the span of any 'optimal' European currency area and has made the economies more vulnerable to (the perception of) competitive distortions through exchange rate manipulation. Other things assumed equal, this has raised the importance attached to a degree of exchange rate stability. Third, at the same time, the progressive liberalisation of capital flows has made exchange rate commitments more difficult to sustain and monetary policies more difficult to co-ordinate. Ultimately, the friction between this second and third development can only be resolved through a definite locking of exchange rates. In this sense, the overview of general considerations affecting the monetary strategy choice sheds light on the continuous quest for a European monetary union.

NOTES

[1] Poole's original analysis is based on a closed-economy Hicksian IS-LM model and is cast in terms of an interest rate or money supply rule. Notwithstanding its limitations, the straightforward and intuitively appealing set-up of the model provides an attractive theoretical basis to gauge the implications of adopting different monetary policy targets. The framework is also applicable to open economies: in the absence of restrictions on capital flows, an interest rate rule is comparable to an exchange rate rule with the interest rate fixed by the external anchor. In this sense, the standard framework amalgamates the instruments, operational targets and intermediate targets of monetary policy; to avoid ambiguity, these are communally referred to as 'targets'.

[2] For an overview of the main issues see B. Friedman (1990). Various extensions are discussed in Argy and de Grauwe (1990); early refinements are presented in Turnovsky (1976).

[3] It goes without saying that under exceptional circumstances different conclusions may apply regarding the optimal monetary target. Goodhart (1989, pp. 340-342) presents a hypothetical case where an increase in incomes raises investment more than savings (such that the IS-curve is positively rather than negatively sloped); however, as long as the interest rate is more potent in stabilising the real sector than the monetary sector (i.e., the slope of

the IS-curve is less steep than that of the LM-curve), the standard conclusions on the stability of the different monetary targets continue to apply.

[4] In principle, the evaluation should take account of all macroeconomic issues of concern to the authorities including, next to output and inflation, objectives for such variables as unemployment, real consumption and the balance of payments. However, this would lead to an excessively complex and unwieldy definition of the authorities' loss function; this is reflected in the literature, where the optimality criterion is most commonly specified in terms of the stability of real output and prices.

[5] At a technical level, the ambiguity is further complicated by the measurement question of whether the stability of output should be assessed relative to its old or new equilibrium.

[6] This point is forcefully made by M. Friedman (1953) in an early article on the benefits of exchange rate flexibility.

[7] This is argued, for example, by Aghevli, Khan and Montiel (1991).

[8] This line of reasoning is also followed by Argy (1990, pp. 36-37), with one exception. He claims that the superior regime is ambiguous under most shocks originating abroad, but that flexible rates are likely to be more stabilising in the case of foreign money demand disturbances. This latter conclusion is, however, questionable. It is based on the assumption that the foreign authorities will adjust interest rates in reaction to the money demand shock; thus, the foreign money demand disturbance ends up looking more like a foreign expenditure disturbance. The opposite conclusion (i.e., that a fixed rate system is likely to be superior) would be drawn if it were assumed that the foreign authorities would fully accommodate the monetary shock (as they should, to promote both price and output stability).

[9] Marston (1982).

[10] Calmfors and Driffill (1988) provide empirical evidence for this hypothesis; their survey includes 10 of the current European Union members. The hypothesis stressing the importance of 'corporatist' wage bargaining is further spelt out in De Grauwe (1997). In a critique, Soskice (1990) questions Calmfors and Driffill's classification of countries, arguing that actual wage setting often differs from the formal structure governing wage bargaining and that the weaknesses of decentralised systems become apparent when other factors (such as lower incentives to invest in human capital) are taken into account. A further amendment of the literature on corporatism is provided by Garrett and Way (1995) who review the influence of 'corporatism' in terms of whether or not the trade union movement is dominated by unions in the tradables sector. They find that if the latter is the case (as in Austria and Finland), the benefit of closer regional monetary and economic integration will be much larger than in countries where this is not the case (as in Sweden). The arguments that link these different views on labour market structure to the monetary strategy choice are essentially similar to those related to the centralised/decentralised case.

[11] This argument becomes more complicated when hysteresis effects are taken into account. But even then, it is doubtful whether continuous accommodation of excessive nominal wage demands increases welfare. Rather, the existence of such effects should prompt all parties concerned to make the transitional period of structural adjustment as short as possible.

[12] Bertola (1989) illustrates the importance of uncertainty using a microeconomic model incorporating uncertainty and adjustment costs related to resource reallocation. His debatable conclusion that stable exchange rates result in greater income variability and thus reduce labour mobility is dependent on the specification of his model and the assumption that the economy is subject to asymmetric terms of trade disturbances. He also disregards issues related to the eventual reconversion of foreign earnings into national currency.

[13] Bini Smaghi and Vori (1993, p. 91) reject migration as an adjustment instrument by emphasising the "social and economic costs that economists generally ignore".

[14] Bayoumi and Prasad (1997) analyse sectoral output, employment and productivity trends, and find that these latter are dominated by country-specific factors in the EU and by industry-specific factors in the United States. Their results also suggest no significant structural changes affecting the degree of integration of European labour markets between 1970 and 1987. Eichengreen (1993) compares labour mobility in Britain and Italy with that in the United States, and finds the elasticity of migration with respect to inter-regional wage differentials is more than five times larger in the United States. The study by Thomas (1994a) analysing labour market flexibility in France, Germany, Italy, the United Kingdom and the United States over a quarter of a century, corroborates these findings.

[15] Kenen (1969) introduced this element into the optimal currency area debate.

[16] See Bayoumi and Eichengreen (1996), who also suggest that the smaller the country, the tighter the constraint on borrowing, and the more limited the scope for stabilisation policies. In empirical research with clear parallels to the European context, Bayoumi and Masson (1998) investigate fiscal stabilisation across Canadian provinces and find significant Ricardian effects: budgetary stabilisers at the local level are estimated to be only one-third to one-half as effective as those at the national level. Overall, however, they recall that studies on the size of federal fiscal stabilisers have generally found these to be modest, offsetting at best 20 to 30 per cent of the initial reduction in income.

[17] At a national level, an exception is provided by Denmark, which has actively used budgetary policy in the 1990s to compensate for asymmetric economic developments.

[18] Polak (1988) provides a lucid overview of the generally unsatisfactory experience in the 1970s and early 1980s with fiscal policies aimed at economic stabilisation.

[19] Reflecting this ambiguity, Aghevli, Khan and Montiel (1991) and Gros and Steinherr (1997) take the view that openness *per se* does not allow any general conclusions on the preferable exchange regime.

[20] This is the position initially set out in the seminal article by McKinnon (1963); more recent supporters include Guitián (1994a), De Grauwe (1997), Masson and Taylor (1992), and Tavlas (1993).

[21] Frankel and Rose (1996) find a strong positive link between the degree of trade integration and the correlation of business cycles using panel data for 20 industrial countries over a 30-year period. Similarly, the European Commission (1990) finds a significant inverse relationship between the extent of trade barriers and the symmetry of sector-specific shocks.

[22] European Commission (1990, p. 43). In an insightful earlier essay on the monetary policy objectives of the European Community, Padoa-Schioppa (1988) speaks of an "inconsistent Quartet" of full trade integration, complete mobility of capital, fixed exchange rates, and autonomous monetary policy; clearly, the first element can be dropped without losing the inconsistency.

[23] For an overview of the movement towards full capital liberalisation in Europe, see Bakker (1996).

[24] In the early 1980s, the G-7 Working Group on Exchange Market Intervention chaired by Jurgensen (1983) already concluded that sterilised intervention did not appear to be an effective instrument to influence exchange rates in the face of significant market pressure; domestic policy adjustments, in particular in the field of monetary policy, were viewed as indispensable to counter such pressure.

[25] At a global level, there is clear evidence that progress with capital liberalisation has been associated with a declining popularity of exchange rate targeting; see Cottarelli and Giannini (1997).

[26] On the risk of self-fulfilling currency attacks in the context of capital mobility, see Eichengreen and Wyplosz (1993) and Obstfeld (1995).

[27] Once market participants become concerned that the exchange rate may be adjusted, the interest rate will need to react vigorously to offset such concerns. For instance, if a portfolio manager takes the view that there is a trifling *one-in-ten* chance of a currency being devalued by just 5 per cent in the next week, the interest rate differential will need to be 30 per cent on an annual basis in favour of the suspect currency to compensate the relatively mild devaluation fears. A vivid description of the difficulty of sustaining a fixed-but-adjustable regime in the face of full capital mobility, based on first-hand experience, is provided by Crockett (1994a).

[28] Kenen (1969), in first highlighting the importance of diversification, correctly took the view that this may be more relevant than the issue of labour mobility.

[29] See European Commission (1996, pp. 71-77). An earlier discussion of the degree of product market integration, based on a study for 1987, is provided in European Commission (1990, p. 142).

[30] See Bini Smaghi and Vori (1993), Helg *et al.* (1994) and Masson and Taylor (1993).

[31] Bayoumi and Prasad (1997), however, find broadly similar degrees of relative specialisation in Europe and the United States, implying that industry-specific disturbances are likely to have a comparable impact in both economic areas.

[32] For example, the monetary policy transmission mechanism is not included in Tavlas' (1993) list of relevant characteristics identified in the literature on optimum currency areas; neither is it included in the costs and benefits of monetary integration discussed in European Commission (1990) and De Grauwe (1997); nor is it mentioned in the optimum currency area criteria set out in Bayoumi and Eichengreen (1996), Frankel and Rose (1996), and Masson and Taylor (1993).

[33] Although insight into the different channels of monetary transmission has been significantly improved by numerous studies during the past decade, the words of King (1994) remain largely valid: "The transmission mechanism of monetary policy is one of the most important, yet least well understood, aspects of economic behaviour."

[34] Borio (1995) provides a comprehensive overview of the structure of credit to the non-government sector in fourteen countries, including nine EU members. His findings confirm the popular classification that, in general, Anglo-Saxon countries are characterised by a relatively high share of credit to households, with a comparatively large share of adjustable rate debt (except in the US), and widespread use of real estate collateral. This difference between Anglo-Saxon and continental European countries is set out in more general terms in Boonstra and Eijffinger (eds.) (1997) in a survey of developments in financial systems and monetary policy in nine industrial countries, including seven EU members.

[35] Using the United Kingdom as an illustration, Eijffinger (1996) stresses that a high short-term interest rate sensitivity may contribute to a perverse incentive structure for the central bank.

[36] These studies have produced very different results and a consensus opinion on the degree of differences in monetary policy transmission has not emerged – not even at a general level (see Kieler and Saarenheimo (1998)). In part, this reflects the diverse methods used in the empirical literature: the studies have included straightforward structural analyses (focusing on differences in financial structures), large macroeconometric models (constructed on a single- and multi-country basis), small macroeconomic models, and structural VAR models. The greatest cross-national differences appear in the studies based on estimates of large, single-country macroeconometric models (see for instance Dornbusch, Favero and Giavazzi (1998)), but the statistical comparability of the results is limited by the variation in model specification. By contrast, the multi-country model approach suggests relatively small

differences in monetary transmission, but this may be attributed to the similar structure that such an approach imposes on all the countries. Given their more aggregated nature, small macroeconomic models may likewise do insufficient justice to cross-country diversity in economic structure. In turn, studies using structural VAR models may be questioned on account of the uncertainties involved in the structural identification schemes. Moreover, even within this specific approach, the results have not been uniform: while Ramaswamy and Sloek (1997) find output responding more slowly but cumulatively more strongly in some EU countries than in others, Barran, Coudert and Mojon (1996) also identify differences in the output response to monetary policy changes (as well as in the response of the final demand components), but find a reasonably similar pass-through in terms of timing. The varying strength of individual transmission channels in European countries is analysed in De Bondt (1999) and Kakes (2000).

[37] In Goodhart's (1984, p. 96) own words, "any observed statistical regularity will tend to collapse once pressure is placed upon it for control purposes".

[38] Based on a global study of 100 countries during the period 1970-94, Cottarelli and Giannini (1997) establish that the average volatility of broad money in countries that targeted this aggregate was one-half of that in the other countries. While it is unclear whether this lower volatility is a cause or a consequence of the policy focus, it would *a priori* seem to indicate that the impact of Goodhart's Law is not very powerful on an aggregated basis.

[39] Hochreiter and Winckler (1995) present evidence for Austria that the exchange rate peg to the Dmark led to adjustment processes which enhanced real wage flexibility and eventually made the country part of an optimal currency area with Germany, even though it clearly was not part of this area at the time the peg was first adopted. Similarly, Kremers (1990) investigates changes in Irish wage formation after the inception of the ERM and finds that inflation expectations in Ireland followed expected price movements in the United Kingdom until 1979 and shifted sharply to the expected price behaviour in the ERM partners thereafter. More generally, while Egebo and Englander (1992) argue that ERM participation *per se* does not provide a direct credibility bonus, they conclude that it does seem to improve policy discipline. Since such discipline is likely to impact labour market behaviour with a considerable lag, credibility benefits in labour markets will only emerge over time.

[40] While its study focused on the consequences of economic integration rather than specifically on exchange rate stability, the European Commission (1990) argues that the increasing product market integration in Europe has tended to be of the intra-industry type, notably in the manufacturing sector; thus, integration reduces the likelihood of asymmetric shocks. Similarly, Frankel and Rose (1996) find that intensified international trade links tend to lead to more closely correlated business cycles between countries. On this basis, they emphasise that since Europe is pursuing trade integration, countries adopting exchange rate links (or joining EMU) may satisfy optimal currency area criteria after the policy switch, even if this was not the case in the past. However, Bayoumi and Eichengreen (1996) present tentative evidence that increasing economic integration in Europe during 1971-1987 has been accompanied by a measurable increase in regional industrial specialisation, thereby reducing the correlation of underlying disturbances.

[41] An early IMF study (1984) on exchange rate volatility and world trade concluded that empirical evidence of a systematic significant link could not be found. In its paper on the benefits of a single currency for the European internal market, the not wholly unbiased European Commission (1990) also recognises the absence of strong empirical proof. A small effect is however found by Gagnon (1993), who estimates that the switch to flexible exchange rates after the collapse of the Bretton Woods regime may have reduced the volume of world trade by approximately 1 per cent. In a comprehensive study, Frankel and Wei (1995) also find a small and declining impact. The decline of this impact over the past three

decades is arguably linked to the increasing availability and use of financial instruments to hedge exchange rate risks – although it should, of course, be emphasised that the use of these instruments is not available for all currencies and maturities and is certainly not without cost. As an exception, Stokman (1995) finds significant effects of exchange rate risk on intra-EC trade: on the basis of a disaggregated product/sectoral analysis he estimates that the combined exports of five major EC countries would have been 3 per cent lower if exchange rate risk during 1987-90 had been at its level in the years preceding the EMS. However, as he only focuses on intra-EC trade, his estimates include both trade creation and trade diversion and may thus overstate the total effect.

[42] Bhandari and Mayer (1990) show that saving-investment correlations during 1975-1987 were substantially lower between the countries participating in the EMS and Austria, than between non-EMS countries. The relationship between saving and investment was also weaker in the post-1982 period (when the EMS hardened) than in the pre-EMS period.

[43] More specifically, based on observations for 1983 and 1993, the cross-country comparison in Borio (1995) does not provide evidence of convergence in the structure of credit between the Anglo-Saxon and the other industrial countries.

[44] Buttiglione, Del Giovane and Tristani (1997) analyse the impact of changes in central bank rates on the term structure of interest rates during 1987-95. They find that central bank rate increases led to decreases in long-term forward rates in Germany, the Netherlands and Belgium, to no change in France, and to rises in Italy, Spain, Sweden and the United Kingdom. While they link this to the past inflation records and indirectly to the credibility of the long-term anti-inflationary commitment of monetary policy, there is a clear-cut relationship with the frequency and size of past adjustments to the central exchange rate parities.

[45] Given the implicit consequences for the trade-off between near-term output and price objectives, it is worth noting that monetary strategies involving a regime commitment (such as an exchange rate arrangement or inflation target) are often decided in the political realm – i.e., by the Government and not by the central bank.

[46] Based on a comprehensive study involving 136 countries over a 30-year time-span, Ghosh *et al.* (1995) find that fixed exchange regimes are associated with lower inflation, but more variable output and employment than flexible regimes. Overall growth performance is not found to differ between exchange regimes. These results are materially unchanged when allowance is made for possible endogeneity of the regime choice. Moreover, no anti-inflation benefit is found to accrue to exchange regimes that are purportedly pegged, but show frequent parity changes in practice.

[47] Papademos and Modigliani (1990, pp. 476-487) provide an extensive comparison of the trade-offs between different money and credit aggregates.

[48] Rogoff (1985) provides a formal analysis of this trade-off. Fischer (1994) presents evidence that, during the period 1960-1992/93, inflation was lower and less variable in Germany than in the United States, but output growth was more variable. (The average growth rates of the two countries were identical during this period.) He attributes this to the greater independence of the German Bundesbank. He acknowledges, however, that his hypothesis is not supported by aggregate data for the industrialised countries.

[49] Whether central bank independence facilitates maintaining price stability is a different question from whether such independence reduces disinflation costs. In this context, De Haan, Knot and Sturm (1993) present evidence that central bank independence promotes a lower level of inflation, but does not reduce the (transitory) disinflation costs of arriving at that lower level. In fact, as discussed in Eijffinger and De Haan (1996), studies suggest central bank independence may even increase disinflation costs.

[50] In an empirical survey of 18 OECD countries in the period 1960-87, Alesina, Cohen and Roubini (1992) find statistically significant evidence of a political monetary cycle of moderate intensity involving an expansionary monetary policy in election years; however, this cycle is not very strong and does not occur at every election.

[51] To a large extent these qualifying arguments are also applicable to the previously mentioned output variability-inflation variability trade-off underlying a direct inflation targeting strategy. But the prioritisation of objectives is less tightly preordained when an independent central bank is given a general price stability objective, than when a central bank is explicitly mandated to aim at a specific, time-bound inflation target. Thus, the short-term trade-off is more likely to favour inflation stability at the cost of output variability under the inflation targeting approach, than under an independent central bank broadly oriented at price stability.

[52] Grilli, Masciandaro and Tabellini (1991), De Haan and Sturm (1992), as well as Alesina and Summers (1993) all arrive at the same conclusion: central bank independence promotes price stability, but has no measurable impact on real output growth nor on real output variability. These studies used industrial country samples that are relevant to the European context. Although Cukierman *et al.* (1993) find a negative relationship between central bank independence and real economic performance in a broader 63-country sample, they find no such significant relationship in separate estimations for the industrial country and developing country sub-groups, suggesting the outcome for the full sample is capturing other differences between the two sub-groups. In a contrary view, Forder (1998) questions the procedures for the measurement of central bank independence employed by Alesina and Summers (1993).

[53] Sargent and Wallace (1981).

[54] Keynes (1936, p. 203).

[55] An overview of the debate is provided in Fischer (1990). See also Barro (1986), McCallum (1987), Goodhart (1989) and Crockett (1994b).

[56] This is essentially the position taken by M. Friedman (1968), who suggests following a passive, fixed money growth rule. McCallum (1987) also subscribes to this view, but proposes an activist rule that targets the monetary base towards a non-inflationary expansion of nominal aggregate demand; simple simulations are shown to produce good results for the United States over a period of several decades.

[57] The breakthrough was made in an article by Sargent and Wallace (1975), who postulated that, with experience, a rational public would fully anticipate monetary measures and that, given this anticipation, such measures only translate into higher inflation and do not influence the real economy.

[58] It has been argued that the central bank will recognise the lack of sense of inflation surprises and that the public will understand this, leading to an equilibrium around price stability. However, with discretionary central bank policy, a risk-averse public that does not know the authorities' true inflation objective will nonetheless build an insurance premium into its inflationary expectations.

[59] McCallum (1995) argues that a truly rational central bank recognises the futility of continually exploiting temporarily given expectations and thus does not behave in a time inconsistent manner. However, this assumes a sufficiently long time horizon and low discount rate, which would not seem to hold in the case of a dependent central bank governed by discretion.

[60] Using a general equilibrium model, Barro and Gordon (1983a) show that reputation can to some degree substitute for policy rules. However, while their reputational outcomes are better than those under a discretionary system, they are inferior to the 'ideal' rules-based results of the model.

[61] This is proposed by Rogoff (1985) as a way to mitigate the time-inconsistency costs of discretion, while maintaining policy flexibility to deal with unforeseen shocks.

[62] Two renowned activist rules are McCallum's (1987) rule, which limits the expansion of the monetary base to the non-inflationary growth rate of nominal demand, and Taylor's (1993) rule, which sets the interest rate to minimise deviations from both inflation and real GDP targets.

[63] Flood and Isard (1989) propose a mixed strategy involving a simple rule that can be overridden in exceptional circumstances; institutional mechanisms are put forward as a way to penalise central banks that exercise discretion in non-exceptional circumstances.

[64] These first two costs are incorporated by Giavazzi and Pagano (1988) in a formal statement of how countries can gain credibility by pegging the exchange rate.

[65] Drazen and Masson (1994) argue that credibility depends on both observing a tough policy line *and* not incurring too high unemployment costs, as this will undermine the viability of the strategy. Given this dual concept, a devaluation may on occasion actually enhance credibility. They draw a parallel with a person seeking to lose weight, who may establish credibility more effectively by at times taking small meals, than by skipping meals altogether. They find support for their hypothesis in the development of interest rate differentials in the ERM, notably between Germany and France. Masson (1995) finds similar evidence during the United Kingdom's ill-omened ERM participation.

[66] Fischer (1994) defines this autonomy as 'instrument independence' and contrasts it with 'goal independence'; the latter applies to central banks that have an imprecisely defined objective and thereby enjoy greater policy latitude.

[67] On this ground, McCallum (1995) contends that the beneficial effects stemming from central bank contracts are overestimated.

[68] In a stark critique of the claim that institutional strengthening improves economic performance, Forder (1996) raises three methodological pitfalls: the threat of a legislative reversal of independence may undermine the purported benefits of that very same independence; established practice may determine that even a central bank with statutory independence predominantly complies with the government's wishes; and an independent central bank may not actually behave in line with the objectives underlying its independence since it may be subject to perverse incentives (for instance, to use monetary policy to advance the electoral prospects of a party that advocates less-inflationary fiscal and public sector wage policies). While these contrarious arguments have some validity, implying that in theory statutory independence may not always promote specified central bank objectives, they do not carry much weight when account is taken of practical considerations such as the difficulty of adapting central bank legislation and the value that central bankers generally attach to their reputation.

[69] De Haan and Kooi (1997) present evidence that, in practice, especially instrument independence is important for inflation performance.

[70] Eijffinger (1996).

[71] Stella (1997) argues that central banks with relatively weak capital bases invariably experience a decline in operational independence and abandonment of price stability as a primary policy goal.

[72] The evidence suggests inflation has an adverse, non-linear effect on growth which is difficult to establish when inflation is relatively low (see Fischer 1996). In a study of inflation in 87 countries (including 13 of the current EU member states) during 1970-90, Sarel (1996) finds a structural break at 8 per cent. Above this level, inflation has a very powerful negative influence on growth. Similarly, using a data set comprising 145 countries over the period 1960-1996, Ghosh and Phillips (1998) establish a negative relationship

between inflation and growth that is both statistically and economically significant and survives a battery of robustness checks. They suggest the relationship is non-linear in two senses: first, at very low rates the relationship is positive (a kink is tentatively estimated at about 2½ per cent) and, second, although the cumulative effect of inflation on growth rises as inflation increases, the marginal effect becomes smaller.

[73] Taylor (1981) and Chowdury (1991) provide evidence of a positive relationship between the level and the variability of inflation. Beyond this, Judson and Orphanides (1996) present tentative calculations, based on a sample of 119 countries over a 30-year period, indicating that the level and the volatility of inflation have independent, significant influences on growth. In particular, they find that inflation volatility is significantly negatively correlated with income growth across time, type of country and level of inflation.

[74] Committee for the Study of Economic and Monetary Union (1989, pp. 25-26). This requirement of institutional independence had not been specified in the earlier proposal for an economic and monetary union in Europe embodied in the Werner Report finalised in October 1970.

[75] A comprehensive overview of the theoretical literature can be found in Cukierman (1992). Outcomes and reviews of the empirical literature are provided in Alesina and Summers (1993), Cukierman *et al.* (1993), De Haan and Sturm (1992), Eijffinger and Schaling (1993), Eijffinger and De Haan (1996), and Grilli, Masciandaro and Tabellini (1991). Of course, these studies are subject to the caveat that empirical correlation need not imply causation: it has been suggested that the correlation may, for instance, primarily reflect a third factor such as the inflation aversion of the population; see Posen (1993). On a more specific point, Forder (1998) has challenged the measurements of independence, and therefore the results, presented by Alesina and Summers (1993).

[76] See Eijffinger and De Haan (1996) and Bini Smaghi (1998). However, the notion that accountability and central bank independence can be two sides of the same coin is at odds with the empirical finding of Briault, Haldane and King (1996) that these elements are actually negatively related. Using a more refined accountability index, De Haan, Amtenbrink and Eijffinger (1998) have confirmed this inverse relationship, establishing that less independent central banks tend to have heavier communication obligations and, especially, are subjected to greater disciplinary mechanisms vis-à-vis the government and Parliament. But this seems to reflect the fact that accountability and transparency have been pursued more vigorously by central banks with weak track records and low credibility – these have typically also been the less independent central banks. In these cases, accountability has therefore largely reflected an initial mistrust of the monetary authority. Over the course of time, this accountability and openness is likely to elicit commensurate policy independence for the central bank, and the inverse relationship may be expected to disappear.

[77] Formal analyses of the optimal contract for a central bank governor are presented in Walsh (1995) and Persson and Tabellini (1993).

[78] Cukierman and Meltzer (1986) highlight the other side of the coin, showing that greater ambiguity makes it easier for the policy-maker to engage in positive surprises when the need for stimulation is seen to prevail and to postpone negative surprises for periods in which inflation concerns dominate. Given the greater uncertainty and higher inflation (expectations) that such ambiguity would entail, as well as the difficulties it would create for central bank accountability, this would be an ill-advised way of increasing monetary policy flexibility.

[79] See in particular Persson and Tabellini (1993). The key role of preannouncement in backward-looking assessments of monetary policy is also emphasised by Bernanke and Mishkin (1992) and Crockett (1994b).

[80] The gradual tightening of the money and credit objectives could theoretically be associated with accelerating money velocity – and thus not with declining inflation – so that the lowering of the target did not genuinely reflect greater policy ambition. However, in practice broad money velocity has declined in most EU countries over the past quarter century.

[81] In 1986 and 1987 the German nominal effective exchange rate appreciated by an average 9 and 6 per cent, respectively. As a result, it was possible to increase the upper end of the money target range by one-half of one per cent in each of these two years, but to base this on a lower implicit inflation target (set at 2 per cent for both 1986 and 1987, against 2 ½ per cent for 1985).

[82] Tobin (1983) advocates simple monetary policy rules on complementary grounds, emphasising the political appeal of simplicity. He draws parallels with the attractiveness of a balanced budget norm and with the powerful imperative of gold convertibility at historic parity.

[83] See also Bernanke and Mishkin (1992).

[84] An example of transparency that would likely cause confusion is if, on account of differences of opinion within the policy setting body, the central bank published more than one inflation forecast under a direct inflation targeting strategy. This is not far-fetched fiction: the Bank of England's Monetary Policy Committee has indicated that it will report separate inflation forecasts if its individual members disagree about the validity of certain aspects underlying the forecasts; see Budd (1998, p. 1793).

[85] This point is made by Goodfriend (1986) in a comprehensive review of standard central bank arguments for secrecy in the implementation of monetary policy. His assessment is based on the US Federal Reserve Bank's defence of secrecy as argued in the 1975-81 court proceedings against the Federal Open Market Committee under the Freedom of Information Act. On balance, he finds the theoretical arguments for secrecy to be at best inconclusive.

[86] Even the minutes of the meetings of the Bank of England's Monetary Policy Committee (renowned for its transparency creed) do not attribute individual contributions to policy discussions. This is done in order to ensure that individual members do not feel restricted in advancing arguments that they may not personally support, but do wish to have fully explored. See Budd (1998, p. 1789).

3 TARGETING OPTIONS FOR MONETARY POLICY

3.1 Introduction

The central element of a monetary strategy is the target at which monetary policy is purportedly aimed in order to achieve its desired final objectives. Such a target can help reduce inconsistencies in the implementation and communication of central bank policies. As Friedman put it, "we are in danger of assigning to monetary policy a larger role than it can perform, in danger of asking it to accomplish tasks that it cannot achieve, and, as a result, in danger of preventing it from making the contribution that it is capable of making. ... By setting itself a steady course and keeping to it, the monetary authority could make a major contribution to promoting economic stability."[1]

Over time, many different variables have been relied upon to fulfil this target role, and even more have been proposed for it. This chapter first reviews the characteristics that a variable must possess to be effective as a monetary policy target. In view of the gaping differences – especially between academicians and policy-makers – on what monetary policy targeting actually means, a practical interpretation of this concept is provided. The pragmatism inherent in this interpretation logically prompts the question why a targeting strategy is to be considered at all. Against the background of the reply to this question, the main targeting alternatives are successively reviewed in an effort to map out their different potential contributions to efficacious and credible monetary policy-making. The following options are appraised: money targeting, domestic credit targeting, interest rate targeting, exchange rate targeting, nominal income targeting, direct inflation targeting, and a combined targeting approach.

The characteristics of an effective target

The importance of the monetary policy target is derived from its role in both the reaction function of the central bank and the communication of this reaction function to the public at large. In weighing different targeting options for monetary policy, both roles must be taken duly into account. As regards the first role, three well-known requirements must in any case be met for a target to contribute directly to the efficacy of monetary policy. First, the monetary authority must be able to influence developments in the target variable in a reasonably predictable manner. Second, these developments, in turn, must have a reasonably predictable (though not necessarily constant) relationship with the end objectives of monetary policy, in particular inflation. And third, in this latter relationship, the target must also lead the end objectives, in the sense that changes in the target serve as a prelude to subsequent changes in the objectives.

The target variable must therefore fall within the scope of the monetary transmission mechanism – at the beginning, such as with a short-term interest rate or base money growth, in the middle, such as with broad money growth or the exchange rate, or at the end, such as with an inflation or nominal income forecast. As is commonly stressed, this implies that the choice of target variable involves a fundamental trade-off between controllability, on the one hand, and relevance for the end objectives of monetary policy, on the other. The former is larger when the target is close to the levers of monetary transmission, whilst the latter is greater towards the end of the transmission process.

But the effectiveness of a target variable depends on more than its controllability and relevance in the process of monetary transmission. Of comparable importance is the role of the target variable in enhancing the transparency, and thus potentially the credibility, of monetary policy. In concrete terms, this depends on the communicability and visibility of the chosen target. Indeed, the more easily understood and observable the target, the greater its impact on the behaviour of economic agents and on the support for the central bank's policies. In this respect, a clearly communicated and readily monitorable target conveys the policy ambition and commitment of the monetary authorities, while simultaneously establishing a basis for accountability. This is also where differences in monetary policy traditions and experiences become relevant, as these make certain policy objectives easier to communicate in some countries than in others.

Finally, at a rudimentary level, the existence of timely, frequent, and reliable data on developments in the target variable crucially determine its operational usefulness. Specifically, timeliness is important because the time span needed for data collection adds to the lag of monetary transmission and thus to the risk that monetary policy is geared to outdated circumstances. Similarly, a high frequency of data collection is essential to allowing gradual changes in monetary policy when shifts occur in the target variable. Finally, the data must be sufficiently reliable (and thus not subject to statistical shortcomings or major later revisions) to enable actual policy measures to be based confidently on the information conveyed by the target variable.

To summarise, the monetary policy target should be: (i) sufficiently controllable; (ii) predictably related to outcomes under the end objectives of monetary policy; (iii) a leading indicator of developments in these end objectives; (iv) readily communicable to the public at large; and (v) monitorable on a timely, frequent and reliable basis. These are *necessary* characteristics, in the sense that any potential monetary policy target must fulfil all these preconditions at some minimum level. But, above this minimum, there are clear differences between alternative potential targets. In the final analysis, it is the trade-offs underlying these differences that determine the optimal monetary policy strategy.

The practical meaning of monetary policy targeting

Before elaborating on the benefits and costs of the prime targeting options, it is necessary to clarify the practical meaning of a 'target' for monetary policy. Conceptually, under an intermediate targeting framework, a central bank first selects a target variable (from amongst controllable, predictable, leading, communicable and monitorable variables), then projects a path for this target variable consistent with its desired policy outcome (in terms of prices and perhaps also real output growth), and finally lets developments in this target variable determine its policy stance. In other words, once the path for the intermediate target has been determined, this target effectively becomes the end objective for monetary policy.[2] Theoretically, monetary policy is then set on an automatic pilot and no room is left for discretion.

In reality, however, the implementation of an intermediate targeting framework is bound to be less mechanical.[3] After all, when setting its day-to-day policy stance, the central bank is expected to review all available information to gauge whether the economy remains on course towards its end objectives. What then is the role of the intermediate target in practice? First, the target variable must be the dominant variable defining the course of monetary policy and monetary policy must ultimately be tuned to this variable. This indicates that the central bank is *a priori* assumed to stick to the preannounced targeted path, but that short-term deviations may be accommodated if there are clear indications that the relationship with the end objective has temporarily shifted. (Of course, the scope for such deviations depends on the target variable and may be limited – as, for instance, with a tight exchange rate target.) A sustained divergence would be inconsistent with a strategy of intermediate targeting. And, second, the target variable must have primacy in the communication of monetary policy to the public. This implies that the intermediate target is preannounced to the public, that policy measures are explained in terms of developments under this target, and that policy can be evaluated on the basis of performance under the intermediate target (contemporaneously according to whether the target is met or deviations can be justified, *ex post* according to the extent the end objectives are met).

In sum, adoption of an intermediate targeting framework for monetary policy does not necessarily mean the switch to a rigid rules-based system. In the same vein, it does not by definition imply eliminating all judgmental or eclectic elements from the monetary decision-making process. Rather, it involves mapping out a consistent forward-looking policy program, preannouncing a target path for the dominant variable guiding monetary policy towards its end objectives, broadly adhering to this target under normal circumstances, explicitly explaining policy measures in the context of this target, and finally also accepting accountability for developments under the target variable.

Why target at all?

In light of the divergence that may arise between intermediate targets and final policy objectives, as well as the risk that central banks may attach undue weight to the former at the expense of the latter, the case for targeting is not self-evident. Indeed, given the compelling arguments for monetary policy decisions based on all available information, and against ironclad monetary policy rules, the question can be posed: why target at all? Why not opt for discretion and for full flexibility to respond to disturbances that inevitably occur? In fact, the US Federal Reserve has implemented such a "Just do it"-approach with remarkable success after it gradually abandoned its money targets in the course of the 1980s.[4]

In first instance, the case for adopting a target can be built on the contribution that a targeting framework may make to consistent and medium-term oriented policy-making. But at least as important is its contribution to the second element of monetary policy strategy – the interaction with the general public. Broadly speaking, announcing a target provides a structure for the external communication on monetary policy-making by, as it were, selecting a common language for this communication. Moreover, an explicit target establishes a nominal anchor to guide inflation expectations and reduce uncertainty, while also clarifying what monetary policy can and cannot do. Besides this, to the extent that a target focuses attention on an early indicator of prospective inflation, this may also bolster confidence that monetary policy is not generating inflationary surprises. On this score, announcing an intermediate target publicly precommits monetary policy and thereby helps resolve the time inconsistency problem facing the central bank. At the same time, by limiting discretion, a targeting framework will make the policy outcome less dependent on the individual personality of the monetary authority and will promote policy continuity. In practice, announcing a policy target will also pressure the central bank to subsequently communicate about developments and divergences under this target. Thus, the adoption of a target may in itself elicit greater policy transparency. Finally, an explicit target in combination with policy transparency creates a basis on which the central bank can be held accountable. In a democratic society, this is no mean benefit.

Of course, these advantages only apply if the target variable meets the necessary conditions enumerated earlier. Also, the magnitude of the advantages differs between the various targeting alternatives. In this respect, it should be borne in mind that the weight of the advantages is determined by their ultimate impact on the credibility of the central bank. In particular, a central bank with high credibility stands to gain little by using an intermediate target. This may explain why the US Federal Reserve, often seen as one of the most credible central banks in the world, has recently been successful without a publicised targeting framework. But, even in such a case, a targeting framework may bring benefits at limited costs, for instance by establishing a policy framework that helps make success durable.

3.2 Money targeting

Against the background of a rising inflationary momentum, and thus of apparent shortcomings in the functioning of existing policy targets, money targeting rapidly gained popularity in Europe in the mid to late 1970s. The academic case for money targeting had been repeatedly spelt out long beforehand (most eloquently by Milton Friedman (1968)), but it was not until after the exchange rate constraints of the Bretton Woods system had vanished and the first oil crisis had sparked a surge in prices that the need for a robust and comprehensive strategy to control inflation became pressing. In late 1974, Germany became the first country to publicly announce a money growth target and, within Europe, the United Kingdom (early 1976), France (late 1976), the Netherlands (early 1977), Spain (1978), Greece (early 1983, based on a long tradition of money growth programming in an eclectic framework), Italy (late 1984), and eventually Portugal (1987) all followed suit.

Benefits

The essence of the case for money targeting is straightforward. In its basic form, it harks back to the quantity theory of money and the mantra that in the long run inflation is a monetary phenomenon. By consequence, a money target provides a clear-cut, infrangible nominal anchor. More specifically, this approach takes as a point of departure the assumption that the stock of money determines the aggregate level of nominal spending and that the demand for money is essentially predictable and controllable – which effectively requires a stable money demand function in terms of a few key variables, notably including nominal income, interest rates and wealth. Under these circumstances, the central bank can effectively secure an end objective for inflation by steering the supply of reserve money on the basis of projections for the money multiplier, broad money velocity, real (potential) output growth and the inflation goal. Alternatively, a short-term interest rate can be used as the instrument variable to keep money growth in line with *ex ante* estimates of money demand, and thus of real output and inflation objectives.[5] In order to precommit monetary policy, the central bank can then preannounce a specific (base or broad) money growth range or point target, which then provides a nominal mooring for prices and price expectations.

Money targets derive much of their appeal from their central position in the process of monetary policy transmission. In this respect, money targets may be seen as achieving a judicious balance between controllability, on the one hand, and relevance for monetary policy's end objectives, on the other. Regarding the former element, money is a variable that is considered within the central bank's span of control – even if there are important differences in degree according to the coverage of the relevant monetary aggregate – and for which the central bank can therefore also be held accountable. As regards the latter element, money expansion is conceptually firmly linked to inflation and is also a precursor to price changes, such that money targets can expedite policy adjustments aimed at controlling subsequent price changes. The fact that money developments are not at the end of the monetary transmission process also means that a central bank controlling money growth within preannounced targets will be able to gain credibility more rapidly than one with no such intermediate targets, where credibility gains have to await outcomes for end objectives, notably prices.

Besides this, at an abstract level, monetary aggregates are an appropriate intermediate target to minimise output and price fluctuations arising from expenditure shocks; when this type of shock occurs, adherence to a money target automatically prompts offsetting monetary policy reactions. Of course, an expedient policy response could, in principle, also be achieved with other target variables – that is, if there is sufficient knowledge of the behavioural relationships driving the economy and of the true characteristics of economic disturbances. But, in reality, such knowledge may often be clouded by the uncertainty and instability underlying these relationships, making money targets conceptually well-suited to guide policies in economies where expenditure disturbances dominate. The same applies in the case of nominal shocks originating abroad.

Money targeting can also contribute to the communication, independence, and accountability of monetary policy-making. First, with respect to the role of targets in advertising policy objectives and orientation, money aggregates have the advantage of being readily understood and thus of being effective signalling instruments. Even though they relate to abstract and intangible concepts, money targets are easily communicable thanks to their extensive use in the past and their simplicity, based on the straightforward perception of a broadly proportional relationship between money growth and inflation. More fundamentally, money targets can be readily broken down into three simple building blocks – the underlying inflation objective, projected real output growth, and changes in money velocity – thereby serving to anchor inflationary expectations and transparently motivating the monetary policy course. Second, the fact that data on monetary developments are timely, frequent and relatively seldom revised – the more so for narrow aggregates – makes policy outcomes easy to monitor. To the extent the potential time horizon for inflation surprises is shortened, this helps preclude time inconsistency in monetary policy. Third, money is directly associated with the central bank's responsibilities. In combination with a relatively high degree of central bank control over money growth and reliable data, this creates a policy framework in which the monetary authority can independently set its policy targets, be closely monitored and be held readily accountable for its (in)actions. By implication, this creates a strong incentive structure to implement appropriate policies, as deviations from policy targets are detected early on and need to be explained in a well-founded manner if the central bank's credibility is to remain intact.

Finally, within the political economy of central banking, money targets can be effective in deflecting criticism of interest rate policy – which is where the pain of monetary policy lies – and thus of anti-inflationary measures. This is because the adoption of money targets essentially makes interest rates endogenous, and thereby also makes assessments of interest rates as being "too high" inherently illogical. Although the role of shielding the monetary authority from political pressure can also be fulfilled by other intermediate targets, money aggregates are particularly well-suited to this task to the extent the central bank can refer directly to the obvious incompatibility of establishing both the quantity and the price of any good, in this case money.

Drawbacks

The principal drawback of money targeting relates to the potential fragility of the short-term relationship between monetary aggregates, on the one hand, and inflation and output, on the other, the latter being the variables policy-makers truly care about. With short-term money demand instability, gearing policy to a money target will imply considerable interest rate volatility, as notably illustrated by the US Federal Reserve's monetarist experiment under Chairman Volcker during 1979-1982. But at a deeper level, when money demand is unstable, the task of predicting a growth rate for base or broad money that would be consistent with a given inflation objective becomes hazardous and any target becomes subject to large margins of error. Consequently, adherence to such a target creates considerable risks: if the money target is pitched too tight, monetary policy will unnecessarily constrain output, while if it is too loose, monetary policy will not achieve its inflation objectives.

When inflation is high, and disinflation needs to be assigned clear priority, these may be risks worth taking. Indeed, the broad-based adoption of money targets in the late 1970s, when there was a perception that inflation was running out of hand, appears to have partly reflected a different trade-off in a situation of sustained rapid price increases. In a situation of low inflation, however, unstable short-term money demand implies that money targets should not be pursued rigidly. In turn, this means that money targets are likely to be missed relatively frequently, thereby undermining any credibility-building effects that the targets may otherwise have.

Key factors behind the instability of money demand are ongoing processes of financial innovation, financial deregulation and capital liberalisation, as well as changes to confidence in the prospective value of the currency.[6] In this regard, money demand shifts are more likely to arise in countries where restrictive regulations are stimulating circumventive innovations, financial stocks are adjusting in the wake of deregulation, or financial flows are prompted by expectations of policy-induced instability (particularly of interest, exchange and inflation rates). By the same token, countries with credible, stability-oriented policies and with an unrestricted financial environment are less prone to money demand instability. And, by consequence, a strategy of monetary targeting is also more likely to be viable. European experience clearly bears this out: Germany, with traditionally stable macroeconomic conditions and relatively liberal financial markets (especially in terms of limited capital controls and direct credit restrictions, as well as a flexible universal bank system) has had a comparatively stable money demand function, whereas for instance the

United Kingdom, with more volatile interest and inflation rates and with a formerly tightly regulated financial system has had quite the opposite.[7]

However, with ongoing innovations of unpredictable pace and scope, no country can escape unexpected changes in the economic significance of any specific targeted money aggregate. Even with unchanged regulation, competition may prompt banks to vary their reaction (between deposit categories) to movements in market rates, or to react in a different manner when rates are rising than when these are falling, thereby making it difficult to gauge the interest elasticity of a targeted monetary aggregate. More generally, the predictability of money demand may also be undermined by Goodhart's Law, according to which the behaviour underlying a money aggregate changes once this aggregate becomes the explicit objective of policy actions. All in all, some money demand instability will inevitably occur – the question is how much, and how this compares to the stability of alternative monetary policy targets.

Money demand instability essentially reflects the difficulty of accurately measuring money, as financial assets provide different degrees of moneyness. As a result, the simple aggregation of various liquid assets may not give a reliable indication of money balances actually held for transaction purposes. Theoretically, this problem can be tackled by calculating so-called Divisia aggregates which weigh monetary assets according to their degree of liquidity. But in practice it is extremely difficult to establish the varying degrees of moneyness of different financial assets. Moreover, the complexity of calculating Divisia aggregates implies that their use would tarnish the transparency and communicability of the money targeting framework.

More practically, the risk of money demand instability can be alleviated by announcing a wide range for the money target, by specifying a longer time horizon during which the target is to be met, or by revisiting the target in mid-year. In this context, supporters of monetary targeting commonly acknowledge that money demand may not be perfectly predictable in the short term, potentially leading to temporary deviations from policy objectives, but that money targeting then still provides a steadfast nominal anchor for price stability over the medium term. However, relatively wide money target ranges, longer time horizons or mid-stream target revisions will weaken the precommitment of monetary policy, thereby reducing the potential credibility gains stemming from the adoption of a rules-based policy framework.

The difficulties posed by short-term volatility in money demand may also be mitigated by selecting a broader money aggregate, thereby internalising portfolio shifts between different liquid assets. In practice, this is what many money targeting countries have done. But such an approach is not free of costs. Specifically, although broad money aggregates usually have a closer relationship with the end objectives of monetary policy, they are positioned further downstream in the monetary transmission process and are thus less sensitive to changes in policy instruments. As a result, an increase in stability is bought at the expense of a decline in controllability. In the extreme, a broad aggregate with primarily interest bearing assets may in the short term even react perversely to monetary policy measures, as a higher interest rate will make these assets more attractive, which may in first instance prompt the targeted money growth actually to accelerate. Clearly, severe controllability problems will hamper the monitoring and communication of a money oriented strategy and, beyond a certain point, will make it unworkable.

A further serious drawback of money targeting, especially in the European context, relates to its implications for exchange rate policy. In particular, a consistent policy strategy of money targeting implies that the central bank explicitly focuses on the quantity of money, and is thus willing to neglect the consequences for the price of money, notably in terms of the exchange rate. By consequence, economic disturbances and cycles are deflected on the external sector. However, in Europe, where economies are relatively open and tightly knit, and where great importance is attached to an unrestricted regional flow of goods and services, there is considerable resistance to allowing mutual exchange rates to fluctuate freely. Exchange rate stability is seen as vital to avoiding calls for trade protection and regional political tensions, and thus to ensuring the viability of the internal European market. Of course, this leaves room for one country (with the anchor currency) to pursue a policy centred on money targets, to which the other countries can peg their exchange rates. But, in general, it argues against a wider regional application of genuine money targeting.

Appraisal

Money aggregates have the attraction of being fundamentally tied to developments in inflation and, further, of being precursors to these developments. At an abstract level, money targets help stabilise an economy primarily faced by shocks in domestic expenditure and foreign prices. Given their intrinsic link to central bank competencies and their (in principle) clear-cut guidance to policy setting, such targets can also shield monetary policy from outside pressures. Moreover, thanks to their relative simplicity and elementary construction, money targets constitute a powerful device to communicate central bank policies to the public at large. And since money growth is objectively measurable, money targets provide a straightforward gauge to monitor central bank policies, thereby limiting the scope for inflationary surprises and creating a basis for accountability.

However, many of these advantages depend critically on whether the relationship between money and price developments is indeed sufficiently stable, and whether controlling money provides a reliable hold on future inflation. In view of the dynamics of ongoing innovation and competition in financial markets, this relationship is, at best, likely to be subject to significant margins of uncertainty in the short run. Such uncertainty can be addressed, in part, by adopting a longer time horizon or a range for the target, and by periodically updating the target. In addition, the stability of money demand may be enhanced by focusing on a broader aggregate, as this will internalise portfolio shifts amongst liquid assets. However, these measures will loosen the targeting framework – thereby reducing the credibility benefits of having one – and risk trading increased stability for reduced controllability. In this broad context, the credibility costs of missing money targets can also be mitigated by providing comprehensive justifications for any past or anticipated deviations. The central bank then effectively accepts the burden of proof for explaining when targets are missed or when these are, in its view, no longer in line with desired end objectives.

Overall, even if public opinion tends to associate money targeting with monetarism and with strict adherence to strait-jacket norms for money growth, in practice this policy strategy will always need to be implemented pragmatically, with a healthy dose of discretion. In such a context, money targeting is adopted primarily for its long-run nominal anchor, its signalling role, its implicit link to central bank autonomy and, more broadly, its contribution to effective communication about monetary policy-making. Beyond this, money targets are conceptually opposite to the objective of exchange rate stability and are thus, from a specific European perspective, potentially at odds with several other dominant Community objectives, notably safeguarding the viability of the internal market. This suggests that although a strict form of money targeting may be appropriate for the region's anchor country, it is *a priori* unsuitable for broad-based adoption across the European continent.

3.3 Domestic credit targeting

During the 1970s, domestic credit targeting was a not uncommon practice, both in Europe and elsewhere. To some extent this seems to have reflected inertia stemming from the Bretton Woods era, when domestic credit ceilings were the logical complement of prevailing exchange rate commitments. Taken together, these two policy targets could help ensure both a degree of price stability and a minimum balance of payments outcome. This was also the motive behind the setting of complementary domestic credit ceilings in a number of European countries (such as the Netherlands) maintaining an exchange rate oriented policy. Besides this, for those European countries with financing arrangements from the IMF, domestic credit limits were a central element of the conditionality of their adjustment program.[8] This was notably the case in Italy (which had an IMF stand-by arrangement covering part of 1977-78), Portugal (1977-78, 1978-79, and 1983-85), Spain (1978-79) and the United Kingdom (1976 and 1977-78). But domestic credit targets were maintained as the central monetary policy target in several countries for a much longer period, including in Italy (until 1983) and Greece (until 1994).

Benefits

Domestic credit targets are often seen as a member of the broader family of money targets. But there is a crucial distinction between these two forms of targeting, which explains both the attraction and the key drawback of credit oriented policy rules. The specific advantage of credit targets over money targets is the potential contribution of the former towards a balance of payments objective. In particular, a country maintaining a managed or fixed exchange rate can strengthen the net international reserves of its banking system by limiting the expansion of domestic credit to below that of money demand.[9] When this happens, the balance of payments becomes the source of money supply for the excess of money demand over domestic credit. In a nutshell, under credit targeting a surplus money demand elicits a strengthening of the balance of payments, whereas under money targeting – and by implication purely floating exchange rates – such a surplus translates itself into exchange rate appreciation and downward pressure on prices. This makes clear the classic trade-off between the external and the inflation objective under these two approaches. It also explains the central role of domestic credit ceilings in IMF supported programs. Since the prime concern of these programs is to redress balance of payments difficulties, the focus is on avoiding excessive domestic money creation, implying ceilings on domestic credit and not on the money supply or the monetary base.[10]

Other considerations that have been advanced to favour bank credit targets over money targets include an allegedly more direct and tighter link to aggregate demand.[11] This greater relevance of credit derives from the unique position of banks in the transmission of central bank policy. In this view, banks do not simply intermediate between savers and investors, but they also deal with asymmetric information between lenders and borrowers. In essence, bank credit is thereby seen as having an independent impact on economic activity, not fully captured by developments in interest rates or, for that matter, the money supply. As a result of credit constraints ensuing from imperfect information, movements in bank credit may be unrelated to that of the interest rate, and may thus also have an independent effect on spending. By consequence, the availability of bank credit, and not that of money, is seen as key to determining aggregate demand. Another aspect supporting the suitability of bank credit as a policy target is that the necessary statistics are available on a reasonably timely, frequent, and reliable basis.

Drawbacks

Although a monetary strategy centred around domestic credit targets has some advantages, these benefits need to be weighed against considerable drawbacks. The principal shortcoming of credit targeting is the lack of a nominal anchor to pin down domestic prices. As mentioned earlier, credit ceilings are effective in strengthening the external accounts, and their implementation can thus potentially contribute to the sustainability of an exchange rate or money anchor. But, by itself, credit targeting in principle does not set any limit to money supply growth, since it does not cap the external sources of money creation. Of course, a nominal anchor could be introduced by ruling out (or strictly limiting) all such external sources of money supply; however, the credit targets would then effectively become money targets. This absence of a nominal anchor makes credit targeting inherently inappropriate as a monetary policy strategy, since it does not provide a watertight hold on the inflation rate. Closely related to this shortcoming is the further disadvantage that credit targets do not, on their own, convey an unambiguous message on the orientation or ambition of monetary policy. In this respect, such targets are not easily communicable to the public and will therefore not contribute towards transparent monetary policy-making.

With respect to the claim that bank credit is more tightly related to economic activity than money, empirical evidence is not clear-cut.[12] More fundamentally, given the intrinsic relationship between bank credit and money as largely offsetting items on different sides of the same balance sheet, these two aggregates will tend to move broadly in parallel. After all, institutions wishing to expand credit activities may generally seek to finance this by attracting deposits, thereby narrowing the distinction between credit and money. Therefore, even though the net domestic assets of the banking system are not rigidly linked to the monetary liabilities – notably on account of movements in banks' net foreign assets and net bond holdings – developments in these items are bound to be closely related. As a result, the relationship between bank credit and real output is subject to essentially the same instability as that between money and real output. In this respect, financial innovation, financial deregulation and capital liberalisation have broadly similar effects on both these financial aggregates, complicating the use of bank credit targets in much the same way as money targets.

The option of focusing on a broad credit aggregate does not offer a viable monetary strategy alternative to bypass these difficulties.[13] In principle this would circumvent the impact of disintermediation on banking system variables. By aggregating all mortgages, consumer credit, other bank loans, as well as the outstanding value of government securities, corporate bonds and commercial paper, this would provide a potentially more relevant concept of credit. But such a broad aggregate would be essentially ill-suited as a monetary strategy's main target, since this aggregate is relatively distant from the instruments under the central bank's direct control and essentially abandons the concept of liquidity being created by banks. More practically, this aggregate is subject to major measurement problems in terms of timeliness and reliability.

Appraisal

In sum, a monetary policy strategy focusing on domestic credit targets may be temporarily appropriate when balance of payments concerns need to be prioritised. On its own, however, targeting domestic credit is not a viable strategy to promote durable non-inflationary growth, because it does not provide the economy with a nominal anchor. It is also ineffective as a communication device with the public at large. Moreover, if exogenous capital flows are large and money demand is unstable, a policy directed at controlling domestic sources of money creation is likely to be just as problematic as one focused on money targets.

At most, credit ceilings may be used to complement another monetary strategy – particularly an exchange rate oriented approach – by precluding excessive domestic money creation from feeding capital outflows and thereby potentially fuelling downward pressure on the currency. But even then the role of credit targets is likely to be modest.[14] In practice, the potential role for credit targets will be smaller, the larger the credibility of the exchange rate peg. With credibility, it is confidence in the central bank's commitment that determines the stability of the exchange rate, making balance of payments flows close to irrelevant.

3.4 Interest rate targeting

The debate on monetary policy targeting has traditionally been cast in terms of controlling quantities or prices, thereby juxtaposing money (and credit) aggregate targeting and interest rate targeting. This has conferred considerable academic attention to the option of targeting interest rates, even if in practice there have only been few periods when interest rates were explicitly used as intermediate targets in the policy process, notably during the early years of the Bretton Woods era.[15]

At the outset, it should be clarified that interest rate targeting is seen as relating to a short-term nominal interest rate. The alternatives of short-term *real* interest rates or *long-term* real or nominal interest rates are not considered serious targeting options because they are not under the systematic control of the central bank.[16] To this can be added the fundamental difficulty with *real* interest rates, in that there is no straightforward way of directly observing inflation expectations and thus of monitoring the developments in these rates in an unambiguous manner.[17] Besides this, a distinction should be made between using the interest rate target as an operational objective, in which case the target is set with a view to achieving another intermediate goal, and as an intermediate objective, in which case the target is treated as an end in itself (on the assumption that this provides excellent prospects for meeting the true final objectives of monetary policy). While many European central banks have used interest rates in the former operational sense, the discussion below considers interest rate targeting in intermediate terms – that is, as the central element of the monetary policy strategy.

Benefits

Interest rate targeting has a number of favourable features. At a conceptual level, interest rate targeting may be considered an optimal strategy if monetary and temporary shocks dominate. In this case, an interest rate rule allows monetary shocks to be automatically and fully accommodated, and also avoids economic adjustment costs in the face of temporary disturbances. At the same time, to the extent that short-term interest rate volatility is viewed as costly in terms of economic instability or risky in terms of financial instability, targeting interest rates brings about the desired interest rate smoothing.

Targeting the interest rate is also attractive insofar as it focuses on a key element of the monetary transmission process and thus on a prime determinant of both inflation and economic activity. In fact, interest rates are arguably the most visible element of monetary policy. By itself, this makes interest rate targeting well-suited to communicating policy intentions. Moreover, as interest rates are well understood and accurately monitorable without any lag or risk of later statistical revision, interest rate targeting can help establish a policy rule to which the central bank can be held directly and precisely accountable. This firm basis for accountability is further enhanced by the tight control which monetary authorities have over interest rate developments. Finally, since interest rates are at the beginning of the monetary transmission process, adherence to such targets can be conducive to building the credibility of the monetary authority – in terms of living up to its policy precommitment – at a very early stage, long before the policy outcomes in terms of inflation and output are known.

Drawbacks

Notwithstanding its attractive features, interest rate targeting faces numerous, overwhelming problems. The key difficulty is that there is no predetermined relationship between the interest rate *level* and the end objectives of monetary policy – inflation and output. By consequence, a policy of targeting an interest rate level for a significant time period is doomed to fail: since the equilibrium level is unknown and also constantly fluctuates as a result of economic adjustments, any pegging of the interest rate risks feeding into an inflationary or deflationary spiral.[18] If the nominal interest rate were set below its equilibrium level, this would fuel demand, thereby raising the equilibrium rate, exacerbating the procyclical impact of monetary policy, and eventually leading to an acceleration of inflation. Conversely, if the interest rate were set above its equilibrium level, the economy would be placed on a deflationary spiral. This makes clear the crucial flaw of interest rate targeting: it does not provide a nominal anchor for the price level. Of course, it could be argued that a policy of interest rate targeting should be pursued dynamically, with continual updating of the target on the basis of incoming information and changing circumstances. But such an approach would tarnish much of the appeal of interest rate targeting. Interest rates *per se* would no longer provide a reliable guidepost for the monetary authorities, policy-making would become largely discretionary, and policy adjustments would have the risk of being too little too late or of overshooting. And, ultimately, interest rate targeting would be characterised by a lack of transparency.

Interest rate targeting leads to an even starker conclusion when the public's expectations are assumed to be rational, since the price level then becomes indeterminate at *any* interest rate level.[19] This derives from the fact that the public expects the central bank to provide full monetary accommodation at a given nominal interest rate for any change in inflationary expectations. By consequence, every expected price level is both rational and possible. This harks back to the crucial shortcoming of interest rate targeting: the absence of a mechanism to pin down the price level. In practice, difficulties with interest rate targeting are thus most likely to arise in periods when inflation and inflationary expectations change and become subject to pronounced shifts. This was the case, for instance, in the wake of the first oil crisis, when the surge in inflationary expectations caused real interest rates to plummet with constant and sometimes even with rising nominal interest rates.

Last but not least, from a political economy perspective, interest rate targeting has the additional drawback that monetary policy is made more susceptible to outside pressures. In particular, since there is no objective measure of establishing whether a specific interest rate target is inflationary or deflationary, monetary authorities will be vulnerable to pressures to adopt a more expansionary policy stance. With no clear-cut way of telling whether monetary policy is loose or tight, short-term considerations are then more likely to prevail and any pre-emptive policy adjustments, which may be crucial in preserving price stability, will be all the more difficult to carry through.

Appraisal

Interest rate targeting automatically accommodates monetary disturbances and smoothes interest rate developments, thereby insulating the economy from shocks to money demand while also enhancing the stability of the financial system. Moreover, interest rate developments have the advantage of being highly visible and tightly controllable, thus strengthening the transparency and accountability of monetary policy-making. However, these benefits are outweighed by the principal drawback that interest rate targets do not by themselves anchor the inflation rate and thus do not provide reliable guidance on whether monetary policy is on course to achieve its objectives.

Against the background of its overriding shortcomings, proposals have been made to combine an interest rate rule with some element of money targeting, thus providing an anchor for nominal prices as well as a clearer indication of the underlying monetary policy stance.[20] In these proposals, there is no immediate and full accommodation of shifts in money demand or other shocks. Money aggregates are essentially kept under long-run control, thereby making the price level determinate, even when the hypothesis of rational expectations is maintained. In principle, however, these proposals further illustrate that interest rate targeting by itself does not constitute a viable monetary strategy. If it is to be used at all, an interest rate rule must therefore be supplemented by other elements in the context of a combined or eclectic strategy. Alternatively, interest rates can be used solely as operating targets or as information variables, thereby serving as important building blocks, but not as the corner stone, of a monetary policy strategy.

3.5 Exchange rate targeting

Exchange rate targets have traditionally played a prominent role in the design of monetary policies in post-war Europe. Unfavourable historic experiences with floating rates, as well as the interwoven nature of European economies and institutions, have contributed to a widespread preference for a co-ordination of exchange rate policy and, by implication, for a certain degree of exchange rate fixity. This is illustrated, for example, by the reference in the Treaty of Rome establishing the European Economic Community that "Each Member State shall treat its policy with regard to rates of exchange as a matter of common concern" (replicated in the Treaty on European Union as Article 124). This avowal came on top of the commitments to exchange rate stability rooted in the fixed (albeit adjustable) exchange rate system that was operative at the time.

Following the collapse of the Bretton Woods system, this intrinsic European preference for exchange rate stability has been reflected in the form of successive regional exchange rate agreements: the tighter mutual European commitments established under the Smithsonian Agreement (the so-called 'snake-in-the-tunnel') in April 1972, the subsequent 'floating snake' that emerged when the fluctuation margins vis-à-vis the dollar were lifted in March 1973, the more comprehensive Exchange Rate Mechanism (ERM) of the European Monetary System established in March 1979 and, of course, the quest for a permanent fixing of exchange rates in the context of Economic and Monetary Union (EMU). In practice, exchange rate targeting has been the dominant strategy in the recent monetary history of Europe. Each of the current EU members barring Germany has, at some time or other, and often most of the time, based monetary policy primarily on an exchange rate target.

Benefits

In an open economy, in the presence of full capital mobility, exchange rate targeting has most of the advantages of interest rate targeting, as the exchange rate commitment effectively ties the interest rate to the level of the external anchor currency.[21] In this respect, exchange rate targets are well-suited to economies that primarily experience disturbances of the monetary or temporary variety, for which the policy stance (notably in terms of interest rates) had best remain unchanged. But, in contrast with interest rate targeting, pegging the exchange rate can provide a solid nominal anchor. Indeed, in countries that are tightly integrated in world markets, the exchange rate is likely to be the most important relative price in the economy, making it an effective instrument to achieve domestic price stability. Besides this, adoption of exchange rate stability as the intermediate monetary policy objective has the benefit of reducing the detrimental effects of exchange rate uncertainty and related risk premia. The larger the tradables sector of the economy, the greater this benefit will be.

At a fundamental level, the crux of the case for sustained exchange rate targeting rests on optimal currency area considerations: whether the country adopting an exchange rate commitment has a similar economic structure, is subject to similar economic disturbances, and has similar policy preferences to the anchor economy. If these conditions are met, a country adopting an exchange rate peg accepts the monetary policy stance of the anchor country, and this policy stance is equally appropriate for both countries. Of course, in reality, such similarities only occur in degrees. Two questions then become essential: first, is there an anchor country pursuing a (more) successful monetary policy and, second, do the two economies to be tied by the exchange rate link move broadly in unison? The first question determines the benefits of exchange rate targeting, the second the costs.

In this regard, a prior assumption of exchange rate targeting is that there is an anchor country successfully implementing stability-oriented policies. When this is the case, a prominent benefit of exchange rate targeting for other countries lies in importing the policy discipline and, therewith, the policy credibility of the anchor country. This greater policy discipline can be attributed to several factors. First, adoption of an exchange rate target increases the costs of higher inflation, especially in terms of a loss of competitiveness. In the context of the European Exchange Rate Mechanism of fixed but adjustable exchange rates, this competitiveness erosion occurs in between realignments and is usually not fully compensated when realignments eventually take place.[22] Second, the political stakes of exchange rate commitments tend to be high. Since devaluation is commonly perceived as a sign of weak domestic policy-making, and thus of political failure, adoption of a peg strengthens the incentives to pursue policies that lower the probability of such an outcome. By implication, a peg serves to promote a policy stance that is as strong as that in the anchor country. Third, the benefit of increased policy discipline results from the fact that the exchange rate is the most visible and readily monitorable of the target alternatives. Exchange rate targeting therefore compels the central bank immediately and continuously to prove its commitment to its policy target. Taken together, these factors explain why exchange rate pegging may enhance credibility more than other monetary policy strategies.

Indeed, since the monetary authority is left with virtually no room for discretion, exchange rate targeting reduces the inflationary pressure and risk premia stemming from expectations of dynamic inconsistency. Scope for time inconsistent monetary policy remains only in the monetary policy of the anchor country, which is *a priori* assumed to be negligible, and in the risk of a surprise devaluation, which can be minimised by unequivocal political commitment and firm supporting macroeconomic policies.[23] In effect, exchange rate targeting in the context of a consistent policy mix leads to a convergence of interest rates to the level in the anchor country, and in due course also to a comparable inflation performance. This has been amply demonstrated in practice by several of the smaller European countries, notably Austria and the Netherlands, where tight exchange rate pegs to the German currency have resulted in practically identical interest rates and, more importantly, similarly low inflation rates in the medium-run.[24]

Exchange rate targeting is also an attractive strategy from the viewpoint of communication about the orientation of monetary policy. Thanks to its virtues of simplicity and visibility, exchange rate targeting makes central bank policy-making highly transparent. In this regard, an exchange rate peg not only sends a powerful signal to anchor inflationary expectations, but also highlights the policy constraints to budgetary authorities and trade unions alike. This combination of communication and policy discipline makes an exchange rate target potentially highly effective in achieving rapid disinflation or maintaining prices firmly anchored once price stability has been more or less reached. A further advantage is that the monetary policy requirements needed to uphold an exchange rate commitment are clear-cut, which can serve to shield the central bank from outside pressure. At the same time, given instantaneous and continuous information on performance under an exchange rate target, as well as general controllability of this target variable, a monetary strategy of exchange rate targeting allows a central bank to be held readily accountable for its policy implementation. This will strengthen the incentives of the monetary authority to live fully up to its policy precommitment.

From a specific European perspective, exchange rate targeting has the additional benefit that it helps safeguard the viability of the regional institutional fabric whose design has been predicated on a reasonable degree of exchange rate stability. This is notably the case, for instance, with the Common Agricultural Policy which denominates food prices in a common unit of account and instituted temporary financial measures (Monetary Compensatory Accounts) to mitigate the adverse impact of exchange rate realignments. These financial measures were implemented in an asymmetric fashion (subsidies to farmers with appreciating currencies tended to be higher and longer-lasting than taxes on farmers with depreciating currencies), further increasing the average intervention price for agricultural products above the world price and causing the Common Agricultural Policy to drain an increasing share of the EEC's financial resources.[25] In itself, this latter development has been enough to institutionalise a preference for exchange rate fixity. Besides this, the fiscal operations of the European Community have been based on a precarious and politically delicate balance between a Community budget in European Currency Units (ECUs) and national budgets in respective currencies, which would be disturbed by greater exchange rate volatility. But, more generally, the EEC has always been a natural advocate of exchange rate stability in view of the Community's original driving objective of achieving a common market free of barriers to trade. Even if the economic costs of exchange rate fluctuations are in some respects difficult to pinpoint, let alone quantify, it is clear that such fluctuations risk fuelling calls for trade protection and thus undermining the viability of the common market project. All told, the institutional view suggests that "Stable exchange rates are needed if the single market is to work, and they are required if the European Community itself is to function."[26]

Drawbacks

Exchange rate targeting has several drawbacks, two of which are especially serious. The first relates to the crucial difference between exchange rate targeting and other strategy options, in that the monetary policy stance is not determined on the basis of domestic considerations. In the context of liberalised capital flows, pursuing an exchange rate target thus implies the loss of monetary sovereignty. In effect, the country adopting an exchange rate peg commits itself to copying the monetary policy decisions of the anchor country, impervious to national economic circumstances. Monetary instruments will no longer be available to pursue domestic stabilisation or to shield the economy from shocks occurring in the anchor country. Any monetary policy divergence on the grounds of domestic developments or national policy priorities weakens the credibility of the commitment to the target and thus directly jeopardises its achievement. This drawback will be large if the structural characteristics, the susceptibility to shocks, and the policy priorities of the pegging country are significantly different from those of the anchor country. In this respect, a strategy of exchange rate targeting will not succeed in promoting monetary stability unless the real exchange rate vis-à-vis the anchor economy is essentially stable, the business cycles of the two economies move broadly in parallel, and the preferences regarding short-term trade-offs between inflation and output are basically similar. Moreover, given the loss of monetary policy independence, exchange rate targeting places a relatively heavy burden on the stabilising properties of other policies – notably fiscal and incomes policies.

A second major weakness of exchange rate targeting strategies lies in the potentially heavy costs of defending an exchange rate commitment in the face of private speculative attacks. These costs have surged over the past decades as capital regimes have been liberalised and global financial markets have expanded on a massive scale. This has made exchange rate pegs highly vulnerable to changes in market perceptions of the authorities' true commitment to the target. Since the sustainability of an exchange rate commitment depends in part on the market-determined costs of maintaining the peg, fixed exchange regimes have become increasingly susceptible to circular forces, whereby market expectations can prompt self-fulfilling crises. In particular, expectations of a prospective devaluation can feed into interest rates, lead to colossal costs, and thereby validate a realignment.[27] In the final analysis, the viability of a peg has thus become a function of its credibility in the market, implying that an otherwise sustainable rate may succumb to abrupt shifts in market sentiments. This is poignantly illustrated by the several European currencies – notably the Danish krona, the French and Belgian francs – that came under unsustainable market pressure within the narrow bands of the Exchange Rate Mechanism in August 1993, but eventually returned to their old parities once the bands had been widened.

On a technical level, central banks have, at the limit, maintained the ability to uphold an exchange rate peg. As long as the level of official reserves plus the borrowing capacity of the central bank exceeds the stock of outstanding high-powered money (which for all practical purposes is always the case), a central bank can redeem its liabilities at the fixed rate.[28] When this redemption occurs, base money tightens and interest rates rise to the level needed to compensate the perceived risk of devaluation. Alternatively, a central bank can actively raise its lending rates to advertise its determination to uphold an exchange rate commitment. Sweden's defence of the krona's peg in September 1992 provides an extreme illustration of this tactic: the marginal overnight lending rate was raised to 500 per cent (for four days) in a temporarily successful attempt to ward off a speculative onslaught.

In reality, however, the costs of raising interest rates may rapidly become prohibitive for a variety of reasons. First, higher interest rates will tend to depress economic activity and employment, particularly if rates are kept high over a longer time period. Second, interest rate action will aggravate banking system fragility, as bank profits typically depend on the spread of long-term over short-term interest rates and, more generally, as interest rate rises will increase the number of non-performing loans. Third, increased interest rates will undermine budgetary performance, as outlays will rise (particularly if public debt is financed primarily in domestic currency and at shorter maturities) and fiscal inflows will decline (on account of weaker economic performance). Against the background of these factors, interest rate action to defend an exchange rate peg may in itself be viewed as unsustainable and thereby prompt further market speculation.

Of course, instruments other than the interest rate can also be activated to uphold an exchange rate under speculative attack, but in practice these alternatives are relatively ineffective and may involve even larger costs. For instance, sterilised intervention can help accommodate the preferred portfolio composition of private agents, but will do nothing to remove the underlying incentives driving the speculation. And, as illustrated by the painful experiences of September 1992 when central bank support in the European Exchange Rate Mechanism reached an estimated \$ 100 billion, such intervention can take on astronomic sums in a very short time period.[29] In November of that same year, 160 billion kroner (over \$ 20 billion) was spent in only six days by Sweden alone, when the Riksbank consciously shifted the emphasis from interest rate increases to sterilised intervention.[30] Another option is capital controls. Indeed, capital restrictions were rife in the early days of the European Monetary System and were even used as late as 1992 to mitigate exchange market pressures within the system. But such controls are costly to administer, constraining to the development of the domestic banking system, and may be easily evaded, particularly beyond the short term and if financial markets are well-developed and innovative. Moreover, introducing capital controls is likely to have an inverse impact in practice, as it may undermine remaining confidence and thereby spur further outflows. Another policy alternative is trade regulations, which can duplicate the effects of a devaluation by tariffying imports and subsidising exports. However, such regulations would create far-reaching distortions and would violate international agreements, not least of which those related to the European internal market. Lastly, corrections in fiscal policy could serve to reduce domestic expenditure and enhance policy credibility. However, this instrument is inherently ill-suited to fine-tuning in the context of exchange market pressures. In all, these unappealing alternatives underscore the potentially heavy costs of exchange rate targeting – costs that come on top of having monetary policy set by another country.

A further problem is that, under certain circumstances, pegging the exchange rate to an anchor country with price stability may be insufficient to wring out inflation. For instance, if there is excessive market confidence in the peg, the exchange rate target will remain sustainable for a protracted period even with unduly expansive domestic macroeconomic policies and relatively high inflation. In this situation, nominal exchange rate stability will result in a real exchange rate appreciation, ultimately necessitating a realignment or abandonment of the peg. This was at play in Europe during the period 1987-1992, when the revivified prospect of Economic and Monetary Union boosted market confidence in regional exchange rate stability, and many countries that experienced nominally stable currencies (or even appreciating within the band) also had deteriorating fundamentals – including significantly higher domestic rates of inflation.[31]

A second circumstance under which an exchange rate peg will not deliver price stability is when a country has differential productivity growth rates in its tradables and nontradables sector. This is the case, for instance, when the export and import-competing industries are undergoing relatively rapid structural and technological improvements. The resulting high productivity gains will set the pace of wage increases for the whole economy, including in the nontradables sector where a lower price elasticity will provide scope for similar wage rises notwithstanding less impressive productivity growth. In this way, a rapid development of the tradables sector leads to higher prices for nontradables, higher overall inflation and a sustained appreciation of the real exchange rate (measured in terms of consumer prices). This phenomenon, commonly referred to as the Balassa-Samuelson hypothesis, may occur in countries that are catching up in their economic development, and seems to have been especially evident in European countries such as Spain, Portugal and Ireland.[32] Although an exchange rate anchor will then not lead to price stability, inflation will be less harmful insofar as the attendant real appreciation will not undermine balance of payments sustainability.

Finally, there is the well-known 'N-1' limitation according to which exchange rate targeting cannot be a solution for all, since there are only 'N-1' independent exchange rates in a world with 'N' countries.[33] If all countries were to pursue exchange rate stability, the system would be overdetermined and the mutual exchange rate commitments would fail to tie down the price level. This implies that there must be at least one country pursuing a different strategy, thereby anchoring prices for itself and for all countries pegged to its currency. In some sense this is ironic: the success of exchange rate based strategies depends critically on the success of a different strategy in the anchor country. Under the Bretton Woods system of fixed exchange rates this anchor role was explicitly assigned to the United States; more recently, in the context of the European Monetary System, this role was implicitly assumed by Germany.

Appraisal

There are several important advantages to a strategy of exchange rate targeting. First, monetary policy automatically insulates the economy from the impact of money demand instability and avoids policy changes in the face of temporary domestic disturbances. Second, adopting an exchange rate anchor serves to reduce the economic costs associated with exchange rate uncertainty. Third, in a mechanical sense, stabilising the exchange rate can be an effective way to stabilise domestic prices in a relatively open economy. Fourth, pegging the exchange rate to a strong currency increases policy discipline and credibility, and thereby facilitates the achievement and maintenance of low-inflation. Fifth, the straightforward nature and visibility of exchange rate targets make for highly transparent and rules-based central banking, thereby limiting the scope for time inconsistency and contributing to a firm anchoring of inflationary expectations. Finally, from a specific European viewpoint, exchange rate stability facilitates the fiscal operations of the Community and enhances the viability of several far-reaching regional objectives, most notably the completion of a common market with an unrestricted movement of goods, services, persons and capital.

The substantial economic and institutional benefits of exchange rate targeting need to be weighed against a number of heavy drawbacks. In particular, sustaining an exchange rate peg implies ceding monetary sovereignty and thereby relinquishing the ability to tailor monetary policy to domestic considerations. The severity of this disadvantage depends on the extent to which domestic economic developments and preferences differ from those in the anchor country. In this context, exchange rate targeting also implies that other policies, especially fiscal and incomes policies, have to take on a greater role in the stabilisation of the domestic economy. To these drawbacks can be added the potentially onerous costs of defending an exchange rate target when it is called into question by the market, which may even occur in the face of sound fundamentals. These costs can take the form of positive interest rate differentials vis-à-vis the anchor country, sterilised intervention, or efficiency reducing restrictions on capital or trade flows. In addition to these difficulties, an exchange rate peg may fail to deliver price stability if, for whatever reason, the market does not fully impose the needed policy discipline on the pegging country, or if productivity growth is substantially more rapid in the tradables than in the nontradables sector. In sum, it is clear that granting primacy to the exchange rate can be very disruptive to an economy, places greater demands on other adjustment instruments, and may not always lead to stable prices.

Of course, the balance between these benefits and costs importantly depends on the specific characteristics of the exchange regime upholding the exchange rate target. In practice, much depends on whether the exchange rate target can be easily realigned, whether the target is defined as a (wide) band, whether the limits of the target are binding in all circumstances, whether the commitment to the target is backed by significant foreign reserves (or even full backing of the monetary base as in currency board arrangements), and whether there is an international intervention support arrangement. Clearly, these modalities can be adjusted to reduce the costs of fixed exchange rates. Although this may end up dissipating the benefits, that need not always be the case. For example, when the ERM exchange rate bands were widened in August 1993, the central parities maintained the role of anchoring policies and expectations, while the intervention limits no longer elicited disruptive market speculation. In general, however, the looser the specifications, the more the 'fixed' exchange rate regime will resemble a floating regime, and the smaller the potential benefits will be.

Viewed over a longer time horizon, it is evident that the costs of exchange rate targeting have grown in tandem with the spectacular expansion of financial flows, as a result of both the liberalisation of international capital markets and the deregulation of domestic financial markets. From a global perspective, this is reflected in a steady decline during the past decades in the number of countries opting for a fixed exchange rate regime (see Chart 4). Barring very small (mostly island) economies and countries that do not have own full-fledged currencies, there were only ten countries in the world in 1998 that had successfully maintained a fixed exchange rate (within ± 1 per cent) vis-à-vis another currency for more than five years: Argentina, Austria, Belgium, Egypt, El Salvador, Estonia, Hong Kong, Lithuania, the Netherlands and Saudi Arabia.[34] Since almost half of these countries (four) implement rigid currency board arrangements, the empirical evidence strongly suggests that exchange rate pegs are difficult to combine with the perception of even a very limited degree of monetary policy discretion.

At the same time, however, the potential benefits of exchange rate targeting have also increased, as economies have become more open and interwoven, and the size of optimal currency areas has widened. This is notably the case in Europe, where the internal market has been brought to completion and regional economic integration has been relatively rapid. Besides this, exchange rate stability has traditionally been high on the list of European political desiderata, as it is customarily placed in the vanguard of regional initiatives to intensify policy co-ordination. In the final analysis, the circle of high costs and high benefits can only be squared through an

Chart 4: Global Evolution of Exchange Rate Regimes (in per cent of total IMF membership)[1]

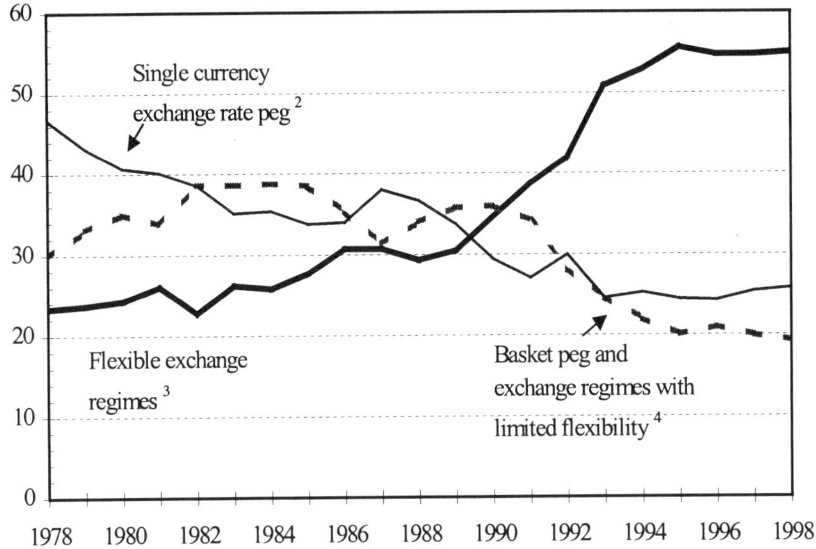

Source: IMF Reports on Exchange Rate Arrangements (including estimates for residual subgroup 'other' in 1978-81).

1 IMF membership covered 137 countries in 1978 and had risen to 182 countries in 1998.
2 Includes all currencies explicitly pegged to a single other currency.
3 Includes all independently floating currencies and all currencies for which the exchange rate is adjusted at relatively frequent intervals on the basis of indicators, or is otherwise flexibly managed.
4 Includes all currencies explicitly pegged to a currency basket, currencies showing limited flexibility against another currency, or currencies co-operating in an exchange rate arrangement (notably the ERM).

irrevocable fixing of exchange rates, as in EMU, thereby mitigating the costs of losing policy independence – since monetary policy will be based on developments in all participating countries – and eliminating the costs of defending a peg in the face of market doubts.

3.6 Nominal income targeting

With consensus that there is no exploitable trade-off between inflation and real output in the long run, with evidence that monetary and credit aggregates may provide unreliable guidance to monetary policy-makers, and with awareness of the problems in adopting interest or exchange rate objectives, considerable attention has been paid to the option of targeting nominal income. Under this approach, the central bank seeks to achieve price stability by steering the expansion of nominal income at the same rate as that of potential output.[35]

While nominal income targeting has never been officially pursued, it has found ardent advocates amongst many distinguished (mostly American) economists, particularly in the 1980s when disillusionment with money targets became widespread.[36] This monetary strategy has not only been suggested as a policy framework for individual countries, but also constituted the core element of the blueprint for the international co-ordination of economic policy designed by Williamson and Miller (1987).[37] Under this proposal, the participating countries (notionally the Group of Seven) would agree to conduct their economic policies with the following assignment of rules and intermediate targets: the *average level* of (more or less global) short-term interest rates would be set on the basis of performance against an aggregate nominal income target, *differences* in short-term interest rates between countries would keep exchange rates within broad prespecified target ranges, and adjustments to national *fiscal* policies would steer domestic demand towards respective national targets. The distinction between nominal income targets at the international level, and domestic demand targets at the national level, reflects the greater relevance of the latter in addressing external payments imbalances.

Benefits

There is an inherent logic to targeting nominal income, since it brings together the two principal macroeconomic objectives that are directly influenced, at least in the short to medium term, by monetary policy – low inflation and high real output. Nominal income targeting thus does justice to the essence of monetary policy-making and casts policy setting in terms of its major underlying motivations. Consequently, nominal income targeting also has the advantage of communicating the basic goals of monetary policy to the outside world. Moreover, next to providing a clear link to the relevant policy goals, nominal income targets have the attraction of ensuring compatibility between inflation and growth objectives, such that one objective cannot be pursued at the expense of the other. In this respect, nominal income targeting addresses the root of the inflationary bias stemming from the short-run trade-off between inflation and output.

In addition to these pertinent benefits, a monetary strategy of targeting nominal income has important stabilising properties.[38] In particular, nominal income targeting insulates the economy in the face of shocks to money velocity, which the central bank would undertake to accommodate. From this perspective, nominal income targets are clearly preferable to money targets. Similarly, monetary policy would adjust to neutralise the effects of disturbances to aggregate demand. In the face of such shocks, nominal income targets would therefore outperform interest or exchange rate targets, under which monetary policy would not adjust to insulate the economy. In fact, at a conceptual level, a strategy of nominal income targeting effectively minimises the destabilising effects of these types of disturbances. In the case of supply shocks, the superior monetary target is ambiguous, since the preferred target then depends on the relative magnitude of the impact on prices and real income growth, as well as on the prioritisation of economic objectives. In this latter context, however, nominal income targeting does provide explicit guidance to policy-makers on how to balance the division of the adjustment burden between a change in the price level and an opposite change in real income. Specifically, by placing equal weight on achieving both the growth and the inflation objective, this approach ensures that the policy response takes both goals duly into account. Only in the case of a temporary shock would a strategy of nominal targeting tend to be inferior to one that keeps policy instruments unchanged, such as with a rigid interest rate rule or exchange rate peg. But, all in all, a monetary strategy of nominal income targeting theoretically offers an effective way to stabilise both output and prices in reaction to unanticipated shocks.

Drawbacks

Notwithstanding its stabilising properties and other strengths, nominal income targeting has considerable shortcomings. A first conceptual problem is that nominal income targets are situated right at the end of the process of monetary transmission and thus are not, by themselves, appropriate leading indicators for future nominal income. As a result of the long, variable and unpredictable lags in monetary policy transmission (whereby the output component of nominal income is generally impacted more quickly than the inflation component), targets at the end of the transmission process such as nominal income make a poor guide for short-term monetary policy decisions, leading either to policy instability or inaction. Specifically, given small short-term effects (mainly on output) and large medium-term effects (mainly on prices), an active monetary policy will run the risk of ultimately overshooting the target, thereby leading to instrument instability in the form of pronounced fluctuations in interest rates. The alternative is to create a policy bias towards inaction and to focus policy on longer-term objectives. Of course, a policy-maker with perfect knowledge on the structural and behavioural characteristics could find a judicious balance between short-term stabilisation measures and inaction, but this scenario is a far cry from the real world, governed as it is by uncertainty.

The problem of the relatively long lags between information on the nominal income target and the transmission of monetary policy changes can be tempered by looking at forecasts for the development of nominal income, rather than at outcomes. Whether this improves policy-making, depends crucially on the accuracy of the forecasts. After all, policies based on inaccurate forecasts will amplify economic volatility and increase uncertainty. Experience suggests that it is particularly difficult, using the techniques currently available, to project nominal income precisely and reliably.[39] In this respect, nominal income targeting can be considered a relatively demanding strategy in terms of information requirements: to be effective, substantial knowledge is needed of current and prospective output and prices, and of how developments in these variables are influenced by monetary policy changes.

A further issue is the equal weight placed by nominal income targets on achieving inflation and output objectives, since it is doubtful whether this parity accurately reflects society's preferences. If, for instance, the public attaches more importance to output stability than to price stability, adhering to nominal income targets leads to excessive output volatility. Of course, the method of targeting nominal income could in theory be refined to do greater justice to the preferred inflation-output trade-off in the social welfare function. This could be done, for example, by allowing policy-makers to permit a larger price deviation per unit of real income deviation.[40] However, such mechanisms to incorporate social preferences into the nominal income targets would expose monetary policy to a tendentious debate on social preferences and would invariably cloud the transparency of the targeting framework.

At the same time, it is unclear whether cumulating two objectives, each of which is desirable in its own right, truly leads to an optimal situation. If the economy is running at full capacity, but there is an unexpected exogenous price drop, should the central bank move to fuel output above its estimated potential? Conversely, if inflation is running at the upper end of what the central bank is comfortable with, but there is an unanticipated slump in output, should price stability be jeopardised to ensure the nominal income target is met? In part, this reverts to the sub-optimality of nominal income targets in the face of transitory shocks. But the issue is of broader relevance, since the duration of disturbances is usually uncertain and prudent policy-makers will generally not put achievements in one field at risk to support performance in another. More fundamentally, the difficulty lies in pursuing two goals (price stability and real growth) with only one instrument (the short-term interest rate); this issue will be tackled more extensively in the context of combined strategies, where monetary policy is explicitly aimed at more than one target.

From a political economy perspective, nominal income targeting has further drawbacks. To start with, it is unreasonable to make a central bank responsible for an aggregate that is crucially dependent on other policy developments – notably fiscal policy, but also structural adjustments – and that is far outside its direct control. By implication, a strategy of nominal income targeting also makes it difficult to hold a monetary authority accountable for the outcome of its decisions. And, by the same token, the central bank runs a greater risk of losing credibility if it adopts a policy target over which it has little control. In this regard, nominal income targets do not help reduce the opacity of monetary policy setting. An additional complication is that it is doubtful whether nominal income targets would be set solely by the central bank. Indeed, given the greater importance of a consistent policy mix in achieving these targets, as well as such targets' implicit inclusion of real income objectives, there is a strong case for political involvement in the setting of nominal income targets. In turn, this introduces the risk that the real growth projections underlying these targets will have a tendency of being set too high, thus loosening monetary policy's nominal anchor.

In terms of communication, it is questionable whether the synthesis of inflation and real income components in nominal income targets would be readily understood by the public. In practice, nominal and real income are readily confused.[41] Viewed from this perspective, nominal income targets will not help increase the transparency of monetary policy-making and will thus not buttress support for the objectives and measures of the monetary authority. In the same vein, these targets may be a less effective instrument to influence inflationary expectations.

Finally, a major – if not prohibitive – practical objection to nominal income targeting relates to the shortcomings in statistical data. In light of the considerable lags before output data become available, the low frequency of such data (mostly only on a quarterly basis), as well as their limited reliability (given numerous and substantive adjustments), national income data make a notoriously poor guide for short-term monetary policy. In particular, lags in data availability add to the lags in the process of monetary transmission and thereby risk leading to unnecessarily protracted deviations from the nominal income target. And when the data are finally available, the limited accuracy effectively makes it hazardous to draw any immediate policy conclusions.

Appraisal

In sum, nominal income targetry has considerable theoretical appeal, insofar as this strategy casts monetary policy in terms of its two main macroeconomic objectives, provides a firm nominal anchor, and also contains commendable automatic stabilisation properties in the face of unexpected disturbances. At the same time, however, nominal income targeting raises a variety of fundamental conceptual, practical, and political economy problems. In particular, since nominal income developments are heavily dependent on policies outside the realm of central banking, related targets will not contribute meaningfully to the transparency, accountability and credibility of monetary policy-making. Moreover, since nominal income developments are situated at the end of the process of monetary transmission, they do not provide timely guidance for policy setting, a drawback that is compounded by difficulties in accurately forecasting nominal income and by the protracted lags, infrequency and limited reliability of actual nominal income data.

Taken together, this leads to the conclusion that nominal income targets are inappropriate for use in short-term operational monetary policy decisions. There could conceivably be a role for a nominal income trajectory in designing the medium-term orientation of monetary policy, based on medium-term inflation objectives and estimates of potential output growth, but such a role may be inadvisable to the extent it risks infringing upon the independence of the central bank. In this context, it seems preferable to divide responsibilities according to the policy instrument that is most effective in achieving a given objective. Thus, the central bank is to be given the task of using monetary policy primarily to control inflation, while the political executive has the task of using structural and fiscal policies to promote sustainable growth in real incomes. This automatically leads to the alternative of targeting only the inflation component of nominal income.

3.7 Direct inflation targeting

Once the instability of money demand had caused discontent with money targets in the 1980s, and the abrupt changes of financial market sentiments had led to disenchantment with exchange rate targets in the early 1990s, the focus naturally shifted to the option of targeting inflation itself. Under this approach, monetary policy is notionally aimed directly at the end objective for inflation with no clear-cut intermediate target. As with nominal income targeting, such an approach has the difficulty that inflation targets are at the end of the monetary transmission process, do not constitute leading indicators for future inflation, and thus risk delaying necessary policy responses. This is resolved by implicitly assigning the role of intermediate target to the inflation *forecast* and by adjusting monetary policy according to deviations between the inflation forecast and the inflation target. The monetary stance is thus not linked to a specific intermediate target, but is based on all available variables containing information on future inflation. In order to avoid boundless discretion – and the inflationary bias that may come with it – monetary policy decisions are cast in a transparent framework: the inflation target is explicit, time-specific (except when it is constant over the medium-term) and well-defined (including in terms of predetermined escape clauses), and comprehensive information is provided on the inflation outlook.

After New Zealand and Canada initially pioneered a monetary strategy of inflation targeting, starting in March 1990 and February 1991, respectively, this approach rapidly gained popularity in Europe when the exchange rate crises of 1992 and 1993 left countries without a nominal anchor, or with only a loose one.[42] The United Kingdom was the first European country to adopt such a monetary policy framework in October 1992, barely three weeks after the pound left the ERM, and was followed shortly thereafter by Sweden (in January 1993), Finland (February 1993) and eventually also by Spain (December 1994). Later, France (January 1994), Italy (May 1995) and Portugal (March 1997) also proclaimed an inflation objective of sorts, but these objectives were less explicit and were not supported by a comprehensive inflation targeting policy strategy.

Benefits

The salient advantage of direct inflation targeting is that it creates a policy framework centred on what monetary policy should primarily be about – controlling inflation. This follows from the proposition that price stability should be the overriding objective of monetary policy and that variables such as real growth or unemployment should only be seen as secondary objectives, to be addressed to the extent consistent with the predominant goal of price stability over the medium term. Put differently, inflation targeting does not reject monetary policy's responsibility for output stabilisation, but it establishes a clear hierarchy of objectives. In turn, this hierarchy is based on the generally accepted hypotheses that, first, there is no exploitable trade-off between real activity and inflation beyond the short term and, second, that stable prices are desirable to promote sustainable economic growth and to avoid arbitrary redistribution of wealth.

A related attraction of inflation targets is that monetary policy is explicitly based on all available indicators of future price developments. This circumvents problems associated with possible instability between (traditional) intermediate targets and the final objective for inflation. Specifically, it avoids the problems ensuing from instability under money targets as well as the difficulties of defending exchange rate targets in the face of volatile market discipline. This does not mean that focusing on inflation targets precludes using intermediate targets, but only that the former always prevail over the latter in case of conflict.[43] In other words, inflation targeting has the advantage of not excluding *any* information that may have a bearing on the inflation objective. This assumes, of course, that the monetary authority has the understanding to recognise such information and, in case of conflicting price signals, is able to draw the correct policy conclusion.[44] In effect, attention is only placed on other variables to the extent this provides *additional* information to the main intermediate policy variable(s). In this respect, inflation targeting by definition gives at least as good, and presumably better, guidance to policy-makers than any strategy that targets one (or few) intermediate variables. For instance, if money targets told the whole story on prospective inflation, the monetary authority could base its policy decisions exclusively on money developments even under an inflation targeting approach. Since this is not the case in the real world, it is clear that taking everything into account provides value added to the policy-maker.[45]

In reality, of course, other monetary strategies with room for policy discretion (thus barring rigid money, exchange rate and interest rate targets) will also be implemented on the basis of all available information. Policy decisions that are at odds with developments under the target variable are then appropriately justified to the public and the additional information is – as it were – internalised into the existing target. Under these approaches, the feedback rules to monetary policy from expected deviations between the intermediate and end objectives are implicit, whereas under inflation targeting these are a central element of the policy-making framework. Thus, inflation targeting avoids the potential credibility costs that would otherwise result from frequent changes to the intermediate target or from repeated target misses. This highlights another area where inflation targeting differs fundamentally from these other monetary strategies – in communication with the public. By seeking to provide full information on the considerations driving monetary policy, rather than emphasising a single intermediate target, inflation targeting provides a better, albeit more complex, picture of what the central bank is actually doing. In this sense, inflation targeting is more forthright; it removes the separation between the internal and external dimensions of monetary policy-making that may exist under other approaches.

Indeed, one of the strengths of inflation targeting lies in capturing the benefits of transparency. Of course, these benefits are similarly applicable to other monetary policy strategies. A case in point is the Bundesbank, which has always sought to educate the public on the relationship between money and prices and to explain the derivation of its money targets. Nonetheless, transparency is a distinguishing characteristic of the inflation targeting framework, because it is key to limiting the otherwise wide-ranging policy discretion under this strategy. In fact, transparency is an intrinsic element of inflation targeting, as it is needed to engender close public scrutiny, reduce the scope for inflationary surprises, and thereby impart credibility to the announced inflation targets. In practice, this transparency is achieved mainly by publishing periodic inflation reports, in which the central bank recounts its views on the factors dominating the inflation outlook, by making the reasons for policy changes explicit and, in the case of the United Kingdom, by publishing (within two weeks) the minutes of the Monetary Policy Committee meetings. As a welcome side-effect, this transparency enhances the predictability of monetary policy and thereby reduces a source of economic uncertainty. More generally, it serves as a pedagogical instrument to explain monetary policy to society at large.

Even abstracting from active efforts to enhance transparency, direct inflation targeting has the advantage that the concept of consumer inflation is reasonably well-understood – more so, probably, than a broad money concept like M3 – thereby contributing to the visibility of the target variable.[46] As a result, an inflation target constitutes not only an effective nominal anchor, but also a powerful instrument to signal monetary policy intentions and steer inflationary expectations. By itself, this can help strengthen the impact (in terms of a larger total effect *and* a shorter transmission lag) of monetary policy on those involved in the wage and price setting process, as well as on financial markets. At the same time, this transparency of inflation targeting – in terms of comprehensibility and visibility – should serve to increase public support for central bank policies.

A further benefit of inflation targeting lies in the realm of accountability. An explicit inflation target against which to measure performance, together with transparency on the motives for (a lack of) policy decisions, provides a basis on which the monetary authority can be held accountable, whether in the abstract form of its reputation, more directly through parliamentary testimony, or in the extreme through changes in its employment conditions.[47] In this way, the combination of transparency and accountability under inflation targeting creates very strong incentives for the central bank to maximise its understanding of the inflationary process and to deliver on its target.

Lastly, also from a political economy perspective, the single-mindedness and transparency of the inflation targeting framework should effectively keep at bay any pressures to divert monetary policy unduly towards other objectives. In this regard, it is noteworthy that all countries pursuing inflation targets have central banks that are independent, at a minimum in the deployment of their instruments towards the target and with respect to the financing of government budgets.[48] Moreover, inflation targets are generally either set in agreement with the government, or later (perhaps implicitly) endorsed by the government, and in any event are not contradicted by it.[49] These aspects further reduce the scope for – and the public's perception of – conflicting objectives in the implementation of monetary policy.

Drawbacks

A dominant drawback of direct inflation targeting lies in the renowned long, variable and unpredictable lags with which monetary policy actions influence inflation. This leads to a limited and more delayed controllability of outcomes under the target variable. By consequence, inflation targets are surrounded by a large degree of uncertainty and performance under these targets can only be assessed after a relatively long time period – probably two years or more. In addition to this, inflation is influenced by a myriad of factors outside the domain of monetary policy, including for instance developments in commodity prices, nominal wages, public goods prices and consumer taxes. This creates difficulties on a number of fronts.

First, since the monetary authority will be pursuing an outcome it does not fully control, it will be vulnerable to a loss of credibility stemming from developments outside its influence. To a degree, this difficulty can be addressed by explaining price developments, by presenting the inflation target as a range, and by publicising inflation forecasts emphatically in terms of a probability distribution rather than as a single rate. But this weakness cannot be eliminated fully. Second, given the long timespan before the outcome under the policy target is known, it will take longer for the monetary authority actually to prove its commitment to its target and thus to achieve full credibility. In this context, third, the central bank may err on the side of caution and implicitly seek to meet the target in a shorter timeframe than the (unknown) full duration of the monetary transmission process. In this way, inflation targeting could generate instrument instability (in terms of greater interest rate volatility) with attendant output variability costs. Since monetary policy generally impacts output before prices, this difficulty is potentially large under inflation targeting (and by implication larger than under nominal income targeting). Explicitly defining the target two years or more in the future – as most inflation targeting countries have done – can help attenuate this drawback. Fourth, since inflation is not fully under the control of the central bank and is dependent on monetary policy implemented as far as 2 years back, it may be difficult to actually hold the monetary authority accountable for performance under the target.

Another major shortcoming of inflation targeting relates to the output or credibility costs of this strategy in case of supply shocks. In particular, although the optimal monetary policy reaction to a supply shock depends on the precise nature of the disturbance, there is usually a strong case to accommodate the first-round price impact without requiring compensating price changes in other areas. For instance, it would be inadvisable to seek offsetting price declines after a sudden increase in oil prices or a jump in indirect taxes, since this would unnecessarily depress real output. Rather, monetary policy should just aim at keeping the one-off influences on the price level from feeding durably into the inflation rate. But, with an explicit commitment to a specific inflation target, the scope to accommodate first-round price effects without credibility loss may be limited, in part because the actual size of the supply shock may not be readily identifiable. Put shortly, targeting inflation is more likely to favour reducing inflation variability over output variability.[50] The difficulty of this trade-off can be alleviated by specifying the inflation target to exclude price changes resulting from certain types of supply disturbances, and by incorporating precise caveats (for instance in case of natural disasters) into the targeting framework. A further option is to define the inflation target as an average over a longer time period, thereby allowing short-term price volatility to net out. More basically, it may be decided in practice not to pursue the target too rigidly – albeit at the price of modifying or missing the target – in order to avoid accentuating output variability. However, these solutions have the difficulty that intricate target definitions and ingenious escape clauses tarnish the transparency and the signalling power of the policy framework; at the same time, pragmatic policy implementation risks eroding the credibility of the targets and introducing an inflationary bias.

This is closely linked to another potential problem, which is the essentially discretionary nature of policy implementation under inflation targets. This is because inflation targeting has a target variable (future inflation) that is not directly and objectively observable – or, if you will, is *not* transparent. By consequence, it is difficult to judge whether the monetary authority is indeed pursuing its inflation target in a consistent manner over time. This risks leading to weaker or delayed decision-making when policy conflicts occur between output and inflation objectives. There are a variety of ways to tackle this shortcoming, but these sometimes give rise to new difficulties. For instance, the monetary authority could be assigned a joint – and mutually consistent – target for both inflation and output, thereby eliminating the incentive to raise output through inflation surprises.[51] In essence, this proposal is similar to nominal income targeting and therefore suffers similar drawbacks – especially that estimates of potential output are notoriously imprecise and that the central bank would be accepting responsibility for an outcome it can hardly secure. Another option is to make the inflation forecast an *explicit* intermediate target.[52] At a theoretical level, this forecast is fully controllable and thus allows a straightforward measurement of monetary policy performance. If this forecast remains on target, but the inflation outturn nonetheless deviates, this will be due to disturbances outside the control of the monetary authority. A first difficulty with this approach is that monetary policy has the aim of delivering an *actual* inflation objective, and not an inflation forecast. To this can be added the practical problem of whose forecast to target: using either that of the central bank or of independent outside forecasters raises a host of complex issues, prominent amongst which are conflicts of interest (given the inevitably judgmental – and thus manipulable – nature of forecasts) and self-fulfilling prophecies.[53] Moreover, if the forecast were to be based essentially on market forces, which are notably volatile and short-term oriented, this approach would likely introduce unnecessary monetary policy instability.[54]

More generally, the opacity of the inflation forecast can be reduced by spelling out its assumed determinants and by increasing the transparency of the policy-making process. This will enhance 'monetary monitoring' by the public, thereby diminishing the expectations of, and the scope for, inflationary surprises. Such an approach has been pursued by all inflation targeting countries. In this context, however, it also deserves emphasis that increasing transparency may have costs. Especially in times of greater uncertainty when the central bank may repeatedly find reason to change its policy course, transparency may highlight fallibility and uncertainty, and therewith contribute to this uncertainty, while also undermining confidence in the monetary authority. Moreover, too much information may weaken the impact of crucial policy signals and may actually reduce the understanding of the prime considerations driving the policy stance.

In addition to these disadvantages, inflation targeting may risk unduly narrowing the focus of the monetary policy on near-term prospects for the specific inflation index that is being targeted, potentially at the expense of attention for price stability in other areas, notably asset prices and the exchange rate.[55] In the European context of tightly knit economies seeking unrestricted regional trade, a policy of benign neglect vis-à-vis exchange rate fluctuations may undermine the mutual support necessary for the communal objectives. Besides this, a strategy of inflation targeting may necessitate far-reaching institutional reforms – especially with regard to the mandate and independence of the central bank. Also, it places heavy requirements in terms of information and, as any central bank with such a strategy will testify, is bound to divert scarce resources towards producing extensive external reports and assessments.[56]

Appraisal

Direct inflation targeting has a host of important advantages. It establishes a clear nominal anchor and focuses on the dominant objective of monetary policy – controlling inflation. By using all information with a bearing on the inflation objective, this approach avoids the difficulties of unpredictable intermediate targets and sets the stage for comprehensive, well-balanced monetary policy-making. At the same time, inflation targeting contributes to the transparency of policy decisions, as the target variable is highly visible and widely understood, and as greater openness in the considerations driving monetary policy is invariably part of the targeting framework. This enhances the monitoring of policy implementation by the public, thereby reducing expectations of time inconsistent policies and promoting central bank credibility. Together with the explicit and unequivocal nature of the inflation target, this protects monetary policy from pressures aimed at other objectives and establishes a yardstick for central bank accountability. In turn, these features increase the central bank's incentives to meet its target, while also fostering public support for the target and the underlying policies. In terms of its bottom line, the benefits of this strategy are supported by empirical evidence: although this took place in an environment of general disinflation, countries with inflation targeting frameworks (including the European ones) have been remarkably successful in meeting their targets and bringing down their rates of inflation to levels broadly consistent with price stability. Although the evidence on whether inflation targeting reduces the sacrifice ratio is mixed, this strategy does strengthen the stamina to bear disinflation costs and to maintain price stability once it has been achieved.[57]

These advantages need to be measured up against various difficulties, rooted in three main handicaps. First, owing to the unpredictability of the monetary transmission process as well as the heavy influence of other factors, the explicit target variable (future inflation) is not under the full control of the central bank. At the same time, the implicit target variable (forecast inflation) is not easily, objectively observable. Second, the singular focus on stabilising prices risks exacerbating output variability, especially if the monetary authority adheres tightly to its target in the face of (seldom easily identifiable) supply shocks. To the extent the goal of output stability is factored into monetary policy, deviations from the inflation target are more likely to occur, which may compromise the credibility of the monetary policy framework. Third, given the broad-ranging and changeable information input, this strategy is essentially discretionary in nature. By implication, it bears the risk of an inflationary bias stemming from the perception that policy tightening may tend to be too little or too late. Within these handicaps, there is a tension between the first two, which suggest defining the target in terms of an appropriately wide band and then pursuing it pragmatically, and the third, which in itself suggests precommitting monetary policy to a narrow target and subsequently sticking closely to it. In essence, there is a trade-off between being able to respond optimally to aggregate supply shocks (as under nominal income targeting) and to maintain a medium-term policy focus, on the one hand, and lowering the inflationary bias of discretionary policy, on the other.

On balance, direct inflation targeting makes for an attractive strategy, particularly in view of its candour on what monetary policy is all about. However, given the limited controllability of the target variable and the incidence of supply shocks, it is inadvisable to pursue this strategy rigidly – a prescription comparable to that for pragmatism under money targets, albeit for a different reason (the issue here is the limited controllability of the target, rather than the potential instability between the target and the end objective). As the attendant policy discretion risks introducing an inflationary bias, it is crucial that such a policy strategy is indeed combined with offsetting steps to strengthen the institutional framework and the transparency governing monetary decision-making. Again, the remedy lies in the adoption of a clear-cut mandate and instrument independence for the central bank, and in the regular provision of comprehensive information on the monetary authority's activities, therewith illustrating its sincerity in pursuing its mandate. While this strategy may thus require substantive institutional and procedural reforms, it is likely to be particularly appealing to countries that have limited credibility and that wish to break decisively with an inflationary past. In this context, it is noteworthy that inflation targeting has been adopted predominantly by countries with a blemished monetary history, and not by countries with a long-standing tradition of monetary stability (such as Germany, Switzerland and the United States).

While this issue has a relevance going beyond this specific strategy, inflation targeting explicitly raises the question of whether monetary policy should target the price *level* rather than its *rate* of change, thereby providing greater long-term certainty on price developments.[58] There are, however, several compelling reasons to focus on the rate rather than the level. First, downward rigidities of nominal wages and prices argue against requiring that temporary price increases, for instance from adverse supply shocks, be followed by periods of deflation to bring the price level back to a stable target. Second, price level targeting would ask the central bank to depart a second time round (but now in the opposite direction) from the inflation range it considers desirable. In effect, greater price level stability would probably be bought at the expense of greater inflation variability. Third, and perhaps most convincingly, it has become increasingly clear that there is a significant upward statistical bias in inflation measurements stemming primarily from unaccounted improvements in quality, adaptations in the average consumption basket and shifts in the location of purchases. By consequence, a target of price level stability would imply deflation. In effect, this wipes out the attraction of aiming for the ideal transparent target of price level stability (and an average inflation rate of zero). And, when the alternative is a level that trends gently upwards, a strategy of rate targeting seems more transparent to the extent it allows constancy in the inflation target and avoids the difficulty of having to explain to a forward-looking public that the inflation target is determined on a backward-looking basis. In all, a strategy of targeting the rate of price increases is preferable to one that targets the price level.

Once the attraction of aiming for the transparency of price level stability is rejected, there seems to be merit in not defining an inflation target symmetrically around effective price stability, but in allowing minimal inflation in order to facilitate the adjustment of real wages as well as the establishment of negative real interest rates in times of recession.[59] However, this rate of inflation needs to remain negligible in order to avoid creating significant distortions in the allocative efficiency of the price mechanism and in the tax system. Against this background, the floor of an inflation target range could be set at the estimated level of effective price stability (perhaps equivalent to about 1 per cent measured inflation in most European countries) while the width of the band could be determined by the unavoidable inflation uncertainty stemming from supply shocks and monetary transmission variability; recent experience in inflation targeting countries suggests that a bandwidth of 2-3 percentage points may be appropriate, even if the target is then still likely to be missed part of the time.[60] The average deviations under the (since 1985 normative) inflation assumption incorporated into Germany's money targets, confirm that a bandwidth of 2 or 3 percentage points would have covered 75 per cent, respectively 88 per cent, of the inflation outcomes since 1975.[61] Alternatively – and this seems preferable – a point target could be set at the upper edge of the range that is considered compatible with price stability (in view of statistical biases of uncertain magnitude, this range has traditionally been set at 0-2 per cent in Europe). Although a point target has the disadvantage that it is likely to be missed, it provides clearer guidance both for inflation expectations and policy-makers, and thus avoids the magnetic field that may otherwise surround the ceiling of the range, or be thought of doing so.

3.8 Combined targeting approaches

The different options for univariate targeting each have their own benefits and drawbacks. In an attempt to soften the individual drawbacks while cumulating the benefits, consideration can be given to adopting a combined strategy that focuses monetary policy on two (or perhaps more) targets. Specifically, under a dual strategy, the central bank stipulates a path for two target variables – ensuring their *ex ante* consistency – and grants developments under both of these targets prominence in its internal policy-making process. With regard to the external element of monetary policy-making, a dual approach involves announcing both targets to the public and explaining monetary policy decisions on the basis of developments under both targets. In principle, a combined strategy does not explicitly prioritise one target above the other.

Mixed strategies have been a common feature in the European monetary landscape. Over the past quarter of a century, exchange rate targets have been combined with money targets (in the cases of France, Greece, Italy, the Netherlands, Portugal, Spain and the United Kingdom), with domestic credit expansion targets (Denmark, Ireland, Italy, the Netherlands, and Portugal), with both money and credit targets (Italy) and with inflation targets (Finland, Spain and, in a low-profile fashion, France, Italy, and Portugal). Similarly, prior to its exchange rate peg, Greece had targets for domestic credit alongside those for money. Germany has also consistently combined its membership of the prevailing European exchange rate arrangement with money targets, although it could be argued that, as the system's anchor country (the so-called Nth country), it was implicitly absolved from its exchange rate constraint in the sense that this external commitment did not effectively bind monetary policy.

Benefits

Pursuing a combined strategy can be attractive for a variety of reasons. A prominent advantage is that the use of two or more targets can serve to spread the risks ensuing from an unstable relationship between an individual intermediate target and the end objective. For instance, a money target may usefully be supplemented by another target to help explain central bank decision-making if money velocity turns out to be unstable. In addition, the adoption of a supplementary target may help anchor policies and expectations when a single target contains undue slack. This may occur, for example, in situations where an exchange rate target is defined as a wide band. A case in point is Spain's adoption of an inflation target after the bands of the ERM had been broadened to ± 15 per cent. More generally, a mixed strategy may prevent monetary policy from being too narrowly focused on prospects for a specific target variable. These advantages essentially boil down to building an extra safeguard into the monetary policy framework. Or, in graphic terms, combining two strategies may be compared to a skydiver wearing two parachutes.

Mixing strategies may also generate political economy advantages. In particular, by employing two or more targets, a combined strategy will alleviate the credibility loss of missing a specific target. Moreover, by highlighting different points in the process of monetary transmission, a combined strategy may enhance accountability. This will especially be the case with inflation and nominal income targets, which are only partly controllable and only observable after protracted lags, and which could therefore benefit from an additional intermediate target that stimulates close and timely monitoring. In this respect, a combined strategy may shift the public's attention to earlier elements of the monetary transmission process and thereby promote a more rapid build-up of policy credibility. To the extent this serves to emphasise a variable that is more fully within the domain of the monetary authority, a mixed strategy may also enhance the autonomy of the central bank.

Besides this, a dual strategy can provide monetary policy with a different coating, thereby making it politically more palatable. A clear example is the combination of an exchange rate oriented monetary policy with a money target: if day-to-day policy is effectively based on the external target, announcement of a complementary money target can convey the impression that domestic considerations are front-stage in the decision-making process. Cosmetically, this may suggest that monetary sovereignty has not been lost. This consideration seems to have motivated the adoption of a combined strategy by France. As a large and leading country in Europe, it has sought to avoid the impression that its monetary policy is determined by the Bundesbank, even if, since 1983, it has effectively granted primacy to its exchange rate target vis-à-vis Germany.

Finally, a combined targeting strategy may be viewed as doing greater justice to the essentially eclectic nature of monetary policy-making. By advertising a greater number of key variables in the central bank's reaction function, a mixed strategy may be seen as conveying a better sense of the multiple considerations occupying the minds of the monetary authority.

Drawbacks

A strategy of multiple targeting does not, however, come without drawbacks. The principal problem is that the different targets may be fully consistent *ex ante*, but will almost certainly deviate during implementation. Conceptually, with perfect foresight, it makes no difference at which target monetary policy is aimed. But, in practice, the alternative target variables will diverge in different manners from their targeted paths and a policy framework with more than one target is bound to prove overdetermined. In essence, the central bank will notionally be pursuing multiple targets with only one instrument (a short-term interest rate), thereby violating the Tinbergen Rule under which the number of policy objectives cannot exceed the number of policy instruments.

At a fundamental level, there is thus an inconsistency in pursuing two targets without prioritising one over the other.[62] For example, the combination of a tight exchange rate target, on the one hand, and a money or inflation target, on the other, is inherently inconsistent because the exchange rate effectively makes monetary policy endogenous (assuming, of course, that capital movements are unrestricted). This not only rules out an independently determined money growth, but also an independently set inflation target, since the domestic inflation rate will not be able to deviate in the medium run from the inflation rate in the country to which the domestic currency is pegged. Similarly, inflation or nominal income targeting cannot conceptually be combined on equal footing with any other strategy, because an intermediate target should by definition be subordinated to a final objective – the only one that society truly cares for.

Indeed, regardless of what the central bank might proclaim, the different targets under a combined strategy will never be of equal standing in practice. Specifically, in any combination with an exchange rate (or interest rate) commitment, this target is likely to dominate on account of its visibility and immediate policy demands. In a similar vein, an inflation target is likely to overshadow most other targets it is combined with, since it is broad-based and is by definition most closely related to the relevant end objective of monetary policy.

These difficulties create costs in terms of transparency and policy credibility. This is because when the central bank has more than one target, every policy measure will trigger the question whether this measure is predicated on the one or the other target, and how long this hierarchy of objectives will last. In this manner, a multiplicity of targets casts doubt on the precedence granted to any target and irrefutably undermines confidence in each individual target. As a concrete example, combining an inflation target with another target will – at a minimum – create confusion regarding the true commitment to that inflation target. By consequence, when the prioritisation of strategic targets is not made explicit, the monetary authority will also experience greater difficulty in steering expectations with regard to prospective policies and desired outcomes. In sum, targeting two potentially inconsistent variables will inevitably cloud the comprehensibility of central bank policy-making, will lessen the credibility of the targeting framework, and will make it more difficult to sustain the target that is actually being prioritised.

Moreover, as the different targets will at times send conflicting policy signals, multiple targeting reduces the rules-based nature of the monetary strategy and risks fuelling a perception of arbitrariness in monetary policy-making. By itself, this greater discretion and policy ambiguity may tend to increase inflationary expectations and undermine central bank credibility. In this latter context, it also needs to be borne in mind that although announcing two targets increases the probability of meeting at least one target, it implies a commensurately greater credibility loss in the event both targets are missed.

Appraisal

Mixed strategies seek to mitigate the drawbacks of individual strategies while cumulating their benefits. In essence, combined strategies aim to build in safeguards in the event an individual target proves to be an unreliable guidepost for monetary policy-making. In this respect, highlighting more than one policy target explicitly broadens the orientation of monetary decision-making and facilitates the communication of monetary policy when a target variable is influenced by unforeseen disturbances. A mixed strategy thus reduces the risk of credibility loss ensuing from the failure to meet any target. In a more political dimension, a dual strategy may make it easier to present an externally-oriented monetary strategy to a public that resists losing monetary sovereignty.

But these advantages of multiple targeting have a price. The co-existence of several targets increases the scope for policy discretion and thereby risks introducing an inflationary bias into the monetary policy-making framework. In addition, mixed strategies reduce the coherence and comprehensibility of the central bank's policies. Not only does the monetary strategy lose the virtue of simplicity, but it also becomes overdetermined and inherently inconsistent. This will tarnish the transparency and weaken the credibility of monetary policy. And even if there is a credibility bonus in a higher probability of meeting a target, this needs to be weighed against the greater credibility loss if both targets were to be breached.

The difficulties of a mixed monetary policy strategy can be ascribed primarily to the fundamental inability to consistently achieve more than one policy target with only one central bank policy instrument. Looking back in time, pursuing two strategic targets can of course be feasible if the instrument of capital restrictions is also available, as was the case in the period directly after the collapse of the Bretton Woods system. This helps explain both the widespread implementation of dual strategies in Europe during the late 1970s, as well as their gradual reduction as capital restrictions were lifted.

On balance, in an environment of free capital flows, a mixed strategy may at most be a second-best solution, to be considered in circumstances when the preferred strategy is politically infeasible. The requirements of consistency, simplicity, transparency and credibility of the monetary policy framework all argue unequivocally for a one-target strategy. To the extent the monetary authority has multiple strategic objectives, these should preferably be announced together with their hierarchy, for example by publicising monitoring ranges for certain key variables alongside a single target for the dominant policy objective.

3.9 Conclusions

Almost as important as what you target, is that you target. This holds in a normative sense for any monetary authority, with the possible exception of one with (close to) full credibility. Internally, a targeting framework promotes the consistency of monetary policy-making and the continuity of the policy thrust. More significantly, targeting externally precommits the central bank and provides a focal point for policy and inflation expectations. In this way, targeting limits discretion, diminishes the inflationary bias of monetary policy, and reduces economic uncertainty. At the same time, targeting enhances the transparency and comprehensibility of monetary policy. This helps bolster the credibility of the central bank – to the level it genuinely deserves – and establishes a basis against which to hold it accountable.

However, these benefits require that the policy target meets a number of preconditions. Specifically, the target must be reasonably controllable, be predictably related to the final policy objective, precede developments in that objective, be readily communicable to the general public, and be statistically monitorable on a timely, frequent and reliable basis. These are the main criteria against which different targeting options need to be measured. Since it is practically impossible that any option will be unequivocally superior on all counts, the selection of a policy target involves pondering a variety of trade-offs. That is what makes the monetary strategy choice both difficult and delicate. But it should not detract from the fact that it is fruitful, in virtually all cases, to make such a choice and to publicly adopt a targeting strategy.

With these criteria, judging the adequacy of a policy target becomes an essentially empirical issue. In general, the outcome will differ both across countries and over time. Selecting a superior monetary policy target is thus a dynamic, country-specific process: continual progress in financial innovation and payments system technology, as well as ongoing changes in financial regulations, institutional structures, central bank communication and behavioural patterns, will invariably shift the long-run relationship between central bank instruments, intermediate policy targets and final objectives over the course of time. Together with adaptations in public preferences, this is bound to cause recurrent adjustments to the superior monetary policy target.

Against this background, Table 6 provides a broad indication, for the various target options, of the general strengths and weaknesses under these five criteria. At the outset, it should be emphasised that the performance of a target alternative may vary substantively from this straightforward overview in practice, depending on the particular character and dynamics of the economic environment, the precise specification of the target, and the degree of pragmatism with which monetary policy is actually implemented. For instance, a country targeting money and undergoing rapid financial system change, may experience transitory money demand shifts, resulting in a temporarily unpredictable relationship between money and the final objectives of monetary policy. And, in the case of an exchange rate target, the relation to the end objectives, as well as the leading indicator properties, may become unreliable if policies go off-track or an asymmetric shock occurs in the anchor country. Besides this, a narrow money target may be readily controllable, but only loosely related to the end objective for inflation, whereas the opposite may be true for a broad money aggregate. Similarly, a central bank targeting inflation may improve its target controllability by aiming at a measure of underlying inflation; this will, however, lessen the target's communicability.

Nonetheless, a few normative conclusions can be distilled. In particular, interest rate and domestic credit targeting are, by themselves, inappropriate monetary policy strategies, since they both leave the monetary policy framework without a nominal anchor to pin down the price level. Credit targets may, at most, be temporarily advisable in the event of an acute balance of payments crisis that necessitates the prioritisation of external viability over the inflation objective. Of the remaining alternatives, nominal income targetry would seem to have the larger drawbacks, since this target variable does not possess leading indicator properties and, with the techniques currently available, can hardly be accurately forecasted.

As a result, nominal income (forecast) data cannot be expected to provide reliable guidance to monetary authorities. Moreover, this approach clouds the transparency of the policy framework, on the one hand by eliciting greater political involvement in the conduct of monetary policy, on the other by making the central bank responsible for output objectives it cannot durably influence. A mixed approach of explicitly pursuing two or more explicit targets is also unlikely to be a first-best strategy. Although the adoption of combined targetsspreads the risk of unreliable signals or uncontrollable developments under any single target variable, multiple targets are bound to prove mutually inconsistent in practice, thereby creating confusion on the true orientation of monetary policy while also increasing the scope for discretion. This essentially leaves three prime strategic alternatives: money, exchange rate and inflation targeting. The choice between these options is determined primarily by the stability and controllability of money demand (a necessary condition for money targeting) and the fulfilment of optimal currency area criteria (a necessary condition for exchange rate targeting), leaving inflation targeting if these requirements are not met.

Table 6: Strengths and weaknesses of monetary policy targeting options

Monetary policy target	Relation to end objectives	Control-lability	Leading indicator properties	Communi-cability	Statistics	Main concern
Money	0	0	+	+	0	Stability/controllability of money demand
Domestic credit	0	0	0	-	0	Absence of nominal anchor
Interest rate [1]	-	+	0	-	+	Absence of nominal anchor
Exchange rate [2]	0	0	+	+	+	Optimal currency area considerations
Nominal income	+	-	-	-	-	Reliability of (forecast) data
Inflation [3]	+	0	+	+	-	Supply shocks
Combined targets [4]	+	-	+	-	0	Consistency of targets

[1] Short-term nominal interest rate.

[2] Assumes broadly similar economic structures, shocks and preferences, as well as stability-oriented policies in the anchor country.

[3] Assumes that forecast inflation, rather than actual inflation, is the policy target; this enhances the leading indicator properties of the target, but complicates its statistical measurability.

[4] Outcome depends on target combination. Here, a dual strategy with money and inflation targets is assumed, as well as pragmatic monetary policy implementation.

Four further issues deserve special emphasis. First, notwithstanding the solid case for monetary policy targeting, there is, in principle, no ground to focus internal monetary policy-making only on one specific target and to neglect all other available information variables. In fact, any monetary policy targeting approach should, at least internally, be prepared in an inherently eclectic fashion. Even when primacy is granted to one target variable, the central bank should nonetheless collect and analyse information on a broad array of other variables, and use this information to decide how closely it should stick to its target variable in practice and, more fundamentally, whether it should continue targeting that specific variable. While there is clearly virtue in maintaining a certain degree of constancy in the strategic approach, this again stresses that selecting a monetary policy strategy is an ongoing activity, with no scope for complacent automaticity.

Second, the superior monetary policy reaction is unlikely to involve strict adherence to a given target, since the central bank will want to be able to accommodate some types of shocks while countering others. Indeed, with the exception of exchange rate (and possibly interest rate) targets – where the need for market confidence in the authorities' commitment is likely to minimise the scope for discretion – it is generally inadvisable to pursue monetary targeting frameworks rigidly. By consequence, these various other targeting options may be very similar in terms of policy prescriptions, as can be readily illustrated at a conceptual level. For example, a money target implicitly incorporates a nominal income target and, in absence of disturbances to money velocity, the two are equivalent. To the extent the central bank seeks to accommodate money demand shocks (as it generally should), policy requirements will be identical under both targets. In the same vein, a money target is necessarily derived on the basis of an inflation target and, barring unexpected deviations in real money demand (for which allowances should be made), policy prescriptions will be equal. Similarly, policy differences between money targeting and credit targeting may be small, especially when in the former case unforeseen money velocity shifts are offset through the balance of payments. By the same token, nominal income targeting is comparable to direct inflation targeting with caveats for supply shocks – whose first-round effects should usually be accommodated to allow relative price changes without incurring the output costs related to downward nominal rigidities. And, of course, a strategy with combined targets can be pursued according to either of its component targets, and even to any policy course in between.

Third, more practically, the absence of reliable day-to-day guidance provided by the target variables other than interest and exchange rates will likely result in an actual policy implementation that is basically the same under these various approaches. In reality, regardless of whether the monetary authority purports to have a money, credit, inflation, nominal income, or combined target, it will process all available information and will use the available margins of discretion to generate the best possible results for its underlying final objectives. In essence, it is then the final objectives rather than the intermediate targets that effectively determine the policy course. And, because the final objectives are basically very similar, the policy course is bound to be so too. To the extent that there are subtle differences between the final objectives (for example between inflation and nominal income goals) under these various targets, this subtlety is likely to become indistinguishable in the noisy environment of practical policy decisions. In the final analysis, the central bank will not disregard the output costs of achieving a dominant inflation objective, but will seek a judicious balance between the stability of price and output growth developments. This is supported by empirical evidence that large countries pursuing an independent monetary policy course (that is, without exchange rate commitments) effectively have similar central bank reaction functions, irrespective of the avowed policy target.[63] Specifically, nominal short-term interest rates are found to be adjusted in a similar fashion to deviations between expected inflation and output from their respective targets.

This leads to a final, important point. Since both the input and the outcome of the internal monetary policy decision-making process is likely to be very similar, the differences between these various targeting frameworks predominantly lies in the external elements of monetary policy strategy. In particular, the presentation of monetary policy to the public, as well as the related political economy aspects, differs considerably between the target options. This suggests that as long as the other four preconditions for a monetary policy target are basically met, special emphasis should be placed on communicability (in the broadest sense of the word). Indeed, this characteristic importantly determines the potential contribution of the target to the transparency, and thus to the credibility, of central banking. Specifically, given a sufficiently close relationship with monetary policy's final objectives as well as an adequate degree of central bank controllability, communicability will determine whether a target variable can sustain a prime role in signalling and justifying monetary policy, and whether it can serve to establish accountability vis-à-vis the general public. Of course, the weight to be attached to this aspect also depends on the extent to which a country's democratic structures require central bank transparency and accountability – Europe's diverse cultures and histories provide limited normative guidance in this respect. Nonetheless, in view of the major contribution communicability can make to the efficacy of a monetary policy strategy, considerable attention should be paid to its various elements – for instance, the comprehensibility and visibility of the target variable, and the degree in which the target signals a central bank's responsibility. Again, these criteria point at three prime target alternatives that are well-understood, readily monitorable and consistent with an autonomous central bank: money, exchange rate and inflation targeting. As will be set out in the next chapters, these are the main alternatives that monetary policy strategies have focused on in Europe over the past quarter of a century.

NOTES

[1] M. Friedman (1968, pp. 5 and 17).

[2] B. Friedman (1994) interprets intermediate targeting in this strict sense, describing it as the adoption of a rigid rule on how the central bank reacts to new information. He contrasts this with an 'information variables' approach, which is broad-based and explicitly includes judgmental elements. He does not, however, consider the role of intermediate targets in precommitting monetary policy, communicating with the public and establishing central bank accountability. It comes as no surprise that – having disregarded these political economy considerations – he advises against intermediate targeting.

[3] In a sense, the adjective 'intermediate' may be viewed as covering all targeting alternatives. Even strategies that focus on variables at the end of the transmission process, such as nominal income and inflation targeting, can be considered variants of the intermediate targeting framework. In both these cases, the *forecasts* for the target variable are the implicit intermediate targets towards the *outturns* under the end objectives.

[4] The term "Just do it"-strategy was coined by Mishkin (1997), then Research Director at the Federal Reserve Bank of New York, in an article where the strategy's disadvantages take up four times the space of the advantages.

[5] Whether a reserve money aggregate or a short-term interest rate should be used to control money growth depends on the interest rate sensitivity and relative stability of the money demand and supply functions. For a discussion of this issue, see Goodhart (1989) and Wenninger (1990).

[6] McCallum (1985) addresses these factors in the context of money targeting.

[7] For a discussion, see Issing (1992) and Kloten (1992). Another viewpoint, set out for example by Kole and Meade (1995), is that the stability of German money demand is also, at least in part, the result of more limited competition and slower financial innovation in German financial markets.

[8] Virtually all IMF programs are centred around credit ceilings, although recently a combination of performance criteria for credit and indicative targets for reserve money has become increasingly common. The design of monetary policy in IMF programs is discussed in Guitián (1994a) and Polak (1997).

[9] This lies at the heart of the monetary approach to the balance of payments; for original essays see Guitián (1972) and Polak and Argy (1971).

[10] A vivid illustration of this elementary distinction between ceilings on domestic credit and on a monetary aggregate is provided in Polak (1991, p. 35). In an IMF consultation with a European country suffering repeated balance-of-payments difficulties (later disclosed by Polak as having been the United Kingdom), the finance minister observes with pride that monetary policy could not be the origin of the problems, as money growth had been kept moderate. He was explained by the IMF staff that "whenever money leaked out through the

balance of payments, it was promptly replaced through new credit so it could leak out again".

[11] This view is set out in Blinder and Stiglitz (1983); see also Alexander and Caramazza (1994).

[12] For a discussion of the evidence for the US, see Radecki (1990) and early work by Fackler and Silver (1983).

[13] A proposal to use total net credit as an intermediate target for US monetary policy is set out in B. Friedman (1983).

[14] In an empirical analysis comparing monetary policy under fixed exchange rates in Austria, Belgium and the Netherlands during 1973-1992, Kool (1995) analyses the rewards of explicitly targeting domestic credit *and* the exchange rate, which was only done in the Netherlands. His findings suggest there may have been benefits in terms of exchange rate and interest rate stability, but that these were marginal at best.

[15] Steindel (1990) sets out the historic experience with interest rate targeting, especially in the anchor currency of the system, the United States.

[16] The option of targeting the slope of the yield curve should be rejected on the same grounds; Steindel (1990, p 296) discusses ineffective past attempts at targeting the spread between short- and long-term rates.

[17] A detailed analysis of the difficulties of measuring real interest rates is provided by Brown and Santoni (1981).

[18] Mote (1988) illustrates this tendency with historical examples of episodes when central banks targeted interest rates and did not move these rates sufficiently actively to achieve stabilisation objectives.

[19] Sargent and Wallace (1975).

[20] See for example McCallum (1981) and Barro (1989).

[21] Exchange rate targeting should be read as setting a *nominal* exchange rate objective. Targeting the *real* exchange rate is inadvisable on account of the limited controllability of this variable. Moreover, a real exchange rate objective leaves monetary policy without a nominal anchor, automatically accommodates domestic price changes, and sets in motion either an inflationary or deflationary spiral depending on whether the underlying real exchange rate is more depreciated or appreciated, respectively, than the target. See also Adams and Gros (1986).

[22] Giavazzi and Pagano (1988) elaborate on this disciplinary influence of ERM membership.

[23] The fact that the ultimate decision on adjustments to exchange rate parities generally rests with the government rather than the central bank further underscores the importance of monetary policy being consistently supported by other macroeconomic policies, if only to make the exchange rate target credible.

[24] Based on developments in German and Dutch consumer prices during the period 1961-91, Berk and Winder (1994) show that the inflation rates in these two countries move in line and are actually co-integrated, implying that the exchange rate peg has anchored the Dutch price *level* to that in Germany. Besides this, they find that two-thirds of the reduction in the Dutch inflation rate between the periods 1961-1979Q3 and 1979Q4-1991 can be attributed to the policy shift of pegging the guilder to the Deutsche mark within the framework of the European Exchange Rate Mechanism.

[25] The impact of exchange rate instability on expenditure in the context of the Common Agricultural Policy is reviewed by Giavazzi and Giovannini (1989).

[26] As stated by Icard (1994b, p. 241), at the time Director General of Research at the Banque de France.

[27] In the literature, a distinction is made between first-generation (or fundamentalist) and second-generation models of speculative attacks. In the former, pioneered by Krugman (1979), currency crises are precipitated by the behaviour of rational investors anticipating an exchange rate collapse as a result of fiscal profligacy. In the latter, currency crises are triggered by self-fulfilling forces that boost the costs of adhering to an exchange rate commitment. As set out for instance in Obstfeld (1995), such crises reflect the government's endogenous response to market expectations and do not require deteriorating fundamentals. In an analysis of the 1992 ERM exchange rate crisis, Eichengreen and Wyplosz (1993) present evidence suggesting that self-fulfilling forces played a role.

[28] Total gross official reserves are sufficient to cover the monetary base in most industrialised countries, even without accounting for borrowing capacity; see Obstfeld and Rogoff (1995) who also discuss the technical feasibility of maintaining an exchange rate target in the face of a domestic bank run going beyond conversion of the monetary base.

[29] Mishkin (1997).

[30] The sharp September monetary tightening had largely exhausted support for interest rate increases in defence of the exchange rate. In late November, when sterilised intervention proved unsuccessful in the face of bandwagon effects, the krona was floated. See Hörngren and Lindberg (1993).

[31] In analysing devaluation risk in the ERM, Thomas (1994) finds that interest rate differentials are only weakly influenced by movements in fundamental variables such as inflation, unemployment, relative unit labour costs, government debt and foreign exchange reserves. Based on research of the credibility of the ERM as a system, Knot, Sturm and De Haan (1998) find that inflation rates, budget deficits, unemployment and current account outcomes have generally had an impact on the system's interest rate differentials; however, they also show that such differentials experienced a sustained decline from 1983 onwards and had all but disappeared by 1991.

[32] In the original analysis of the validity of this hypothesis for the main industrialised countries, Balassa (1964) highlights the potentially misleading signals that price developments (and purchasing power calculations) may provide on the need for exchange rate adjustments. On the basis of an analysis of inflation in eight EU countries during 1975-93, Alberola and Tyrväinen (1998) simulate that inflation differentials of up to 2 percentage points may be attributed to the Balassa-Samuelson effect. In a separate report, the Banco de Portugal (March 1997 Economic Bulletin, p. 8) finds that inflation in the non-tradables sector was 2 to 4 percentage points higher than in the tradables sector during the early 1990s.

[33] For a discussion of the related problems in the Bretton Woods era, see Giavazzi and Giovannini (1989).

[34] This follows the definition of a fixed exchange rate that prevailed under Bretton Woods, as set out in Obstfeld and Rogoff (1995) and Rogoff (1998).

[35] In this broad analysis, the expression 'nominal income' can be used interchangeably with 'nominal GNP' or 'nominal GDP'. The subtle differences between these variables do not materially affect the thrust of the arguments set out in general terms for nominal income targeting. Proposals have also been made to target final sales, since this has the technical advantage of circumventing the impact of inventory changes; such a target may, however, be less well understood and thus less useful in communicating the prime considerations driving monetary policy.

[36] The case for nominal income targeting has been made, amongst others, by Tobin (1983), Taylor (1985) and McCallum (1987 and 1996). Reviews of the debate are provided by Hilton and Moorthy (1990) and Clark (1994).

[37] In a more loosely defined framework, Frankel (1990) similarly proposes the use of nominal income targeting as an international policy co-ordination device between the G-7 countries.

[38] For a formal exposition of the stabilising properties of a nominal GNP rule, see Frankel and Chinn (1995). Using a wide variety of empirically based open-economy models, Flood and Mussa (1994) similarly illustrate that monetary policy rules directed at nominal income perform better in terms of output stability and inflation stability than rules focused on the exchange rate or the money supply.

[39] Meltzer (1987) argues that forecast errors for output growth are generally large and that discretionary policies based on these forecasts are unlikely to stabilise the economy. Based on the US experience, Kahn (1988) finds inevitable imprecision and at times large errors in nominal GNP forecasts.

[40] Taylor (1985, 1993) presents a policy rule that can be adjusted according to the relative welfare effects of output and inflation fluctuations. As an alternative approach, Hall (1985) proposes an 'elastic price standard' under which the central bank is instructed to stabilise prices at a particular level, but is allowed to depart from this level when unemployment deviates from target. The magnitude of the permissible price level departure is equal to the deviation of unemployment multiplied by a predetermined elasticity. This elasticity effectively determines the short-run trade-off between inflation and unemployment; Hall suggests it be set between 5 and 8.

[41] Mishkin and Posen (1997).

[42] In the more distant past, Sweden explicitly pursued a policy of price-level stabilisation in the 1930s, making it the first country on record to have aimed monetary policy openly at a price target; it is also the only country to date to have targeted the price level stability rather than an inflation rate. This early Swedish experience is set out in Jonung (1979) and Berg and Jonung (1999).

[43] Leiderman and Svensson (1996).

[44] M. Friedman (1968, p. 15) rejected this assumption, although he acknowledged that: "Perhaps, as our understanding of monetary phenomena advances, the situation will change."

[45] Haldane (1995a) draws a parallel between the target choice and decisions on an optimal asset portfolio, where the precept applies that all eggs should not be placed in one basket.

[46] In a formal comparison between inflation targets and monetary targets, Cukierman (1995) assumes that visibility is the main advantage of the former.

[47] In New Zealand, the governor's employment contract can be discontinued if the inflation target is breached. See Debelle (1997).

[48] Masson, Savastano and Sharma (1997). The Bank of England was an exception, however, as it did not have instrument independence during the United Kingdom's first 4½ years of inflation targeting.

[49] This was originally not the case in Sweden, as the Government initially had a different inflation objective and only officially accepted the Riksbank's target after 2½ years of inflation targeting.

[50] In this context, Cecchetti (1997) presents data suggesting that the inflation-output variability trade-off is extremely steep, as small declines in inflation variability are associated with steep increases in output variability. By contrast, using simulation techniques, Haldane and Batini (1998) show that an inflation forecast-based rule with a judiciously chosen targeting horizon naturally embodies the desired degree of output-smoothing. Indeed, Goodhart (1999) summarises the evidence that – for the United

Kingdom at least – the trade-off is not large, as long as the central bank chooses an appropriate time horizon to meet its inflation target.

[51] Green (1996).

[52] Svensson (1997).

[53] Woodford (1994) criticises the use of indicators that forecast future inflation, rather than variables that are proximate causes of inflation, as a guide to the conduct of monetary policy. In particular, he emphasises the danger of self-fulfilling prophecies when a policy rule is adopted that feeds back from an indicator that is itself sensitive to policy expectations. Bernanke and Woodford (1997) elaborate on the risks of using private sector inflation forecasts as a guide to monetary policy. While such forecasts can provide useful information, they find that the central bank must ultimately rely on an explicit structural model of the economy to guide its policy decisions.

[54] With an element of jest, Blinder's Law of Speculative Markets states that markets usually get the sign right, but tend to exaggerate by a factor between three and ten; see Blinder (1997).

[55] Goodhart (1995) echoes the call by Alchian and Klein (1973) that the orientation of monetary policy should be broadened beyond consumer prices to include asset prices. In his view, this would focus policy on a more relevant concept of inflation (since asset price increases are a direct source of future consumer inflation), while also countering the procyclical influence of monetary policy through the credit channel. However, this approach has numerous problems, prominent amongst which are the difficulty of correctly identifying the inflationary component of asset price increases and the instrument volatility this would imply. For a discussion of the monetary policy implications of asset inflation, see Capel and Houben (1998).

[56] The Curriculum Vitae of M. King, Executive Director and Chief Economist of the Bank of England, is said to make reference to the fact that he used to play tennis until the United Kingdom adopted inflation targetry.

[57] Of course, it is still early to come to a firm judgement on the efficacy of direct inflation targeting. Strictly, the jury remains out until there is a broad-based experience across a full cycle (or two) and under a wide variety of shocks. In this respect, Groeneveld, Koedijk and Kool (1998) juxtapose the performance of three inflation targeting countries (the United Kingdom, Canada and New Zealand) with three comparator countries (Germany, the United States and Australia, respectively) and do not find strong evidence of a structural break in the relationship between inflation and interest rates at the time countries switched to inflation targeting. This is also the conclusion reached by Bernanke *et al.* (1999). However, based on a comparison between seven inflation targeting countries and four control groups, Almeida and Goodhart (1998) present tentative evidence suggesting that the adoption of inflation targeting reduces the sacrifice ratio of disinflation in terms of unemployment and especially foregone output growth.

[58] See Fischer (1994 and 1996), Goodhart and Viñals (1994), McCallum (1996) and Summers (1991).

[59] On the first point, Akerlof, Dickens and Perry (1996) present evidence that nominal wages are downward rigid. In a zero inflation environment, this reduces the scope for real wage adjustments and leads to an unnecessarily higher rate of unemployment. However, their findings are not uncontested (see Yates (1998) for an overview of the inconclusive empirical literature). Also, in a context of generally increasing labour productivity, there will usually be scope for some adjustment in real labour costs even when nominal wages remain stable. On the second point, Fuhrer and Madigan (1997) show that the adjustment of the economy to adverse shocks is significantly slower in a zero-inflation climate, since nominal interest rates cannot be set below zero in practice, thereby constraining the central bank in its ability

to establish negative real interest rates and to cushion the output decline. Their conclusions are corroborated by Orphanides and Wieland (1998), who simulate the impact of typical stochastic shocks on the US economy and find that monetary policy effectiveness is significantly reduced when inflation is targeted between 0 and 1 per cent. As a result, recessions become more frequent and longer lasting. The consequences of the zero nominal bound are found to be negligible for inflation targets of 2 per cent or more. See also Fischer (1996) and, for the original essay on this issue, Summers (1991).

[60] While the prominent study by Boskin *et al.* (1996) concludes that the US Consumer Price Index exaggerates inflation by 1.1 percentage point per year, subsequent studies for European countries suggest a somewhat smaller measurement bias. For instance, the Bundesbank study carried out by Hoffmann (1998) indicates that the overall bias in Germany may be in the order of 0.75 percentage point per year.

[61] The deviations under the inflation assumptions built into Germany's money target are presented in Appendix VI. It has been assumed that deviations above 1.0 percentage point (respectively 1.5 percentage points) would have fallen outside a hypothetical bandwidth of 2 percentage points (respectively 3 percentage points). Over the past twenty-four years, the average absolute deviation has been 0.9 percentage point, with a standard deviation of 1.1.

[62] The only country in Europe to have explicitly pursued more than two targets is Italy, which combined targets for money, credit and the exchange rate in the 1980s. Outside Europe, a notable example of the mixed results to be expected from multiple targeting of nominal anchors is provided by the Philippines, where base money and inflation targets were combined with in practice overriding exchange rate targets in the mid-1990s; see Houben (1997). In principle, the basic arguments against strategies with two targets hold *a fortiori* against strategies with three targets.

[63] For example, Clarida, Galí and Gertler (1997) find that since 1979 each of the G3 countries – as well as the United Kingdom after it relinquished its exchange rate commitment in 1992 – has followed a remarkably similar forward-looking policy rule, whereby nominal interest rates are adjusted in response to changes in expected inflation and the output gap. Thus, notwithstanding different declared monetary policy strategies, each of these countries has effectively pursued an inflation target with some allowance for output stabilisation – a strategy which they coin "soft-hearted inflation targeting". Chadha and Janssen (1997) corroborate these findings with evidence that changes in official interest rates in each of the G3 countries plus the United Kingdom have been prompted by a similar set of variables through time, regardless of the announced policy rule. These authors venture an interpretation that central banks combine a stated policy rule with discretion and, in practice, pursue something like a state contingent inflation target or a nominal income rule. In a similar vein, Bernanke and Mihov (1997) find that the most ardent advocate of money targeting, the German Bundesbank, in fact hardly reacts to changes in forecasted money growth and "is much better described as an inflation targeter than as a money targeter."

PART TWO

THE EUROPEAN EXPERIENCE

4 THE HISTORICAL SETTING

4.1 Introduction

Selecting a monetary policy strategy is an ongoing activity. Changing circumstances, adaptations in preferences, and advances in the understanding of how economies work each imply that the strategic orientation of monetary policy needs to be kept under continuous review. At the same time, given the uncertainty inherent in economic relationships and in decisions on prospective developments, as well as the importance of stabilising expectations, constancy in the monetary strategy choice runs at a premium. The adage 'if it ain't broke, don't fix it' clearly applies to the domain of monetary strategy. In this respect, the evolution of monetary policy strategies in Europe over the past quarter of a century is characterised by a degree of inertia, with changes often prompted by a financial crisis. Indeed, this evolution should be seen against the backdrop of the collapse of the international monetary system of Bretton Woods, which necessitated a fundamental adaptation of European monetary policy frameworks and prompted greater soul-searching in the monetary strategy choice.

4.2 The background of Bretton Woods, 1946-1971

Under the Bretton Woods system, monetary policy strategies were essentially rules-based. The United States maintained a fixed rate between the value of the US dollar and that of gold, and thus provided the system's anchor, while the other participating countries based their monetary strategies on maintaining a fixed exchange rate vis-à-vis the US dollar (within a range of ±1 per cent). The system's discretionary element lay in the possibility of adjusting the dollar exchange rate, which was subject to international oversight. At a deeper level, countries maintained a further limited degree of national monetary policy discretion on account of the unrestricted allowance for capital account controls.[1]

This fixed but adjustable exchange rate system was associated with unprecedented economic success. Particularly after the European countries adopted full current account convertibility in 1959, the Bretton Woods system experienced the highest and most stable per capita real GDP growth rates (expanding at an average annual rate of around 4 to 5 per cent in most European countries) of any monetary regime on record, in combination with an inflation rate that remained low (for the region as a whole on average below 4 per cent) and remarkably stable.[2]

This success can be attributed to a number of factors in the monetary strategy environment. First, the system unquestionably exerted a disciplinary influence on national policy choices. The focus on the dollar exchange rate provided countries with a strong incentive to pursue non-inflationary policies, as these would alleviate their dollar shortage while avoiding the admission of policy failure associated with currency devaluation. Second, especially during the system's first two decades, there was general scepticism – rooted in the experiences of the thirties – regarding the effectiveness of an active monetary policy.[3] Of course, given ebullient economic performance, there was also less pressure for expansionary monetary policy. But the general monetary policy orientation towards nominal objectives enhanced the system's stability. Third, the system operated in the context of limited capital mobility. This created scope to combine exchange rate stability with some deviation in national monetary policy. In turn, this lowered the cost of maintaining a multilateral system of exchange rate targeting, since monetary policy could still be partly attuned to asymmetric developments in the domestic economy. Fourth, the system's endurance over a quarter of a century may be attributed in part to the relatively small demand and supply shocks it faced.[4] From this perspective, it is doubtful whether the system could have survived the disruptions of the massive oil price hikes in the 1970s.

In many respects, it is the reverse-side of these same characteristics that ultimately contributed to the system's downfall. Central amongst these factors is the faulty design structure – the so-called Triffin dilemma – that predestined the system to collapse under its own success. According to the implacable logic underlying this dilemma, the rapid expansion of global production and trade demanded a sustained growth in the supply of global liquidity. In the face of an inadequate supply of monetary gold, this basically required the United States to furnish the alternative reserves component (dollars) by persistently running substantial balance of payments deficits. At the same time, however, these very same external deficits increasingly undermined the United States' ability to maintain its gold convertibility, as outstanding dollar liabilities rose cumulatively above the value of its declining monetary gold stock.[5] As a result of this intrinsic inconsistency, it was not a question of whether, but only of when, the system would collapse.

More practically, the need for global liquidity implied that the system's policy discipline was imposed on all participants, except the Nth country – the United States. And when policies in this anchor country started to slip on account of the financing requirements of the Vietnam War and President Johnson's Great Society Program, other countries' fixed exchange rate strategies effectively imported the inflationary consequences. This also reflected a general resistance on the part of surplus countries to revalue against the dollar. In this regard, the Bretton Woods system suffered the standard weakness inherent in any fixed exchange rate strategy, namely the reduced ability to offset asymmetric developments within the fixed rate area. Indeed, the system's design had initially aimed at maintaining a degree of domestic policy autonomy at the expense of capital convertibility. But, notwithstanding these controls, capital was becoming increasingly mobile, including through leads and lags in trade flows.[6] As a result, the system became more susceptible to speculative attack and more dependent on credibility. This was problematic because, fundamentally, the system lacked credibility: the commitment to gold convertibility was blatantly unsustainable and the adjustable and politicised nature of the fixed exchange rate commitments prompted increasing speculation.

In all, the Bretton Woods system provided a stable policy framework that allowed the global economy to flourish as never before. But in terms of the monetary policy strategy implications for participating member countries, the framework could not deliver sustained stability. In particular, the use of gold as the ultimate nominal anchor made the system vulnerable to the vagaries of the gold market and especially to the fact that gold production did not grow reliably in line with real liquidity demand. In turn, this fuelled the demand for dollars, thereby exempting the US from monetary discipline and loosening the exchange rate anchor used by the other participants in the system. Besides this, with capital controls becoming increasingly porous, countries' scope to combine an exchange rate peg with a domestically oriented monetary policy was diminishing. And since the countries bonded by the global exchange rate commitments clearly did not constitute an optimal currency area, diverging monetary policy needs of individual participants – not least of which the major European partners – were straining the system. In effect, this further eroded the system's dwindling credibility. By the early 1970s, it was clear that the European countries needed another framework for their monetary policy strategies.

The European perspective

Although well-predicted, the disintegration of the Bretton Woods system was a slow process, spread over the course of several years. Unmistakable signs of the upcoming collapse were already evident in the late 1960s, particularly in the 1968 separation of the official market for gold from the private market (where a floating market price applied). And the resuscitation of the system under the Smithsonian Agreement of December

1971 could not fully disguise the structural weaknesses of the global fixed exchange rate system, notwithstanding the introduction of some flexibility in the form of 'temporary' margins of 2.25 per cent above and below the newly established central dollar rates. In this light, the European countries had ample opportunity to review their monetary policy bearings long before the system's definite collapse and the general switch to managed floating in March 1973.

From the European perspective, the Bretton Woods system had the fundamental shortcoming that the system's policy thrust was unduly oriented at the priorities and preferences of the United States. This had been acceptable – and even welcome – in the early stages of the post-war recovery when Europe confronted a massive dollar balance of payments need and when a dollar exchange rate anchor served to boost confidence in the revamped European currencies. But as the European recovery progressed, with economic growth rates usually substantially above those in the US, and as monetary policy credibility returned, with inflation rates generally close to and in the German case mostly under those of the US, this asymmetry became untenable.

In this context, the European countries had already set their sights on a more regionally oriented monetary policy course. Indeed, towards the end of the Bretton Woods era, as the prospects for fixed exchange rate links vis-à-vis the US bleakened, European monetary initiatives sought to tighten exchange rate links vis-à-vis each other. This was evidenced by the 1970 Werner Report, whose objective of a regional economic and monetary union was endorsed by the European Council in March 1971, and by the subsequent short-lived agreement amongst the EC central banks to narrow the fluctuations between their currencies beyond that required under the Bretton Woods system.[7] It was also reflected in repeated, predominantly German, calls in the spring of 1971 for a concerted European float against the dollar.[8] But Europe's most tangible joint action was the creation of a regional exchange rate 'snake' within the confines of the global Smithsonian framework.

4.3 The experience under the snake, 1972-1979

The 'snake' was Europe's response to the disintegration of the Bretton Woods system and to the global trend towards flexible exchange rate policies.[9] Under this Common Margins Agreement of March 1972 , the EC central banks pledged to limit the bilateral fluctuations of their currencies to ± 2.25 per cent, thereby tightening the Smithsonian Agreement's ± 4.5 per cent margins between non-dollar currencies (based on maximum deviations of ± 2.25 per cent from the dollar parities).[10] Besides this, the central banks of Belgium and the Netherlands had earlier agreed to limit fluctuations between the Benelux currencies to ± 1.5 per cent.[11] In figurative speech, the different exchange rate agreements had thus created a Benelux 'worm' within the European 'snake' within the global Smithsonian 'tunnel'. The regional exchange rate limits were supported by mutual intervention commitments at the outer margins as well as unlimited very short-term credit facilities. These latter facilities were covered by an exchange rate guarantee and were settled monthly. Furthermore, it was agreed in principle that intervention needed to keep EC currencies within the snake would be conducted in these respective currencies, while intervention to keep the snake within the tunnel would take place in dollars. In all, the snake arrangement constituted the first practical undertaking towards monetary integration in Europe.

The snake arrangement had a troubled history, characterised by recurrent exchange rate realignments and frequent membership withdrawals (see Chart 5). It started out with broad regional coverage, as the six original members (Germany, France, Italy, the Netherlands, Belgium and Luxembourg) were joined within weeks by the United Kingdom, Ireland and Denmark, and shortly thereafter also by the associated member Norway. At the time of the definite collapse of Bretton Woods and the emergence of the snake from the tunnel in March 1973, Sweden similarly associated its currency with the arrangement. Thus, a total of eleven European countries were, at some time or other, members of the snake. Moreover, at the sidelines, Austria unilaterally shadowed the currencies in the arrangement from March 1973. However, the arrangement only met with partial success in terms of actually stabilising regional exchange rates: the system experienced nine realignments and eight withdrawals (including two by France) in less than seven years, and ended with a membership of just five countries, including only one of the major European economies.

This uneven performance can essentially be attributed to three interrelated factors: inconsistent policy priorities, acute external shocks, and limited commitment to the exchange rate agreement. Put differently, the mixed results can be ascribed to fundamental inconsistencies in monetary policy strategy, exacerbated by global financial turmoil, leading to deficient credibility. Specifically, the snake arrangement first had to cope with the massive capital flows associated with the final crumbling of the Bretton Woods system in March 1973 and the subsequent instability as a result of the outbreak of the first oil crisis in October 1973. In turn, these disturbances highlighted differences in national policy priorities. While some countries focused on softening the adverse impact of the terms of trade shock on the real economy, others granted precedence to containing the inflationary momentum and the external financing need. The resulting

Chart 5: The Snake Arrangement, 1972 - 1979 [1]

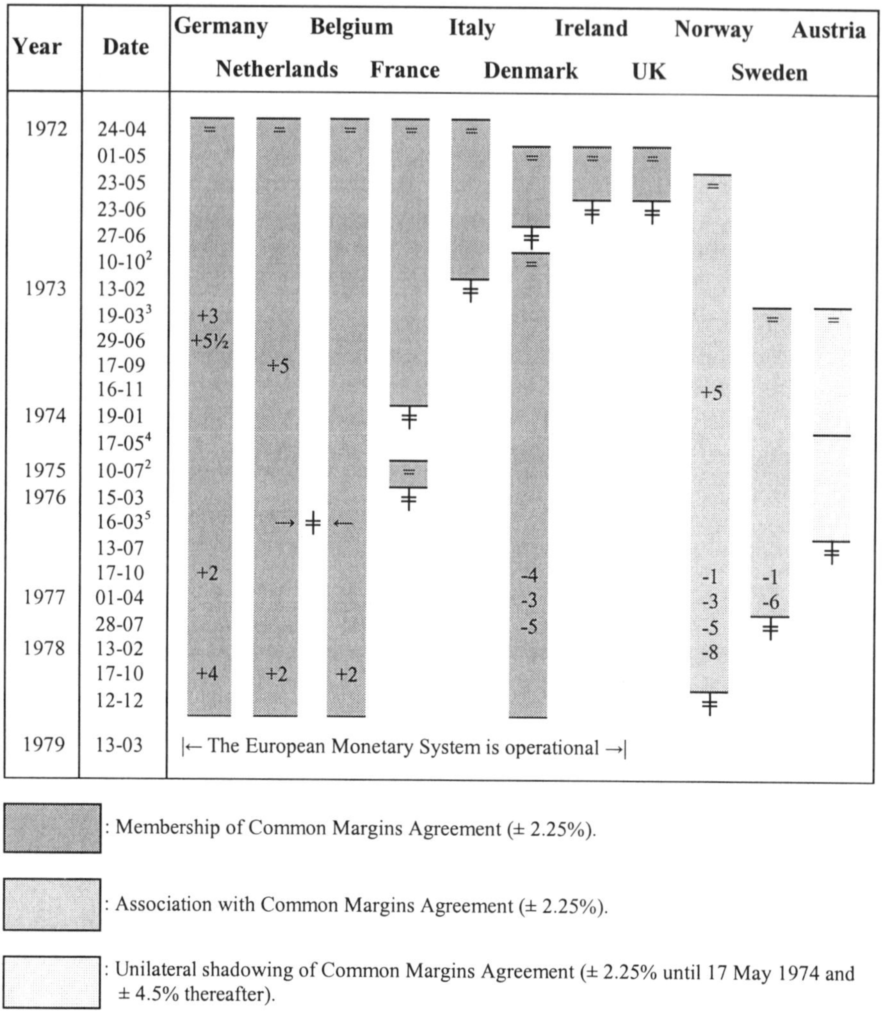

1 Chronology of the 'snake' indicating the accessions to (=) and withdrawals from (ǂ) the exchange rate agreements, as well as the percentage revaluations (+) and devaluations (-).

2 Both Denmark and France returned to the snake at their previous official exchange rate parity.

3 On 19 March 1973 the intervention obligations to maintain fixed margins against the US dollar ('tunnel') were discontinued, marking the start of the European joint float.

4 On 17 May 1974 Austria widened the fluctuation band with which it unilaterally shadowed the snake from ± 2.25% to ± 4.5% in order to be able to maintain a tight link to the Deutsche mark, which had appreciated against the other snake currencies.

5 On 16 March 1976 the Benelux countries discontinued their mutual ± 1.5% narrow margins agreement (the 'worm') that had been in force since 19 August 1971.

policy divergence led to sharp differences in price performance (for example, in 1974-75, price increases in France were twice those in Germany) that were incompatible with fixed nominal exchange rates.

Besides this, the institutional parameters were insufficient to uphold the credibility of the exchange rate arrangement. In particular, the majority of the central banks did not have the policy autonomy to pursue their exchange rate targets, while the political authorities' commitment to these monetary policy targets was at times flauntingly meagre. Moreover, the snake was based on a 'monetarist'approach towards policy co-ordination, whereby commitments were made in monetary policy matters without any supporting 'economist' agreements in other macroeconomic policy areas, such as the budget.[12] By consequence, there was little institutional pressure to stimulate convergence in national policy trends in order to underpin the desired mutual exchange rate stability. In addition, as regards the one area where agreements had been reached, the intervention mechanism was not perceived as powerful, especially on account of the very short (one-month) payback period and the settlement at the official parity.[13]

Finally, in the context of increasingly mobile capital, the snake experience provides an early illustration of the then already rising importance of consistent communication on monetary strategy objectives. For instance, when confidence in sterling was ebbing in April 1972 and supportive statements were called for, the UK Chancellor of the Exchequer precipitated the currency's downfall by announcing that "It is neither necessary nor desirable to distort domestic economies to an unacceptable extent in order to retain unrealistic exchange rates." [14] Indeed, in its post-mortem of the UK departure from the snake, the Bank of England took the view that adverse expectations had played a larger role in the loss of confidence in sterling than the economy's actual position, noting with understatement that: "There had also been considerable talk about ... the need to take action on the exchange rate".[15]

In hindsight, the break-up of Bretton Woods gave rise to diverging monetary policy strategies, at the surface with respect to the commitment to exchange rate agreements, at a deeper level with respect to what the prime objective of monetary policy should be. Within the framework of the snake, this was evidenced by the system's inability to dovetail the monetary policy orientations of the major European countries: the United Kingdom, Italy and France each successively abandoned the arrangement, leaving only Germany with a number of smaller countries. With regard to the monetary policy outcome in terms of price increases, this divergence was manifest in the wide spectrum of average annual inflation rates during 1973-78, ranging from 4.7 per cent in Germany, to 10.6 per cent in France, and about 17 per cent in Italy and the United Kingdom.

In the aftermath of Bretton Woods, this primarily reflected how exchange rate developments had lost much of their disciplinary influence – especially for the larger countries. Given the global switch to floating, these countries could avoid the stigma of devaluation by quitting the system as soon as their currency came under heavy pressure, justifying this with commonly accepted arguments about prioritising domestic real economic concerns. In fact, the chronicle of the snake reveals that whenever a large country's currency came under untenable pressure, it always left the arrangement, whereas in similar circumstances smaller countries generally stayed in the arrangement and accepted an exchange rate devaluation. In its barest form, the snake was thus an agreement whereby a number of smaller countries oriented their policies towards the large country with the strongest currency and accepted the constraints this imposed, while that country – Germany – charted its own policy course paying very little, if any, heed to the needs of the others in the arrangement.[16] Such asymmetry was acceptable to the smaller countries as long as Germany's monetary policy could be counted on to deliver domestic price stability, or something very close to that. Besides sufficient fulfilment of optimal currency area considerations, this required an independent and effective monetary policy strategy in Germany. This is the background against which Germany, initially on an experimental basis, pioneered money targeting.

NOTES

[1] The IMF's Articles of Agreement only commit members to full convertibility on current account transactions (Article VIII), and even this commitment is open-ended (existing restrictions are grandfathered under the transitional arrangements of Article XIV). An amendment to incorporate an objective of capital account convertibility into the Articles is currently under discussion.

[2] Although inflation had been lower during the classical gold standard (1881-1913) and the inter-war period (1920-38) including the short-lived restoration of gold exchange, it was most stable during the convertible period of Bretton Woods (1959-1971); see Bordo and Jonung (1997).

[3] Guitián (1994) and Shigehara (1996).

[4] Bordo and Schwartz (1997).

[5] In an "intrepid attempt to prophesy history and to deflect its course" Triffin (1960) warned against this dynamic instability and showed that foreign countries' dollar holdings first exceeded the value of the US monetary gold stock in 1959. He advocated a solution whereby the IMF would be reformed to provide a new medium of reserves that would meet the legitimate need for global liquidity. However, in line with Triffin's warning, and notwithstanding the creation by the IMF of Special Drawing Rights (SDRs) as a new reserves currency, the gold coverage ratio of the US showed a more or less continuous decline until the system's gold anchor was jettisoned in August 1971. With masterful political dexterity, President Nixon presented the US suspension of gold convertibility as a bold new initiative (see Volcker and Gyohten, 1992).

[6] Solomon (1982) describes how interest rate differentials induced increasingly sizeable capital movements under the Bretton Woods system. While major speculative flows already occurred in the 1950s, these rose to formidable proportions in the late 1960s and early 1970s (pp. 32, 213-214).

[7] According to this agreement concluded in April 1971, the EC currencies were to fluctuate by no more than ± 1.2 per cent of each other, against an effective margin for cross parities of ± 2 per cent under the Bretton Woods accord (as implied by the ± 1 per cent margin for individual currencies against the US dollar). However, the EC central banks suspended their agreement before its scheduled implementation in June, as Germany and the Netherlands had temporarily allowed their currencies to float in May. For a discussion of the decisions in response to the Werner Report, see Ungerer (1997, pp. 114-116).

[8] Solomon (1982, pp. 179-180).

[9] For elaborate expositions on the motives and design of the snake, see Kruse (1980), Oort (1979) and Szász (1999).

[10] The ± 2.25 per cent fluctuation band, copied from the Smithsonian agreement, was to remain a central feature of European exchange rate agreements for more than two decades. Although the two decimal point bandwidth suggests great precision and well-founded institutional motives, Oort (1979, p. 194) recalls that the decision "was taken in a rather offhand manner, without preparation of any kind and determined as an average of the US desire for even wider margins and the European wish to go less far."

[11] The Benelux arrangement lasted until 16 March 1976.

[12] Kruse (1980, pp. 62-70) reviews the debate on monetarist and economist strategies of monetary integration that was conducted in the 1960s and early 1970s. France, Belgium and Luxembourg were advocates of the former, Germany, Italy and the Netherlands of the latter.

[13] The first occasion on which intervention was needed to keep a currency within the snake was the defence of sterling in June 1972. However, activation of the financing mechanism failed to boost confidence in the sustainability of the exchange rate. Within a week, after concerted purchases of sterling had risen to £ 1 billion, the United Kingdom withdrew from the intervention arrangement. An elaborate description is provided in Bank of England, *Quarterly Bulletin*, September 1972.

[14] James (1996, p. 239).

[15] Bank of England, *Quarterly Bulletin*, September 1972, p. 326.

[16] Oort (1979, p. 200) states that "Although the major targets of West German economic and monetary policy have not, as far as I know, ever been amended as a result of discussions in the snake, the timing of intended policy measures has occasionally been geared to the requirements of the snake."

5 THE EVOLUTION OF MONEY TARGETING, 1975-1998

5.1 The rise of monetary targeting

The rise of money targeting has its roots in the 1960s, when 'monetarism' gained academic prominence and the preoccupation of policy-makers started to shift gradually away from interest rates towards monetary aggregates.[1] But the eventual adoption of money targets for the most part reflected a pragmatic policy reaction to the changed global economic circumstances of the early 1970s, rather than any strong 'monetarist' convictions. Two developments notably spurred the advance of money-based strategies in Europe. First, the collapse of Bretton Woods and the limited, brittle scope of the snake granted monetary authorities greater control of domestic monetary developments and, by implication, also bestowed them with greater responsibility for monetary policy outcomes. Whereas the exchange rate had previously served as the primary (intermediate) monetary policy target, the new international monetary environment left the central banks of the large European countries without a nominal anchor at which to gear their instruments. Second, the first oil crisis and the concomitant near quadrupling of oil prices – representing the largest supply-side price shock in modern history – sparked a global inflationary momentum. This shock occurred at a time when monetary conditions were already loose, partly on account of the massive exchange market intervention in the terminal phase of the Bretton Woods system. Given unabated money growth in 1974-75, direct price effects were accommodated and inflationary pressures continued to build. In itself, this wrenching experience contributed to wide acceptance that rapid growth in the money stock and in prices go hand in hand.

In many respects, central banks were in uncharted territory. As a result of the surge in inflation, nominal interest rates ceased to be a reliable indicator of the tightness of the monetary policy stance. Moreover, given the pronounced slowdown of output growth, there was considerable pressure to orient monetary policy at real objectives. This complicated the task of increasing nominal interest rates prior to, rather than in reaction to, price increases and thus inhibited the implementation of a necessarily pre-emptive monetary policy. The combination of these factors resulted in generally negative real interest rates in the mid-1970s. In addition to these considerations, central banks did not have an effective instrument with which to communicate their intentions and precommit their policies. Previously, the fixed dollar exchange rate had served to signal the limited scope for price and wage increases, but this disciplinary influence had vanished with the switch to more flexible exchange regimes. Although exchange rate management potentially constitutes a signalling instrument, an activist exchange rate policy risks destabilising the real economy, undermining external viability and exacerbating general economic uncertainty.[2]

Money targeting offered a way out of this quandary. First, money targets provided an unequivocal nominal anchor at which to aim monetary instruments, and developments under these targets gave an unmistakable interpretation of the policy stance. Second, with poor performance on both the price and the output front, announcing money targets underscored that the central bank's prime concern lay with money growth and inflation control, rather than with production and employment. In this regard, third, focusing on money developments endogenised the short-term interest rate and thus facilitated timely interest rate increases. Given political resistance to higher interest rates in the context of weak economic growth, this shift of emphasis buttressed monetary authorities' efforts to remain in front of the curve of rising inflation. And, fourth, money targets offered a straightforward way to signal policy intentions and thus to help avoid the first-round price effects of the oil crisis from becoming entrenched in inflation expectations.

The German origins of money targeting

It is not entirely surprising that *Germany* was the first country to embark on a monetary policy strategy of preannounced money targets. Under Bretton Woods, German inflation was on average lower than that of any other country and, especially in the last decade, the Deutsche mark had been subject to intense and recurrent revaluation pressures. In view of considerable opposition to upward realignments, including from within the German government that was primarily responsible for exchange rate policy, membership of the fixed exchange rate system had actually constrained the central bank in its monetary control, and thereby in its inflation objectives.[3] Indeed, with the benefit of hindsight, the German central bank perceived the end of participation in the Bretton Woods system as something of a liberation: "By releasing the Bundesbank from its duty to intervene in the foreign exchange markets ... the Federal Government freed monetary policy from the obligation to create central bank money involuntarily via purchases of foreign exchange."[4]

After the collapse of Bretton Woods, the challenge was how to maintain price stability independently – a challenge that was made more pressing by the outbreak of the oil crisis. For Germany, the monetary policy prioritisation between near-term output and inflation objectives was relatively clear-cut. The central bank had an overriding statutory aim of safeguarding the currency (as enumerated in Article 3 of the Bundesbank Act), was independent in the implementation of its policies, and had traditionally pursued its price stability objective with rectitude. More fundamentally, the German public had a deep aversion to inflation, rooted in the devastating experience of having hyperinflation wipe out the value of its currency twice within a century. Accordingly, in 1974, as the energy shock fuelled German inflation to unprecedented post-war levels (almost 8 per cent), there was an urgency to signal this prioritisation and to highlight that monetary developments would not be allowed to contribute to a rising price level.

The innovative elements of German money targeting were the singular focus on money growth developments and the public preannouncement. Actually, it is solely on account of these elements that the Bundesbank is commonly considered the pioneer of money targetry. In the early 1950s, long before Germany's launch of this strategy, Greece and the Netherlands had already started making use of money oriented targets.[5] However, these targets formed part of an encompassing policy framework that also included an exchange rate commitment, implying a combined strategy that was broader than just money targeting. Subsequently, in the early 1970s, when the crumbling global exchange rate system allowed money to take on a more dominant role, a number of other central banks were also ahead of Germany in specifying money targets for their internal policy-making.[6] Specifically, the US Federal Reserve had adopted in-house monetary targets as early as 1970, with targets for M1 and M2 growth being set by the Federal Open Market Committee (FOMC) for the periods between its bimonthly meetings.[7] These targets served to guide policy discussions (with money market rates being subordinated to a proviso role) and were not disclosed to the public. Similarly, after its exchange rate commitments were lifted, the United Kingdom adopted informal targets for M3 growth starting in late 1973.[8] Both the French and the Spanish monetary authorities also introduced confidential targets for M2 and M3, respectively, in 1973.[9] Germany itself started pursuing initially unpublished targets for the central bank monetary stock in 1974.[10] However, since the money targets only played an internal role in each of these latter cases, the targets did not precommit the central bank, hardly placed real constraints on monetary policy setting, and did not serve to steer public expectations. In this sense, the adoption of these generally short-term money targets did not constitute a full-fledged strategy of money targeting.

Indeed, the external aspect of the new monetary policy strategy was crucial. In fact, in the case of Germany, the need for more effective communication with the public was the driving force behind the new approach. At a tactical level, this was a reaction to the experience during the previous year, when the Bundesbank had indicated by means of unquantified statements that monetary policy would be non-accommodating, but both trade unions and employer organisations had been left largely unimpressed.[11] At a strategic level, this also reflected the desire to tackle the credibility gap in the Bundesbank's staying power, which stemmed from the Bretton Woods experience when German monetary policy had often been powerless in the face of massive money creation through the external accounts.[12] Money targeting, the central bank hoped, would address this shortcoming by explicitly defining the monetary scope for the growth of output and prices.

The spread of money targeting in Europe

Once Germany had launched the new monetary policy strategy in late 1974 by announcing a precisely quantified target for central bank money for a full twelve-month period (through December 1975), money targetry gradually swept across the major countries of the European Community. The first regional partner to follow Germany's example was the *United Kingdom*. Again, the need for more effective communication with the public was a prominent factor behind the strategy switch: the declaration of a UK money target in July 1976 occurred in the midst of a sterling crisis and was part of a broader publicity campaign to shore up financial confidence in the pound. It was hoped that the announcement would help arrest the declining policy credibility prompted by the sharp rise in inflation (which had reached 20 per cent in mid-1975 before the reimposition of direct wage controls), the weak exchange rate and the loose fiscal stance. When recourse was made to IMF borrowing later in the year, both the associated limits for domestic credit expansion and the tightened budgetary financing path were consistently determined within the framework of the money targets.

In a sense, however, the true advent of money targeting in the United Kingdom occurred later when the Thatcher Government introduced its monetarist-inspired Medium-Term Financial Strategy (MTFS) in 1980. Under the MTFS, monetary policy would expressly prioritise the control of inflation by lowering money growth. The aim was to break categorically with the 'unbelieving monetarism' of the previous Government's monetary policy, which along with fiscal policy had remained essentially Keynesian in character.[13] The new strategy sought to put in place a more rules-based system, with a clear monetary policy precommitment and a consistently supportive budgetary position.[14] Furthermore, in an effort favourably to influence expectations, the declining target ranges for money growth were announced for a multiyear horizon and were given the highest political blessing.

In *France*, the adoption of money targets took place in a relatively propitious setting. In general, the development of monetary policy had been reasonably stable, with monetary growth rates virtually in line with unpublished targets for the years 1973-76 (with the exception of a sizeable overrun in 1975, when unemployment reduction had been temporarily prioritised).[15] This steadiness had been achieved with the support of prudent budgetary policies and effective credit limits on dominant banking institutions, which remained the principal source of funds. The switch to public targets for 1977, proclaimed shortly after France had left the snake exchange rate arrangement, reflected the authorities' overriding aim of strengthening confidence in their anti-inflationary policy stance, both at home and abroad. However, the approach to reducing inflation was gradualist: the money growth targets indicated a deceleration, but remained in double digits during the first six years.

From a broader perspective, political economy considerations have also played a key role in France's adoption and maintenance of money targets. Specifically, France has traditionally viewed money targets as indispensable to stress the independent character of French monetary policy-making, even if in practice the exchange rate (especially vis-à-vis Germany) has repeatedly functioned as the overriding monetary policy anchor. In fact, the Banque de France has at times explicitly motivated the use of money targets by pointing at its responsibility for monetary stability within the whole franc zone, for which the objective of exchange rate stability was not viewed as sufficient.[16]

The Netherlands was the first of the smaller and more open EC countries to adopt a form of money targeting, aiming specifically for a given ratio between the amount of liquidity and nominal national income. Interestingly, a quantified target for this ratio had been announced by the central bank as early as 1969, although this was not conveyed as an overriding monetary policy orientation and was made conditional on the development of public finances, the external accounts and the degree in which inflation was considered to be driven by cost-push rather than demand-pull factors.[17] In April 1977, in the context of a sustained increase in the liquidity ratio over the previous five-year period and of a rising inflationary momentum, and in line with the general monetarist awakening, the central bank switched to announcing an unambiguous quantified target for this ratio. The target had the dual aim of reducing the available liquidity, while also gearing liquidity expansion clearly to the trend growth of nominal income. Of course, it should be emphasised that this target served as an auxiliary anchor, since Dutch monetary policy was also explicitly focused on the exchange rate, consecutively under Bretton

Woods, the Snake arrangement and the ERM. The monetary authority's ability to combine a money target with an exchange rate commitment, notwithstanding the considerable openness of the economy, reflected pervasive capital controls and segmentation of the money and capital markets.[18] Indeed, to help meet the money target, 1977 also saw the introduction of direct restrictions on domestic money creation by banks.

While *Spain* had introduced money growth guidelines in its internal decision-making process as early as 1973, the switch to publicly announced money targets was not made until 1978. Following a year during which the exchange rate had experienced a major depreciation and inflation had accelerated to an unprecedented rate of close to 25 per cent, this announcement was a central feature of a new policy framework (notably also including agreements on incomes policy) aimed expressly at moderating expectations about future price developments.[19] The intermediate money targets were viewed as strict limits and were pursued primarily through control of the quantity of bank reserves. As part of the strategy shift, interest and exchange rates were allowed to fluctuate more freely. The autonomy of monetary policy from foreign developments was further enhanced by tight restrictions on external capital flows.

Against the background of a rising inflationary tide and a wage explosion in the mid-1970s, a combined concern about inflation and external viability led to an eclectic monetary policy approach in *Greece*. In an effort to signal disinflation objectives and to shield the central bank from pressures to ease monetary conditions, while also strengthening the balance of payments, targets were simultaneously announced for two money aggregates and two credit aggregates. In practice, the credit targets were more closely adhered to in the 1970s. After a new surge in inflation in the wake of the second oil crisis, Greece switched to a more focused form of money targeting in 1983.[20] However, as money targets were still coupled with credit targets, and later also with an increasingly prominent exchange rate objective, Greek monetary policy strategy consistently maintained an eclectic character.

Italy was a latecomer in the realm of money targetry, adopting money targets at a time when many other countries had already started de-emphasising their role.[21] Ironically, Italy had been one of the first countries to publicise targets for financial aggregates (starting in April 1974), but these targets had related to credit and thus did not veritably prioritise the containment of inflation. Indeed, the decision to cast the policy objective in terms of credit – in the context of successive IMF stand-by arrangements in 1974 and 1977 – reflected the imperative need to address the precarious external position and halt the loss of official reserves. Besides this, the profligacy of the public finances constituted a further binding constraint on effective monetary policy. In practice, massive and persistent overruns in the financing needs of the public sector led to systematic large breaches of the broad credit ceilings: these targets were only met once in their twelve-year existence.[22]

Several developments in the early 1980s paved the way for the Banca d'Italia's eventual switch to money targeting. First, while the external constraint was heavily binding in 1980-82, balance of payments pressures subsided and ceased being an overriding concern from the mid-1980s on. Second, the degree of dominance of fiscal policy over monetary policy was gradually lessened, including through the continuous deepening of the Italian financial markets and the repeal in 1981 of the obligation for the central bank to purchase those Treasury bills that remained unsold at auctions. Third, in 1983 the central bank abolished direct credit restrictions and switched to indirect instruments of monetary control. Against this background, a money target was finally launched in late 1984, together with a twin target for a more limited (private sector) domestic credit aggregate. However, in view of the poor track record and thus limited credibility of the previous credit targets, as well as the combination with both a new credit target and the prevailing ERM exchange rate commitment, the money targets did not take on a dominant role in the monetary policy strategy. This also reflected the Banca d'Italia's rejection of straightforward monetarism, on account of the perceived complexity of monetary policy transmission (with important transmission channels besides money growth), underscoring the need to focus on a wide array of policy indicators and to attach weight to analyses based on structural econometric modelling.

The last of the European countries genuinely to adopt money targeting was *Portugal*. This occurred against the background of the 1985 graduation from IMF supported programs (with credit ceilings) and of the 1986 accession to the European Community, which placed heavy emphasis on successful disinflation. After unabated expansion of domestic demand had suggested an overly accommodating monetary policy and money growth in fact overshot the internal 1986 program objective by more than one-third, the central bank switched to publicly announced money targets. These targets were envisaged as a complementary nominal anchor, next to a crawling peg exchange regime with a gradually reduced rate of depreciation. At the same time, the first steps in the gradual process of financial liberalisation prioritised domestic deregulation over the freeing of capital movements, thereby fostering monetary policy autonomy.

As a sidenote to the European experience with money targets, in the late 1980s *Denmark* launched a proposal for the adoption of a system of common and mutually consistent monetary policy targets, in the hope that this would prompt a strengthening of monetary policy co-ordination within the European Community. As its own contribution to this system, notwithstanding a monetary policy strategy that had been focused on the exchange rate for as long as memories could tell, Denmark announced a target range for the growth in domestic money creation (effectively more akin to a credit target) in 1991 and 1992.[23] Given that the target was introduced solely for international political motives, it only figured low-key in domestic official publications and certainly never triggered adjustments in the monetary policy stance. In the event, the proposal did not marshal the support of regional partners. After the target range was vastly undershot in 1992, no new target was officially announced for 1993 and the target was essentially abandoned.

The adoption of money targets in the large majority of European Community countries was, of course, part of a global shift towards this strategy. In fact, all major industrial economies followed Germany's suit within the course of the subsequent decade. Outside the European Community, the United States announced target ranges for two monetary aggregates in early 1975. At roughly the same time, the Swiss National Bank publicly declared a specific target for a narrow monetary aggregate. In late 1975, Canada also announced a wide range for the growth rate of a narrow money aggregate. Australia subsequently switched to money targetry in March 1976, focusing on a 'guideline' range for broad money. And, in 1978, Japan started publishing official quarterly 'projections' for broad money.

5.2 The diversity of money targeting frameworks

In European monetary history, the family of money targeters has encompassed many birds of different feather. The wide-ranging diversity is especially well illustrated by the varied, and varying, choices regarding: (i) the money aggregate being targeted; (ii) the specification of the target as a point, range or ceiling; (iii) the time horizon of the target and the periodicity of updates; and (iv) the presentation of the target. This mainly reflected dissimilar institutional arrangements, policy preferences, financial structures, and economic circumstances. A certain convergence in the implementation frameworks can, however, be detected over the course of the years, as central banks have adapted their money target parameters to those that apparently produced the better results in practice.

The choice of money aggregate

In the design of a money targeting strategy, the choice of target aggregate is crucial. In first instance, this choice is driven by the trade-off between the controllability of the aggregate, on the one hand, and the tightness of fit with the growth of nominal output, on the other. While controllability is likely to be greater in the case of narrow aggregates, which are more sensitive to interest rate changes on account of the larger share of non-interest bearing components, broad aggregates are likely to provide a better indication of potential money spending in the economy. Of course, this trade-off has not always been clear-cut, especially as many countries with broad money targets have complemented the interest rate instrument with quantitative credit controls. In addition, considerations related to communication aspects and statistical availability have also featured prominently in the choice of aggregate, as well as the relevance of the aggregate in the existing framework for analysis and forecasting. In practice, countries have assigned different weights to these various considerations. This is reflected in the fact that, within Europe, the choice of target aggregate has ranged across the full spectrum of possible candidates.

Germany initiated the new monetary strategy in 1974 on the basis of a composite aggregate: central bank money. Besides being sufficiently controllable, reasonably stable vis-à-vis domestic expenditure, and reliably and promptly available statistically, this target variable represented the central bank's direct contribution to money growth and was therefore seen to underscore the central bank's responsibility for monetary policy.[24] The alternatives also had specific shortcomings: the greater interest elasticity of M1 would have required larger changes in the money targets over the course of time, which was at odds with the aim of stabilising expectations; econometric studies could not find a sufficiently stable money demand function for M2; and data on M3 were only available on an end-of-month basis (rather than as monthly averages) and with a two-week delay relative to central bank money stock data.

However, while central bank money could be considered a relatively narrow aggregate on account of its large currency component (hence strengthening the link with the transactions demand for money), it was essentially equivalent to M3 weighted by the constant reserve ratios of its components.[25] This weighting was seen to do justice to the different degrees of moneyness of the M3 components. At the same time, by virtue of its definition, central bank money moved broadly in parallel with M3. Nonetheless, the central bank recognised early on that the selection of this relatively narrow aggregate made the strategy vulnerable to changes in the currency to deposit ratio – a factor that came home to roost in the second half of the 1980s. Following exceptionally rapid growth in the share of currency in the central bank money stock in 1986 and 1987, the central bank switched to targeting M3 in 1988, although it cited this as a minor adjustment and emphasised the similarities between the two concepts of money (the components are identical, but the weights are different). M3 consistently remained the target variable thereafter. In all, Germany's choice of aggregate has thus been characterised by a large degree of constancy.

Most other European countries set out with a broader aggregate. In the case of the *United Kingdom*, the announcement in mid-1976 of a target for M3 (adjusted marginally to £M3 later that year in the context of the IMF arrangement) reflected the desire to anchor the monetary objective in a comprehensive framework for overall macroeconomic management. In an accounting sense, the broad money target incorporated the Public Sector Borrowing Requirement (PSBR), bank lending to the private sector, external monetary flows, and non-bank absorption of government debt. Thus, the target provided a consistent framework with implicit guidelines for the fiscal deficit, credit ceilings, external objectives, debt management, and prevailing price and wage policies. In part, this reflected the United Kingdom's institutional context at the time, where the ultimate responsibility for both the fiscal and the monetary policy domain rested with just one authority – the Treasury.

However, more than any other country, and in sharp contrast with the German constancy, the United Kingdom subsequently vacillated in its choice of aggregate, trying out every serious money target candidate (with the exception of M2) and commonly employing several of them at the same time. Paradoxically, this wavering had its roots in the 1979 switch to a more monetarist inspired anti-inflation policy, which granted great prominence to the single aggregate £M3. But, as a result of concurrent far-reaching financial and capital liberalisation (notably the abolition of Exchange Control in the autumn of 1979 and of direct credit controls in the summer of 1980), as well as the perverse rise in the savings component of the aggregate when interest rates increased in reaction to monetary tightening, £M3 proved to be a flagrantly unreliable monetary policy compass. The former factors undermined the stability of the demand for £M3, whereas the latter factor reduced its controllability. In 1980/81, while £M3 was growing very rapidly, narrow aggregates were not, interest rates were very high, the exchange rate was remarkably strong, and the economy was moving into recession. Put differently, while M3 growth suggested monetary policy was very loose, virtually all other variables indicated that it was actually quite tight. It is no small irony that a Government extremely committed to its money target, on the one hand, was confronted by an unprecedented money target overrun, on the other hand. In these circumstances, the authorities decided to spread their risks and supplemented the existing £M3 target with identical target ranges for both a narrower and a broader aggregate – M1 and Private Sector Liquidity (later rechristened M4).

Notwithstanding that all targets were prodigiously met in 1982/83, maintaining three different money targets was recognised as sending a rather muddled signal about the conduct of monetary policy.[26] Following a change of Chancellor, 1984 then saw the replacement of the M1 and M4 targets by yet a new aggregate M0, with the explicit indication that the M0 and (higher) £M3 targets would be assigned equal weight in monetary policy-making.[27] In effect, £M3 was maintained on account of its visibility with the financial markets and the public at large (having been in use for the better part of a decade), while M0 was added on the basis of its strong empirical track record. Subsequently, when £M3 again went wayward in 1985, the related target was temporarily suspended, to be abandoned altogether in 1987.[28] M0 therefore remained the only targeted aggregate. As it turned out, M0 proved to be a remarkably stable aggregate: the average absolute deviation under this target was smaller than for any other targeted aggregate in the EC (see Table 7 below) and the target achievement ratio of 75 per cent was also highest (albeit in part thanks to relatively wide target ranges). But this came too late: by the time M0 was launched, money targeting had lost credibility in the UK. Subsequently, when the UK switched to direct inflation targeting in 1992, money was altogether downgraded to an indicator status, with monitoring ranges for M0 and M4 established by the Treasury. As both aggregates were notably unstable following the regime shift, they were finally abolished in 1997 when the Bank of England achieved operational independence. The Bank's Monetary Policy Committee concluded that the uncertainty about the path of money velocity was simply too great to justify even a monitoring range status.[29]

France initially selected M2 as its target aggregate, both when it pursued unpublished money targets in the period 1973-76 and when it made its money targets public starting from 1977. The preference for M2 (contrary to custom initially also including all foreign currency deposits and non-residents' franc deposits) was related to its controllability, on account of the quantitative restrictions which the central bank imposed on its counterparts. As regards the alternatives, M0 was considered insufficiently correlated with the broader aggregates and, thus, with nominal output; M1 was seen as having inadequate coverage of transactions balances (some of which French statistics located in M2 but not in M1); and the central bank's grip on M3 was perceived as significantly weaker.[30] The Banque de France narrowed its chosen aggregate slightly in 1984 and 1985, when it targeted M2R, which excluded non-resident M2 holdings and corresponded more closely to the M2 definition used in other major industrial countries.

A period of wavering between targets for M2 and for M3 subsequently set in. This was primarily a reaction to financial innovations that were increasing the supply of monetary assets outside M2 and undermining the stability of demand for M2 money. The innovations were spurred by the financial liberalisation that had commenced in the early 1980s, culminating in the complete removal of quantitative credit controls in 1987 and the full elimination of capital controls by the end of the decade. In this setting, the authorities redefined their monetary aggregates in late 1985 and switched to a novel M3 target aggregate for 1986. Although the outturn was spot on target, the substitutability of financial assets between M2 and M3 was still viewed as problematic, prompting the central bank to adopt dual targets for M2 and M3 (maintaining their revised definition) for 1987. Subsequently, after the M3 target was massively overshot (the outcome was double the target), the authorities moved back to targeting just M2, opting to focus on the aggregate that was viewed as more closely linked to the transactions demand for money.[31] Financial innovation continued to plague the stability of this aggregate, however, and the boom in high-yielding money market investments as well as the introduction of new savings instruments (particularly the Plan d'Epargne Populaire) actually led to a nominal decline in M2 in 1990. In this context, the Banque de France reverted back again to a target for M3 in 1991, on the grounds that this aggregate would be less sensitive to asset substitution. At the same time, the M3 definition was revised to include the hugely popular money market funds. Notwithstanding continued instability of this aggregate on account of further (also fiscally motivated) financial innovation, France subsequently stuck with M3 targets. However, following a particularly pronounced velocity shock in 1996, the money targets for 1997-98 were actually vaguely defined, with reference made to an evaluation of liquidity growth not only on the basis of M3, but also of narrower and broader aggregates – with explicit mention of M1, M2, and M3+P1 (P1 being an investment aggregate for contractual savings products that are considered close substitutes of M3 monetary assets).

The *Netherlands'* choice of target – the liquidity ratio – was unique. Although based on a broad money aggregate, the liquidity ratio (equivalent to M2 over nominal income) expressly linked the growth of this aggregate to changes in nominal output. In this respect, it was emphasised that the liquidity ratio target was implicitly comparable to a money growth target, but had the analytical advantage of also incorporating the expected growth trend in real output and the inflation forecast. The direct comparison of money expansion with the growth of nominal income would make more clear whether the monetary policy stance was accommodating and, if so, to what extent.[32] Moreover, since the liquidity ratio targets are expressed as a level rather than as a rate of change, the targets also reflect the amount of liquidity already in the economy, which is relevant, for instance, in cases of monetary overhang.

However, a liquidity ratio target has a number of conceptual and practical difficulties. First, since the target includes developments in the real economy besides those in money, it is not tightly controlled by the central bank. Second, the liquidity ratio does not provide a nominal anchor, since price developments are included in both the numerator (money) and the denominator (nominal income). As a result, a constant liquidity ratio could be consistent with any inflation rate, especially when expectations reduce the time lag between money expansion and price increases. Third, the delays in publication and limited periodicity of nominal income data, as well as the customarily substantial revisions of these data, make the liquidity ratio an unreliable guide for monetary policy decisions.[33] Of course, these shortcomings need to be seen in the Dutch context, where the liquidity ratio effectively served as an ancillary target to the exchange rate peg. In this situation, particularly when the scope to support the liquidity ratio targets with credit ceilings and capital restrictions diminished, the central bank's control over the money component of the liquidity ratio decreased anyway. Against this background, it is not surprising that the liquidity ratio targets were short-lived.

Following four years of satisfactory experience with this aggregate in an internal targeting framework, *Spain* first announced public money targets in 1978 on the basis of M3. This broad aggregate was selected on account of the relative stability of the related money demand function, reflecting a high substitutability of its different components. Moreover, the M3 aggregate had important statistical advantages over other aggregates, especially in terms of the promptness, frequency, and reliability of the data.[34] However, the nexus of increasingly large budget deficits (primarily financed through recourse to the Bank of Spain), compulsory cash requirements, and a high and variable inflation rate was spurring financial innovation which, especially from mid-1982 on, caused unpredictable and pronounced shifts in the demand for M3. In this light, the central bank switched to an even broader aggregate ALP (comprising a wide range of liquid assets held by the public, effectively M4) starting in 1984. This aggregate includes a group of financial assets (notably short-term public sector financing instruments) that are comparable to bank deposits in terms of liquidity and return, but are not covered by M3. Hereafter, ALP remained the money target, but the definition of this aggregate was repeatedly modified to accommodate financial innovations.

Greece's experience with money targets indicates a changing emphasis from narrow to broad aggregates. In fact, while the central bank has traditionally communicated multiple monetary policy targets, the attention was initially directed at strict M1 targets (comprising only currency in circulation). In 1983, the emphasis on money targets increased and shifted to M3. However, the deregulation of the banking system as well as high cash reserve requirements stimulated the design of new financial instruments and substitution out of M3 deposits, thereby prompting money demand instability. The central bank reacted by considerably widening the definition of M3 in 1991 and by announcing ranges for a broader measure of liquidity (M4) as a new supplementary monetary indicator.

While *Italy* was relatively late in adopting a money target, it had been early in announcing financial targets to guide monetary policy. Its initial choice of target in 1974 was dominated by three concerns: first, the need for a quantitative framework that co-ordinated monetary and fiscal policy in a way that ensured (at least *ex ante*) consistency between the financing of the private sector and the viability of the external and public sectors; second, the substitutability of money and other financial assets (since money balances other than cash were interest bearing in Italy); and, third, the interchangeability between bank credit and other forms of financing (in particular loans from the Special Credit Institutions and bonds). These first two factors led the authorities to favour a credit target, while the third factor made them select a particularly broad aggregate (Total Domestic Credit – TDC).[35] This target aggregate was maintained until 1984, when it was replaced by the announcement of twin targets for money and credit. The money target related to M2, which had begun to show a remarkably stable relationship with nominal output.[36] The credit target was narrowed to the private sector component of TDC. Subsequently, however, when the information content of the credit variable proved to be unreliable and the targets were systematically and substantially overshot, their role in the policy-making process and in the public's perception gradually declined. By contrast, the continued empirical stability of M2, as well as Italy's relative successful performance in targeting it, enhanced this aggregate's role in monetary policy-making.

Finally, in its short stint of money targeting, *Portugal* consistently opted for the wide aggregate L- (approximately M3 plus Treasury bills held by non-financial residents). This aggregate fitted in well with the internal monetary programming practices as well as with the system of direct credit ceilings that were then still in place.

The specification of the target: a point, range or ceiling?

In addition to diversity in the choice of targeted aggregate, European countries have differed in the specification of the target itself. This diversity has related primarily to the question of whether the target is defined as a point, as a range or as a ceiling.

A *point target* has the advantage of sending an unambiguous signal to anchor expectations and of providing unequivocal guidance regarding the required policy stance. To illustrate the latter, money growth well within the upper half of the target range may suggest the need for policy neutrality in the case of a target range, while it would signal the need for policy tightening in the case of a point target. In this respect, a point target conceptually represents a more rules-based approach to policy-making. This may contribute to greater policy predictability, while also reducing the scope for time inconsistency. At the same time, however, a point target has the disadvantage that it is practically never met and thus requires considerably more explaining to the public. More fundamentally, a point target may be seen as overstating the controllability of the target aggregate, the short-run stability of money demand and the reliability of the statistical measurement of the targeted aggregate.

By contrast, a *target range* does justice to the uncertainties inherent in the target projections and especially to those exogenous factors that limit the near-term accuracy of money targeting. In this regard, the use of target ranges helps avoid an unduly mechanical and hence misguided interpretation of monetary policy-making. A narrow but attainable target range can thus simplify the communication and accountability of monetary policy, especially if it provides a realistic yardstick against which to measure policy success. This is because a range provides a clear measure of when monetary policy is to be considered on track, while a point target does not. Moreover, a range is attractive insofar as it offers a two-dimensional objective: the central bank sets both the level and the bandwidth of the target. This means that target ranges can be tailored more closely to dominant monetary policy concerns. In particular, a range can be narrowed when the central bank wishes to emphasise a motive that would otherwise suggest adopting a point target (for example, the strength of the policy signal) and can be widened when the central bank wishes to highlight a motive for adopting a range (for example, temporarily higher money demand uncertainty). As regards the decision on bandwidth, there is thus a trade-off between the credibility-enhancing effects of choosing an ambitiously tight target, and the credibility-weakening effects of subsequently missing it.[37] At the same time, however, it should be recognised that an unduly tight target range may not be credible to start with.

The alternative of using a *ceiling* may be considered in situations where only the upper limit of an otherwise announced target range is viewed as binding and where the central bank wishes to stress this maximum. In particular, a ceiling may be appropriate when policy tolerance is asymmetric, such as when a considerable undershooting of the target would be welcomed, whereas an overshooting would not. This may be the case, for instance, in a situation of substantial monetary overhang. Furthermore, ceilings are generally opportune when a credit aggregate is being targeted, as this is usually motivated by balance of payments concerns and as any undershooting of the credit ceiling will lead – with a given money demand – to overperformance in the external accounts. Nonetheless, defining a target as a ceiling has the drawback that the monetary policy framework is left without a definite nominal anchor and that expectations are provided somewhat ambiguous guidance. Moreover, in the case of money targets, ceilings fail to signal that just as monetary policy is employed to reduce inflation, it will be also be used to counter deflation.

Money targeting was initiated by *Germany* with a point target. This reflected the prime concern spurring the publication of money targets, namely to provide explicit and unequivocal guidance to expectations about prospective monetary policy. Indeed, at the outset, the Bundesbank expressly wished to limit any perception of (output oriented) policy discretion under the target. However, the central bank subsequently experienced difficulty in explaining technically motivated target breaches in a credible fashion to the public, a task that was made no easier by persistent target overruns during the first four years. Against this background, the Bundesbank switched to publishing target ranges in 1979. The width of these ranges was set at either 2 or 3 percentage points depending on the prevailing uncertainty and the desired stringency of the policy signal.[38] The only exception was the imprecise point target for 1989 (M3 was to grow by "about 5 per cent"), announced after three years of substantive target range overshooting. This point target was determined at the upper limit of the range that the standard method would otherwise have suggested (3 to 5 per cent) and sought to provide the Bundesbank somewhat more flexibility to deal with prevailing uncertainties, especially greater money demand instability linked to the introduction of a withholding tax on capital income and a greater demand for Deutsche Mark notes abroad.[39] Barring this one exception in the past twenty years, Germany has staunchly stuck to the practice of announcing ranges.

France's experience with different target definitions is intriguing, in that this country initially preferred a point target, then switched to a target range, and later reverted back again to a point target. Specifically, it maintained point targets during 1977-83 (with the sole exception of a range in 1982 to allow for year-end accounting discrepancies), switched to target ranges during 1984-93, and subsequently went back to point targets from 1994 on. In the early years of money targeting, this reflected relatively accurate monetary marksmanship in the context of tight direct credit controls and a gradualist approach to disinflation. Following the switch to ambitious disinflation and the progressive dismantling of credit ceilings, a tightened point target for 1983 was hugely overshot and France joined the ranks of most other countries with target ranges (usually setting a bandwidth of 2 percentage points). In the event, the effective prioritisation of the exchange rate objective as well as ongoing capital and financial liberalisation subsequently led to even greater variation in money growth outcomes. Against this background, France returned to point targets in 1994, but emphasised their approximate and medium-term character.

The experiences of the *United Kingdom* and *Spain*, and from the mid-1980s also *Italy* and *Portugal*, are fairly similar, in that these countries predominantly made use of target ranges with relatively wide bands (of usually 3 or 4 percentage points). This partly reflected a higher absolute level of these target ranges (with double digit figures until the second half of the 1980s), but in the United Kingdom the ranges remained wide even when trend money growth had been brought down. After a lengthy use of point targets, *Greece* also adopted the practice of using target bands in the late 1980s. In 1995, with an explicit switch to direct inflation targetry in Spain and an implicit switch in Italy, both countries ceased using ranges in the context of a progressive de-emphasising of money targets.[40] As the nominal anchor was evidently being provided by another variable, the money target took on a more parochial role as a limiting condition. Accordingly, both countries eventually switched to announcing ceilings beneath which money growth would not be considered a risk to the prevailing, overriding inflation objective.

Ceilings had also been used earlier in the case of *Italy*'s credit targets (1974-85) and the *Netherlands*' liquidity ratio objectives (1977-80). In the former case, the use of ceilings was related to the dominant balance of payments concerns, since any undershooting of the credit target – the larger the better – would serve to underpin the external position. (This assumes, of course, money demand developing as envisaged; any higher-than-envisaged money demand would strengthen the external accounts even with credit expansion at the ceiling.) However, primarily as a result of overruns in public sector credit, the targets were not met in any year except the first and the ceilings did not fulfil their envisaged role. In the latter case, the liquidity ratio targets were broadly defined as a minimum objective over a multiyear horizon. The specification in terms of a ceiling was chosen on account of the uncertain magnitude of the excess liquidity that was perceived to have accumulated over the previous years as well as the asymmetric policy concerns of the Netherlands Bank at the time.

In all, point targets were more common in the early period of money targeting, as countries simply made public their internal practice of using a single figure as an unambiguous policy compass. Over the course of time, as central banks increasingly wished to communicate the uncertainties governing money targets, and as the uncertainties themselves also grew on account of financial liberalisation and of the broad-based shift to indirect instruments of monetary control, money targeting frameworks converged towards the use of ranges. In those cases that money targets were subsequently de-emphasised, the use of loosely defined point targets and ceilings re-emerged.

The money target time horizon and the periodicity of updates

European countries have generally specified their money targets for calendar years or, in the case of the United Kingdom, budget years. Implicit in this choice of time horizon has been the assumption that money growth is sufficiently controllable in the course of the year, thanks to its position midway the monetary policy transmission process. The prominent advantage of an annual time horizon is that it has allowed the monetary framework to be made consistent with budget intentions, as well as with GDP and balance of payments projections. Moreover, an annual cycle serves the target's communicability, as this is the interval the general public is most accustomed to. In this respect, targets have usually not been updated in mid-stream, as frequent updates would water down the signalling power of the targets as well as their rules-based character. However, there have been notable exceptions to these regularities.

For instance, money targets have occasionally been proclaimed for a multiyear rather than an annual time horizon, thereby emphasising their essentially medium-term orientation. This was the case in the *Netherlands'* 1977 announcement of a liquidity ratio target, which aimed at a gradual decline in this ratio over a four-year period (entailing an average 1 percentage point per year fall in 1977-80). With early deviations from the medium-term path, the liquidity ratio objectives subsequently became less specific and were de-emphasised. Similarly, multiyear money targets lay at the core of the *United Kingdom*'s Medium-Term Financial Strategy (MTFS) when it was first introduced in 1980. These targets stretched out four years ahead and spelt out a progressive and sustained decline in annual money growth (see Appendix XIVb). The aim was not only to cast monetary policy expressly in a medium-term framework and to dismiss any expectations of a monetary policy contribution to short-term economic management, but also to anchor expectations more firmly onto a downward path by signalling the ambition of the Government's more distant inflation objectives. Against the background of a massive overshooting of the target in the first year – reflecting £M3 instability rather than monetary policy looseness – subsequent MTFS programs only identified a target for the first year, with 'illustrative ranges' being set for outer years. These illustrative medium-term ranges were maintained through the early 1990s (see Appendix XIVb).

In another departure from custom, *France* explicitly ceased setting annual money targets in 1994 after several years of poor targeting performance owing to M3 volatility. Rather than abandon money targets altogether and pursue only an external policy target, the authorities set a medium-term money growth target of approximately 5 per cent. Of course, this shift to more flexible money targets was effectively the consequence of assigning priority to the exchange rate in day-to-day policy-making, hence limiting control over money developments. On the basis of similar considerations, *Spain* also granted its privileged money indicator a medium-term character after the adoption of formal inflation targeting in 1995. For different reasons, *Germany* also switched to announcing a two-year money growth target in 1997 and 1998, although it combined this with a more accurate specification of the annual target at the outset of each year.[41] The underlying motive was to provide an early signal on the continuity of the monetary objectives and targeting framework and therewith to dispel any uncertainty about the orientation of German monetary policy in the run-up to the third stage of EMU.

At a more technical level, European countries have differed considerably in the definition of the time period covered by the money targets, even when these have been essentially annually oriented. In particular, the definition of target time periods has varied between December to December, fourth quarter to fourth quarter, and annual average growth rates.[42] On the one hand, money targets expressed in December to December growth rates are vulnerable to random fluctuations and end-of-year effects. On the other hand, the use of annual averages implies that money growth outcomes not only reflect developments in the targeted year, but also those in the previous base year. As a result, the outcomes only partly represent the authorities' policy efforts during the relevant target period. Targets defined in terms of fourth quarter to fourth quarter growth rates (or a different 3-month average of a 12-month growth rate) attempt to strike a balance between these two extremes. In general, on the basis of practical experience, European countries have converged somewhat towards using such a definition: Germany and Italy eventually settled for fourth quarter to fourth quarter targets, as did France in the decade until 1996, even though none of these countries had initiated their money targeting on this basis. France's eventual decision to re-adopt a December to December schedule reflected the de-emphasised role of its money targets (more akin to reference points), according to which a simple 12-month growth rate was seen as more transparent. In so doing, it joined Greece and Spain, which have consistently used December to December targets.

With regard to the periodicity of updates, the general practice has been to maintain money targets without adjustment until the expiration of the (usually annual) target period. An all but exceptional use of review clauses enhances policy precommitment and limits policy discretion, thereby providing clear guidance to expectations. In addition, it serves to iron out short-term random influences and to reduce the scope for (inflationary) base drift. However, notwithstanding these considerations, an active use of mid-stream reassessments has occasionally been part of the money targeting framework. For example, in 1978, the *United Kingdom* explicitly adopted rolling targets, according to which the money growth objectives were to be reviewed at six-month intervals. These reviews, it was argued, would allow changing circumstances to be taken fully into account.[43] More specifically, a periodic reassessment would avoid the disruptive impact of undue efforts to bring – or keep – money growth in the target range, especially towards the end of the target period. The practice of rolling targets was not, however, taken over by the Thatcher Government that came to power in 1979. Similarly, during the first years of money targets in *Spain*, the central bank sometimes formally redefined its target range in the course of the year, but more recently it has preferred to explain its willingness to tolerate departures form original targets.[44]

Formal reviews of the money target are also conducted at mid-year by *Germany*'s Bundesbank. Again, the main motive is to enable policy-makers to take explicitly into account any additional information that has arisen in the course of the first half of the year.[45] However, in practice such reviews have only once involved revising the money target – in the wake of German unification in 1991. Hence, disregarding this extraordinary circumstance, the reviews have never been used to rebase, suspend or otherwise revise a prevailing target. At most, the reviews have served to increase the precision of the existing target. In particular, during each of the five years from 1979 to 1983, the target ranges were kept relatively wide on account of the then prevailing economic uncertainty and the mid-year review was used to specify which part of the target range (e.g., 'lower half') the central bank was actually aiming for. These reviews thus did not entail greater discretion, since they mainly served to implement a rules-with-feedback system whereby the Bundesbank spelt out in advance (at the time it initially announced the target range) the conditions that would determine the content of the mid-year specification.

The presentation of the target

In the field of presentation, European countries have used a variety of methods to enhance the strength of the message conveyed by their monetary policy targets. These methods have related to the political as well as the technical aspects of such targets. The former have sought to communicate the broad-based nature of the support for the target, whereas the latter have aimed at clarifying the derivation of the target, thereby making it more transparent. In general, these methods reflect the considerable value that countries have attached to presentation in order to strengthen the credibility of the monetary policy strategy and therewith its external signalling power.

With regard to the politics of money targets, most countries have sought to present the targets in a way that clearly communicates a sense of governmental backing. The need for such backing has been considered important even in countries with an independent central bank. For instance, in *Germany*, the novel monetary framework was launched at the end of 1974 with outspoken support from the Federal Government as well as of the independent Council of Economic Experts. Moreover, it subsequently became a tradition that the Bundesbank's money targets were publicly endorsed in the Federal Government's Annual Economic Report, in which the main macroeconomic objectives for the coming year are set out.

To the extent political support is valued in countries with an independent central bank, such support is indispensable in countries where this is not the case. In the *United Kingdom*, where the central bank did not achieve policy autonomy until 1997, the money targets were effectively determined by the Treasury and political backing was imperative. Nonetheless, there was an awareness that the publicity of this backing could contribute to policy efficacy. Indeed, at the time the Medium-Term Financial Strategy was introduced in 1979 and policy commitment genuinely shifted towards the money targets announced therein, the Prime Minister expressly made a point of sanctioning the strategic objectives.[46] Similarly, in *France*, money target announcements were customarily made by the Prime Minister, thereby incontestably signalling the Government's support, and particularly its intention not to undermine the target through excessive monetary financing of the budget.[47] An even starker example is provided by *Spain*, where money targets were traditionally announced during the presentation of the State Budget to Parliament. And, in the case of *Italy*, money targets were first publicised in the context of the autumn Parliamentary presentation of the Ministry of the Budget's macro-economic projections for the following year.[48]

In several countries, the presentation of money targets has also comprised an explanation of their technical derivation. In general, the provision of this information seeks to contribute to a greater understanding of the otherwise 'abstract' money targets, thereby enhancing their transparency and credibility. More specifically, information on the breakdown underlying a money target (in particular between the nominal and real components) can strengthen the guidance to expectations, convey a clearer sense of monetary policy's final objectives, and provide a more comprehensive measure against which to assess the central bank's performance. In addition, by publicising the implicit inflation objective, a central bank as it were hedges the risks of money demand instability: if such instability becomes evident, it is easier to deviate from the money target with reference to the specified ultimate goal for inflation.

The first and finest example of such an external presentation policy is provided by the patent fashion in which *Germany* has traditionally disclosed the breakdown of its money target (see Appendix VI on Germany's monetary policy targets). To be sure, in its own way, the Bundesbank attached credence to the concepts of transparency and accountability long before they came in vogue in the central banking world of the 1990s. From the outset at end-1974, it has publicly spelled out the exact magnitude of the different components on which its money target is built: (i) estimated potential real output growth, initially corrected for desired changes in capacity utilisation; (ii) expected medium-term rate of change in money velocity; and (iii) 'unavoidable' inflation, a concept that was replaced in 1985 by a constant normative medium-term price assumption of 2 per cent. By focusing the target on potential output growth, trend velocity changes and 'unavoidable' inflation, the aim was to make monetary policy more resistant to fine tuning in the face of transitory changes in output and prices. In particular, the use of potential output growth as it were introduced an automatic counter-cyclical stabiliser into monetary policy, since money growth would tend to be above target in years that real output grew at a higher rate than potential output (implying a restrictive policy stance), and below target in years that the opposite occurred (implying an expansionary policy stance). At the same time, the publicity for the implicit inflation objective (and the velocity assumption) can be viewed as an early indication that there was no intention of pursuing a strict monetarist doctrine. Indeed, the distinct manner in which the Bundesbank has always identified the assumed price development – or, crudely put, the inflation objective – underlying its money target indicates that its strategy of money targeting is a close relative of inflation targeting.[49] However, the choice to advertise the money rather than the inflation goal reflects a preference to communicate with the public on the basis of a leading monetary variable, thereby signalling that the main element driving policy-making falls directly within the realm of the (independent) monetary authority.

Although Germany has been in a league of its own as regards the clarity and consistency of presenting how money targets are derived, some other countries have also consciously sought to enhance public insight into the technical basis for their money targets. For example, in *Spain*, after the targets are first announced during the autumn presentation of the State Budget, the central bank traditionally provides a detailed analysis of the assumptions underlying the monetary targets in the first issue of the year of its Economic Bulletin. Similarly, in *Italy*, subsequent to the Parliamentary debate on the macroeconomic projections for the following year, the central bank discusses the financial targets in its October Economic Bulletin. When *France* switched to announcing a medium-term point target for money growth in 1994, it emulated Germany's example by quantifying the underlying medium-term projections for the final inflation objective (being annual price increases of '2 per cent or less') as well as for real GDP growth potential (generally set at 'about 2½ per cent').

One example where the derivation remained opaque is the *Netherlands*' liquidity ratio targets. While there was clearly an initial intention to combine the presentation of these targets with the implicit money targets, in practice this did not occur.[50] And an example where the explanation was deliberately kept minimal is the *United Kingdom*'s announcement of money targets in its first Medium-Term Financial Strategy: the statement was kept simple in the belief that, given the environment of high inflation at the time, straightforward communication would have the greatest impact on expectations.[51]

5.3 The money targeting experiences in perspective

Overall, the development of monetary policy strategies in Europe over the past quarter of a century indicates first an increase, and then a decline, in the popularity of money targeting. This runs parallel to the global experience of industrialised countries.[52] The initial popularity may partly reflect the greater usefulness of money targets in a high inflation environment, such as existed when each of these countries first adopted money targetry. In such a situation, the priority attached to disinflation is more likely to outweigh the perceived risk of money demand instability. Of course, this attraction recedes once inflation is brought back under control. Besides this, liberalisation of international capital flows, such as was largely completed in the EU by the late 1980s, sharpens the conflict between money targets and the other desideratum of monetary policy – exchange rate stability. And, at an operational level, a greater reliance on indirect monetary instruments reduces the immediate controllability of money developments.

From a broad perspective, European countries have commonly had considerable success in bringing down inflation in their initial phase of money targeting. For those countries that adopted money targetry in the mid-1970s, consumer price inflation was generally reduced by at least one-half by 1985; for the latecomers, all in Southern Europe, comparable success was booked somewhat later. However, in absence of the counterfactual, it is impossible to gauge the extent to which this decline can be attributed to money targeting. In fact, in terms of the bare outcome under the money targets, the record is dismal: the targets were missed in more than half of the cases in all countries that maintained money targets for longer than three years (see Table 7). Even Germany, the most successful money targeter in terms of the smallest average absolute deviation from target (with the exceptions of the Netherlands, which used irregular liquidity targets that it failed to achieve, and Portugal, which only pursued money targets a short period) met its target in no more than 42 per cent of the time. Indeed, the average absolute deviation under Germany's money targets (1.7 percentage points) was actually twice as large as the average absolute deviation under the inflation assumption (0.85 percentage point) that was explicitly built into these money targets. In short, the leading indicator properties and controllability of money over a period as brief as one year have proven to be relatively unreliable in practice. On a European level, the results are even more telling. The region's average absolute deviation was not only large (about 3 percentage points), but also widely dispersed. As a result, despite wide target ranges (3 percentage points on average), European targets were missed in more than two thirds of the cases.

It should be stressed, however, that the effectiveness of monetary policy in the different European countries cannot be evaluated simply on the basis of the deviations from target. This is because these deviations reflect three different influences: (i) the policy-maker's efforts to keep the money supply growth in line with the target; (ii) unanticipated shocks (e.g., in domestic demand) which the policy-maker has not yet been able to offset due to monetary policy transmission lags; and (iii) unanticipated shocks (e.g., of a monetary or temporary nature) which the policy-maker has deliberately sought to accommodate through deviations from the preannounced target. Basically, policy effectiveness can only be judged in terms of success relative to the end objectives of policy, that is the stability of prices and of output growth. Moreover, a comparative evaluation should strictly speaking also take account of the degree in which individual countries have been struck by asymmetric shocks. That would correct for the impact on performance of idiosyncratic events such as, for instance, the sudden financial sector liberalisation in the United Kingdom in the early 1980s and the unification of Germany in the early 1990s. By implication, Table 7 does not say the final word on whether monetary policy has been judicious in the different European countries. Rather, it assesses money targeting marksmanship, and thus the appropriateness of a policy strategy based primarily thereon, in these countries.

The poor marksmanship record seems to imply that the main contribution of money targets has not been to the internal monetary policy decisions, nor to the external monitoring of the dynamic consistency of

Table 7: Money targeting marksmanship in Europe, 1975-1998

Country	Period [1]	Average deviation [2]	Average absolute deviation [3]	Average width of target range [4]	Target achieved [5]
Germany [6]	1975-98	0.98	1.70	2.53	42%
CBM	1975-87	0.92	1.72	2.67	38%
M3	1988-98	1.05	1.69	2.40	45%
France	1977-98	-1.00	2.53	1.88	22%
M2	1977-85,1987-90	-0.11	1.60	1.71	23%
M3	1986-87,1991-98	-2.16	3.74	2.10	20%
UK	1976/77-1991/92	2.93	3.34	4.00	42%
£ M3	1976/77-1986/87	4.24	4.74	4.00	25%
M1	1982/83-1983/84	3.70	3.70	4.00	0%
PSL2	1982/83-1983/84	2.60	2.60	4.00	50%
M0	1984/85-1991/92	0.86	1.34	4.00	75%
Netherlands [7] Liq. ratio	1977-80	0.45	0.45	..	0%
Italy (M2)	1984-98	0.81	1.87	2.78	33%
Spain	1978-94	2.00	2.80	3.59	47%
M3	1978-83	0.57	1.40	4.17	83%
ALP	1984-94	2.78	3.56	3.27	27%
Greece	1975-97	1.33	5.02	2.50	11%
M1	1975-87	0.22	6.02	..	15%
M3	1983-97	2.29	4.16	2.50	7%
Portugal (L-)	1987-89	0.98	1.58	3.63	67%
EU average [8]	1975-98	1.14	2.91	3.00	31%

Source: Appendix Tables.

[1] Relates to the period during which money targeting was implemented, respectively the sub-period during which a specific money aggregate was targeted.

[2] Indicates the average deviation (in per cent of the initial money stock) between the money growth outcome and the point target or the mid-point of the target range.

[3] Indicates the average absolute deviation (in per cent of the initial money stock) between the money growth outcome and the point target or the mid-point of the target range.

[4] Indicates average range width in years that target ranges (rather than point targets or ceilings) were announced.

[5] Percentage number of targets achieved. Point targets are assumed to have been met when the outcome was within ± 0.5% points of the target.

[6] On the basis of rounded figures, the Bundesbank considers the money targets in 1980 (5-8%), 1981 (4-7%) and 1991 (3-5%) to have been met (outcomes 4.9%, 3.5% respectively 5.2%). This would improve the overall target achievement ratio from 42% to 54%.

[7] Target related to the *minimum* decline in the Liquidity ratio, (i.e., M2 as a percentage of GDP); deviations are expressed in per cent of GDP.

[8] Excludes the Netherlands which expressed money targets in per cent of GDP rather than in percentage growth rates.

these decisions. Indeed, the prevalence of velocity instability suggests that policy setting and policy monitoring based on money aggregates is not without risks. Rather, the prime contribution of money targets should be sought in the communication of policy ambition, the orientation of monetary policy towards a variable that falls under the responsibility of the central bank, and the disciplinary impact on the central bank itself.

A further important point is that money targets were on average significantly overrun in all countries except France. This seems to confirm that these targets have generally been used to set out a somewhat more ambitious policy path than what the monetary authorities were actually prepared to settle for. At first glance, this suggests that central banks have indeed engaged in time inconsistent policies, by first announcing an ambitious policy and later implementing a looser one. However, there are also indications that these ambitious targets may in some cases have been part of a (probably not premeditated) central bank ploy to facilitate the achievement of the final inflation objective. In particular, a central bank that tends to set a conservative intermediate money target by erring on the upside in its money velocity projections, may find it easier to tighten monetary policy when needed to meet its inflation goal, as it will usually be able to point to money growth above the target mid-point. The German case provides evidence on this score, as the Bundesbank has consistently used overly conservative assumptions on money velocity when constructing its money targets. This is illustrated by the fact that the average overshoot of the money target mid-point (1.0 percentage point) has been about three times larger than the average overshoot of the inflation assumption (0.3 percentage point) built into this target. Of course, such a ruse only works as long as the announced target is considered credible; in turn, this highlights the importance of measures to enhance this credibility, in particular regarding the political presentation and transparent communication of the target.

In the final analysis, money demand instability as well as increasing prioritisation of exchange rate targets ultimately rendered money targeting infeasible in all EU countries except Germany. Nonetheless, these countries were generally reluctant to renounce money targets altogether. This seems to have reflected the efficacy of these targets in signalling a nominal anchor for medium-term inflation and in communicating a domestic orientation of an otherwise externally determined policy stance. Even in the case of Germany, however, the track record testifies that pursuing money targets does not come without hitches. But the cumulated credibility invested in this strategy has, in itself, represented a legitimate motive to sustain it.

At a detailed level, four further issues stand out in these countries' diverse experiences with money targetry: first, the importance evidently attached to the announcement of money targets, second, the vulnerability of money targeting in the face of money demand instability, third, the pragmatism with which money targeting strategies have invariably been implemented and, fourth, the learning process that has characterised the evolution of money targeting.

The eagerness to announce money targets

The communication aspect of monetary policy has been a driving influence in the evolution of money targeting. Indeed, the importance of signalling the objectives and responsibilities of monetary policy largely determined the initial announcements of, as well as part of the subsequent adjustments to, the money targeting frameworks. In particular, the first declaration of a money target by Germany was clearly motivated by the Bundesbank's wish to emphasise its overriding responsibility for a nominal objective and therewith to signal to wage setters that monetary policy would not accommodate an inflationary momentum. More generally, the announcement of money targets has been used to advertise a renewed priority for disinflation and to increase the political costs of not delivering on this prioritisation. This is well illustrated by the emphasis that the Barre and Thatcher Governments placed on these targets in France and the United Kingdom when price pressures mounted in the wake of the oil crises. It is also apparent in Portugal's adoption of money targets in 1986, when accession to the EC underscored the need for convergence, especially in terms of price developments. In a more abstract sense, monetary authorities undoubtedly also envisaged a didactic role for money targets in explaining the link between money growth and inflation, and hence the constraints determining their policies. A prime example where this consideration seems to have been at play is in the Netherlands' selection of a target for the liquidity ratio, which related money growth directly to the growth of nominal income.

It is an interesting question whether the eagerness to publicise money targets reflected overconfidence in the stability of the relationships determining money demand. In retrospect, the zeal with which money targets were commonly launched, in conjunction with the initially widespread use of point targets (without caveats) and of December through December target periods, indeed suggests this was the case. But there are also indications that monetary authorities were forewarned of the dangers of money demand instability. For instance, shortly before the genesis of practical money targeting, a 1974 synthesis report of OECD monetary policy studies concluded that "it is not surprising that the central banks concerned have not rigidly geared the operation of monetary policy to any narrowly prescribed course for any one variable. ... On the contrary, there is a need for constant re-evaluation of the main sources of instability in the light of the most recent observed developments and prospects."[53] At best, the evidence available in the turbulent macroeconomic environment of the early 1970s suggested that money was only the "least unstable" of the potential policy targets.

As a more specific illustration, the Bank of England adopted money targets in 1976 notwithstanding a severe breakdown in its £M3 demand-for-money function in 1973 (which ironically occurred not long after the Bank published econometric results that suggested this relationship was stable). And when the United Kingdom moved to money targets in earnest in 1979, the Government was expressly warned that the weight being placed on the money targets was excessive in relation to the stability that could reasonably be expected in money demand.[54] Later, when the framework with multiple money targets was streamlined in 1984, £M3 was maintained – despite its instability – primarily on account of its communicability.[55]

These examples serve to illustrate the general point that monetary authorities have repeatedly decided to grant a publicity to money targets that was disproportionate to the risk of divergent money velocity developments.[56] In turn, this testifies to the importance attached to the external signalling and task-setting roles of money targets, and to the ready acceptance of having to deal with the possible consequences (in terms of explaining legitimate deviations from target) later.

Money demand instability and the viability of money targets

Beyond short-term announcements effects, the communication potential and disciplinary impact of money targetry depends crucially on the stability of the relationship between the targeted aggregate and the end-objectives, particularly inflation. In this respect, money targeting has proven to remain viable in circumstances of limited money demand instability, but has also shown to be futile once such instability takes on too great a magnitude. The experiences of European countries have differed considerably on this point, both in relation to each other and over the course of time.

In explaining the differences in money demand stability, two key factors feature prominently: domestic financial deregulation and innovation, and external capital account liberalisation. Essentially, the shifts to a more liberal financial environment in Europe over the past quarter of a century have tended temporarily to prompt portfolio adjustments and permanently to change financial behaviour. In turn, this has altered the information content of given monetary aggregates as well as the central bank's control over them. Besides this, the orientation of monetary policy at other nominal variables than the money supply (notably the exchange rate) has, by itself, tended to lower the stability of money velocity. And a diminished emphasis on money aggregates has also reduced the value attached to more specific stability enhancing measures, such as timely adaptations of aggregate definitions and restrictions on potentially destabilising financial instruments. Together, these considerations essentially constitute the antithesis to Goodhart's Law: the less policy focuses on stabilising a given monetary variable, the more likely that variable will become unstable.

It should be emphasised, however, that it is difficult to say anything conclusive about the true underlying stability of money demand in any country based on observed variability in the past. In particular, it is impossible to separate instability that leads central banks to deviate from their targets, from instability that is caused by these same central banks. This is pertinent in Europe, especially in countries where money demand instability appears to have been fuelled by monetary policy variability. But it is also relevant for the countries where increasing prioritisation of the exchange rate objective in the context of a liberal financial and foreign exchange system has limited the scope to steer money growth.

The European experiences cover the full spectrum. At one extreme, *Germany* has traditionally experienced a relatively stable money demand function, thereby facilitating its strategy of money targeting.[57] This seems to reflect the fact that all direct controls on credit, interest rates or foreign exchange had been removed well before money targets were launched. In addition, a consistent implementation of stability-oriented policies, resulting in the on average lowest and least variable inflation and interest rates in the EC, has fostered stable money demand.[58] This has had a self-reinforcing effect: Germany's macroeconomic stability contributed to its anchor role in the ERM and thus to pursuing a largely autonomous monetary policy; this, in turn, enhanced the central bank's control over money aggregates. At the same time, sustained macroeconomic stability has kept incentives for financial innovation at a minimum (perhaps strengthened by the traditionally conservative nature of the domestic banking community as well as restrictions on specific financial instruments). In more recent years, temporary deviations from target have been caused by special factors such as the impact of high demand for German currency in eastern Europe, the (re-)introduction of a withholding tax, massive Deutsche Mark intervention in the context of the September 1992 ERM crisis, and of course German unification. However, despite these factors, studies generally lend tentative support to the conclusion that German money demand has remained largely stable over the past two and a half decades.[59]

This stability is reflected in a relatively favourable performance under money targets. In practice, barring the exceptional and short-lived cases of

Portugal and the Netherlands, the Bundesbank's marksmanship has been the most accurate of all European central banks: over its 24 years of money targetry, the average absolute deviation from the target mid-point amounted to only 1.7 percentage points. The fact that Germany did not meet its targets more often than all the other money targeters in Europe, can be fully attributed to the preference for relatively narrow target ranges. Against this general background, it is not surprising that Germany's monetary policy strategy has undergone the least changes of any country in Europe and that the framework in place through 1998 essentially remained comparable to the one that initiated money targeting in 1975.

At the other extreme, the *United Kingdom* has faced considerable money demand instability from the outset of its sincere money targeting in 1979/80.[60] This was related to the simultaneous removal of all capital restrictions and the (thus unavoidable) abolition of direct credit control under the 'corset'. The combination of these factors led to a money growth explosion that was roughly double the target in each of the two following years, thereby genuinely ruffling the financial markets.[61] In fact, while broad money generally continued to grow much faster than expected and intended, headline inflation fell precipitously from over 20 per cent at its peak in 1980 to below 3 per cent in 1986. Given the limited reliability of the leading indicator properties of the targeted money aggregate, the central bank diversified the attention over both a narrower aggregate, that was less influenced by the accumulation of wealth, and an even broader aggregate, that provided more comprehensive coverage of spending potential (in particular through the inclusion of building society deposits). However, velocity changes in these aggregates did not prove to be sufficiently explicable either and, in practice, the United Kingdom's targeting record hardly improved. A subsequent new target aggregate turned out to be relatively stable, but this came too late. Money targets had already become unworkable on account of their lack of credibility and, especially from 1986 on, were de-emphasised.

The experiences of the other European countries fall in between these two extremes, although perhaps closer to that of the United Kingdom. Again, welcome progress in domestic financial deregulation and innovation, as well as in external capital account liberalisation, was at the root of money demand instability. Subsequently, the increased prioritisation of the exchange rate objective in the context of a free capital regime further fuelled this instability. This is well-illustrated by the cases of *France*, *Italy*, and *Spain* where financial deregulation and innovation during the 1980s blurred the distinction between money and securities, and between banks and other financial institutions. This spurred significant portfolio shifts and prompted the central banks to repeatedly redefine or change their targeted money aggregate. Following full capital account liberalisation, the early

1990s added substantial currency substitution and delocation, other fiscally motivated portfolio adjustments, and a monetary policy that effectively granted primacy to the exchange rate.[62] Under these circumstances, velocity proved insufficiently stable for a credible strategy of money targeting and the central banks of France and Italy eventually shifted to a loosely defined medium-term oriented money target. Similarly, in the case of Spain, the money target was downgraded to a medium-term reference ceiling tailored to meeting the inflation target; when the velocity instability persisted, the reference rate was allowed to lapse altogether at end-1997.

Even more telling examples of this evolution are provided by the experiences of the smaller and more open EU countries with money targets. In these countries, money targets were generally maintained as long as capital movements remained restricted. This was the case in the *Netherlands* in the 1970s, *Portugal* in the 1980s, and *Greece* in the 1990s. Once capital markets were deregulated and exchange restrictions were fully liberalised, the respective central banks effectively ceased viewing money as an intermediate target and opted to use the exchange rate as their sole monetary policy compass.[63] A temporary exception was the Netherlands' attempt in the second half of the 1980s to combine the (in practice overriding) exchange rate commitment with targets for the growth of domestic credit.[64] Consistent with the endogeneity of money expansion under the exchange rate target, the aim was to keep the domestic component of money creation in line with the trend growth in domestic money demand, and thereby to avoid persistent capital outflows that might otherwise jeopardise the exchange rate commitment. As a stable domestic money demand trend could not be established, and the relationship between capital outflows and exchange rate pressure proved ambiguous anyway, credit targets were effectively abandoned in 1991.[65] In the case of Greece, money targets also continued to be announced during the period when the ECU was being unilaterally targeted, but these were downgraded to monitoring ranges as soon as the country entered the ERM in early 1998.

The prevalence of pragmatism

The distinguishing feature of the European experiences with money targeting is the pragmatism with which this policy strategy has been pursued. Indeed, despite the dogmatic traits that characterise monetarism, money targeting has invariably been implemented with a considerable degree of elasticity. This pragmatism can be illustrated at a fundamental, technical and practical level.

At a fundamental level, the decisions to adopt, degrade, suspend or abandon money targets have mostly been driven by pragmatic considerations rather than firm convictions of the policy relevance, or irrelevance, of the quantity theory of money. In particular, a high level of inflation and resistance to monetary tightening often made adoption of money targets opportune, while the achievement of relatively low inflation in the context of volatile money demand made their degradation or discontinuation acceptable.

At a technical level, pragmatism is apparent in the cross-country differences in money targeting frameworks and in the evolution of these frameworks over time. Specifically, targeted aggregates have been redefined or changed; targeting frameworks have been expanded to cover two or more money aggregates; target time horizons have been adjusted; targets have been subjected to mid-stream updates; targets have been temporarily suspended; target specifications have switched between point targets, ranges (of varying widths) and ceilings; and target presentations have varied according to the explicitness of political backing and of the target derivation.

But, most importantly, the predominance of pragmatism is evidenced by the fact that, in all countries where these have been pursued for a period of more than three years, money targets have more often than not been breached.

The lessons learnt

Stretched over eight countries and more than two decades, the European experience with money targeting represents a gradual learning process. At a general level, a first lesson has been that pragmatism is necessary for money targeting to be workable in a dynamic environment with ongoing financial innovation and portfolio shifts. In practice, pragmatism helps ensure the viability of money targeting strategies when difficulties related to short-term money demand instability or reduced controllability inevitably crop up. This need for flexibility relates to both the specification of the target parameters and the actual interpretation of the target limits. In this respect, money targeting has proven to be a rules-based approach that nonetheless needs to contain considerable room for discretion.

However, in those cases where substantive and persistent money demand instability has led to blatant pragmatism and where the policy strategy has tended to degenerate towards unheeded discretion, money targeting has been rendered futile. In particular, frequent adjustments to the targeting framework make it difficult to advertise money targets as secure supports for the reputation of monetary policy.[66] By implication, a second lesson has been that credible money targeting requires a degree of continuity in the design of the targets, in the performance under the targets, and in the external communication about the targets. Thus, while pragmatism is a necessary precondition for successful money targeting, the same holds for continuity. This is well illustrated by the fact that the most credible money targeting in Europe is seen to have been conducted by the Bundesbank, which at times has adjusted its targeting framework, but on the whole maintained the highest level of constancy in terms of unchanged target parameters, smallest deviations under target, and consistent policy communication based on these deviations.

Where this continuity requirement cannot be met, particularly owing to an effective prioritisation of the exchange rate in the context of open capital account, the European experience suggests the signalling power of money growth objectives can be sustained through specification of a medium-term time horizon or through reclassification of money as a privileged indicator. By contrast, credit targets have shown not to be viable in such circumstances and have in fact become all but extinct in Europe. Without prejudice to their role as an information variable in the monetary policy-making process, credit growth objectives have proven to fall short of what is needed for a targeting variable, especially on account of their limited communicability.

At a more detailed level, the evolution of money targeting in Europe brings out several lessons that have been drawn with regard to the specific design of the policy framework. For instance, there has been a general shift towards using broader money aggregates in order to internalise portfolio shifts between the components of narrow aggregates and other liquid assets. This shift is supported by empirical evidence that broad aggregates are more stable.[67] Since broad aggregates are typically less controllable, this shift has also reflected an increasing dominance of stability over controllability considerations in the selection of targeted aggregate. To the extent that broad aggregates were already being used in the 1970s and 1980s, this was primarily for a different reason: the broad aggregates dovetailed with the counterparts analysis on which direct credit controls and budget financing projections were based.

A further lesson is that money targets have increasingly been defined in a way that acknowledges the underlying uncertainties, notably regarding the stability of money demand. This has been achieved mainly through the adoption of ranges or of loosely defined point targets. Moreover, given the constraint of having only one main policy instrument (the short-term interest rate) and the need to focus the communication of policy objectives, central banks have generally shifted to advertising only one policy target or, in those cases with multiple targets, to indicating the policy prioritisation. In the case of non-dominant money targets, this has been done by classifying certain money growth objectives as monitoring ranges or as supplementary indicators, or by significantly loosening the target definition, for instance through specification of a medium-term time horizon.

There has also been a tendency to hedge the uncertainties governing intermediate money targets by providing a clear indication of the central bank's final objectives, notably for inflation. In particular, following the time-honoured practice of the Bundesbank, since 1994 the Banque de France has spelt out the inflation assumption built into its money target. Similarly, in Spring 1995 the Governor of the Banca d'Italia initiated a custom of announcing the inflation rate he views as feasible for the year. Such specifications of the underlying inflation objective make it easier for the central bank to deviate from its money target for the sake of safeguarding its final objectives. More generally, the European experience suggests it is important to complement the announcement of money targets with an indication of broad political backing, even in those cases where the central bank has far-reaching independence. As the efficacy of monetary policy is intertwined with that of other policies, such support can serve to enhance the credibility, and thus the external impact, of the targets.

Besides this, consensus has emerged normally not to set specific targets beyond a one-year time horizon. This reflects the experience that longer-term targets are subject to such uncertainty that any policy precommitment beyond that time scope should, at most, only relate to a vaguely defined medium-term objective. At the same time, however, European central banks have also converged towards not conducting mid-year revisions. This reflects the perception that frequent revisions risk watering down the strength of policy signals and confusing the public. Rather, the preference has been to maintain unchanged targets and explicitly to communicate the justification for any departure from target. In this way, upholding original targets exerts a disciplinary influence on the central bank and avoids the risk of unwarranted discretion that would accompany frequent target changes. Credibility has thus come to be viewed as more dependent on whether the justification for a deviation is convincing than on whether or not a target is met. Finally, on a technical note, several countries have settled for the practice of setting fourth quarter to fourth quarter targets, rather than December on December targets or annual average growth rates. This has served, on the one hand, to focus attention on developments in the target year, while, on the other, smoothing out random fluctuations and end-of-year effects.

NOTES

[1] On the former development see M. Friedman (1968), on the latter OECD (1979).

[2] During the brief period in 1971 that the German mark and the Dutch guilder floated (from shortly before the end of gold convertibility until the Smithsonian Agreement), the

Bundesbank intervened to generate an appreciation of the mark and thereby to signal the need for wage and price restraint; see Solomon (1982, p. 181). In a similar vein, Austria's official revaluation against the Deutsche Mark in September 1979, at the beginning of the autumn wage bargaining round, was expressly aimed at preventing a lag between revaluation and wage response; see Hochreiter and Winckler (1995, p. 93).

[3] On the differences of opinion between the Bundesbank and the German government regarding currency revaluation during the Bretton Woods era, see for example, Berger and De Haan (1999) and Giavazzi and Giovannini (1989, p. 23-24). In this context, it should be noted that the views within both the Government and the Bundesbank were generally divided.

[4] Schlesinger as quoted in Issing (1992, p. 291).

[5] For the early use of money targets in Greece, see Cottarelli and Giannini (1997, p. 25); for the Netherlands, see De Greef, Hilbers and Hoogduin (1998). Dutch monetarism has its roots in the interbellum and was translated into operational terms in the 1950s; it had a strong influence on the subsequent development of the monetary approach to the balance of payments. Kessler (1958) sets out the main concepts underlying this method of monetary analysis. Fase (1987) provides an academic review of Dutch monetarism.

[6] Next to the specific country cases mentioned, money targets also started playing a role at the supranational level at a relatively early stage. In 1972, the European Council recommended that the member states' central banks adopt such targets; see Von Hagen (1999, p. 688). More specifically, in late 1973 the EC Economic and Finance Ministers agreed that member countries should strive gradually to lower money growth to the targeted rate of nominal GNP expansion; see McClam (1978, p. 9).

[7] The primacy granted to the money growth target ranges was subject to key money market rates (chiefly the Federal funds rate) not moving outside a stated range. See Wallich and Keir (1978) and Kole and Meade (1995).

[8] Foot (1981, p.15) and Richardson (1978, p. 33).

[9] For France, see Cobham and Serre (1986, p. 24); for Spain, Escrivá and Malo de Molina (1991, pp. 161-162).

[10] Kloten (1992).

[11] OECD (1979).

[12] Schlesinger (1983).

[13] Fforde (1983, p. 53).

[14] Lawson (1993, pp. 45 and 66-87) provides a vivid account of how seriously the Government initially took its money targets, expressly opting for a new monetary policy framework with less discretion.

[15] Cobham and Serre (1986, p. 27).

[16] See for instance the views of Banque de France official J-P. Patat set out in Eijffinger (1993, p. 174).

[17] Fase (1985) presents a comprehensive account of the Dutch experience with monetary control aimed at the liquidity ratio.

[18] A conceptual description of how the Netherlands' exchange rate and liquidity ratio targets were combined is provided by Wellink (1989).

[19] Ayuso and Escrivá (1998).

[20] Pringle (1995).

[21] For a more elaborate discussion of Italy's long road towards money targetry, see Angeloni and Passacantando (1991), Argy (1990), Caranza and Fazio (1983), and Passacantando (1996).

[22] The public sector share in total annual domestic credit expansion soared from around 35 per cent in the early 1970s to more than 65 per cent a decade later; see Caranza and Fazio (1983).

[23] The Danmarks Nationalbank Monetary Review of February 1991 refers to the new target as follows: "As an element of strengthening co-operation between the central banks of the EEC countries on the prior co-ordination of national monetary-policy objectives, the Nationalbank has decided to use as its indicator the domestic money creation. ... A range for growth in domestic money creation has been set at 4-7 per cent from the 4th quarter of 1990 to the 4th quarter of 1991." While the bank's Annual Report over 1991 (p. 38) expressly links the outcome of "just over 1 per cent" to the target (4-7 per cent), the Annual Report over 1992 no longer relates the outcome to the target. This is not surprising given that performance under the target (3-6 per cent) would have been difficult to explain: domestic money creation fell in absolute terms by 9 per cent during that year.

[24] Although the statistical differences between central bank money and the monetary base are small (mainly on account of the latter's inclusion of banks' excess reserves and reserve requirements on external liabilities), the Bundesbank repeatedly emphasised the major conceptual differences between these two aggregates in a targeting framework. Specifically, rather than advocate a strategy of direct money base control, the German central bank has underscored the intermediate character of its central bank money target, to be achieved indirectly by influencing money market conditions. On the motives behind the selection of central bank money as target variable, see also Schlesinger (1979 and 1983) and Kloten (1992).

[25] Central bank money consisted of currency in circulation, plus 16.6 per cent of sight deposits, 12.4 per cent of time deposits, and 8.1 per cent of savings deposits below four years. These weights corresponded to the reserve ratios applicable in January 1974 and sought to do justice to the varying liquidity of the different components of M3. Currency effectively accounted for about half of the central bank money stock and roughly ten per cent of M3.

[26] Later data revisions indicate that only two of the three targets had in fact been met. More importantly, the success in 1982/83 was partly cosmetic, as it was met through overfunding. With this technique, the Treasury sold more gilt-edged securities than needed to finance the public deficit in order to attract money that would otherwise have been left with banks. Over the period 1981/82 through 1984/85, overfunding is estimated to have reduced £M3 growth by nearly 4 per cent a year; see Lawson (1993, pp. 458-460).

[27] Fforde (1983) and Lawson (1993) provide animated chronicles of the United Kingdom's struggle to find an appropriate money aggregate to target. See also Cobham and Serre (1986) and Townend (1991).

[28] In the words of Prime Minister Thatcher's personal advisor Alan Walters: "M3 was a dog that barked too often to be taken seriously"; as quoted in Lawson (1993, p. 482).

[29] The decision to abandon monitoring ranges for M0 and M4 is set out in the Bank of England's November 1997 Inflation Report (pp. 8-9).

[30] Raymond (1983) and Argy (1983, 1990).

[31] Fournier and Alleron (1991).

[32] Zijlstra (1985).

[33] The liquidity ratio figures were actually subject to enormous data revisions and substantive definition changes. In fact, the Annual Reports of the Nederlandsche Bank for the period 1976 through 1980 contain different historical figures each year, whereby the magnitude of the statistical adjustments at times even exceed the size of the targeted change.

[34] Rojo and Aríztegui (1984, p. 182).

[35] OECD (1979), Caranza and Fazio (1983), and Vaciago (1985).

[36] Angeloni and Passacantando (1991). As an illustration of the apparent changes in the stability of money demand, an OECD (1979) study had earlier concluded that it could not find one conventionally defined money aggregate that could be considered a reliable guide for monetary policy in Italy.

[37] Goodhart and Viñals (1994).

[38] In practice, the Bundesbank fudges at the margins in order to improve its targeting record. Specifically, by rounding actual growth figures to the nearest percentage point (notwithstanding targets sometimes expressed in half percentage points), outcomes that otherwise fall outside the announced target range can be classified as having been kept within it. This was the case in 1980 (outturn 4.9 per cent, target 5-8 per cent), 1981 (outturn 3.6 per cent, target 4-7 per cent) and 1991 (outturn 5.2 per cent, target 3-5 per cent), years in which the target was met according to Deutsche Bundesbank (1995, p. 79) and Issing (1997, p. 69). Since this rounding practice effectively widens the target range by half a percentage point at both the lower and upper limit (implying bandwidths of three or four percentage points), it is inconsistent with the statement (Deutsche Bundesbank p. 84, Issing, p. 71) that the target ranges are typically two or three percentage points. With this elastic interpretation of its money targets, the Bundesbank improves its success rate in meeting money targets from 42 per cent to 54 per cent.

[39] Anticipation of this withholding tax had prompted large shifts into cash in the previous half year; the tax was rescinded in mid-1989. See Kole and Meade (1995, p. 924).

[40] The increasingly prominent role of inflation targets in Italy, particularly after 1993, is set out in Visco (1995).

[41] The Bundesbank rejects using only multi-year targets, as this risks weakening policy discipline by creating a wait-and-see attitude to target deviations; see König (1996, p. 123).

[42] An exceptional position is taken in by the United Kingdom where, in line with the different coverage of the fiscal year, targets have generally extended from March to March. As a further peculiarity, the United Kingdom had money targets during the first half of the 1980s that referred to a fourteen-month period (February to April) thereby reducing the impact of irregularities linked to the end of the fiscal year.

[43] Bank of England Governor Richardson (1978, p. 37) was a firm advocate of six-month rolling targets, but considered quarterly reassessments – such as those then conducted by the US Federal Reserve – as too much of a good thing.

[44] Escrivá and Malo de Molina (1991).

[45] Issing (1997, p. 71).

[46] In the words of Thatcher (1993, p. 97): "The MTFS would only influence expectations insofar as people believed in our determination to stick to it: its credibility depended on that of the Government - and ultimately, therefore on the quality of my own commitment, about which I would leave no one in doubt."

[47] Raymond (1983) provides a detailed description of the decision-making procedure for the monetary target, at the time involving the Prime Minister, the Minister of the Economy and Finance, and the Governor of the Banque de France.

[48] This presentation includes an address by the Governor of the Bank of Italy. More generally, the Italian central bank is intimately involved in the preparation of the Ministry of the Budget's macro-economic projections. It is also noteworthy that although all financial targets fell under the final responsibility of the Government, the Governor customarily proposed the monetary policy targets and these targets were never rejected; see Angeloni and Passacantando (1991).

[49] On this basis, Von Hagen (1995) suggests that the strategic orientation of the Bundesbank should not be classified as monetary targeting, but rather as "monetary and inflation targeting".

[50] In discussing monetary targets in its Annual Report for 1976, the Netherlands Bank noted that "it is desirable that published targets as to the liquidity ratio should be accompanied by their implicit targets with respect to money supply growth, given the expected rise in net national income in real and nominal terms."

[51] Townend (1991, p. 206).

[52] For the group of industrialised countries as a whole, the use of money targets surged in the second half of the 1970s, stabilised at close to 50 per cent in the first half of the 1980s and declined to below 25 per cent over the course of the next decade. Monetary targetry has remained relatively rare among developing countries, although a slight increase has been apparent in recent years; see Cottarelli and Giannini (1997).

[53] Shigehara (1996, p. 11).

[54] Goodhart (1997) provides a colourful account of the Bank of England's vainglorious attempts at finding a stable money demand function and of the warnings to the Government, including by himself, that inordinate emphasis was being placed on the money targets.

[55] Lawson (1993, p. 456).

[56] Monetary authorities initially sought to cover this risk with minimal references to uncertainty. For instance, the United Kingdom's first MTFS opened with a footnote stating "The way in which the money supply is defined for target purposes may need to be adjusted from time to time as circumstances change." The fact that Germany originally only adopted money targets on an experimental basis could also be seen as conveying the prevailing uncertainty, albeit more implicitly. However, this dimension of targeting frameworks was not given much prominence. Indeed, highlighting the uncertainty governing a target does not sit well with the desire to strengthen its signalling role. Anyhow, as recognised by Lawson (1993, p. 68) on the basis of first-hand experience, such nuances about uncertainty are unlikely to be picked up by the public, including academic commentators.

[57] Early studies already indicated the superior money demand stability in Germany: see for example OECD (1979), Atkinson *et al.* (1984), and Isard and Rojas-Suarez (1986).

[58] The fact that Germany has combined the lowest variability in interest rates and in money growth illustrates that, contrary to the intuitive view, there is not necessarily a trade-off between these two variables; see Bernanke and Mishkin (1992, p. 202).

[59] An overview of the recent studies is provided in Kole and Meade (1995). König (1996) presents further evidence that the long-run demand for money function has remained stable and predictable even after reunification.

[60] In a study of money demand stability in Europe over the period 1971-1989, Fase and Winder (1993) find the United Kingdom to have the least stable money demand function for each of the aggregates M1, M2 or M3 of any of the then eleven EC currencies (with the singular exception of greater M1 demand volatility in Greece).

[61] Lawson (1993, p. 80) and Goodhart (1997, p. 407). The Bank of England had previously made a rough estimate that the abolition of the 'corset' direct credit rationing scheme (which penalised banks' growth of interest-bearing deposits above a certain allowable rate) would raise £M3 by somewhat over 2 per cent; in reality, the contribution to money growth was nearly 5 per cent.

[62] Vega (1994) analyses the deterioration of ALP money demand stability in Spain, suggesting a structural break in 1989 related primarily to the lifting of restrictions on capital movements. Although incorporating foreign interest rates in the long-run ALP demand

function restores an appearance of stability, this also implies a reduced controllability, thereby bleakening prospects for a money targeting strategy.

[63] The study by Fase and Winder (1993) confirms that money demand stability in individual EC countries has generally been inversely related to the size of the country.

[64] There is a subtle distinction between credit ceilings as instruments towards achieving another intermediate money target (such as with the credit ceilings supporting the liquidity ratio targets in the period 1977-80) and credit ceilings as an intermediate monetary target in their own right: the strategic focus of the central bank switches from the liability side to the (domestic) asset side of the balance sheet. Hilbers (1998) discusses the changing design of the various credit controls in the Netherlands.

[65] The shift away from a dual strategy combining an exchange rate target, on the one hand, with a liquidity ratio or domestic money growth ceiling, on the other, and towards singular exchange rate targeting is explicitly acknowledged in the Nederlandsche Bank's Annual Report over 1991.

[66] A prime illustration of the detrimental effect of excessive changes in a money targeting framework is provided by the United Kingdom's announcement of novel targets for M0 in 1984. After having recently targeted £M3, M1 and PSL2, the new target failed to have a real impact. In the words of the then Chancellor Lawson (1993, p. 457): "The financial markets [were] inclined to believe that any departure from the original rules was politically expedient and therefore economically unsound. ... In time it became clear that the real problem with M0 was that it lacked street credibility. ... The achievement of the M0 target – or even its undershooting – had no great effect on inflationary expectations." The irony is that M0 subsequently proved to be more reliable and stable than any other aggregate targeted in Europe (and probably the world).

[67] Fase and Winder (1993) present evidence on the greater stability of broad aggregates for each of the EC member countries. Monticelli and Strauss-Kahn (1992) discuss the preference for broad aggregates in Europe.

6 THE EVOLUTION OF EXCHANGE RATE TARGETING

6.1 Exchange rate targeting under the European Monetary System, 1979-1998

6.1.1 The rise of regional exchange rate targeting

Exchange rate targeting had fallen out of favour in the first half of the 1970s. The collapse of Bretton Woods signalled a global shift towards greater exchange rate flexibility and the European response in the form of the 'snake' common margins agreement did not offer a broadly acceptable alternative. Indeed, as participation dwindled, the snake symbolised how limited the common ground was on the strategic objectives of monetary policy and how pitifully little was left of Europe's collective monetary ambitions. But, despite its shortcomings, the snake did constitute a nucleus of monetary stability in Europe. It was around this nucleus that new monetary initiatives could be built once greater like-mindedness in monetary policy objectives returned.

The support for such initiatives increased as dissatisfaction with the monetary state of affairs grew. This dissatisfaction stemmed from a variety of sources.[1] First, the consequences of floating exchange rates became increasingly clear. While Bretton Woods had led many economists to believe that exchange rates would stay closer to their real equilibrium level when not hindered by monetary authorities' resistance to realignments, practical experience refuted this view. It became manifest that, once left to the markets, foreign exchange rates tended to fluctuate substantially more relative to shifts in fundamentals. Second, the use of the exchange rate as an adjustment instrument towards both a higher level of output and a stronger external position was increasingly challenged as the cost in terms of inflation became more evident. In particular, the sharp devaluations in 1976 of many European currencies had led to price developments that were proving difficult to control in these countries. As containing inflation climbed up the list of economic policy priorities, greater importance was attached to stabilising the nominal exchange rate. In fact, by 1977 the three large European countries outside the snake, France, Italy and the United Kingdom, had each embarked on stabilisation programs. More generally, increased inflation aversion serves to explain the (partly overlapping) rise of both exchange rate and money targets in Europe during this period. Third, notwithstanding the ability to offset imported inflation through exchange rate appreciation, the countries with strong currencies were concerned that excessive appreciation would undermine progress towards economic recovery. This was particularly true of Germany, where inflation had returned to acceptable levels and the Bundesbank intervened to the tune of DM 11 billion in the last quarter of 1977 to keep the Deutsche mark down.[2] Fourth, there was discontent with the effects of US dollar instability on intra-European exchange rate relations both outside and within the snake. In the latter context, during the two years through October 1978, dollar weakness strained the system, as reflected in five realignments and the withdrawal of Sweden. Finally, at a deeper level, the increasing divergence of nominal economic developments in Europe was weighing heavily on the continent's erstwhile alluring monetary aspirations. Indeed, from a political perspective, monetary co-operation was seen as a vehicle to reinvigorate the stagnating process of European integration. This catalysed the search for a common recipe.

To be acceptable, a joint framework for exchange rate targeting strategies needed to be cast in a mould that accommodated the concerns of the different countries. These concerns were primarily rooted in past experiences with asymmetry, which had undermined the viability of exchange rate targeting under both Bretton Woods and the snake. But the concerns about asymmetry were diametrically opposed. On the one hand, Germany – broadly supported by Denmark and the Netherlands – was bent on avoiding the asymmetry of Bretton Woods, when a rigid exchange rate peg to an inflating currency effectively forced participants to import price increases. More specifically, this concern reflected the fear that parity adjustments would be unduly resisted and that asymmetric policy discipline would entail excessive intervention obligations to support weaker currencies, thereby loosening the Bundesbank's control over the domestic money supply. On the other hand, the larger deficit countries – especially France, but also Italy and the United Kingdom – were adamant to avoid the asymmetry of the snake, when Germany's restrictive monetary policy effectively obliged other central banks in the system to adopt a disinflationary bias. This form of asymmetry, implying the risk of an overly tight monetary policy stance in countries with weaker currencies, subsequently received the most attention. To resolve these opposite concerns, the successor arrangement to the snake had to be more symmetric in design, but also to include a simple realignment safety valve.

The symmetric design of the European Monetary System

In terms of design, the European Monetary System (EMS) was indeed created with an appearance of symmetry.[3] Together with the prevalence of capital controls, this would attenuate one of the major economic costs of the strategy of exchange rate targeting – the loss of monetary policy independence. Politically, it would allow countries with diverging monetary policy track records to participate (at least seemingly) on an equal footing. This semblance of symmetry was embodied in several features:

- First, exchange rate realignments were explicitly made joint decisions, subject to mutual agreement between all participating countries. This co-operative element went significantly further than the limited, essentially unilateral consultation procedures under both Bretton Woods and the snake.
- Second, the intra-EMS exchange rates were not only defined in terms of fixed bilateral limits, but also against a common divergence indicator. Unlike the bilateral limits, the indicator thresholds did not entail an obligation to intervene. Rather, they warned when the exchange rate of a currency diverged markedly from the weighted average of the others, thereby objectively signalling the country that should consider adjusting its policies. This could just as well be a surplus as a deficit country. Inaction by this country would trigger joint consultations.
- Third, a novel common currency, the ECU, was placed at the centre of the system, thereby giving it a supranational, European look. The ECU served as a common denominator for the exchange rate parities, the divergence indicator, and the operations under the intervention and credit facilities, as well as being a new reserve asset and settlement vehicle for the EC central banks.
- Fourth, unlimited and automatic credit lines were opened for support at the fluctuation margins, where central banks of both weak and strong currencies were obliged to intervene. To this end, a 'Very Short-Term Financing Facility' (VSTF) was set up that converted related claims and liabilities into ECUs and channelled these through a common fund. Interest on these balances was determined as the average of the official discount rates of all EC central banks weighted by their shares in the ECU basket.[4] Settlement was due within 45 days of the end of the month during which the intervention had taken place, with the option of three months' automatic extension (subject to a ceiling) and a possible further three months deferral (subject to the agreement of the creditors). This intervention support scheme was considerably more extensive – and was thus viewed as more credible – than that under the snake.
- Fifth, other financing arrangements were substantially expanded to alleviate the adjustment burden on weaker currencies. In particular, the existing short- and medium-term credit facilities were expanded by a factor of nearly three.[5] Moreover, a system of resource transfers was set up to facilitate the convergence of economic policies in the poorer

countries, with access limited to participants in the exchange rate mechanism. This especially aimed to smooth participation for Italy and Ireland, the only initial recipients.[6]

Thus, in contrast with the design of Bretton Woods which was centred around the US dollar, the rules and obligations of the EMS treated all participants alike and did not contain a formal element of asymmetry. And, although the EMS inherited a host of features from the snake, including fixed but adjustable bilateral exchange rate parities and intervention financing at the limits of a narrow ± 2.25 per cent fluctuation band (with the exception of a novel and transitional ± 6 per cent band for Italy), it had more elaborate and refined technical features, as well as a more acceptable political framework. This latter aspect is evidenced by the fact that the system's Exchange Rate Mechanism (ERM) encompassed three of the four largest EC countries as well as all the other member states.

6.1.2 The evolution of the European Monetary System

Over the course of the past 25 years, while the rest of the world was characterised by a tendency towards greater exchange rate flexibility, European countries have placed increasing emphasis on exchange rate fixity. During this period, the EMS has embodied the desire for regional exchange rate stability and has provided standard modalities for a strategy of exchange rate targeting. This system, it is widely accepted, has been broadly successful in the objective of creating a zone of monetary stability in Europe. In particular, there is firm evidence that the EMS has contributed to greater exchange rate stability between participating countries, both in nominal and real terms, and that this has not been achieved at the cost of greater short-term interest rate variability. Moreover, at a general level, it appears that the EMS has facilitated the convergence process to low inflation in participating countries.[7]

However, the contribution of the EMS to the coherence of policies in and amongst its member states has differed markedly over the course of time. Indeed, the system has experienced a changeful history, with varying implications for the strategy choice of exchange rate targeting. In broad terms, four phases can be distinguished: (i) from the system's inception until the beginning of Spring 1983, (ii) from Spring 1983 until the beginning of 1987; (iii) from early 1987 until mid-1992; and (iv) from mid-1992 until the start of EMU in 1999.[8]

The EMS during 1979-83: Learning by not doing

The EMS had a turbulent start. Notwithstanding that the system's creation stemmed from the desire for greater exchange rate stability in Europe, there were no less than seven exchange rate realignments during the first four years (see Chart 6). Participants essentially wanted the outcome of exchange rate stability but were not willing to do much in terms of domestic financial policies to achieve it. Different domestic policy reactions to the second oil crisis and, more fundamentally, different policy priorities gave rise to recurrent exchange market strains. In fact, economic developments diverged relatively strongly within the ERM: the differences in general government budget balances, external current account positions, wage increases and consumer price developments were larger within the ERM than amongst other industrialised countries.[9] This divergence was reflected in an increasing size and greater frequency of realignments in the course of this first phase.

Participation in the ERM hardly implied a monetary policy strategy of exchange rate targeting during the initial years of the system, since many countries continued to prioritise domestic policy objectives. This was notably illustrated by the shift to expansionary policies in France in 1981 (after the election of a socialist government) at the same time as Germany tightened policies to contain its current account deficit and rising inflationary pressures. During this period, evidence mounted that expansionary policies were translating into unacceptably high inflation, particularly in France, Ireland, and Italy, and that inconsistent policies in the partner countries were keeping the coveted exchange rate stability out of reach – in other words, that the benefits of exchange rate targeting could not be reaped without bearing the costs. In a nutshell, this was a phase of 'learning by not doing'.

Moreover, the first phase of the EMS brought home the lesson that intervention policy could be used to buy time when exchange rate tensions mounted, but that market pressures could not be durably resisted unless strong domestic policy measures were taken to correct the underlying cause of imbalances. This lesson was also drawn by the G-7 Working Group on Exchange Market Intervention, which concluded in 1983 that intervention – especially when sterilised in monetary operations – did not seem to be effective in countering significant market pressure unless supported by domestic policy adjustments.[10]

Analysis of the evolution of the EMS during this period indicates that the realignment decisions took on an increasingly collective character and that this strengthened the disciplinary impact of the exchange rate commitments.[11] Given the shared aim of avoiding competitive devaluations

Chart 6: The European Monetary System, 1979 - 1998 [1]

Year	Date	Germany	France	Netherlands	Belgium	Denmark	Ireland	Italy	Spain	UK	Portugal	Austria	Finland	Greece
1979	13-03	=	=	=	=	=	=	=						
	24-09	+2				-2.9								
	30-11					-4.8								
1981	23-03							-6						
	05-10	+5½	-3	+5½				-3						
1982	22-02				-8½	-3								
	14-06	+4¼	-5¾	+4¼				-2¾						
1983	21-03	+5½	-2½	+3½	+1½	+2½	-3½	-2½						
1985	22-07	+2	+2	+2	+2	+2	+2	-6						
1986	07-04	+3	-3	+3	+1	+1								
	04-08						-8							
1987	12-01	+3		+3	+2									
1989	19-06								=					
1990	08-01[2]							-3¾						
	08-10									=				
1992	06-04										=			
	14-09	+3½	+3½	+3½	+3½	+3½	+3½	-3½	+3½	+3½	+3½			
	17-09							≠	-5	╪				
	23-11								-6		-6			
1993	01-02						-10							
	14-05								-8		-6½			
	02-08[3]													
1995	09-01											=		
	06-03								-7		-3½			
1996	14-10												=	
	25-11							=						
1998	16-03						+3							=
1999	01-01	EMU and ERM-II become operational												

: ± 2.25% fluctuation margins.

: ± 6% fluctuation margins.

: ± 15% fluctuation margins.

[1] Chronology of the European Monetary System indicating the accessions to (=), withdrawals from (╪), and suspension of commitments under (≠) the Exchange Rate Mechanism, as well as the percentage revaluations (+) and devaluations (-).

[2] When Italy switched from the broad (±6%) to the narrow (±2.25%) fluctuation margins, the lower intervention limits remained unchanged, implying a 3.75% devaluation.

[3] On 23 August 1993 the general ERM margins were widened to ± 15%, except for Germany and The Netherlands, which formally agreed (outside ERM) to maintain a ± 2.25% margin for their bilateral exchange rate.

and fostering nominal convergence, the joint nature of the decision-making process implied that individual devaluation requests were no longer automatically accommodated. In practice, such requests were increasingly judged in the context of the corrective domestic policy measures proposed together with the realignment.[12] Moreover, a tendency emerged not to compensate fully for cumulated past inflation differentials. As a result, the countries with the highest inflation, Italy and Ireland, and to a lesser extent also France, experienced a loss of competitiveness during 1979-83.

The changed nature of exchange rate targeting under the EMS came to the surface during the realignments of February 1982 and March 1983. On the occasion of the former realignment, the two countries involved – Belgium and Denmark – had to settle for a significantly smaller devaluation than what they initially requested.[13] But the breakthrough came with the latter realignment, which was the most comprehensive parity grid adjustment to date (all but one official bilateral exchange rate were changed) and powerfully established the link between realignment and domestic policy adjustment. France, in particular, abandoned its expansionary policy creed and announced a major package of restrictive measures in the budgetary and monetary field, thereby signalling a fundamental reorientation towards price and exchange rate stability.[14]

The EMS during 1983-87: Work in progress

The second phase from Spring 1983 until early 1987 was a period of tightened exchange rate commitments generally based on commensurate policy adjustments. During this phase, the EMS was characterised as a disciplinary device in the more inflation-prone members, on the one hand constraining their policy discretion, on the other enhancing their anti-inflation credibility. In fact, the system entered a virtuous cycle, as domestic policy adjustments aimed at underpinning the exchange rate commitments led to falling inflation and interest rates, as well as to declining differentials. By way of illustration, average inflation in the ERM countries was brought down from almost 11 per cent in 1979-82 to 2 per cent in 1987, while the standard deviation was reduced from 5 percentage points to 2 per cent in the same period. The greater policy efforts of this second period were also apparent in the pattern of disinflation relative to other industrialised countries: while disinflation was slower in the EMS countries than in the non-EMS (OECD) countries during 1980-83, it was significantly faster thereafter, arriving at a lower inflation level in 1986.[15] However, although there were some improvements in fiscal policy, it was notably monetary policy that became more consistent amongst ERM countries.[16]

This greater monetary policy consistency reflected an increasing focus of central banks' policies (including especially intramarginal intervention) on maintaining a stable exchange rate vis-à-vis Germany. Thus, notwithstanding the semblance of symmetry in the EMS' design, the Deutsche mark emerged as the system's anchor. Evidence on foreign exchange intervention, sterilisation coefficients and interest rate linkages increasingly indicated that monetary policy in Germany was having a strong influence on that in the other ERM countries, with hardly any influence in the opposite direction.[17] In practice, the divergence indicator proved technically deficient, as currencies commonly reached their intervention limits without even crossing the divergence threshold. But, fundamentally, countries willingly oriented their policies at exchange rate stability vis-à-vis Germany in order to buttress their disinflationary efforts with a firm nominal anchor. After all, the Deutsche mark was the only currency that had at no time devalued against any other currency in the EMS or, for that matter, in the snake. In this regard, the issue of asymmetry during this phase was not the concern that the system allowed one country to set monetary policy in light of the business cycle of its own real economy, with other countries being forced to adjust regardless of their cycle. Rather, the origin of asymmetry was primarily a difference in policy discipline and credibility, whereby the anchor country set a standard which the system subsequently facilitated the other countries to live up to.

Given improvements in nominal convergence, realignments became less frequent (on average one a year) and relatively smaller. The practice of agreeing on realignments that did not fully compensatefor inflation differentials was consistently pursued during this phase, reflecting the view of the exchange rate as a disciplinary instrument to foster stability rather than as an adjustment instrument for external expansion and output growth. Significantly, the greater exchange rate calm was achieved despite major dollar instability, as marked by the September 1985 New York Plaza agreement seeking to guide the dollar downwards in an orderly fashion. In the past, especially during the first EMS phase, a declining dollar had customarily spurred disproportionately large capital flows into Deutsche marks, thus causing severe tensions within the system.

Of more than symbolic importance for the monetary strategy choice, this phase saw a major advance in the common ambitions of the EC, especially through the February 1986 signing of the Single European Act. The Act spelt out the goal of achieving a unified market with unrestricted flows of goods, services, labour and capital by end 1992 and reaffirmed the aim to strengthen monetary co-operation towards establishing EMU. From the exchange rate targeting perspective this was relevant on two accounts. On the one hand, the fair competition and allocative-efficiency benefits of deeper trade integration increased the European penchant towards exchange rate stability. Indeed, the renewed commitment to monetary integration foreshadowed a strengthening of monetary policy co-ordination. Once this strengthening became credible – which it initially certainly was not – exchange rate stability would be easier to maintain. On the other hand, the commitment to free capital flows implied relinquishing an instrument that could otherwise make such stability easier to achieve. In effect, this liberalisation would further tighten the constraint on domestic economic policies and would make performance more dependent on policy credibility in the markets.

In this latter context, the increased power of the financial markets came to the fore during the last realignment of this period, in March 1987, which marked a second turning point in the evolution of exchange rate targeting under the EMS. Contrary to all previous parity adjustments, this relatively small realignment was precipitated by market forces rather than by a need to adjust for competitiveness difficulties. This was the official view at the time, but was subsequently validated when market fears of a resumption in French inflation – which together with dollar weakness had been a prime cause of the overwhelming speculative flows – did not materialise.[18] The main lesson of the second phase was clear: with well-developed financial markets and without capital controls, credibility and well-attuned monetary policies became dominant factors in sustaining an exchange rate target. In practical terms, this lesson was translated into a concerted EC effort to find ways to strengthen the operational resilience, and therewith the credibility, of exchange rate targeting in the EMS framework.

The EMS during 1987-92: Too good to be true

The third phase stretched from early 1987 until mid-1992 and represented the heydays of exchange rate targeting in Europe. For more than five years, no realignment took place in the standard narrow band of the EMS.[19] And the success was contagious: the European zone of exchange rate stability was broadened by the decisions of Finland, Norway and Sweden unilaterally to peg their currencies to the ECU.[20] During the initial years of this phase, most ERM countries that did not yet have fully liberalised capital flows – especially Denmark, France and Italy – dismantled remaining controls, thereby making the sustainability of their exchange rate targets even more dependent on the confidence of financial markets. At the same time, however, the institutional and political deepening of European integration bolstered these markets' confidence in the capacity and will of monetary authorities to uphold their exchange rate commitments. To the extent that this allowed the achievement of exchange rate stability without a corresponding convergence in underlying economic developments, the targeting success was too good to be true. And, thus, too good to last.

The deepening European integration during this phase was achieved primarily in the monetary field. A first important landmark was the Basle-Nyborg agreement of September 1987, representing the official response to the increased clout of the financial markets.[21] This agreement refined the modalities of exchange rate targeting in the EMS in a number of ways. In particular, participants agreed: (i) to use the full width of the fluctuation band more flexibly, (ii) to use interest rates more aggressively to defend exchange rates near the intervention limits; (iii) to reduce the size and frequency of realignments; (iv) to allow recourse to the VSTF for the financing of intramarginal intervention; (v) to expand the borrowing limits as well as the payback periods under the VSTF; and (vi) to intensify the surveillance of the system. In effect, these changes sought to make speculation against a currency more costly (in terms of foregone interest), less profitable (since a realignment that was smaller than the system's bandwidth could leave a market exchange rate largely unchanged), more risky (given the prospect of exchange rate appreciation within the band once a speculative attack was fended off) and less likely to succeed (given the strengthening of central banks' instruments and surveillance). As a whole, the Basle-Nyborg package contributed significantly to the credibility of the system's exchange rate targets, particularly after it had survived the test of exchange market turmoil in the wake of the October 1987 stock market crash.

Several milestones were subsequently passed on the road to EMU, each of which further boosted market expectations of EMS exchange rate stability. The first of these was the completion of the Delors Report in April 1989, providing an official blueprint for a three-staged route to EMU that would culminate in an irrevocable fixing of the exchange rate parities and elimination of the fluctuation margins. This was followed by a series of steps in the development of EMU: the Delors Report was formally accepted as a basis for further preparatory work on EMU in June 1989; the first stage of EMU entered into force in July 1990; the Intergovernmental Conferences (IGC) on EMU and political union were launched in December 1990; and, finally, the Treaty on European Union was signed in Maastricht in the small hours of 11 December 1991, stipulating the creation of a European Central Bank and of a single European currency by 1 January 1999 at the latest. Significantly, the Treaty even identified exchange rate stability within the "normal" fluctuations margins of the ERM "without severe tensions for at least two years" as a convergence criterion for participation in EMU.

As a result of these political advances, exchange rate stability came to be built on the anticipation of monetary union and of limited devaluation risk, rather than on actual policy convergence. In this respect, the EMS took on excessive – or undeserved – credibility during this phase, as differentials in inflation and in external and fiscal deficits persisted, and in several cases even increased, between the traditional hard core ERM countries and the other participants. In effect, the greater monetary interdependence in the ERM was paradoxically limiting the scope for tight interest rate policies in those countries with the largest imbalances. For instance, while inflation was highest in Italy and ERM-newcomer Spain, the lira and peseta fluctuated near or at their upper limits during much of 1989-91, thereby precluding interest rate increases. Similarly, after strengthening on the basis of anticipated ERM membership, the Portuguese escudo directly moved towards its upper limit the moment it finally joined in 1992. The most poignant illustration of the perverse impact of exchange rate targeting in the ERM is provided by the United Kingdom's lowering of interest rates, despite a much higher inflation rate, immediately upon entry in October 1990. The credibility enhancing impact of ERM membership was therefore employed to achieve a nominal convergence in interest rates rather than in price developments. Ironically, monetary easing in a high-inflation country was precisely the crux of the 'Walters Critique' that had motivated the UK Government's long-standing resistance to ERM entry.[22] Overall, exchange rate targeting was not imposing discipline in these countries, but was spurring capital inflows in excess of current account deficits while also allowing interest rate levels that stimulated domestic demand.[23] In short, during this phase the nature of exchange rate targeting in the ERM changed dramatically, prompting speak of a 'New EMS'.[24]

But this was only half the problem of the increased monetary interdependence in the ERM during this in appearance successful phase. The other half lay with asymmetry that originated in Germany, where public and private spending had soared in the wake of unification. This was a different type of asymmetry, stemming from a disequilibrium in the anchor country and heavily straining those countries that had their monetary policy tied to this anchor. While a fiscal tightening through substantial tax increases would have been a first best solution to address emerging imbalances and sustain ERM stability, Chancellor Kohl had pledged not to do so during the election campaign. As a consequence, Germany's real exchange rate needed to appreciate in order to channel part of the domestic demand expansion abroad. Nominal Deutsche mark appreciation may then have been a second best solution, but this was initially ruled out by EMS partner countries, where the Deutsche mark-peg had come to symbolise policy credibility and the momentum towards EMU. By default, the real appreciation had to come about through relatively higher inflation in Germany. And, given Bundesbank resistance to price increases (although inflation was allowed to rise to just over 5 per cent in 1992), this implied inordinate disinflationary pressure on the other EMS countries.[25]

In sum, notwithstanding persistent economic divergence due to insufficiently restrictive policies in the traditional deficit economies, as well as an excessively tight monetary stance stemming from a highly unbalanced policy mix in the anchor country, the EMS functioned as a de facto fixed exchange rate system during this period, glued together by an overly sanguine market sentiment. Such providence is not conducive to judicious policy-making; the need for policy discipline would return with a vengeance.

The EMS during 1992-98: The search for stability

The combined tensions came to a head in the summer of 1992 and reverberated for about a year until the system found a new balance under adjusted modalities. The proximate cause of the eruption was the rejection of the Maastricht Treaty in the Danish referendum of 2 June 1992. This raised wide-ranging doubts about the institutional and political viability of EMU and thus shifted markets' focus back to economics. As underlying imbalances surfaced, the need for higher interest rates to compensate for an increased perceived exchange rate risk exacerbated the inconsistency between domestic interest rate requirements and those needed to keep up with the Deutsche mark. In the course of the following year, the United Kingdom left the ERM, Italy suspended its participation, five realignments took place, capital controls were temporarily reintroduced in Ireland, Portugal and Spain, and the unilateral ECU-pegs of Finland, Norway and Sweden all foundered.[26] At the same time, the system itself experienced an increased volatility of exchange rates and interest rates, and a widening of interest and inflation differentials.

The period of strain culminated in the more existential EMS crisis of August 1993. The French economy was finding German interest rate levels increasingly hard to bear and French officials fuelled market scepticism about the sustainability of the exchange rate link by calling for lower interest rates in Germany and pre-emptively reducing their own short-term rates beneath those for the Deutsche mark. At this point, the crisis could hardly be resolved within the existing EMS framework. The option of a realignment was essentially contrary to the spirit of the EMS, as it would have involved adjusting currencies against the grain of fundamentals: France would have devalued against Germany despite a lower inflation, smaller budget deficit and stronger external current account. An alternative would have been to float only the Deutsche mark, which was indeed the position taken by France during the crisis. But this was unacceptable to the Netherlands, which saw no reason to break its longstanding Deutsche mark-peg. And if the Netherlands stayed the course, so would countries like Belgium and Denmark, thereby eroding the effectiveness of the whole exercise. Other alternatives such as reintroducing widespread capital controls or temporarily suspending the ERM were basically inconsistent with the achievements of the single market and progress towards EMU. This left the option of broadening the fluctuation margins to such a width that the intervention guarantees would no longer elicit any further speculative attacks.

The crises of 1992-93 underscored several truths about exchange rate targeting, all of which were well-known beforehand but had been insufficiently taken to heart. First, that an exchange rate target in the context of a liberalised capital account leaves virtually no scope for independent monetary policy-making. Accordingly, other policy instruments must be used to ensure both sufficient economic convergence and offsetting forces in the case of asymmetric shocks. And optimal currency area characteristics matter. Second, that the sustainability of an exchange rate target is crucially determined by its credibility in financial markets, implying that monetary policy actions and external communication about monetary policy objectives must readily accept the limitations ensuing from the exchange rate commitment. In this regard, the speculative attack on the French franc could not be classified as genuinely 'self-fulfilling' to the extent that the market pressures were elicited by authorities' actions and communications. And, third, that if these principles are not respected, financial flows are likely to become highly disruptive, and unpredictably so. These truths were powerfully evidenced by those countries – notably Austria and the Netherlands – whose exchange rate targets weathered the storm unscathed. In these countries, optimal currency area considerations were favourable, the exchange rate link to the Deutsche mark had been relatively tight, and external communication about monetary policy had consistently acknowledged prioritisation of the exchange rate target. However, as experience testified, these preconditions were too demanding for most European countries. In part this reflected a half-hearted acceptance of Germany's anchor role and, especially in France, a continuous struggle for monetary leadership. But it was also because a different – less acceptable – type of asymmetry had taken over the system. Whereas, in previous phases, the asymmetry had mainly stemmed from inadequate policy discipline in the weaker countries, in the fourth phase policy discipline was more widespread while the anchor was slipping.

The general widening of the fluctuation bands to ± 15 per cent constituted the switch to a less demanding form of exchange rate targeting in Europe and thereby marked the third turning point in the evolution of the ERM.[27] From then on, exchange rate targeting in the EMS formally became much looser and intervention obligations at the margin no longer served to keep exchange rates within a narrow band or, as you will, to trigger speculative attacks. In effect, by making exchange rate commitments less rigid and allowing for greater fluctuations, exchange rate risk became more two-sided and the scope for speculative onslaughts was greatly reduced. The crucial change was that, although markets could now drive exchange rates further down from their central parities, a subsequent rebound could result in an equally large appreciation (which would not be the case if the parity were devalued), wiping out any previous speculative gains.

But, on the downside, the nominal anchor provided by the exchange rate was made less secure and there was a genuine risk that convergence efforts would lose their focal point. In fact, an additional nominal anchor was adopted by several countries that maintained or reinstated EMS exchange rate targeting in the aftermath of the crises: Spain complemented its exchange rate target with an overriding inflation target, Portugal announced reference values for inflation alongside its exchange rate commitment, Finland only reverted to exchange rate targeting in the context of a firmly established inflation targeting framework, and Italy similarly returned to the ERM but combined this with increased emphasis on the inflation outlook, notably through an annual announcement by the Governor of the inflation rate he considered achievable in the current year.

Indeed, the very wide fluctuation margins clearly changed the character of exchange rate targeting in the EMS. Whereas previously the desire to avoid reserve losses through intervention or, worse, currency devaluation, had provided incentives to tailor domestic policies towards sustaining the exchange rate target, this disciplinary influence largely disappeared with up to 60 per cent fluctuation scope (that is, ± 15 per cent for each of the two currencies determining the exchange rate). In practice, however, the disciplinary spell was taken on by another device: the central rates. As prospective EMU members proceeded towards the definite, irreversible locking of their currencies, central rates became focal points for policy setting. Given the 'no devaluation' criterion in the Treaty, as well as the desire to sustain exchange rate stability and nominal convergence in the run-up to EMU, EMS central banks prevented large exchange rate deviations from central rates (with the exception of the Irish central bank which saw its currency pulled vigorously upwards in the wake of sterling appreciation). As a result, contrary to most expectations, monetary and exchange rate policies were not individually loosened and exchange rates soon returned to within what would otherwise still have been the narrow band.

During the rest of this phase, intense domestic policy adjustment efforts contributed to impressive declines and reduced differentials in inflation, and thus to convergence in monetary policy needs and improved prospects for sustainable exchange rate stability within the EMS. Towards the end of this stage, exchange rate stability between prospective EMU members was further buttressed by the preannouncement of bilateral conversion rates into the Euro. In light of the convergence achievements and the staunch political will to deliver on EMU, the preannouncement was judged credible by the markets and exchange rates stabilised around their conversion rates – in line with prevailing, declining interest rate differentials.

6.2 The hardening of exchange rate targets in individual countries, 1975-1998

Over the past quarter of a century, each current member of the EU has at some time or other adopted a monetary policy strategy of exchange rate targeting, although the implicit anchor country (Germany) did so with an additional degree of freedom. In a number of cases, notably Austria, Belgium (and by implication Luxembourg) and effectively also Denmark, this strategy has been exclusively and consistently pursued during this period. From a broad perspective, exchange rate targets hardened in virtually all EU countries from the 1980s on, even though the modalities of policy implementation (particularly within the EMS) changed considerably. And, of course, during the final years in the run-up to EMU, exchange rate targeting effectively became the dominant strategy in all prospective euro area members.

While the EMS provided the basic framework for exchange rate targeting in Europe, the evolution of this strategy has actually differed widely from country to country. In general, exchange rate policies in the smaller countries closest to Germany were the first to harden– in the sense of an exchange rate target that is tightly pursued and flanked by a compatible policy mix. In the larger countries as well as the smaller countries further from the geographical centre of the Union, exchange rate policies also hardened over the course of the years, but encountered recurrent difficulties, primarily because asymmetric economic developments led domestic monetary policy needs to diverge relatively strongly and because the disciplinary policy standard imposed by external capital flows proved highly erratic and unpredictable. Although the reputation of exchange rate targeting has been tarnished by the various EMS crises, it is testimony to the potential strength of this strategy that seven of the eleven countries (Austria, Belgium, Denmark, France, Germany, Luxembourg and the Netherlands) entering EMU did so on the basis of nominal exchange rate targets that had been set twelve or more years earlier. A review of the different paths taken by EU countries during the hardening of their exchange rate targets illustrates how, in practice, the success of this strategy depends on a myriad of different conditions.

Germany

Notwithstanding the cosmetics providing the EMS with an appearance of symmetry, Germany soon emerged as the anchor country in Europe. The theoretical mechanics that determined this outcome are straightforward. Given a monetary policy that was relatively more restrictive (that is, in terms of the balance of payments) in Germany than in the other countries in the system, these countries could only uphold their exchange rate commitment by selling external reserves (the stock of which is finite, even if expandable through borrowing) or otherwise tightening policy relative to Germany. More practically, Germany's emergence as the anchor country was a logical consequence of its heavy weight in the European economy in combination with an unrivalled domestic price inflation since September 1949 – the last time the Deutsche mark had been officially devalued against any other major currency. An early signal of Germany's hegemony in the EMS was given barely half a year after the system's inception when, on the occasion of the first realignment, the Deutsche mark was revalued vis-à-vis every other currency in the system. This established a constant feature in the evolution of the EMS, just as it had been during the snake: the Deutsche mark was the currency to keep up with. Barring the exceptional revaluation of the Irish punt in 1998 (reflecting a much larger appreciation of the pound sterling outside the ERM), no currency was ever revalued against the Deutsche mark during the system's 19 realignments in 20 years.

As the Nth member in a system with N-1 exchange rates, Germany's anchor role provided it with the freedom of participating in an exchange rate targeting agreement while actually targeting money and pursuing a largely independent monetary policy. In fact, the Bundesbank originally had serious misgivings about participating in the EMS out of fear that the obligation to provide undue support for weaker currencies would undermine its money supply control. This is evidenced by the famous 'Emminger letter' in which the Bundesbank president agreed with the Government in 1978 that mandatory interventions at the EMS margins could be temporarily suspended if they began to threaten domestic monetary stability. More subtly, after four unsatisfactory years of large money target overruns and difficulties in credibly communicating monetary policy to the public, the Bundesbank Council nonetheless decided to maintain money targets in late 1978 primarily to underline the independent character of Germany's monetary policy-making in the EMS.[28]

But this is not to say that Germany's monetary policy has been implemented oblivious of exchange rate developments. In practice, the money targets have been pursued flexibly and the Bundesbank has been willing, from time to time, to accord considerable priority to external considerations. This was explicitly the case in the period 1979-83 when the

Bundesbank adopted the custom of announcing relatively wide money target ranges and specifying at mid-year, mainly on the basis of exchange rate developments, which part of the range it was actually aiming for. Of course, the relevant exchange rate developments included those outside the EMS, but these were usually consistent with the interests of the other EMS members – for example, a lower dollar was typically associated with downward pressure on the weaker EMS currencies, and both developments allowed Germany to aim for the looser part of its money target range. Indeed, although the Bundesbank generally sterilises foreign exchange intervention fully in the short run, there is evidence that this is often not the case in the long run, particularly if the Deutsche mark is either strong or weak against both the EMS currencies and the dollar.[29] The substantive money target breaches in 1992-93, following massive foreign exchange intervention in the context of the successive EMS exchange rate crises, further testifies to the weight at times attached to exchange rate developments.

Austria

The hardening of exchange rate targeting strategies in Europe was a gradual and uneven process, encompassing two decades and culminating in the irreversible locking of exchange rates in EMU. The first country where a hardening occurred is *Austria*, which deliberately used the exchange rate as an instrument to trigger wage and price discipline. Following the collapse of Bretton Woods, Austria had pioneered exchange rate targeting with a currency basket, but as the composition of this basket was not published and was frequently adjusted, it failed to provide a clear policy compass. Besides this, Austria had also shadowed the snake during 1974-76, but this experience had encountered difficulties on account of the devaluations of many snake currencies and the Austrian wish to mitigate inflationary pressures by keeping up with the Deutsche mark. In the event, when a widening of the fluctuation margins (to ± 4.5 per cent) proved insufficient to accommodate the increasing Deutsche mark orientation, the snake was abandoned and Austria officially targeted only the somewhat opaque currency basket. However, within the context of this policy, the schilling was allowed to lose ground (about 3 per cent) against the Deutsche mark in 1977-78, including through an official devaluation (of 1 per cent) that was classified as a 'technical correction'.

The breakthrough for the hard currency strategy finally came in 1979. This occurred against the background of the second oil crisis, which threatened to increase the already large external deficit, unemployment and inflationary pressures. The policy views in Austria were split.[30] On the one hand, the Federal Chancellor, Mr. Kreisky, had previously urged currency devaluation and had received the support of industry. Internationally, the IMF and OECD also questioned the viability of Austria's exchange rate policy, suggesting a devaluation remedy. On the other hand, the finance minister, central bank and, surprisingly enough, trade unions advocated a hard currency strategy to contain the inflationary momentum and preserve real wages. Following the inception of the EMS, this group had rejected the option of pegging to the ECU on the grounds that this would unduly weaken the schilling – much in line with the Austrian experience of shadowing the snake. In the end, the latter view carried the day when the schilling was revalued in September 1979, at the outset of the annual wage bargaining rounds. Shortly thereafter, industry dropped its opposition to the hard currency strategy, additionally buttressing its credibility. Over the course of the subsequent year, notwithstanding the external deficit and competitiveness concerns, the schilling was nudged further upwards (by a cumulative 4.5 per cent) to establish unequivocally the determination of policy-makers to restore stability. Following this tough signal, the Deutsche mark-peg was durably tightened. Much later, upon joining the EU in 1995, Austria entered the ERM, but this had no influence on exchange rate policy which remained focused on the tight bilateral exchange rate vis-à-vis Germany. Overall, the Austrian schilling has not only been the most stable European currency against the Deutsche mark, but is also the only currency to have appreciated relative to Germany over the period 1975-1998 (see Table 8).

Besides its timeliness, Austria's unparalleled success with exchange rate targeting stands out for three reasons. First, the simplicity and communicability of the Deutsche mark-peg – in contrast with the previous snake and basket orientation – is viewed to have contributed substantively to monetary policy credibility. In fact, the central bank considers the support of an easy-to-understand nominal exchange rate rule for stable expectations as one of the main pillars of its exchange rate targeting success.[31] Indeed, credibility has not emanated from the institutional set-up or disciplinary influence of the EMS, since Austria was not a member. Second, the link to the Deutsche mark has been exceptionally tight and the exchange rate has only been allowed to fluctuate minimally – generally within a range of less than ± 0.1 per cent. This has required a permanent presence of the central bank in the foreign exchange market as well as relatively frequent adjustments in short-term interest rates. By these means, policy-makers have sought to reduce to a minimum any uncertainties about the future exchange rate. High and rising capital mobility have increased the importance attached to this objective.[32] The ease with which Austria's exchange rate link, despite being unilateral and informal, weathered the

Table 8: Exchange rates in Europe vis-à-vis Germany, 1975-1998 [1]

Country	Period	*Annualised rate of devaluation / depreciation*					Total Cumulative Depreciation
		Snake [1]	ERM [1]	Other official peg [1]	Floating [1]	Total [1]	
Austria	12/74 – 07/76	0.0					0.0
	07/76 – 01/95			0.0			- 1.0
	01/95 – 12/98		0.0				0.0
	12/74 – 12/98					0.0	- 1.0
Belgium / Luxembourg	12/74 – 03/79	0.9					5.5
	03/79 – 12/98		1.3				30.4
	12/74 – 12/98					1.3	37.6
Denmark	12/74 – 03/79	4.3					18.6
	03/79 – 12/98		1.6				36.2
	12/74 – 12/98					2.1	62.5
Finland	12/74 – 10/77				8.2		24.7
	10/77 – 08/92			1.3			50.0
	08/92 – 11/96				2.0		8.9
	11/96 – 12/98		0.0				1.3
	12/74 – 12/98					3.1	106.3
France	12/74 – 03/76	0.0					-0.2
	03/76 – 03/79				7.7		24.9
	03/79 – 12/98		1.8				45.8
	12/74 – 12/98					2.5	81.7
Greece	12/74 – 01/95				13.4		1152.0
	01/95 – 03/98			3.7			11.1
	03/98 – 12/98		0.0				-3.0
	12/74 – 12/98					11.5	1249.0
Ireland	12/74 – 03/79			0.0			47.2
	03/79 – 12/98		2.1				54.9
	12/74 – 12/98					3.5	127.9
Italy	12/74 – 03/79				12.8		66.9
	03/79 – 08/92		4.1				70.1
	08/92 – 11/96				6.2		29.0
	11/96 – 12/98		0.0				0.4
	12/74 – 12/98					5.6	267.3
Netherlands	12/74 – 03/79	0.9					3.9
	03/79 – 12/98		0.2				4.5
	12/74 – 12/98					0.3	8.5
Portugal	12/74 – 08/77				21.6		69.6
	08/77 – 04/92			1.8			384.5
	04/92 – 12/98		2.4				22.0
	12/74 – 12/98					10.1	902.8
Spain	12/74 – 06/89				7.2		173.4
	06/89 – 12/98		2.7				33.5
	12/74 – 12/98					5.5	265.1
Sweden	12/74 – 08/77	2.4					23.2
	08/77 – 10/92			2.3			80.4
	10/92 – 12/98				4.4		28.2
	12/74 – 12/98					4.6	185.0
United Kingdom	12/74 – 10/90				4.2		91.5
	10/90 – 08/92		0.0				5.8
	08/92 – 12/98				0.1		0.3
	12/74 – 12/98					3.1	103.2

[1] All figures reflect the devaluation/depreciation vis-à-vis the Deutsche mark, except the column 'Other official peg' which indicates the devaluation against the official exchange rate target. Moreover, while figures for the 'Snake', 'ERM' and 'Other official peg' relate to the average annualised rate of *official* devaluations, figures for the 'Floating' and 'Total' periods relate to the average annualised rate of *market* depreciation. On account of these differences in definition, figures across columns and through sub-periods do not necessarily add up.

turbulence of foreign exchange markets in 1992-93 validates this view. Third, broad-based support, particularly of labour organisations, made possible a co-ordinated supply-side response to underpin the hard currency policy. In fact, on the basis of real wage behaviour, the Deutsche mark-peg was basically credible from 1979 onwards. Essentially, the corporatist trade union structure allowed the macroeconomic benefits of the monetary strategy to be internalised in the centralised bargaining process. This facilitated the adjustment process to the various asymmetric shocks that afflicted the Austrian economy, including in particular the structural problems in the large nationalised industries sector. In this regard, Austria serves as an example of a country where optimal currency area prerequisites were not met when the rigid exchange rate target was first implemented, but where structural adjustments subsequently helped bring these prerequisites about and where real wage flexibility mitigated transitional difficulties.[33]

The Netherlands

Inside the EMS, the first country to harden its exchange rate strategy was the Netherlands. Previously, during the snake arrangement, the Netherlands' monetary policy had been conducted broadly in tandem with Germany and, in fact, the guilder had been the snake currency that had remained closest to the Deutsche mark. But it had not managed to keep up fully, losing about 8 per cent over the snake period. Moreover, while the exchange rate was a prime policy focus, international financial market restrictions provided scope for the central bank also to adopt intermediate money targets during 1977-1980. As the integration of international money and capital markets progressed, however, this dual strategy became increasingly difficult to sustain. In the late 1980s, while accepting that the money supply had been rendered largely endogenous, the central bank started to target its composition, seeking to keep the expansion of domestic credit in line with projected money demand growth. But the overriding priority already lay with the exchange rate: the targets sought to avoid an excessive credit expansion that could fuel sustained capital outflows and place downward pressure on the exchange rate. When it became clear that the assumptions on which this strategy was built – especially the predictability of money demand and the correlation between capital outflows and exchange rate pressures – did not hold, the central bank reverted to targeting just the exchange rate.

The hardening of the Netherlands' exchange rate policy took place in the EMS period and came about largely in two steps. The first marking point was the September 1979 ERM realignment, when the authorities were torn between the desire, on the one hand to keep up with the Deutsche mark and, on the other, to preserve fixed rates amongst the Benelux countries (notionally to avoid having to reintroduce border controls on account of diverging domestic agricultural prices within the Benelux customs union). During the commotion of the politicised realignment negotiations, Benelux solidarity prevailed, although not without serious misgivings on the Dutch side which had wanted to match the German revaluation. A central bank analysis of the realignment drew the conclusion that a future devaluation against the Deutsche mark was to be avoided by continuously keeping the guilder close to the anchor currency in the foreign exchange market. This would create the presumption during any – unpredictable – prospective realignment discussion that the two currencies should be adjusted in parallel.[34] The practical implication was that exchange rate policy would need to be much tighter than the bandwidth permitted under the EMS.

The second occasion that marked the definite adoption of a tight Deutsche mark-peg was the March 1983 realignment, when the government decided against the advice of the central bank not to duplicate the adjustment of the Deutsche mark – revaluing by 6 per cent against France and Italy, but lagging 2 per cent relative to Germany.[35] This move squandered part of the monetary policy credibility that had been carefully and consistently built up over the course of the previous three and a half years, during which the guilder had been kept close to and on average clearly above the official Deutsche mark parity. Following the devaluation, financial markets came to doubt the hardness of the exchange rate commitment and short-term interest rates had to be raised significantly above comparable rates in Germany. When it became increasingly conspicuous that it had been a mistake not to revalue fully with the Deutsche mark, the Government let it be known that this would not happen again.[36] In practice, it took more than five years for the short-term interest differential to disappear.

In many respects the evolution of the Netherlands' exchange rate strategy has thus been comparable to Austria's, especially the gradual tightening of the link to the Deutsche mark. Credibility was accumulated by consistently showing a readiness to increase short-term interest rates, if needed substantially, to defend the exchange rate anchor. There is also a marked similarity insofar as other economic developments adjusted to the external constraint and fostered the fulfilment of optimal currency area criteria with Germany.[37] Specifically, in the early 1980s, at roughly the same time as the exchange rate anchor hardened, a crucial trilateral agreement (between trade unions, employer organisations and the government) was reached to moderate wages and a process of budgetary consolidation was initiated.

But Dutch exchange rate targeting has characteristics of its own. In particular, the Netherlands has consistently sought to frame exchange rate policy in the context of multilateral and bilateral institutional arrangements – first the snake, then the EMS and finally, when the ERM bands were widened to ± 15 per cent, an exclusive German-Dutch agreement to maintain a mutual ± 2.25 per cent fluctuation band. Moreover, in practice, its exchange rate target has been pursued relatively rigidly (± 0.5 per cent). While perhaps not as tight as Austria (which could not, however, draw on any institutional credibility provided by multilateral or bilateral support arrangements), this target was considerably tighter than that of any other ERM participant and implied a different policy implementation than the Basle-Nyborg prescription of using the full scope of the fluctuation band. At the same time, there has been interaction between the institutional framework and the hardness of the exchange rate anchor. Just as the tightening of the Deutsche mark-peg was initially motivated by the aim to strengthen the Netherlands' position in the institutional realignment procedures, so the later institutional agreement with Germany sought to strengthen the resilience of the peg. The credibility of the Netherlands' monetary and exchange rate policy was amply demonstrated during the EMS crises of 1992-93 when the guilder appreciated to above its Deutsche mark central parity and interest rates even declined somewhat beneath those in Germany.

Belgium and Luxembourg

Exchange rate policy also started to harden relatively early on in Belgium and, by implication, in Luxembourg, which had transferred the responsibility for monetary and exchange rate policy to the National Bank of Belgium.[38] The hardening occurred consistently within the frameworks of the European exchange rate arrangements, the snake and ERM, in which Belgium participated without interruption from the outset. But the process was very gradual and actually took the better part of a decade. In particular, following the major devaluation of the Belgian franc in 1982, the objective of exchange rate policy as formulated at the time of realignments was progressively tightened from keeping the Belgian franc steady against the average for the EMS partner currencies to maintaining its value against the strongest EMS currencies.[39] The final step came in June 1990, when the Deutsche mark had weakened to the bottom of the EMS fluctuation band on account of concerns about the financing costs of German unification and thus, for once, was close to the Belgian franc. In this circumstance, the central bank seized its chance and publicly announced that henceforth it would undertake to fasten the Belgian franc to the most stable EMS currencies, in practice the Deutsche mark and the guilder. The announcement was initially credible and the Belgian currency rose smoothly to the top of the EMS band – where it had virtually never been before – in parallel with the Deutsche mark and the guilder. In fact, for more than a year, it was even the strongest currency in the system. But the novel Deutsche mark orientation foundered temporarily under the massive exchange market pressure of the mid-1993 ERM crisis when the bands were widened to ± 15 per cent. In contrast with the Netherlands, Belgium could not count on the support of a bilateral agreement with Germany to maintain a narrow ± 2.25 per cent band and it did not have an esteemed tradition of hard exchange rate targeting. By consequence, the Belgian franc slipped to a maximum of some 6 per cent beneath its Deutsche mark parity, before rejoining these currencies in early 1994 – a company it maintained until the start of EMU.

The initially limited ambition of the exchange rate strategy in Belgium has reflected a two-minded approach according to which the exchange rate was gleefully accepted as a stability anchor, on the one hand, while the constraints this imposed were consciously minimised and at times even ignored, on the other. The not fully committed nature of the exchange rate policy was apparent, for instance, in the Belgian policy of systematically keeping interest rates as low as possible within the confines of the external commitment, implying that the Belgian franc was virtually always the weakest currency in the system's narrow band, until the policy hardening in mid-1990. The desire to lessen the external constraint was also evident in the maintenance of two-tier exchange rate regulations stipulating that current account transactions had to be conducted at the official exchange rate – for which the snake and ERM provisions applied – while capital account transactions were settled at a freely floating exchange rate. The original aim of the system (established in the early 1950s) had been to liberalise financial transactions without jeopardising the level of official exchange reserves, under the assumption that the free market rate would find its own balance through small fluctuations. But in practice the deviations became very large in the early 1980s (reaching a yearly average of 7½ per cent in 1982, with daily deviations of up to 16 per cent), indicating that monetary policy was generally insufficiently tight to uphold the exchange rate anchor in absence of the restrictions underlying the dual exchange market. As exchange rate policy hardened, the deviations steadily became smaller (usually remaining beneath 1 per cent after 1984) until the dual market was finally abolished in March 1990, clearing the way for the tight linkage to the Deutsche mark.

The originally inadequate commitment to the exchange rate target was more visible in the implementation of macroeconomic policies that were clearly inconsistent with the external constraint. Wage policy was notably incompatible, especially indexation practices that limited the resilience of the external peg to adverse external disturbances. In this regard, it is illustrative that indexation mechanisms were only temporarily suspended – and not abolished – after inadequate real wage adjustment to the second oil shock had contributed to a balance of payments crisis. The indexation system has subsequently remained a liability for the exchange rate strategy, although safeguard measures have been taken by excluding energy prices and indirect taxes from the mechanisms and by allowing the government to suspend indexation in the face of competitiveness problems. The limited dedication to the external target was also blatantly evident in budgetary policy and particularly in the financing of the ballooning deficits. Specifically, the budget deficit was allowed to surge in the 1970s, reaching a high of 13 per cent of GDP in 1981, and was only brought back gradually to fall under the 3 per cent of GDP-mark in 1997. Detrimentally, the deficits were importantly covered through monetary financing, with one-half of the deficits over the period 1979-82 financed in this way.[40] While monetary financing was effectively reduced in the second half of the 1980s, advances to the government were only formally limited in January 1991 and abolished in July 1993.

Denmark

The evolution of Denmark's exchange rate policy was in many respects similar to Belgium's. In particular, exchange rate targeting has effectively been the only monetary strategy and, over the past quarter of a century, this strategy has consistently been conducted within the scaffolding of the European exchange rate arrangements.[41] Moreover, although Denmark had difficulty in living up to the discipline of the snake and initially also the ERM, exchange rate policy hardened impressively during the 1980s, culminating in a public precommitment closely to track the most stable currencies within the EMS. In addition, in the early 1980s Denmark and Belgium both confronted a rising inflationary momentum on account of widespread wage indexation as well as exorbitant budget deficits. In early 1982, these two countries together requested substantial devaluations – roughly double what they eventually got – reflecting how the exchange rate was then primarily seen as an instrument to strengthen competitiveness, rather than as an anchor to which other policies should adapt. Overall, the currencies of both countries lost roughly a third of their value against the Deutsche mark during the EMS period – the best performance in the EU behind Austria and the Netherlands (see Table 8).

Characteristic of Denmark's hard currency policy is that it followed a very resolute turnaround. Indeed, the stabilisation program adopted in the fall of 1982 contained a host of measures designed to underpin the renewed objective of a fixed exchange rate target – that is, without the creeping devaluations of the past. Under the new conservative government, capital flows were liberalised, wage indexation was abolished by law and fiscal policy was significantly tightened, allowing a deficit of nearly 10 percent of GDP to be eliminated by 1986. The commitment of the authorities was soon put to the test as Sweden, the second most important trading partner, devalued its currency by 16 per cent within days of the program's announcement. In the event, the authorities held the line and the seemingly deflationary policy package yielded spectacular results: monetary policy credibility surged, external capital streamed in, interest rates declined swiftly and substantially, and growth took off to well above the community average. In this respect, Denmark counts as a classic example of a country where sizeable fiscal retrenchment and tough monetary policy can be expansionary.[42]

A further crucial attribute of Denmark's more recent approach to exchange rate targeting has been its use of fiscal policy to compensate for deviations between domestic economic developments and those in the anchor country. This stems from the fact that Denmark, given its heavy trade links with other Nordic countries and the United Kingdom, does not seem to form an optimal currency area with the core ERM countries. Against this background, a clear understanding was reached between the government and the central bank that fiscal policy should actively provide an offsetting impulse at times when Denmark experiences an asymmetric economic development.[43] This approach has on occasion led to policy adjustments, most recently through the adoption of an additionally restrictive budget in 1998 on account of the country's relatively favourable business cycle. In this respect, Denmark forms a notable exception to the general rule that budgetary policy has not been tailored to the monetary strategy choice. Besides this, it is important that Denmark's financial structure does not seriously constrain the use of the interest rate to defend the exchange rate anchor, as it is dominated by fixed rate long-term borrowing (up to 30 years).

Exchange rate targeting in Denmark underwent three further developments in the 1990s. First, early on in the decade, Denmark complemented its external target with a domestic credit target. Similar to the Netherlands' credit targets in the late 1980s, the design of this target respected the endogeneity of money growth under an exchange rate commitment and only sought to influence the composition of money expansion. But the target primarily had a political purpose, as it was announced in the context of a Danish initiative to foster closer consultation on national monetary policy targets in Europe. After the initiative met insuperable resistance, the target was discontinued; it had never effectively influenced monetary policy setting which remained exclusively exchange rate-oriented.

Second, exchange rate policy was fundamentally challenged during the ERM crises of 1992-93, which had been triggered by Denmark's own rejection of the Maastricht Treaty. Notwithstanding its strong track record in the exchange markets, as well as solid macroeconomic fundamentals – a relatively small budget deficit, a substantial external surplus and the lowest inflation rate in the EC – the krone came under inordinate pressure. When the widening of the exchange rate bands left the central bank alone in the defence of the krone, the Prime Minister announced that "the objective of Danish exchange rate policy will be to maintain a stable exchange rate against the core EMS countries" while the Governor publicly indicated that "a considerable narrowing of the wide fluctuation margin temporarily fixed at ± 15 per cent will be sought".[44] But, together with a substantial interest rate differential (increased to 4 percentage points), this could not keep the krone from depreciating some 8 per cent. However, as the authorities maintained their relatively tight policy stance, the currency gradually recovered. This forcefully reaffirmed the hard currency policy.

Third, in the early autumn of 1998, following a seemingly unwarranted new bout of speculative pressures against the krone, agreement was finally reached on a strengthening of the common institutional framework supporting the Danish exchange rate target. The speculative pressures had reflected contagion effects from the currency crises in Asia and Russia, but financial markets were evidently focusing on Denmark because it was not a first-round EMU participant. (Finland, which stood to suffer more heavily from the Russian fall-out, did not experience exchange market strains.) In these circumstances, the authorities reacted not only by raising interest rates significantly above those of the other ERM members, but also by reaching an agreement with regional partners that the krone would participate in the successor exchange rate mechanism (ERM II) within a narrow ± 2.25 per cent fluctuation band. Although this agreement would only take effect from the outset of EMU, its pre-announcement served to signal broad support for the Danish intention of maintaining a tight exchange rate target.[45] In the event, during the run-up to EMU, the 'opt out'-krone was able to remain just as close to its Deutsche mark parity as the currencies of the initial monetary union participants.

France

Of the large European countries, France was the first and only truly successful country to implement a strategy of exchange rate targeting. The acceptance of the external constraint did not come easily, however. During the snake period, France had generally prioritised domestic objectives and when the franc came under untenable downward pressure, it had opted to leave the system rather than accept a devaluation – an approach common to all the large countries at the time. This had first been the case in January 1974 and was repeated in March 1976, as a consequence of an expansionary policy package (including rapid credit growth) implemented only shortly after rejoining the snake in July 1975. The inconsistency between domestic and external policy objectives persisted during the initial EMS period. This policy discrepancy was especially striking following the election of a socialist government in June 1981 that had not been involved in the making of the EMS and that attempted to overcome the domestic recession through budgetary expansion, a major increase in the minimum wage, and an initial shortening of the work week. In the domestic monetary policy field, the money growth target was loosened from 10 to 12 per cent. Again, the exchange rate target would have to give. But a major difference with France's earlier approach is that the authorities accepted to resolve the frictions caused by their deviant policy preferences within the context of the exchange rate system: the franc was devalued by 8½ per cent against the Deutsche mark in October 1981 and by a further 10 per cent in June 1982 – the largest bilateral adjustment in the history of the EMS or, for that matter, of the snake.

The incompatibility between the exchange rate target and the domestic policy objectives came to a head at the beginning of Spring 1983 when a new foreign exchange market crisis prompted the franc to be devalued by a further 8 per cent vis-à-vis the Deutsche mark. Given three major devaluations within one-and-a-half years, it was clear that the digressing national policy course could not effectively be combined with a fixed exchange rate. In fact, within the French administration, an intense policy debate had taken place on whether to continue with expansive policies and switch to a flexible exchange regime, or to remain in the ERM and genuinely to adopt the policy discipline that was necessary to make the exchange rate strategy credible.[46] The evidence against France's policy strategy had mounted: the franc had cumulatively lost almost one-third of its value against the Deutsche mark since the inception of the EMS and almost two thirds since it definitely left the snake in March 1976. Moreover, a withdrawal from the EMS would likely deliver a fatal blow to the process of European monetary integration. In the event, France opted for a switch to a hard currency policy, abandoning its expansionary fiscal and social policies and granting priority to the sustainability of the external target and, by implication, to achieving price stability. As part of the stabilisation package, the domestic money growth target was this time tightened from 10 to 9 per cent. Henceforth, a strategy of 'competitive disinflation' would be pursued, with external competitiveness attained through domestic cost control rather than external currency devaluation.

The hard currency policy was mastered over the course of the next four years, with two last devaluations of decreasing size (6 respectively 3 per cent relative to the Deutsche mark) in April 1986 and January 1987. In this period, wage indexation was abolished, the budget deficit was halved (to 1.7 per cent of GDP in 1987) and a relaxation of capital controls was initiated. While the link between the French franc and the Deutsche mark-block was never tightened within the fluctuation band, the sustained strengthening of French fundamentals validated the exchange rate parity vis-à-vis Germany, which remained unchanged from 1987 on, eventually determining the conversion rate into EMU. In practice, during the second half of the 1980s it became obvious that of the two monetary policy objectives, the exchange rate had clear priority, with the money supply target serving solely to signal a medium-term goal of controlling inflation.[47] This was reflected, with a lag, in a slow but steadily increasing credibility of the exchange rate peg in the financial markets: the French-German long-term bond yield spread which had amounted to almost 7 percentage points in 1982, had all but disappeared by 1991.

The exchange rate strategy survived the ERM crises of 1992-93, although barely so. France had finally restored solid macroeconomic fundamentals – in addition to the relatively small budget deficit, a large current account surplus and the lowest inflation rate in over 30 years – but unemployment, at 10 per cent and rising, made the high interest rates due to German unification well-nigh unacceptable. Against this background, France overplayed its hand by publicly calling for a reduction in German interest rates, while taking the lead and reducing its own short-term rates beneath those in Germany. Notwithstanding official statements underlying the commitment to the external target, this naturally raised market doubts as to whether France truly had the stamina to sustain the hard currency peg or whether it would change its monetary policy course to allow a reduction in interest rates and the exchange rate. Given massive speculative flows against the franc and other currencies judged to be inadequately committed, as well as a lack of agreement between the EMS partners on a new structure of the central rates, the fluctuation bands were widened to ± 15 per cent. Nonetheless, although this offered scope to tailor interest rate policy more closely to the needs of the French economy, the Banque de France maintained interest rate policy roughly in line with that of the Bundesbank, thereby upholding the crucial element of the hard currency policy even in absence of intervention margins. By consequence, after slipping to a maximum of about 6 per cent beneath its Deutsche mark parity, the initial bilateral exchange rate position was gradually regained, forcefully reaffirming France's hard currency preference.

Ireland

The monetary policy strategy of Ireland has always been exchange rate targeting. But in its history, Ireland has implemented two different types of exchange rate targeting, one of which proved to be straightforward and relatively easy, the other complicated and difficult. The former was the exchange rate link to the pound sterling that lasted from the introduction of the Irish currency in 1928 until the inception of the EMS more than half a century later. During this period, the Irish pound was tied by a one-for-one peg with no margins or charges to the British pound. Originally set up as a currency board arrangement, Ireland's monetary policy gradually experienced an accretion of broader central bank activities, but retained several of the conservative policy characteristics of a currency board system right up to the severance of the sterling link in early 1979.[48] Interest rates were basically driven by those in London and price developments in the two countries showed an essentially parallel development. Given tight trade links between the two countries as well as a reasonable degree of stability in UK policy, the exchange rate orientation was a logical choice that was simple to implement and on the whole produced satisfactory results.

The break with sterling and accession to the EMS in 1979 involved a fundamental restructuring of exchange rate policy. Besides obvious political considerations, three main issues motivated the switch.[49] First, ERM membership was expected to improve prospects for disinflation. The relatively rapid price increases in the United Kingdom following the collapse of Bretton Woods, resulting in an inflation rate on average 13 percentage points a year higher than Germany during 1975-78, had weakened commitment to the sterling link. Second, Ireland was seeking to reorient its economy towards continental Europe, which had shown greater post-war economic dynamism. In this respect, ERM entry was expected to reinforce an ongoing adjustment process: although the United Kingdom was still the largest trading partner, accounting for about one-half of exports and imports in 1978, its trade share (particularly of exports) had shown a steady decline that had accelerated following Ireland's accession to the EC. Third, participation in the ERM harboured the promise of significant resource transfers from the community credit facilities.

But the new exchange rate strategy was much more difficult to implement. A tight exchange rate peg setting monetary policy on an automatic pilot was out of the question, since the central bank faced a dual policy objective. On the one hand, inflation expectations and policy discipline needed to be tuned to developments in the other ERM countries; on the other, the fluctuation margins and the scope for realignments had to be used actively to mitigate the heavy influence of fluctuations in a non-ERM currency, the British pound. In essence, the dilemma stemmed from a shortage of optimal currency area attributes with the other ERM participants, as the economy remained dominated by developments in the United Kingdom, which had decided not to participate in the ERM. This difficulty contributed to a terrible start in the ERM, during which the mechanism provided Ireland with quite the opposite of a hard currency support. Within a month, the sterling link had to be broken on account of an appreciation of the British pound and, over the next two years, tight UK monetary policy in combination with a petrocurrency status lifted sterling by some 25 per cent against the Irish pound. Thus, although the Irish exchange rate remained broadly stable against the other ERM currencies, it depreciated by almost 15 per cent in nominal effective terms. The inflationary impact of exchange rate policy was exacerbated by a profligate fiscal policy that resulted in a primary budget deficit (that is, excluding rising interest payments) of on average 7.2 per cent of GDP during 1979-81. Against this background, it is not surprising that wages failed to fall in line with the requirements of a durably stable ERM exchange rate.[50] Together, these developments allowed inflation to reach by far the highest rate in the narrow ERM band, peaking at over 20 per cent in late 1981 and boosting prospective disinflation costs.

The switch to a genuinely hard currency policy occurred at roughly the same time as that of France, taking hold in 1982-83. While rapid inflation was no longer compensated by an appreciating British pound, monetary policy was tightened to sustain the external target, resulting in high short-term interest rates and an erosion of competitiveness against both the ERM countries and the United Kingdom. At the same time, a forceful fiscal correction was initiated, reducing the primary deficit by 4½ per cent of GDP in two years. Under these circumstances, inflation plummeted, coming to a virtual halt by 1988. And, as the credibility of the strategy increased, interest rates declined, facilitating much-needed further budgetary consolidation. But the tough policy line had a severe toll on the real economy, as unemployment soared from 12 per cent in 1982 to 19 per cent in 1987 – a figure that would have been even higher if extensive emigration had not taken place.[51] Thus, the monetary policy strategy finally proved effective, but success had come at a high price.

In practice, Ireland has pursued its own breed of exchange rate targeting, focusing on its ERM commitments as well as the effective (trade weighted) exchange rate or, more simply put, on both the Deutsche mark and the British pound. Specifically, Ireland has respected the constraints of the ERM, except when exchange rate developments outside the ERM caused undue competitiveness loss (this applies in particular to the major devaluations of 1983 and 1986 that reflected pronounced developments in sterling and the dollar). In other words, realignments have not been used to accommodate inadequate domestic price control and have generally not allowed the nominal effective exchange rate to depreciate. In this regard, exchange rate targeting temporarily became much easier once the United Kingdom joined the mechanism in 1990. But, by the same token, Irish monetary policy faced tremendous difficulty when sterling withdrew from the ERM and fell sharply in the autumn of 1992. Although the government with the support of trade unions strenuously tried to avoid devaluing, the force of the financial markets proved overwhelming and the authorities ultimately had to accept a sizeable devaluation (of 10 per cent, somewhat less than the depreciation of sterling).[52]

The dual character of Irish exchange rate targeting became more visible after the widening of the ERM bands to ± 15 per cent in August 1993, as the Irish pound was the currency that made most conspicuous use of the full bandwidth. This first became evident during the exchange market turbulence of early 1995, when the Irish pound was allowed to depreciate to almost 10 per cent beneath its Deutsche mark parity following dollar and sterling weakness in the wake of the Mexico crisis. But it became especially apparent in 1997 when the Irish currency rose in the slipstream of sterling strength to close to its upper ERM limits against all the other currencies. On the eve of EMU, shortly before the preannouncement of the conversion rates of national currencies into the euro, this prompted a unique occurrence in the history of the EMS: the Irish pound became the only currency at any time to be revalued against the Deutsche mark. While it may be argued that the revaluation was on the small side (3 per cent), the realignment illustrated that Ireland's exchange rate policy was of a hard variety, even if it was loose within the confines of the ERM.

Finland

Exchange rate targeting was the mainstay of Finnish monetary policy until 1992. Within a few months of the final collapse of Bretton Woods, Finland had introduced a trade-weighted currency index as the exchange rate policy compass, thereby pioneering (alongside Austria) the use of currency baskets in exchange rate policy. With an open economy and a motley composition of trading partners, this broad-based policy approach aimed to avoid changes in international exchange rates from affecting the average competitiveness of the Finnish economy. The new exchange rate policy was made official in November 1977, concurrent with the legislative changes under the second Amendment of the IMF Articles that formalised the establishment of a global system of floating exchange rates. At that time, the external value of the markka was explicitly defined in terms of the currency index and a fluctuation band of ± 2.25 per cent was officially introduced.

The currency basket regime remained largely unchanged over the next 15 years, barring a few technical adaptations. First, in 1984, the Soviet rouble was removed from the index in order to avoid artificial adjustments in the value of this non-convertible currency from affecting Finland's competitive position vis-à-vis western trading partners. This implied a significant change as buoyant bilateral trade had caused the weight of the rouble gradually to rise to close to 25 per cent in the index. Second, the width of the fluctuation band itself oscillated back and forth between ± 2.25 and ± 3 per cent, as the authorities sought to tighten their nominal anchor, on the one hand, or increase the scope for an independent monetary policy, on the other. Some asymmetry is evident in these band adjustments, however, as a narrow band was generally selected at the time of, or shortly after devaluations (as in 1977 and 1982), whereas the band was widened when the currency faced strong upward pressure (as in 1979 and 1988). Third, in 1991 the trade-weighted index was replaced by the ECU basket as part of a broad effort – also pursued by Sweden and Norway – to tighten economic links with the EC. The basket switch left the fluctuation bandwidth unchanged at ± 3 per cent and did not alter the external value of the markka; in fact, the fluctuation limits hardly varied because the ECU currencies, plus the other currencies pegged to the ECU, accounted for over 85 per cent of the old basket.

Although the structure of the exchange rate regime remained broadly constant until 1992, exchange rate policy did, however, undergo a substantive hardening in the early 1980s, particularly with respect to discretionary realignments of the band. Initially, exchange rate policy had been oriented primarily at preserving competitiveness; on top of the fact that the currency index comprised a large share of relatively soft currencies, the markka was devalued three times (by a cumulative 17½ per cent) in 1975-78. These devaluations conformed to a well-established Finnish devaluation tradition, according to which the exchange rate was substantially devalued at lengthy intervals, temporarily increasing growth and employment, but causing inflation to catch up sooner or later (depending on the success of incomes policy) and erode the benefits, until a new devaluation was implemented. As evidence cumulated that this policy did not seem to have a permanent effect on growth or employment, but was rather a source of cyclical fluctuations, proposals were made for a stability-oriented exchange rate policy.[53] Indications of a change in attitude came around the turn of the decade when three minor revaluations (totalling 3 per cent) marked the first serious attempt to renounce the devaluation instrument. Finally, the policy objective of nominal exchange rate stability – rather than of safeguarding competitiveness – was proclaimed in the program of the new Government that took office in early 1983; this remained a constant feature in subsequent programs (in 1987 and 1991), surviving changes in the political affiliation of governments.[54]

Overall, two features are characteristic of Finland's exchange rate targeting: its basket orientation and its unilateral nature. The first attribute limits fluctuations in the nominal effective exchange rate and thus contributes to a broad stability of competitiveness. In fact, Finland had a remarkably stable real effective exchange rate in the 1970s and 1980s.[55] Given a geographically diversified trade pattern, the variability of the real exchange rate would clearly have been much higher if the currency had been pegged to, say, the Deutsche mark or the dollar. This policy also implied, however, that the Finnish economy was steered towards the average, rather than the best, inflation performance of trading partners. As a result, even before the impact of official devaluations, the markka lost on average almost 2 per cent per year against the Deutsche mark during the period of the basket peg. Moreover, the policy target was relatively opaque and difficult to communicate.[56] The second characteristic – the unilateral nature of the peg – increases the flexibility of the authorities to adapt the policy framework as circumstances and preferences evolve, but misses the disciplinary influence and intervention support that multilateral agreements can give, thereby reducing the credibility of the policy target. In this regard, it is telling that the Finnish exchange rate peg was the first to succumb in the European exchange market turbulence of 1992-93.

Fundamentally, however, the exchange rate peg collapsed on account of the different structure of the Finnish economy – especially its idiosyncratic production composition, financial sector and trade pattern – and the evident need for monetary instruments to offset country-specific developments in domestic demand. In particular, the economy is susceptible to commodity price fluctuations in its large resource-based (forestry) sector, as occurred during 1986-89 when the country's terms of trade rose each year for a cumulative total of about 20 per cent.[57] At that time, credit growth was booming in the wake of financial deregulation, further fuelling domestic demand. Even though fiscal policy was activated to temper the overheating economy (as evidenced by growing central government surpluses, reflecting the impact of automatic stabilisers as well as initial discretionary measures), it did not prove possible to implement a sufficiently tight package. With capital flows almost fully liberalised over the past years, recourse was made to a variety of monetary measures that fitted roughly within the constraints of the exchange rate regime. In late 1988, the room for monetary manoeuvre was expanded by widening the fluctuation band (from a total of 4.5 per cent to 6 per cent); in early 1989 an auxiliary credit target was introduced (supported by a supplementary interest-free cash reserve requirement); and a few weeks later the currency was revalued (by

4 per cent). The a-synchronised cycle turned sharply around during the next year, with the downturn amplified by the collapse of trade with the Soviet Union and banking system fragility, and the exchange rate subsequently suffered recurrent bouts of downward pressure. Although the switch to the ECU basket initially enhanced credibility and provided a reprieve, massive speculative flows ultimately led the authorities to implement a sizeable 12.3 per cent devaluation in November 1991. However, when the foreign exchange market unrest endured and even intensified in the context of a broader questioning of exchange rate targets in Europe, the authorities threw the towel in the ring and floated the markka in early September 1992.

Finland seemingly returned to exchange rate targeting when it joined the ERM in October 1996. But this policy move was motivated solely by the need to ensure Finland's meeting of all the EMU convergence criteria, including the requirement of at least two years' ERM membership.[58] The existing policy framework of direct inflation targeting was, for all intents and purposes, maintained unchanged. The central rate was determined slightly below the prevailing market rate, at about the average of the previous two years, and in line with the central bank's estimates of the real equilibrium rate using PPP and macroeconometric model calculations. Of course, as EMU approached and was judged credible, this rate became a focal point for market expectations of the conversion into euro and for official interest rate convergence. Somewhat ironically, exchange rate developments were therefore more stable during the last two years prior to EMU under the direct inflation targeting approach than during most of the previous twenty years of exchange rate targeting.

Sweden

During the past quarter of a century, exchange rate targeting has also been the dominant monetary policy strategy in Sweden. But the evolution of the Swedish exchange rate regime is exceptional, insofar as its orientation has gradually shifted away from the European anchor currencies. In particular, Sweden pegged its currency to the European snake arrangement from the moment of the final collapse of Bretton Woods in March 1973, switched to a broad-based currency basket in 1977 and, after a brief period of ECU-pegging during 1991-92, abandoned its exchange rate objective altogether.

More specifically, an incompatible policy response to the first oil shock cast a shadow over Sweden's association with the European snake soon after its inception. While Sweden prioritised employment and engaged in fiscal stimulation during 1974-76, Germany geared its policies to containing inflationary pressures, setting itself relatively tight money targets. Diverging inflation performance from 1974 onwards was initially accommodated by two devaluations (totalling 9 per cent) in late 1976 and early 1977, but sustained policy deviation made the exchange rate target untenable and the krona dropped out of the snake in late 1977. Although the switch may to a limited extent have reflected concern over an inadequate weight of Sweden's main trading partners in the exchange rate orientation, it primarily stemmed from the rejection of a hard currency policy. This is poignantly illustrated by the large devaluation (of 10 per cent) that was implemented concurrent with the withdrawal from the snake and the adoption of a trade-weighted currency basket. In this respect, the weaker discipline implied by a link to the average inflation performance of trading partners, rather than that of Germany, also provided a closer match of the prevailing Swedish policy preferences.

Exchange rate policy started to tighten in late 1982, but only after it had been considerably softened. Notwithstanding adequate competitiveness (the real exchange rate had remained roughly stable following the 1977 correction), the exchange rate was massively devalued (by 10 per cent in 1981 and 16 per cent in 1982) as part of a policy program that sought to mitigate the adverse unemployment impact of a pending fiscal consolidation effort. In effect, the large up-front devaluation was part of a classic adjustment mix, comprising both expenditure reducing (budgetary) and expenditure switching (exchange rate) measures which, at least that was the plan, would steer demand towards the tradables sector and would contribute to high employment, healthy public finances, a strong balance of payments and reasonably stable prices. The latter was importantly to be achieved by committing to exchange rate stability after the 'one-off' devaluations. In fact, the original plan had been to tie the Swedish currency to the Deutsche mark immediately after the 1982 realignment in order to make the switch to a hard currency policy more visible, but this fell through at the last moment on account of uncertainty about the Bundesbank's attitude on unilateral Deutsche mark-pegs.[59]

Over the course of the next years, successive measures were taken to buttress the credibility of the hard exchange rate commitment. Starting in 1983, domestic credit market controls – which had previously been geared towards tangential policy objectives such as housing policy – were gradually lifted. Monetary policy operations were adapted in steps to reduce the degree of sterilisation and interest rate smoothing, and therewith to bolster the central bank's capacity to tighten policy in reaction to capital outflows. Also, in 1984, an Act was passed prohibiting the government from borrowing abroad on a net basis. This not only sought to increase fiscal discipline by obliging the government to pay the high domestic interest rates that follow from large budget deficits, but also to constrain monetary policy by requiring that foreign exchange outflows are offset by interest rate adjustments. This measure thus formed an integral part of the fixed exchange rate regime.[60] Moreover, in mid-1985, in an effort to make the exchange rate peg more transparent, the Riksbank announced an official fluctuation margin of ± 1.5 per cent around the target value for the currency basket. In practice, this involved a tightening of the commitment, as the central bank had previously been working with an (undisclosed) margin of ± 2.25 per cent. By reducing market uncertainty about the authorities' objectives and raising the (reputation) costs to the authorities of deviating from the target, the publication of the margin bolstered the credibility of the exchange rate target, allowing the interest rate differential vis-à-vis the peg to be substantively lowered. Finally, in 1991, shortly after Sweden's decision to apply for EC membership, the central bank announced a switch to a unilateral ECU-peg in a move that kept the fluctuation band and the overall exchange rate unchanged.[61] At the same time, the Riksbank publicised that it would seek a formal association agreement with the EMS, the ultimate goal being participation in the ERM. These political and institutional intentions signalled that the switch was more than simply a change of currency basket and thus served (albeit temporarily) to underpin the credibility of the exchange rate target, as again illustrated by a decline of the interest rate differential.

In the event, the exchange rate commitment was indeed met without interruption for a decade following the 1981-82 competitive devaluations. But this external stability masked major domestic imbalances that made a break inevitable. In particular, Swedish inflation was consistently substantially higher than that of the trade-weighted (and the ECU) basket until late 1991. Next to the direct price impulse of the devaluations, this reflected the expansionary impact on the tradables sector, where output picked up rapidly, while the non-tradables sector did not become commensurately slimmer. Furthermore, financial liberalisation measures and tax deductibility of nominal interest payments triggered a credit boom that also led to a surge in asset prices. Meanwhile, although a general government deficit of 7 per cent of GDP in 1982 had been transformed into a sizeable surplus by 1987, structural budgetary policy was insufficiently tight to rein in the overheating economy.[62] When the cycle finally turned in the early 1990s, the underlying weaknesses were quick to surface: the general government deficit plummeted to under its previous low, asset price declines led to banking system frailty, and a surge in unemployment cast doubt on the authorities' true commitment to the external anchor – especially against the background of the real accommodation in the past.

In hindsight, it is impressive that, given these developments, Sweden managed to keep an unchanged exchange rate within such a narrow band for such a long time. To a degree this can be attributed to the undervaluation of the krona when the exchange rate commitment first hardened. But it also reflected the progress that was gradually made towards mastering the art of sustaining a hard exchange rate target. Actually, during the first half of 1992, Swedish inflation was running below that of the ECU basket and the necessary real adjustment process – although belated – was finally taking place within the constraint of the nominal exchange rate peg. Moreover, in the face of the speculative onslaught on the European currency markets in the fall of 1992, the Swedish defence of the krona was exceptional in its tenacity. Where Finland, Italy and the United Kingdom opted to float their currencies, Sweden, facing comparable pressures, raised the overnight rate to 500 per cent and kept it there for four days, allowing agreement to be reached on an overdue package of fiscal measures and confidence to be temporarily restored. This policy response was unsustainable in light of the weak economy and vulnerable banking system, and when pressures resumed in mid-November, the Riksbank shifted away from the interest rate instrument and resorted to massive use of sterilised intervention, spending over 160 billion kronor of foreign reserves in just six days (equivalent to 12 per cent of GNP and almost a quarter of the broad money stock).[63] In turn, when this unilateral effort proved insufficient to halt – let alone turn – the speculative tide, the sapped Riksbank abandoned its exchange rate target and switched to a floating exchange regime. Since Sweden did not wish to join EMU from the outset, ERM participation (a criterion for EMU entry) was not considered opportune when the EU was joined in 1995 – notwithstanding the prospect of ± 15 per cent fluctuation bands and multilateral support. Thus it came to happen that Sweden was the only EU country, together with the United Kingdom, not to have an exchange rate target on the eve of EMU.

Italy

Over the past twenty-five years, Italy has been a champion in combining different monetary policy targets. Next to the exchange rate, it has intermittently pursued credit, money and indicative inflation targets, usually aiming for two, and often three, of these targets simultaneously. The weights accorded to the individual targets have varied, however, depending on the underlying objective that was being prioritised – output growth, balance of payments strengthening or inflation control. While exchange rate targeting has arguably been the main monetary policy strategy, this is far from clear-cut as there have been protracted periods when an exchange rate commitment was either absent (until early 1979), relatively loose (from early 1979 until the mid-1980s during which a wide fluctuation band was combined with frequent realignments), or suspended (from September 1992 until November 1996). Overall, given the uneven character of exchange rate targeting, as well as pervasive capital controls until 1990, the other quantified targets have fulfilled at times similarly prominent, or even temporarily dominant, roles in the framing of monetary policy.

The patchy exchange rate targeting record starts with the European currency snake, of which Italy was a founding member. But the external target was soon subordinated to domestic policy objectives and, after the introduction of a dual exchange market failed to provide relief, Italy dropped out of the arrangement in February 1973 – even before the floating of the dollar and the global switch to flexible exchange rates. Given a precarious external current account, credit targets were introduced under an IMF supported arrangement in 1974 and the exchange rate was essentially left to its own devices. Credit targets remained the only explicit monetary policy goal for the next five years, during which an unprecedented budgetary expansion in combination with widespread agreements on wage indexation boosted inflation to way above the levels in most trading partners. The external value of the lira made the consequences of these unrestrained policies irrefutably clear, as the exchange rate suffered a pronounced decline and untenable downward pressures even necessitated a temporary closing of the exchange market for five weeks in early 1976. Following this exchange rate crisis, policy adjustment under a second IMF agreement strengthened the balance of payments and contributed to a more stable exchange rate, but inflation remained conspicuously higher than in the other EC countries.

Against this background, and given the judgement that nominal convergence could only be gradual, Italy negotiated an exceptional wider intervention threshold (± 6 per cent) when it resumed an exchange rate commitment at the inception of the EMS in 1979. Intended as a temporary measure, the lira remained in this wide band for over a decade, reflecting a limited commitment to the exchange rate target. This limited resolve was equally evident in the relatively high frequency and large magnitude of lira devaluations, which averaged one a year and totalled a cumulative 55 per cent until 1987. In appearance, Italy's ERM policy thus resembled a crawling peg more than a fixed exchange rate regime. But the devaluations did not fully offset Italy's inflation differential vis-à-vis the other EC countries and the real exchange rate underwent a gradual appreciation. In absence of firm macroeconomic policy measures outside the monetary realm during this period, it was mainly this influence on price and wage setting behaviour, particularly in the tradables sector, that supported a gradual but sustained process of disinflation.

After 1987, when the 'new' EMS was born, mistaken expectations of lasting regional exchange rate stability allowed Italy to avoid devaluing altogether and even to join the system's narrow band in 1990, despite an inflation rate that was still 3 percentage points higher than the average of the other ERM countries during each of the years 1987-90. Moreover, soon after entering the narrow band, the lira bounced against the ceiling of the system, thereby constraining the scope for monetary policy tightness and accommodating a continued inflation differential. The stabilisation of the exchange rate during this phase was thus more a product of the system's increasing credibility than of a hardening of underlying policies. With the benefit of hindsight, an exchange rate collapse was inevitable. It is not surprising, then, that the lira was the first ERM currency to come under attack in the summer of 1992. Following massive intervention support and failed attempts to engineer a broad ERM realignment, the lira was initially the only currency to devalue (by 7 per cent against the rest). But once Italy had broken the spell of ERM stability, exchange markets became more anxious to test the true strength of policies and commitments in the system. Within a day, the lira fell to its new ERM floor, where it was joined by the British pound. When a tendentious news report circulated that the Bundesbank president did not rule out one or two currencies coming under further pressure, speculative flows became overwhelming and Italy suspended its ERM participation. Only at end-1996, after the nominal effective exchange rate had fallen by roughly one quarter and domestic policies had been strenuously tightened (as notably evidenced by an inflation rate finally in line with the system's average despite the effects of currency depreciation), did Italy rejoin the ERM to fulfil the related EMU entry criterion. Supported by a relatively tight monetary policy (Governor Fazio was bent on avoiding any risks to EMU qualification), exchange rate stability was comfortably achieved thereafter and the lira closely shadowed the system's hard core currencies until the start of EMU.[64]

While this mixed track record creates the impression that Italy paid little heed to the policy requirements of an exchange rate commitment, a series of measures was actually implemented to underpin the external target, even if the pace at which this occurred was tediously slow. These measures related to the three issues of monetary policy autonomy, stability oriented wage bargaining procedures and budgetary strengthening, in absence of which any monetary policy strategy in Italy would have been doomed to impotency.[65] On the first issue, an important step was the so-called 'divorce' agreement of 1981 that relieved the central bank of the obligation to act as the residual buyer at public debt auctions. Although the central bank had previously been able to sterilise the monetary impact of its debt purchases through open market sales, the divorce facilitated a non-accommodating monetary policy and made budgetary financing difficulties more transparent. This latter point is vividly illustrated by the 1982 showdown that forced the government to go to parliament for an extraordinary one-year special advance to cover its financing needs. The process of institutionalising monetary policy autonomy took more than a decade to complete, however, as the central bank governor was only formally empowered to set the official discount rate in February 1992 and direct advances to the Treasury were only legally forbidden in November 1993. On the second issue, some progress was made under the influence of the exchange rate target in 1984, when indexation was temporarily linked to the government's inflation objective rather than the outcome. After a proposal to restore uncompensated excess inflation was rejected in a referendum, a new indexation scheme was introduced in 1986 that substantially reduced the degree of coverage. But it took until July 1992 for the 'scala mobile' indexation system to be completely abolished. Progress was similarly slow on the third issue of the public finances. While the budget deficit started to decline after 1985 (from a peak of 12½ per cent of GDP), the consolidation process was initially insufficient to turn the adverse debt dynamics, allowing the debt stock to continue to rise until 1994 (reaching 125 per cent of GDP). Moreover, the adjustment measures largely spared those sectors that were most in need of structural adjustment, including pension schemes, health services and public sector employment. Ironically, consensus was only reached on fundamental reform measures in these sectors on the day after the lira fell out of the ERM, when the exchange rate crisis had sparked a sense of urgency.

Overall, Italy has had a chequered exchange rate targeting experience, characterised by an adjustment process that was unfortunately too gradual to ensure its sustainability. But the exchange rate commitment does seem to have catalysed adjustments that would unlikely have been implemented in its absence. While the credit targets did not provide a nominal anchor nor an objective yardstick to communicate domestic policy shortcomings, money targets would not have functioned well under the marked money demand instability of the early 1980s and may have been subjected to greater political scheming. At the same time, inflation targets could not have delivered price stability in absence of far-reaching institutional strengthening, for which the political climate was then not ripe. By contrast, the exchange rate measured economic performance in an objective manner relative to regional partners, thus carrying the weight of national prestige, and also bore the promise of participation in the deepening European integration. In this respect, the external target elicited substantial adjustment in Italy, even if it imposed insufficient policy discipline during 1987-92 when market expectations provided undue support to exchange rate stability. Moreover, it is telling that exchange rate crises were highly effective in exacting long-delayed adjustment measures, notably in 1976 and 1992. And, in the final analysis, Italy did ultimately achieve a hardening of its exchange rate commitment in 1997-98, just in time for its coveted participation in EMU.

Spain

Spain was a latecomer to the European realm of exchange rate targeting. Following the collapse of the global fixed exchange rate system in the early 1970s, Spain had embarked on an independent monetary policy course directed primarily at domestic objectives. The choice of a floating exchange regime had reflected the relatively closed nature of the Spanish economy at the time and had served to foster – as a complement to tight capital controls – autonomous decision-making under a new money-oriented policy framework. While the money targets were initially internal, an inflationary surge (to almost 25 per cent) in the wake of a sizeable depreciation in 1977 prompted a tightening of policy setting, accompanied by the preannouncement of these targets to the public. But the adjustment path underlying the money targets remained moderate and inflation, although declining, stayed relatively high. In turn, the exchange rate experienced a sustained nominal decline as well a relatively high variability, both in nominal and real terms.

During the 1980s, the exchange rate made a gradual comeback as a monetary policy target.[66] This stemmed, first, from a growing disenchantment with money targeting, as financial innovation caused severe instability in the targeted money aggregate (M3), particularly from mid-1982 on. While this instability was mainly addressed in 1984 by switching to a broader, though less controllable aggregate (ALP), it also spurred the development and monitoring of a new exchange rate indicator that registered the nominal effective peseta rate against main industrial country trading partners. A second motive for the increasing prominence of the exchange rate was a growing awareness of the detrimental effects of exchange rate volatility in combination with Spain's ongoing integration in the international economy, notably marked by Spain's accession to the EC in 1986. In this latter context, the exchange rate indicator was narrowed to record just the nominal effective position against EC countries, excluding Greece and Portugal. Although this indicator had initially only played a very limited role in the monetary policy framework, it now became a prominent variable in the decision-making process.[67] Subsequently, in 1988, the indicator was again changed, when the index was replaced by the peseta's bilateral nominal exchange rate against the Deutsche mark. This completed a telling evolution in Spain's exchange rate indicator that suggests the aim was initially on minimising average competitiveness shocks to the tradables sector (by highlighting a broad, trade-based currency basket), subsequently on fostering regional convergence (by monitoring an EC currency basket), and finally on maximising the disciplinary influence (by focusing solely on the anchor currency of the EMS). In practice, Spain's managed floating exchange rate policy informally kept the peseta broadly within a fluctuation band of ± 6 per cent of the other EMS currencies during 1986-88.[68] During this period, money growth also deviated from its targets to a previously unprecedented degree.

The eventual decision in 1989 to adopt an explicit exchange rate commitment in the ERM and to do so within the mechanism's broad (± 6 per cent) fluctuation band reflected a number of further motives. A prime factor was that, although the system's limits had been largely adhered to over the course of the previous years, this monetary policy constraint had not been effectively communicated to wage and price setters. In this regard, ERM membership was expected to stabilise expectations and to enhance the disciplinary and credibility impact of exchange rate policy. Besides this, ERM entry would help cap the peseta appreciation that had been underway since early 1987, as it would limit speculative inflows driven by expectations of further strengthening. From a broader perspective, political considerations linked to more visible participation in the deepening European monetary integration – the Delors Report on EMU had just been finalised – evidently contributed to the announcement of ERM entry on the eve of the 1989 EC summit in Madrid. The decision to enter the transitory broad fluctuation band logically followed from the still high inflation differential (of 4 percentage points in 1988-89) vis-à-vis the ERM participants and the still uncertain balance of payments impact of the forceful ongoing tariff and trade quota reduction program implemented pursuant to EC membership.

Spain's exchange rate strategy did not harden successfully within the ERM, as prospects of durable exchange rate stability were undermined by persistent inflation differentials. This lack of success in first instance reflected a severe conflict between the internal and external objectives of monetary policy. Specifically, in the late 1980s, domestic demand soared way over the expansion of production and over growth elsewhere in the EMS, causing a rapid deterioration in the external current account and, following ten years of decline, an acceleration in inflation. At the same time, the scope for interest rate increases was limited by the exchange rate target, as the peseta reached the upper range of its ERM band soon after its entry into the system. Under these circumstances, the central bank took recourse to the temporary introduction of credit restrictions and of capital controls to preclude their circumvention. The effectiveness of these measures was questionable and certainly decreasing over the course of time, however, and the restrictions were rescinded within eighteen months. The incapacity of monetary policy was well-illustrated by developments relative to the money targets, which had been maintained to serve as a reference point for liquidity growth consistent with the medium-term viability of the ERM exchange rate, but were being consistently overrun.[69] At a deeper level, the absence of success in the monetary field therefore reflected the lack of support from other elements – notably in the fiscal and wage domain – to temper an exuberant domestic demand. In particular, the cyclically adjusted budgetary deficit rose by over 4 percentage points during 1987-91 and wage settlements remained significantly above the inflation targets set by the government.

The incompatibility of the policy mix came to a head in 1992 when the growth cycle turned and contrasted sharply with that in Germany, where monetary policy was overburdened with countering the inflationary effects of unification. This friction was system-wide and called an end to the self-validating market expectations of exchange rate stability, triggering an abrupt and heavy attack on the peseta. However, the Spanish authorities were quick to adjust to the changed market disposition and, only weeks after the peseta had been at the system's ceiling (against the British pound), the exchange rate was significantly devalued (by 5 per cent) and limited capital restrictions were shortly reimposed (for two months). When market pressures persisted, two further large devaluations (of 6 and 8 per cent) were carried through in November 1992 and May 1993, respectively. As a result, what had been the strongest currency in the system over the previous three years, now came to be the weakest. But, to the authorities' credit, the market pressures were orderly managed and Spain remained within the confines of the existing exchange rate system – a feat also achieved by Ireland and Portugal, but not by Italy, the United Kingdom or the Nordic countries with ECU-pegs.

When a new escalation of system-wide pressures led to the general widening of the exchange rate fluctuation band to ± 15 per cent in August 1993, the central bank essentially left the thrust of interest rate policy unchanged, but broadened the assessment of monetary policy needs in light of domestic cyclical conditions. In this context, an increasing emphasis was placed on a policy outcome in terms of inflation that was comparable with the core EMS countries. Given sluggish demand and muted domestic price pressures, the exchange rate was therefore allowed to weaken significantly within the band. However, this created uncertainty about the genuine priorities of the central bank and raised the spectre of an unduly discretionary monetary policy. After all, the combination of an evidently loose exchange rate target with a relatively wide and not very credible money target implied that monetary policy was left without a firm nominal anchor. Against this background, in late 1994, the monetary strategy was officially switched to direct inflation targeting. With an inflation rate similar to that in the core ERM partners now adopted as an overriding target, exchange rate stability against these countries was no longer a policy target but an expected policy outcome. In the event, this approach bore the anticipated fruit and, following a last devaluation within the new policy framework in 1995, the exchange rate stabilised in the run-up to EMU.

United Kingdom

The United Kingdom's experience with exchange rate targeting is an unfortunate one, marked by short-lived targets that typically ended in crisis. In essence, the country never really got to the point of adopting a hard exchange rate commitment, as these targets were plagued by cyclical differences vis-à-vis exchange rate partners, differences in financial and economic structure (including the impact of predominantly variable rate lending on monetary transmission and of large oil reserves on the balance of payments), and a lack of consistent support by other policies, especially fiscal policy, to mitigate these differences, partly owing to further differences in policy preferences. In addition, more than in any other European country, the monetary policy strategy of the United Kingdom has been heavily influenced by the vagaries of the prevailing political climate, as the Bank of England only achieved independence to set interest rates in 1997. By consequence, monetary policy credibility has generally been weak and highly dependent on the cohesion and standing of the Government in power.

The poor track record starts under the European snake arrangement that was joined in the Spring of 1972, but had to be abandoned within two months in the face of massive speculative pressures. Although these pressures were triggered by official statements emphasising that domestic economic concerns had to be granted precedence over exchange rate considerations, the underlying cause was a pronounced balance of payments weakening that elicited an increasing policy focus on credit control. Eventually, continued weakness of the external position led to the implementation of an IMF supported adjustment program in late 1976 centred around credit ceilings. However, these ceilings were not ends in themselves, but served as policy instruments within a money targeting framework that had been announced as part of a confidence shoring package adopted in July. The money oriented approach had the perceived advantage that domestic objectives could be prioritised, although this came at the cost of large nominal and real exchange rate fluctuations.[70] Indeed, in practice large exchange rate overshootings occurred as a result of changing domestic policy objectives (output growth in 1976, disinflation in 1979-80) amplified by sterling's rise as a petrocurrency status in the latter part of the decade (North sea oil production started in 1975). During this period, with the unfavourable experience under the snake still fresh in the mind, participation in the ERM was ruled out by both political sides, albeit for diametrically opposite reasons: while the Labour government disapproved on the grounds that ERM membership would prejudice competitiveness, the subsequent Conservative government objected – in keeping with its monetarist creed – that it would constrain the policy scope to counter inflation.

In the 1980s, the exchange rate moved slowly from the wings to the centre stage of monetary policy-making. Initially, as spelt out in the first Medium-Term Financial Strategy (MTFS) in 1980, the exchange rate was explicitly "assumed to be determined by market forces" – in effect a strategy of benign neglect. However, after huge money target overruns in 1980-81 owing to velocity instability caused disillusionment with the monetarist experiment, opinion began to swing in favour of exchange rate targets. Analyses of the dramatic rise in sterling as a costly overshooting contributed to the changing sentiment.[71] By 1982, the exchange rate had become a privileged indicator that featured prominently in the MTFS: "... the Government considers it appropriate to look at the exchange rate in monitoring domestic monetary conditions and in taking decisions about policy."[72] In practice, it was increasingly evident, especially during 1984-85, that interest rate moves were often driven by developments in the exchange market rather than in money growth.

When money targets were de-emphasised from the mid-1980s on, the exchange rate was the natural candidate to take their central place in the policy-making framework. But the change of strategy was held hostage to a political conflict between, on the one hand, the Prime Minister who was staunchly opposed to exchange rate targeting and, on the other, the Chancellor who had become an ERM convert as early as 1981.[73] While the official line remained an indefinite postponement of ERM entry 'until the time was ripe', the 1987 G7 Louvre Agreement to stabilise key exchange rates provided the Chancellor the opportunity to achieve his objective, albeit unilaterally and informally. Despite the fact that the Louvre Accord only explicitly related to the exchange rate of the dollar against the Deutsche mark and the yen, the Chancellor used it as a ploy also to seek to stabilise sterling against the Deutsche mark around its prevailing market rate. By consequence, for nearly a year from March 1987, intervention and interest rate policy were geared to maintaining a rate of three Deutsche mark.

This exchange rate targeting episode proved disastrous, for a host of reasons. First, the Deutsche mark was shadowed at far too low a rate, having fallen precipitously in the previous two years (from four Deutsche mark in July 1985). By resisting an exchange rate recovery, the inflationary consequences of the earlier depreciation were locked into the economy.

Second, given much higher interest rates in the United Kingdom than in Germany, the perceived objective of exchange rate stability elicited sizeable capital inflows. Next to a large increase of foreign exchange reserves (which more than doubled in 1987), these inflows prompted successive interest rate reductions (from 11 to 8½ per cent), at a time when a sharply recovering domestic economy and a credit boom spurred by financial liberalisation required quite the opposite. Third, fiscal policy did not contribute to dampening excess demand pressures, as the 1988 Budget provided a stimulus to the economy.[74] Fourth, given the unofficial nature of the exchange rate commitment, monetary policy communication did not direct wage and price setters at the new target, which would otherwise have underscored the need for an inflation objective broadly in line with Germany. In the event, the target was abandoned in March 1988 when capital inflows persisted and the authorities were no longer willing to hold the exchange rate down. In the aftermath of this episode, headline inflation surged from about 3 per cent in 1987 to over 10 per cent in 1990.

Notwithstanding the unfavourable effects of this period of exchange rate targeting, pressures formally to adopt an ERM target continued to build. From the monetary perspective, this reflected the lack of coherence of the then anchorless policy framework as well as the wish quickly to re-establish anti-inflation credentials. Moreover, the enduring stability of nominal exchange rates within the ERM was clearly augmenting its attraction to outsiders. But non-monetary considerations also played a heavy role, especially the notion that the United Kingdom would have little influence on the imminent design of EMU if it were not even in the regional exchange rate system.[75] As a first significant step, on the occasion of the 1989 European Summit in Madrid, the government spelt out the conditions under which the time for ERM entry would be considered 'ripe'.[76] Subsequently, within little more than a year and despite these conditions not all being met, sterling was brought into the system. With inflation way above that in other participants, interest rates at 15 percent and a sizeable external current account deficit of 3½ per cent of GDP, Spain's example was followed and broad fluctuation margins (± 6 per cent) were selected. In light of the previous experience with the informal exchange rate target (that had clearly been set too low), the central parity was now established above the prevailing market rate and disinflation was emphasised. Against the common ERM modalities, the United Kingdom selected this parity unilaterally, announcing it to the press prior to the internal discussions in the relevant EC bodies, thereby effectively precluding any negotiation on the appropriate (probably lower) parity. Besides this, the credibility of the new commitment was not helped by the half-hearted official support and an interest rate decline announced concurrent with the decision to join.[77]

This further attempt at exchange rate targeting was as calamitous as the previous ones. The prime cause was a sharp divergence in cyclical developments vis-à-vis Germany. In the United Kingdom, the economy reacted more sharply than anticipated to the high interest rates: while inflation came down quickly, the country moved into recession at about the time of entry into the system. By contrast, ERM interest rates remained dominated by Germany, where tight monetary policy was needed to contain the inflationary momentum created by unification expenditures. In these circumstances, the Bank of England made full use of the scope to loosen policy within the constraints of the system. But, in part owing to the appreciated parity that had been selected, this scope was limited as sterling remained close – if not at – its ERM floor. When money market rates had been lowered virtually to the German level, further declines clearly had to await an initiative in that direction by the Bundesbank. The ways out of this conundrum were all cut off: the Bundesbank was not willing to tailor its policies to the United Kingdom's needs, a sterling devaluation was not acceptable to the UK authorities, and agreement could not be reached within the system on a broad-based realignment or a unilateral Deutsche mark revaluation or float. By consequence, huge speculative flows built up against sterling, particularly once Italy had broken the spell of nominal exchange rate stability. Mindful of the fragile domestic economy, the United Kingdom initially reacted through very heavy intervention, spending 15 billion dollars – about half its entire stock of reserves.[78] When this proved ineffective, interest rates were also raised in a last-ditch attempt to turn the tide; but given the blatant inappropriateness of higher interest rates for the economy, speculative pressures did not ease. In part, this also reflected the limited political viability of an interest rate defence that directly impacted payments by most mortgage-holders and could not be attributed to an independent central bank. The only option left was ERM withdrawal.

Shortly after the ERM exit, the United Kingdom adopted a new policy strategy of direct inflation targeting, according to which no further objectives are set for the exchange rate. In this context, sterling fell by around 20 per cent in the wake of the ERM crisis, but subsequently recovered to above its previous levels against European partners. The size and timing of this recovery is difficult to explain on the basis of the customary macroeconomic variables and thereby conforms to the unpredictable pattern of sterling developments over the past quarter of a century.[79] This again suggests the inappropriateness of exchange rate targeting for the United Kingdom, as does the fact that interest rate differentials have remained substantial vis-à-vis continental Europe despite a similar inflation performance.

Portugal

Exchange rate targeting, in a variety of different and generally loose specifications, has been the principal monetary policy strategy of Portugal. The tone was set in the second half of the 1970s, when exchange rate policy was designed primarily with an eye to safeguarding competitiveness. Initially, the escudo had held its own following the demise of Bretton Woods, but a persistent deterioration in the external position eventually triggered a steep exchange rate decline that started as a market-driven, creeping depreciation in 1976 and culminated in an official devaluation of 15 per cent in February 1977. However, exchange rate policy was then still largely discretionary and, given political and institutional unrest following the revolution, the monetary policy framework was not fleshed out. This changed in August 1977 when the authorities introduced a comprehensive crawling peg regime, according to which the exchange rate was set to devalue at a preannounced monthly rate against a trade-weighted currency basket. The rate of crawl was originally determined at 1 per cent a month, but was frequently adjusted and complemented by further discretionary exchange rate adjustments. Together, these measures aimed at offsetting the adverse impact of high domestic inflation and trade liberalisation on external competitiveness so as to preserve a sustainable foreign balance. Essentially, a real exchange rate rule was implemented. At roughly the same time, credit targets were adopted under an IMF first credit tranche arrangement; these targets similarly assigned priority to promoting external viability.[80]

But the combination of credit targets with a crawling peg regime implicitly targeted at the real exchange rate left the economy without a nominal anchor for domestic price developments. This was reflected in an effective decline in the Portuguese currency that was amongst the sharpest in the OECD area during the 1970s. Moreover, following a failed attempt in 1980 to halt the inflationary dynamics by revaluing the currency and reducing the rate of crawl, Portuguese inflation consistently accelerated – at the same time as average inflation in the EC consistently declined – reaching 30 per cent in 1984. Clearly, given the increasing momentum of the wage-price spiral as well as the prospect of EC participation in 1986, the time had come for a strategy that placed greater emphasis on inflation control.

Against this background, exchange rate policy started to harden in late 1985. First, in order to moderate inflation expectations, the government temporarily suspended the downward crawl. Subsequently, starting in April 1986, the crawling peg was resumed but at a slightly lower and gradually declining pace (reduced in steps from 1.0 per cent a month before the policy tightening to 0.25 per cent a month in 1988). During the next five years of the crawling peg regime, the authorities also renounced the instrument of discretionary devaluations. Besides these policy changes, the greater focus on disinflation was reflected in the 1987 adoption of money targets that complemented the switch to a non-accommodating exchange rate crawl. The change in policy orientation could hardly be more perceptible: in a short time period Portugal changed from having no nominal anchor, to having two.

The sustainability of this dual targeting framework was predicated on capital controls that, however, were largely ineffective.[81] In practice, monetary policy measures (notably intervention) to keep the exchange rate from appreciating above the targeted crawl were at odds with efforts to keep money growth from increasing above the targeted growth range. In this light, the money targets were dropped after 1989 (although the Bank of Portugal maintained such targets for internal policy monitoring purposes), leaving the exchange rate as the sole monetary policy target. But this external target was also proving increasingly difficult to sustain, as the combination of a porous capital account, growing confidence in European exchange rate stability and relatively high Portuguese interest rates was attracting massive net capital inflows. Eventually, in September 1990, the magnitude of these inflows drove the authorities to abandon the predetermined crawl and to switch to a more flexible exchange rate regime, under which the escudo was managed within an (unannounced) band around a trade-weighted basket of the main currencies participating in the ERM.[82] This move sought to deter inflows by increasing two-sided exchange rate risk while also – as a prelude to ERM participation – aligning monetary policy closer to that of Portugal's regional partners. Although the exchange rate commitment was now more flexible, it was actually harder, as the policy anchor no longer had an in-built downward crawl.

Over the course of the next one-and-a-half years, exchange rate policy became the cornerstone of the authorities' disinflation efforts: despite domestic price increases that were significantly higher than in the anchor countries, the nominal exchange rate was kept broadly stable and was even allowed to appreciate slightly. At the same time, however, the economy remained inundated by large net capital inflows that seemed inverse (while official reserves more than tripled in 1988-91, the real exchange rate appreciated by over 20 per cent) and that frustrated the central bank's efforts at maintaining a tight policy stance. In these circumstances, the ERM was joined in April 1992 within the wide ± 6 per cent margins but at a central rate that was slightly lower than the market rate, thereby limiting the scope for further appreciation. Indeed, within weeks of joining, the exchange rate settled at the system's ceiling. But this position was short-lived, as the escudo became a target of speculative pressures when markets reassessed the underlying strength of currencies during the ERM turmoil that started in September 1992. Besides a vigorous intervention and interest rate defence, Portugal accommodated these market pressures through two large devaluations in November 1992 (by 6.0 per cent) and May 1993 (by a further 6.5 per cent) until relief was offered by the general widening of the ERM bands in August 1993.

Like most other countries, Portugal did not take advantage of the greater scope for exchange rate fluctuation but successfully sought to keep the escudo well inside the old 6 per cent band against the Deutsche mark. However, the authorities also took separate account of exchange rate developments against the one important trading partner – Spain – that was not part of the core ERM group. In this respect, the Portuguese situation was similar to that of Ireland. Thus, when neighbouring Spain devalued its currency by 7 per cent in March 1995, the Portuguese authorities followed course but with a smaller (3.5 per cent) devaluation. Thereafter, the currency tracked the Deutsche mark tightly within the system and exchange rate policy hardened decisively, as reflected in an impressive further decline in inflation. But the central bank was not fully comfortable that the exchange rate strategy would on its own deliver the desired price stability, especially given the singular importance attached to this objective in light of the EMU inflation criterion. In this context, to anchor price and wage behaviour more tightly, the central bank published a sweeping appraisal of the inflation outlook in March 1997 and announced reference values for inflation in conducting monetary policy.[83] However, it was explicitly indicated that these reference values would in principle still be pursued through the intermediate objective of ERM exchange rate stability. In the event, there was no conflict between the two potentially inconsistent targets as inflation declined more rapidly than envisaged and the EMU entry criterion was met with ease.

Greece

Greece's monetary policy strategy has traditionally had an eclectic inclination, according to which the exchange rate was, at most, one of several policy focal points. The basic policy framework has typically been a monetary program with multiple objectives, including one or more credit targets (primarily for total domestic credit expansion, but at times also for domestic credit to the private sector), one or more money targets (with an emphasis on M1 until 1982, and on M3 thereafter), occasionally an exchange rate target (until 1975 and during 1983 in terms of the US dollar) and an underlying inflation projection (given increasing prominence during the 1990s). When Greece finally precommitted to an exchange rate target in 1995, it was the last EU country to do so. This is not to say, however, that the Greek government was not, in principle, a supporter of greater exchange rate stability and of the related regional agreements.[84] Rather, it reflects the progressively large domestic imbalances, particularly during the 1980s, that stood in the way of granting serious consideration to the adoption of an external nominal anchor before meaningful convergence to EU norms had taken root. Of course, the switch to a more rules-based policy strategy – especially a transparent, exchange rate oriented one – would have limited the scope for swings in policy controlled variables and may thereby arguably have dampened their magnitude, but the intemperate forces in the domestic political dominion would have made this a risky undertaking.

Under these circumstances, the principal monetary policy focus was on credit growth and the exchange rate was employed to ensure external viability in the face of the large domestic policy – especially budgetary – shocks. In practice, this dominant view of the exchange rate as an instrument to maintain competitiveness was reflected in a relatively high, accommodating rate of depreciation (of on average a little over one per cent a month during 1975-90) and a major drachme devaluation (by 15 per cent) at the outset of a stabilisation attempt in 1985-87. In fact, the failure of this attempt poignantly contrasted the readiness of the authorities to activate the exchange rate instrument with their apparent inability during the 1980s to address domestic policy slippages, particularly in the fiscal area.

Exchange rate policy started to harden, albeit gradually, in mid-1989, when the central bank launched a policy of depreciating the currency by less than the full inflation differential relative to the ECU. However, this 'hard drachme' policy was initially pursued loosely, as the exchange rate continued to depreciate significantly in nominal terms and was only allowed to appreciate marginally in real (CPI-based) terms. Nonetheless, the non-accommodating rate of depreciation was slowly reduced over the course of the next years (from 11 per cent in 1990 to 6 per cent in 1994) as the necessary tightening in other policy areas took hold: the abolishment of wage indexation was followed by an austere incomes policy, and the primary accounts of the budget underwent a major turnaround (from a deficit of 6 per cent to a surplus of 2 per cent of GDP during the same period). At the same time, the domestic financial market and the external capital account were liberalised, impairing the stability of money demand and reducing the reliability of money targets. In this context, the exchange rate progressively became the main monetary policy compass, which was validated by a slowly declining inflation differential vis-à-vis regional partners.

Exchange rate policy hardened further in 1995 when the Bank of Greece officially announced a specific exchange rate target. In line with the government's convergence program, the drachme would be allowed to depreciate by only 3 per cent against the ECU during the year and a broadly stable drachme/ECU exchange rate would be targeted in 1996 and beyond. This commitment was subsequently judged credible by the markets. Despite international financial turbulence that led to realignments of the peseta and the escudo, to relatively strong depreciations of the lira and pound sterling and more broadly to emerging market turmoil (notably the collapse of the Mexican peso), the drachme ECU-peg showed remarkable stability and resilience. In fact, the targeted exchange rate path was exactly met in both 1995 and 1996. However, the market credibility elicited major capital inflows that not only allowed official reserves to reach historical peaks, but also caused nominal and real interest rates to decline, thereby frustrating efforts aimed at rapid disinflation towards the level of the exchange rate peg and causing a substantial real appreciation of the currency. In many respects, this adverse side-effect of exchange rate targeting was similar to that experienced by Italy, Spain and Portugal in the ERM during the late 1980s. Against this background, in an effort to raise the risks faced by investors, the central bank loosened the exchange rate target somewhat in 1997, defining it more cryptically in terms of the 'currencies comprising the ECU', rather than the ECU itself, and allowing slightly greater fluctuations against the peg than in previous years.

In the event, market sentiment shifted in 1997 and, rather than capital inflows, the central bank faced recurrent and intense downward pressures on the drachme. While the exchange rate target was vigorously defended – and broadly met – through foreign exchange intervention, interest rate increases and moral suasion on the predominantly state-owned banking sector, the sustainability remained subject to repeated market questioning. In this setting, Greece switched to an unequivocal exchange rate targeting strategy in March 1998, when the drachme was introduced into the ERM and the money targets were downgraded to monitoring ranges. Given the government's objective of EMU entry shortly after its inception, this decision was importantly driven by the EMU entry criterion of at least two years' ERM membership. Indeed, the concurrent large devaluation (by about 12 per cent relative to the ECU peg) was determined on the basis of the desired prospective euro conversion rate rather than an assessment of the prevailing equilibrium and the market rate only depreciated by part of this adjustment. With policies explicitly oriented at a stable and overriding nominal exchange rate target against the European currency block, Greece clearly positioned itself to join the eurozone soon after the monetary union had taken off.

The lessons learnt

Europe's rich history of exchange rate targeting harbours a host of lessons, some of which were drawn gradually, others in a context of crisis. In general, almost all EU countries have assigned an increasingly dominant role to the exchange rate in their monetary policy strategies, as the expansion of tradables sectors strengthened the exchange rate channel of monetary transmission and as money demand instability in the context of liberalised capital flows reduced the attractiveness of quantity oriented policy approaches. More specifically, *hard* exchange rate targets have steadily gained in popularity, even if the institutional modalities of such a strategy (in particular the potential fluctuation bandwidth around the target) have generally become looser. By contrast, the European record indicates that a soft currency strategy aimed at ensuring a competitive real exchange rate level – such as implemented in the Scandinavian and Southern European countries through the better part of the 1980s – brings about higher inflation (expectations) rather than higher growth; in no country has such a strategy survived the test of time.

There does, however, seem to have been a shift in the effectiveness of the exchange rate as an adjustment instrument. While experience in the 1970s and 1980s suggested this efficacy was limited, it proved quite powerful in the 1990s when a number of countries (especially Finland, Italy, Portugal, Spain, Sweden and the United Kingdom) underwent sizeable depreciations that did not trigger commensurate domestic price increases and that therefore translated into durable real exchange rate improvements. In each of these cases this can be attributed in part to the revamping of the monetary policy strategy in the wake of currency falls and especially to explicit emphasis on a target or reference value for inflation. With tight inflation control, nominal depreciations were more effectively translated into real competitiveness gains.

European monetary history also shows that exchange rate targeting agreements, whatever their formal design, are almost by nature predestined to end up being asymmetric, with the anchor role taken up by the larger country pursuing the tightest and most stable policies. The follower countries have the important benefit of enhanced policy discipline, but at the prime cost of a loss of monetary policy autonomy. In this context, the division of roles between anchor and follower countries has proven to be governed by considerable inertia, which underscores the influence of track records in monetary policy strategy. In fact, once its anchor role had been clearly established, Germany's dominant position in Europe's exchange rate arrangements survived major domestic policy slippages, including periods when economic developments in other large European countries (notably France) were significantly more stable, both internally and externally. This inescapable asymmetry, as well as its inertia, is powerfully illustrated by the fact that, with one anomalous exception, the Deutsche mark never devalued against any other currency within the framework of either the snake or the EMS.

From a broad perspective, the European experiences demonstrate that a prolonged period of exchange rate stability does not mean that the nominal convergence necessary to underpin this stability is actually taking place. In fact, the exchange rate targeting experiences of Ireland in the early 1980s, of Finland, Italy, Portugal, Spain, Sweden, and the United Kingdom during the next ten-year period, and of Greece during the late 1990s, all show that it is possible to maintain an exchange rate peg for a considerable time period even when the domestic inflation rate and the underlying policies are clearly inconsistent with this external anchor. In other words, the link between the exchange rate target and the macroeconomic policies that largely determine its sustainability is loose at best. By consequence, the disciplinary influence of an exchange rate target is unpredictable and abrupt. And, as many European countries can testify (notably Sweden and the United Kingdom, which both subsequently abandoned this strategy altogether), this difficulty is compounded by the fact that failure to uphold an exchange rate target can bring with it massive costs – in terms of intervention losses, diminished monetary policy credibility and collateral damage from unduly high interest rates during the defence of the peg. These costs are evidently much higher than in the case of missing, say, a money or inflation target.

The European experiences further highlight the importance of broadly parallel macroeconomic developments between countries maintaining mutual exchange rate links. In this respect, the existential EMS crises of 1992-93 harshly brought home the lesson that a-synchronised economic developments can undermine exchange rate stability as forcefully as divergent policy discipline can. This accentuated the relatively heavy burden that exchange rate targeting places on fiscal and wage policies, not only because of these policies' impact on the long-run sustainability of the target, but also on account of their contribution to the short-run stabilisation of the domestic economy. Indeed, with monetary policy aimed at an external target, other policies have to be tailored more keenly to the needs of the internal economy than in the case of domestically oriented monetary policy strategies. This change of emphasis is especially apparent in the institutional design of EMU (a fixed exchange rate agreement of sorts), where the 1991 Maastricht Treaty on European Union emphasised the need to limit budgetary deficits and debts, while the subsequent Stability and Growth Pact (concluded after the 1992-93 EMS crises) stressed the need to create adequate scope beneath these ceilings for stabilisation policy.

Developments in Europe have also vividly illustrated how exchange rate targeting becomes more demanding once capital flows are freed of restrictions. While intervention policy could previously be used to buy time for apparently necessary domestic policy adjustments, the liberalisation of capital flows drastically shortened the duration of any period of respite, rendering the intervention instrument all but impotent. In this context, the widening of intervention limits around an exchange rate target and the concomitant enlarging of two-sided exchange rate risk have proven to be effective ways of limiting the scope for speculative attacks. In principle, this weakened the strength of the exchange rate anchor; in practice, increased emphasis on central parities has precluded a significant softening of exchange rate targets.

Moreover, the European record seems to confirm that the opening up of capital accounts makes exchange rate targets more susceptible to volatile market sentiments and thereby minimises the scope for monetary policy actions or communications aimed at anything other than the exchange rate target. This was poignantly illustrated by the downward pressures on the French franc in mid-1993, which were triggered by domestically oriented signals from the monetary authorities and occurred despite solid fundamentals. Within the group of most successful exchange rate targeters, this was also shown by the fact that the countries with the tightest and longest-standing exchange rate pegs (Austria and the Netherlands) survived the 1992-93 EMS crises unscathed, whereas the countries with somewhat looser or more recent pegs (Belgium and Denmark) came under heavy speculative pressure.

Besides again emphasising the contribution of continuity to the credibility of a monetary policy strategy, these combined experiences thus suggest that exchange rate targeting – in contrast with money targeting – is best pursued tightly, even when the targeting framework provides room for flexibility and discretion. In general, European practice suggests that exploiting any flexibility to deviate from an exchange rate target, or communicating that this may occur in the future, risks raising market doubts about the true commitment to the external anchor. In this respect, experience indicates that exchange rate targets can hardly be combined in a meaningful manner with other monetary policy targets for credit, money, inflation or whatever. To the extent that countries have maintained such auxiliary targets, these targets have either played no effective role in actual policy setting, or in practice have not seriously conflicted with the exchange rate target.

In sum, Europe's extensive experience with exchange rate targeting conveys a mixed message. On the one hand, the preconditions for success in a context of free capital flows are highly demanding: macroeconomic developments need to run broadly parallel with the anchor country, the scope to orient monetary policy at anything other than the exchange rate is strictly limited, and fiscal and wage developments need to contribute relatively strongly to the strategy's sustainability. Moreover, the costs of failure are relatively steep. On the other hand, Europe provides ample evidence that exchange rate targeting can still be viable with an open capital account and that this strategy can be highly effective in providing a stable policy framework. Moreover, amongst the countries pursuing the tightest exchange rate regimes (notably Austria and the Netherlands), there is evidence that economic structures gradually adjust to the regime choice in a way that enhances optimal currency area attributes. On balance, most European countries have opted to stick with a monetary policy strategy of exchange rate targeting, even if under looser institutional arrangements. But in several countries the 1992-93 experience led to the conclusion that the preconditions for successful exchange rate targeting were simply not, or no longer, met. Since these countries had previously exhausted the existing alternatives, there was high demand for a new monetary policy strategy.

NOTES

[1] Kruse (1980), Thygesen (1979) and Ungerer (1997). A political analysis of the motives leading to the EMS is provided in Ludlow (1982) and Szász (1999).

[2] Thygesen (1979, p. 94-108)

[3] Monticelli and Papi (1996) provide an extensive review of asymmetry in monetary policy co-ordination.

[4] In an effort to increase the attractiveness of holding official ECUs, the yield was adjusted in 1985 to the average of national money market rates, typically about 1 percentage point higher than the average of national discount rates.

[5] While the short- and medium-term credit facilities were accessible to all EC countries, regardless of whether they participated in the ERM, it was agreed that the enlarged quotas of the United Kingdom in the former facility were only to be used after this country had joined the ERM; see Ungerer (1997).

[6] Although the size of these transfers was originally modest, they played a significant role in the negotiations on the creation of the EMS; see Kruse (1980) and Ludlow (1982). The issue featured particularly prominently in Ireland, where ERM participation involved severing the exchange rate parity with the British pound that had lasted for over fifty years; see Honohan (1997).

[7] These issues were the objects of intense empirical study during the first decade of the EMS. Evidence on the reduced volatility of bilateral exchange rates and lower variability in short-term interest rates is presented in Artis and Taylor (1988), Padoa Schioppa (1985), Ungerer, Evans and Nyberg (1983) and Ungerer *et al.* (1986). Evidence on the contribution of the EMS to disinflation is more tentative since disinflation was a world-wide phenomenon in the 1980s; see for example Collins (1988) and Giavazzi and Giovannini (1988). A formal analysis of the EMS as a disciplinary device fostering inflation convergence is set out in Giavazzi and Pagano (1988).

[8] European Commission (1989), Giavazzi, Micossi and Miller (eds.) (1988), Gros and Thygesen (1992), Monticelli and Papi (1996), Ungerer (1997) and Ungerer *et al.* (1990).

[9] This can be illustrated by comparing the average outcomes for these variables during the periods 1975-78 and 1979-1982 between the ERM countries (excluding Luxembourg which did not have its own currency), on the one hand, and a group of seven other industrial countries (Canada, Japan, Norway, Spain, Sweden, UK and US – selected on the basis of data availability for all four variables), on the other. In the case of the general budget balance, the standard deviation of the outcomes increased in the ERM countries from 2.6 during 1975-78 to 3.6 per cent of GDP during 1979-82, against an increase from 2.4 to only 2.7 per cent of GDP in the control group of other industrial countries. For the external current account, wage and consumer price changes, there was an increase in the standard deviation of the outcomes for the ERM countries (from 2.1 to 4.2 per cent of GDP, from 3.6 to 5.4 per cent, and from 3.7 to 4.9 per cent respectively) against a *decrease* in the other industrial countries (from 2.6 to 1.5 per cent of GDP, from 7.6 to 4.2 per cent and from 4.4 to 2.9 per cent respectively). Substitution of Austria, Australia or Switzerland in the control group leads to broadly the same conclusion. The background data are drawn from Tables 13, 17, 19 and 31 in Ungerer *et al.* (1990).

[10] Jurgensen (1983).

[11] Gros and Thygesen (1992), Padoa Schioppa (1985) and Ungerer (1997).

[12] An overview of the adjustment measures announced in connection with the realignments through 1990 is provided by Ungerer (1990).

[13] Belgium and Denmark asked for devaluations of 12 and 7 percent, but ultimately agreed to 8½ and 3 per cent respectively; see Gros and Thygesen (1992, p. 76).

[14] The stabilisation package was supported by an ECU 4 billion loan through the EU medium-term facility.

[15] This can be deduced from the evidence presented in De Grauwe (1990, p. 148).

[16] Folkerts-Landau and Mathieson (1989).

[17] Mastropasqua, Micossi and Rinaldi (1988) and Giavazzi and Giovannini (1989). Gros and Thygesen (1992, pp. 136-57) provide an overview of the findings in other asymmetry studies and conclude that asymmetry tests fare best in the 1983-86 period.

[18] Gros and Thygesen (1992, p. 84) and Ungerer *et al.* (1990, p. 14-15).

[19] Although the bilateral central rate for the lira was devalued by 3.75 per cent when Italy moved from the wide (± 6 per cent) to the narrow (± 2.25 per cent) band in January 1990, this did not increase the scope for lira depreciation as the lower intervention points remained unchanged.

[20] Norway, Sweden and Finland pegged their currencies to the ECU in October 1990, May 1991 and June 1991, with fluctuation margins of ± 2.25, ± 1.5 and ± 3 per cent respectively.

[21] The texts of the Basle-Nyborg communiqués are provided in Ungerer *et al.* (1990, Appendix II).

[22] See Walters (1986, pp. 125-132).

[23] The analysis in Eichengreen and Wyplosz (1993) that the persistently higher inflation and rising labour costs in these countries did not cause competitiveness and balance-of-payments problems, but reflected the Balassa-Samuelson effect, is unconvincing. With the benefit of hindsight, it is easy to refute this analysis by pointing at the massive subsequent devaluations by Portugal (12½ per cent cumulatively between mid-1992 and end-1993) and Spain (19 percent) within the ERM framework, and the depreciations by Italy (32 per cent between the mid-1992 Deutsche-mark parity and the end-1993 market rate) and the United Kingdom (15 percent) outside it. With the exception of the United Kingdom, the real exchange rates of these countries remained broadly around their newly found levels thereafter. If the Balassa-Samuelson effect had previously been a driving force behind the

inflation differentials, the initially higher real exchange rate levels would have proved sustainable.

[24] The term 'New EMS' originates from Giavazzi and Spaventa (1990).

[25] In a study of monetary conditions in the EMS during this period, Clarida, Galí and Gertler (1997) show that Germany's interest rates were indeed too high for the economic conditions of other countries in the system. By applying an estimated reaction function of the Bundesbank to France, the United Kingdom and Italy, they find that the inflationary pressures from German unification led to unreasonably high interest rates and thus to untenable economic stress, particularly in the first two of these countries.

[26] Finland, Sweden and Norway severed their ECU-pegs on 8 September, 19 November and 19 December 1992, respectively.

[27] At the time of the widening of the fluctuation bands, Germany and the Netherlands mutually agreed, outside the ERM, to maintain the ± 2.25 per cent margin for their bilateral exchange rate. Szász (1999) describes the astute political manoeuvres by the Netherlands that elicited this exceptional deal, notwithstanding the opposition of countries such as France that were bent on avoiding a differentiated treatment.

[28] Von Hagen (1999, p. 694).

[29] Von Hagen (1989) shows that the empirical results for short-run and long-run sterilisation are very different and that the latter generally did not occur throughout the 1980s. The pattern of long-run sterilisation can be clearly linked to the exchange rate developments of the Deutsche mark against both the dollar and the EMS currencies.

[30] Hochreiter and Winckler (1995).

[31] Gnan (1994, p. 32).

[32] Glück, Proske and Tatom (1992, p. 168).

[33] Hochreiter and Winckler (1995) present evidence that asymmetric shocks dominated until the mid-1980s and that real wage flexibility allowed Austria to become part of an optimal currency area with Germany. In particular, they show that the variability of the schilling's real exchange rate vis-à-vis the Deutsche mark was significantly higher than that of, for example, the Dutch guilder during 1980-87, but that it was clearly lower than that of all other EC and EFTA currencies during 1987-92.

[34] In the words of then central bank official Boot, the main lesson of the unsatisfactory realignment outcome was the importance of creating "an undeniable political fact regarding the guilder in as far as this is possible: an unassailable position in the market, implying that next time a deviation from the German mark would not be credible"; see Szász (1999, p. 199).

[35] In the Netherlands, monetary policy is the domain of the central bank, but exchange rate regime and realignment decisions are governmental responsibility. When such decisions are taken, the central bank provides a public recommendation.

[36] Szász (1999, p. 201).

[37] Using correlation coefficients for GDP, inflation, unit wages, and short- and long-term interest rates as broad indicators for the fulfilment of optimal currency area criteria, Wellink (1994) finds that the economy of the Netherlands is more tightly linked with Germany than any other EMS country – with Belgium a close second – and that this linkage was generally tighter for the period 1989-1993 than for 1983-93, suggesting increasing convergence.

[38] Luxembourg did not have its own central bank. The exchange rate between the Belgian franc and Luxembourg franc was fixed in 1936 and rescaled to a rate of one-for-one in 1944. However, Luxembourg did give its opinion on the monetary and exchange rate policies pursued by Belgium, occasionally voicing its disapproval and raising the spectre of a break-up of the Belgium-Luxembourg Economic Union. This was, for instance, the case

when Belgium requested a disproportionately large devaluation in 1982; see Gros and Thygesen (1993; p. 76).

[39] Michielsen (1994, p. 66).

[40] Quintyn and Vuchelen (1992). Monetary financing is defined as the total of direct and indirect borrowing by the Treasury from the central bank, including foreign borrowing whereby foreign exchange proceeds are sold directly to the central bank.

[41] Denmark was continuously a member of the snake and the ERM, with the exception of a short interruption in 1972 when the snake was abandoned in the wake of the United Kingdom's withdrawal. However, the krone was kept within the margins and Denmark formally rejoined the arrangement at its original parity within four months.

[42] De Grauwe and Vanhaverbeke (1990) attribute the Danish success primarily to the impact of the one-off capital liberalisation, which allowed the external inflows that fuelled the domestic consumption and investment boom. They arrive at this conclusion in a comparison with Belgium and the Netherlands, which also initiated adjustment programs in the early 1980s, but could not count on such an impact as their capital flows were already essentially free. However, it seems the much more forceful and comprehensive nature of the Danish policy package was the key distinguishing factor.

[43] Christensen and Topp (1997).

[44] Denmark was the principal – and unsuccessful – advocate of a general return to more narrow bands. The August 1993 statements by the Prime Minister and the central bank Governor are reproduced in Christensen and Topp (1997, pp. 22-23).

[45] The pre-announcement expressly mentioned the agreement of the euro area ministers and the ECB. Although the central rate around which the narrow fluctuation band would be positioned was not specified, the press communiqué did spell out that Denmark had had an unchanged parity within ERM since January 1987.

[46] James (1996, p. 476-77) offers a colourful account of the heated debate on exchange rate strategy in France during 1982-83.

[47] In an interview with Le Monde on 20 December 1989, Finance minister Bérégovoy indicated that the stability of the exchange rate vis-à-vis Germany had become the "cornerstone of policy-making". From the perspective of the Banque de France, Icard (1994a and 1994b) recognises that the exchange rate has been given precedence in monetary policy setting since the mid-1980s, but conjectures that the money supply target continued to fulfil an important role in influencing expectations by stressing the authorities' abiding commitment to price stability. However, it is clear that the prospect of exchange rate stability, which had to be upheld in daily monetary operations, has had a much more powerful influence on expectations than the annual announcement of a money target that was more often than not missed. Thus, the role of the money targets primarily seems to have been a political one: to provide a domestic coating to an externally oriented monetary policy.

[48] The central bank of Ireland was set up in 1943, but domestic lending operations remained on a very modest scale through the 1970s. From 1971 on, adjusting the exchange rate no longer required legislative change, but could be decided by the minister of finance after consultation with the central bank. Honohan (1997) provides an insightful review of the gradual evolution of Ireland's currency board arrangement.

[49] Leddin and Walsh (1995).

[50] The exchange rate strategy was apparently not credible in the labour market during the initial period of ERM membership. In 1979, following entry into the arrangement, determined efforts to have wage agreements based on a single digit inflation forecast failed and wages subsequently fuelled the inflationary spiral; see Walsh (1983).

[51] Dornbusch (1989) assesses the first decade of Ireland's EMS membership and concludes – given the costs in terms of unemployment, emigration and government debt – that the stabilisation program was a failure and that EMS participation did not furnish a credibility bonus. While he considers an overly tight exchange rate policy to have been a prime cause of this failure, a major shortcoming was that this policy, if anything, was initially unduly loose. His appraisal would most probably also have been quite different if he had known of the impressive, drawn-out Irish recovery that would be built on the painful stabilisation efforts of the 1980s. More specifically, Kremers (1990) finds twofold empirical evidence that ERM entry actually did influence policy credibility: first, in 1979 inflation expectations shifted away from the United Kingdom towards the rest of the ERM and, second, during the ERM period – and especially 1981-82 – competitiveness became an important determinant of expected inflation, with competitiveness losses expected to be recouped by adjustments in Ireland's inflation rather than by exchange rate correction.

[52] Leddin and Walsh (1995) recount the authorities' attempt to avoid devaluation based on considerations of adequate domestic competitiveness, the need to defend the ERM against speculators, the desirability of breaking the dependence on the United Kingdom, and the lack of durable benefits from devaluation. It is testimony to the authorities' efforts that the Irish devaluation only occurred four months after the United Kingdom withdrawal from the mechanism.

[53] The Finnish markka had previously been devalued by over 30 per cent in both 1957 and 1967 and by about 10 per cent in 1971-73. Korkman (1978), for instance, provides a sharp theoretical critique of the Finnish devaluation cycle; Halttunen and Korkman (1983) present econometric simulations of the detrimental impact of this cycle.

[54] Lehmussaari, Suvanto and Vajanne (1992, p. 10).

[55] Gylfason (1990) finds that the standard deviation of Finland's real exchange rate (2.0, calculated on the basis of the IMF's Multilateral Exchange Rate Model) during 1975-88 was notably lower than that of for instance Norway (6.4), the United Kingdom (10.0) and the US (15.4, over 1978-88).

[56] At a technical level, the central bank did, however, strive to increase the transparency of the basket, for instance, from 1984 on, by publishing the index daily rather than as a monthly average, thereby facilitating public monitoring of the exchange rate within the band; see Puro (1984). In addition, the switch to the ECU basket in 1991 undoubtedly enhanced policy communicability.

[57] Lehmussaari, Suvanto and Vajanne (1992) offer a sweeping account of Finland's boom-bust cycle in the late 1980s and early 1990s.

[58] Pikkarainen *et al.* (1997, p. 39).

[59] Hörngren and Lindberg (1993) provide an elaborate and compelling account of Sweden's endeavours to turn the krona into a hard currency.

[60] Hörngren and Westman-Mårtensson (1991, p. 176).

[61] In contrast with the common institutional set-up elsewhere in Europe, Swedish exchange rate policy – including the regime choice – has traditionally fallen exclusively under the central bank, although the government had to be consulted prior to major decisions; see Hörngren and Westman-Mårtensson (1991, pp. 173-174).

[62] In interpreting budgetary policy in Sweden, it needs to be borne in mind that this country is estimated to have had the most cycle-sensitive budget of the current EU members; see European Commission (1995).

[63] The intervention total is reported in Hörngren and Lindberg (1993).

[64] In the advent to EMU, Italian interest rates were the last to converge to the commonly agreed level (3 per cent), only reaching that level in the last week of 1998.

[65] Progress in each of these three fields was in fact identified in 1981 by the central bank governor as a prerequisite for a stable currency; see Passacantando (1996) and Visco (1995).

[66] Ayuso and Escrivá (1998).

[67] In an empirical study of the Bank of Spain's reaction function, Escrivá and Santos (1991) find that, prior to 1986, the exchange rate was not a variable systematically affecting policy-making. They also establish that the exchange rate against other EC currencies had a consistent influence on the interest rate thereafter and that, from mid-1987 on, the authorities' policy response was essentially governed by the behaviour of the peseta-Deutsche mark rate.

[68] If it is assumed that the peseta would have been realigned in parallel with the French franc (implying devaluations of 6 and 3 per cent against the Deutsche mark in April 1986 and January 1987), the peseta would have appreciated against its upper ceiling in late 1988; see Viñals (1990, pp. 209-210).

[69] Escrivá and Malo de Molina (1991) underscore this signalling role of the money targets.

[70] Ungerer *et al.* (1990, p. 66) show that the variability of the United Kingdom's effective exchange rate, in both nominal and real terms, was higher than that of any other of the then EC countries and about twice their average during 1975-78 and 1979-89 (the ERM period before UK entry).

[71] Particularly influential was the critique of the MTFS program by Buiter and Miller (1981), who modelled how the government's tight money approach was leading to a transitory real appreciation and a decline in output below potential capacity. Their analysis of exchange rate overshooting was based on the standard proposition that, with liberal capital flows and a floating exchange regime, restrictive monetary policy is immediately reflected in the nominal exchange rate, whereas, owing to wage and price inertia, it only affects domestic costs with a lag.

[72] Artis (1990) provides a verbatim chronicle of the increasing emphasis on the exchange rate in the evolving MTFS.

[73] Thatcher (1993) and Lawson (1993) provide first hand accounts of their fundamental discord.

[74] Townend (1991, p. 210).

[75] George (1998, p. 180).

[76] At this summit, the Delors Report was certified as a starting point for the architecture of EMU. The conditions to be met for ERM entry were specified as: a lower inflation rate in the United Kingdom; the removal of exchange controls within the ERM; sufficient progress towards the single EC market including the liberalisation of financial services; and agreement on competition policy.

[77] The announcement to enter ERM in combination with a lowering of interest rates was politically timed on the eve of the annual Party Conferences. Prime Minister Thatcher insisted on the rate cut against the advice of the Treasury and the Bank of England, and placed heavy emphasis on it in presenting the decision to join the ERM. It is more than curious that a Prime Minister entering an exchange rate commitment should point at money supply figures as a sign that inflation will decline in the near future: "I for my part was determined to demonstrate that we would be looking more to monetary conditions than to the exchange rate in setting interest rates." See Thatcher (1993, p. 724).

[78] Buiter, Corsetti and Pesenti (1998) provide a detailed reconstruction of the 1992-93 ERM crises.

[79] George (1998, p. 181) concedes that the Bank of England cannot explain the marked appreciation of sterling against European currencies in the second half of the 1990s, even when taking account of interest rate differentials. This seems to echo the conclusion of

Hacche and Townend (1981) who dramatically failed to find a stable relationship between exchange rate developments during 1972-80 and the main (monetary and other) variables which theoretical considerations suggest may be its chief determinants.

[80] The system of credit ceilings remained in place until 1990 and was mostly supplemented by administratively set interest rates. These combined regulations not only served a monetary function, but also levied an implicit tax on the banking system that represented a major source of financing for the large public sector deficits during this period.

[81] On the basis of a relatively high ratio of (short-term and overall) capital flows to GDP as well as of onshore/offshore interest rate differentials, Torres (1990) concludes that Portugal's capital controls were largely ineffective from mid-1986 on.

[82] The new currency basket comprised the Deutsche mark, the Spanish peseta, the French franc, the Italian lira and the British pound; the weight of the Deutsche mark was adjusted upwards to reflect the importance of trade with the Benelux countries.

[83] The comprehensive inflation assessment was not published as a separate inflation report but was included in the central bank's quarterly Economic Bulletin and updated after a semi-annual interval; see the March and September issues of Banco de Portugal (1997).

[84] On the favourable Greek attitude to European objectives for greater exchange rate stability, as well as the scant Greek contribution to these objectives owing to the dominant national political business cycle, see Papademos (1990).

7. THE EVOLUTION OF INFLATION TARGETING, 1992-1998

7.1 The rise of inflation targeting

The rise of direct inflation targeting in Europe during the 1990s was spurred by conceptual advances in monetary policy strategy, technical progress in the analysis of inflation, as well as practical problems with prevailing strategies. On the first issue, the inflationary experiences of the 1970s and early 1980s had brought home the lesson that there is no durable positive trade-off between inflation and unemployment (at least, in case of high inflation) and that, if anything, this relationship is negative in the longer run. Moreover, the view gained ground that a monetary policy focus on real variables introduces an inflationary bias. As a result, it became increasingly accepted that monetary policy should prioritise the establishment and maintenance of price stability. In Europe, this shift was apparent in institutional changes that spelt out an overriding price stability objective for monetary policy and that granted central banks the related policy autonomy. This was most notably the case in the 1991 Maastricht Treaty setting out the creation of a European System of Central Banks (ESCB), constituted of independent, price stability oriented entities.

At a technical level, considerable progress had been made during the 1970s and 1980s in the analysis and forecasting of inflation, especially with regard to the transmission of monetary policy measures and to the identification of information variables with leading indicator properties for future price developments.[1] Although these insights had not resolved the imperfect controllability of inflation in the short and medium term, they facilitated a broadening of the monetary policy focus – and the communication about this focus – beyond a single intermediate target such as a money aggregate or the exchange rate. In itself, this paved the way to aim monetary policy directly at its end objective for inflation.

Finally, on the practical front, the 1992-93 EMS crises had left the European central banking landscape in a state of disarray. Several countries (Finland, Italy, Sweden and the United Kingdom) had been forced to abandon their monetary policy strategies of exchange rate targeting, while others (notably Portugal and Spain) were left with wide fluctuation bands around sharply devalued exchange rate targets. This created concern that expectations regarding prospective policies and price developments were being given insufficient guidance. Moreover, in the wake of the crises, these countries' weak monetary policy track records were further blemished by continued downward pressure on the currency. In these circumstances, there was a need to re-establish a firm anchor for monetary policy. Given the manifest difficulties of tight exchange rate targets, as well as the unhappy earlier experiences under other traditional intermediate targets (especially for money and credit), it was evident that a new monetary policy strategy was needed. The new strategy basically had to meet three requirements: first, the policy target should provide a strong signal about the authorities' ambitiousness regarding future price developments; second, the success of monetary policy should no longer be made dependent on an intermediate target that had an uncertain relationship with the relevant end objective for inflation; and third, the strategy should allow an expeditious build-up of monetary policy credibility, so that it could be readily adopted by central banks with lack-lustre track records.

In this setting, direct inflation targeting swiftly came of age. By highlighting a target for inflation, the strategy gave direction to those in the wage and price setting process, and in financial markets, on the authorities' prospective policy course. And, by focusing policy on a broad-based forecast for the central bank's final inflation objective, this monetary strategy was less vulnerable to instability between individual variables in the monetary transmission process. Thus, the main weakness of the customary intermediate targets was circumvented. At the same time, by placing heavy emphasis on central bank policy autonomy and transparency, the new approach sought quickly to address any lingering doubts about the monetary authorities' true commitment to the new target. This made the strategy attractive to countries seeking to short-cut the accumulation of policy credibility.[2] There was, however, some friction between the second and the third requirements, since the inflation forecast is not easily and objectively observable. This made external monitoring more difficult and implied that monetary policy – other things equal – essentially became more discretionary, widening the scope for time inconsistent decision-making. In general, this increased the weight attached to the elements underlying short-term policy credibility, especially to the autonomy, transparency, and incentive structure governing central bank policy decisions.

The origins of inflation targeting

By any practical standard, the origins of inflation targeting lie in New Zealand. After years of relatively poor macroeconomic performance, a disappointing experience with money targeting, and an acute foreign exchange crisis, New Zealand pioneered inflation targeting as part of a far-reaching reform package designed to restore macroeconomic balance and improve microeconomic efficiency. In a radical break with the past, monetary policy was cast in an exceptionally coherent and clear-cut new framework that prioritised inflation control, established central bank independence for policy adjustments, stressed transparency in policy implementation, and created accountability for policy outcomes. The monetary re-orientation involved a major institutional restructuring, legally underpinned through the passage (in 1989) of a new central bank Act and operationally launched (in March 1990) through a first Policy Targets Agreement between the central bank Governor and the Minister of Finance. This latter agreement publicly committed the Governor to a reach a specific inflation range by a specific date, although it allowed for temporary departures from the target to accommodate price movements caused by certain predefined shocks. Subject to this proviso, inadequate performance under the target was explicitly established as a reason to dismiss the Governor. Moreover, the central bank was obliged to report twice a year to Parliament on progress under the target, including by disclosing a two-year inflation forecast. The example of New Zealand was first followed by Canada, where the government and central bank jointly announced an inflation target in February 1991, also after a protracted period of relatively high inflation and disappointment with money targets. However, the strategy switch was not as comprehensive as that of New Zealand: it was not accompanied by institutional reform of the monetary policy framework, the price stability target was not legislated, and periodic reports on developments under the inflation target were not introduced until the Spring of 1995.

In the more distant past, inflation targeting also has European roots. In fact, the first country on record to have focused monetary policy explicitly on a price target is Sweden. This country pursued a policy openly geared to price-level stabilisation from the moment it left the gold standard in September 1931 until the krona was pegged to the British pound in July 1933.[3] Subsequently, price level stability remained the prime monetary policy target alongside the exchange rate commitment until 1937, when the Riksbank was given additional objectives including full employment. At a general level, it is notable that the price stability target was supported by an institutional structure that, by current standards, was surprisingly transparent and accountable. After Parliament had endorsed the monetary program designed to stabilise the domestic price level, it monitored the central bank's activities through regular reports and periodic questioning of the Governor. Furthermore, in the context of the 1930s, the Swedish experience shows how a form of inflation targeting can aim at countering not only the risk of rising prices, but also of deflation. Overall, however, this early practice does not seem to have directly influenced the spread of inflation targeting in Europe some sixty years later, except perhaps in Sweden itself.[4] At most, the underlying writings of Knut Wicksell may have had an indirect impact. Rather, the return of inflation targeting is a re-invention of the wheel that illustrates how the optimal monetary strategy is liable to change over the course of time, as economic structures and policy preferences adjust and as the understanding of economic processes progresses.

The spread of inflation targeting in Europe

The first European country to introduce direct inflation targeting was the *United Kingdom.* Following poor results with discretion and repeated failures under a wide variety of different intermediate targets, the United Kingdom, for want of better, opted directly to target an end objective for inflation. The new strategy was launched on 8 October 1992 and was accompanied by an official downgrading of money growth targets to monitoring ranges (with a broadened coverage of two aggregates, M0 and M4). Over the course of the next five years, the inflation targeting framework was developed in steps to produce one of the most comprehensive examples of its sort. Thus, coming from far behind, the United Kingdom managed to re-establish its position in the vanguard of monetary policy-making.

The United Kingdom's switch to inflation targeting stands out on two counts. First, the new strategy was introduced remarkably quickly, being announced within three weeks of the hapless collapse of the EMS exchange rate commitment. This promptness powerfully illustrates the United Kingdom's urgency to restore an anchor for inflation expectations, even before the aftershocks of the exchange rate crisis had subsided. In this regard, although the official records nowhere relate the adoption of the inflation target to inspiration derived from the earlier initiatives of New Zealand and Canada, it can hardly be a coincidence that the novel strategy was expeditiously introduced in Europe by an Anglo-Saxon country. In fact, inflation targeting has maintained something of an Anglo-Saxon glow.

Second, politics played a heavy role in the birth of the new strategy. The inflation target announcement was made by the Chancellor at the highly politicised occasion of a Conservative Party Conference (the details of the framework were set out in a concurrent letter by the Chancellor to the Treasury Committee of the House of Commons). This contrasts with the introduction of inflation targeting elsewhere in Europe, where central banks had the lead. Moreover, the duration of the first inflation target was proclaimed "for the remainder of this Parliament" (May 1997 at the latest) and was thus explicitly linked to the British political cycle. This may have cast doubt on the longer-term prospects for the new commitment to low inflation.[5] Finally, and most importantly, the announcement did not include any changes to the institutional framework governing monetary policy decisions. Clearly, in contrast with the movement towards central bank independence elsewhere in Europe, developments in the United Kingdom's monetary strategy were constrained by the desire to preserve the primacy of politics in monetary decision-making. In fact, although the United Kingdom's inflation targeting framework showed an impressive evolution over the following years, particularly in the fields of transparency and accountability, it took until the "next Parliament" for the Bank of England to be granted the policy autonomy that necessarily goes with the strategy it was advertising so proficiently.

Sweden was the second European convert to inflation targeting. After an exceptionally vigorous exchange rate defence, first using interest rate policy and then intervention policy, Sweden concluded that the costs of sustaining its ERM commitment were prohibitive. But the decision to withdraw from the ERM on 19 November 1992 caught the authorities off-guard: it had been close to sixty years since the country had had a flexible exchange regime for any substantive time period and the Riksbank did not have a contingency plan for the new policy environment.[6] Under these circumstances, the Governor requested various prominent academics as well as central bank staff expeditiously to write a series of articles on Sweden's monetary strategy options and the experiences of other small open economies with floating exchange rates (notably Canada, New Zealand, Switzerland, and Sweden itself in the 1930s).[7] Subsequently, on 15 January 1993, the Riksbank's Governing Board unilaterally announced an explicit inflation target. Given the uncertainties then governing the new policy framework and the unclear impact of the sharp exchange rate depreciation (by over 10 per cent relative to the previous ERM limit), the new target was set to apply only two years in the future (starting in 1995); in the meantime, monetary policy would aim at preventing a rise in the underlying rate of inflation.

From Sweden, inflation targeting spread to neighbouring *Finland.* Having been the first casualty of the European exchange market turmoil in the late summer of 1992, Finland had landed in a vicious circle of low policy credibility and economic contraction.[8] While high real interest rates exacerbated the depressed state of the economy, sustained downward pressure on the exchange rate boosted the domestic value of the large foreign currency debt, further weakening the banking system and the public accounts. Under these circumstances, agreements on public expenditure cuts and a general wage freeze failed to bolster confidence, as these measures implied a downward influence on domestic demand. At the same time, the lack of a nominal anchor to guide expectations on monetary policy was reflected in pronounced financial market instability. And the continued depreciation of the markka raised concerns about an acceleration of inflation. Against this background, after an almost five-month intermezzo without a clear monetary policy strategy, the central bank of Finland unilaterally adopted inflation targeting on 2 February 1993. Similar to the example set by Sweden, the inflation target was to be reached by 1995; however, no guidance was given on the (indicative) inflation path to be pursued during the transitional years 1993 and 1994.

Finland maintained a strategy of inflation targeting right up to the incorporation of the markka into the euro at the start of 1999. This was the case even after the country joined the ERM on 14 October 1996 in a step that was primarily undertaken to ensure the fulfilment by Finland of all the EMU convergence criteria. While this step involved paying increased attention to the goal of broad exchange rate stability within the system's wide fluctuation margins, the central bank indicated that low inflation was to remain the overriding objective of monetary policy and that the conduct of this policy would be essentially unchanged. This reflected the view that the two policy targets were compatible over the short time horizon remaining until EMU, as Finland's inflation target was in line with the implicit inflation target in the core ERM countries.[9] In this regard, Finland followed the example of Spain, which had launched a similar hierarchy of policy goals one year earlier.

Indeed, at the outset of 1995, *Spain* had become the fourth European country to join the ranks of inflation targeters. The initial motive for the strategy switch lay in the August 1993 widening of the ERM fluctuation bands, which had taken place shortly after three sharp exchange rate devaluations and had thus left the economy without a firm anchor at a time when inflation expectations risked surging. But, given continued participation in the ERM, the need for a new strategy was felt less sharply and Spain weighed the target alternatives for more than a year. A tighter exchange rate anchor was out of the question as this would imply an interest rate level that was probably inappropriate for the relatively closed domestic economy (as indicated by the previous years' experiences) as well as an undue interest rate variability to defend the target – particularly given Spain's recently weak track record of exchange rate targeting. Relying more heavily on the existing money supply anchor was not an option either, as the money demand function had become very unstable in the early 1990s in the wake of capital account liberalisation.[10] Although the stability of this function could be restored by including foreign interest rates in its determinants, this also implied a reduced controllability of the money target, making it an inadvisable policy compass. Actually, given greater uncertainty about future money demand, the target range for money growth was somewhat de-emphasised and was widened from 3 to 4 percentage points in 1994.

A number of factors prompted the eventual announcement of an inflation target in December 1994.[11] From a macroeconomic viewpoint, brightened prospects for cyclical recovery had raised the need for a firm anchor, which the prevailing eclectic strategy of wide exchange rate fluctuation bands, broad (and soft) money growth limits, and a qualitative orientation at inflation trends failed to provide. At the same time, the deepening monetary integration in Europe had increased the value attached to inflation convergence between Spain and the core ERM countries. And, from an institutional perspective, the Bank of Spain had been granted autonomy in June 1994, with price stability explicitly highlighted as the overriding monetary policy objective. Against this background, the switch to inflation targeting entailed the adoption of a tighter and more transparent strategy that would guide monetary policy towards an inflation performance in line with that in the other prospective EMU countries and with the central bank's new statutory mission.

But when Spain introduced the new strategy, effective from 1995 on, it faced major uncertainties on the price front. Not only was the targeted rate of inflation substantially lower than the then actual rate, but inflationary pressures were expected to intensify on account of the significant exchange rate weakening during 1994, the anticipated upturn in economic activity and prospective increases (in early 1995) in indirect taxes. Against this background, the inflation target (< 3 per cent) was set at a relatively distant time horizon (for 1997, effectively three years later), with a shorter-term reference range (of 3½-4 per cent) for the opening months of 1996. At the same time, Spain preserved the two mooring points of its previous strategy, although these were explicitly subordinated to the inflation anchor. Specifically, Spain maintained its ERM exchange rate commitments, the fulfilment of which constituted an EMU entry requirement. In the new framework, exchange rate stability came to be viewed more as an outcome of successful price control, than an *ex ante* policy target, as illustrated by the major peseta devaluation (by 7 per cent) that occurred shortly after the new strategy was launched. In addition, the central bank retained a benchmark for ALP money growth, although this variable was explicitly downgraded from a policy target to a privileged indicator. Under the new strategy, this indicator signalled a maximum medium-term money growth rate that was considered consistent with the inflation target. In the event, with continued money demand instability, the announcement of such a reference rate was discontinued after 1997.

In a broader sense, many other European central banks have also moved in the direction of inflation targeting by emphasising the inflation *objective* underlying their monetary policy-making. But these central banks have all stopped short of publicly committing to a quantified, and in monetary policy terms explicitly overriding, inflation *target*. For instance, in the case of *France*, shortly after legislative revisions had determined price stability as the primary objective of monetary policy, the newly established – and autonomous – Monetary Policy Council publicly specified its practical interpretation of this objective. In particular, in early 1994 the Council spelt out that the 'overall price increase should not exceed 2 per cent in 1994 and the medium-term' – a formula that was repeated annually until the start of EMU. However, while this final objective featured prominently in monetary policy press releases, the central bank also expressly indicated that it would be pursued through the dual intermediate targets for the ERM exchange rate and the medium-term money growth trend. In practice, of course, the exchange rate commitment vis-à-vis the Deutsche mark remained the dominant policy target.

In the case of *Italy*, numerical inflation objectives slowly evolved from an inflation path hoped for by the government (during the 1980s), to a governmental co-ordination device for wage and pricing decisions (from July 1992 on, after the abolishment of *scala mobile* wage indexation system).[12] And, after the lira had dropped out of the ERM in September 1993, inflation objectives automatically gained in importance as a guide to policy-makers and private agents alike. In these circumstances, proposals were made to increase the clarity and credibility of Italian monetary policy by switching to full-fledged inflation targeting.[13] Although this advice was not followed through, the central bank did take a step in this direction. Starting in 1995, the Governor adopted the custom of announcing, in the concluding remarks to the central bank's Annual Meeting in May, the inflation rate he considers achievable for that year.[14] On the first occasion, he also indicated that the central bank would actually calibrate its policies towards the stated objective, thereby bringing the policy framework very close to direct inflation targeting.[15] Beyond this, the re-entry of the lira into the ERM in November 1996 and the exchange rate focus this implied, effectively precluded a further evolution in that direction.

Similar examples are provided by *Greece* and *Portugal*, where the inflation objectives underlying monetary programs gained prominence in the 1990s. In the case of Greece, a gradually heavier weight was placed on the inflation objective within the eclectic policy approach, until the country joined the ERM in March 1998. In the case of Portugal, an increasing emphasis on inflation projections culminated in the publication of reference values for inflation in March 1997. This move was driven by central bank concerns that the relatively loose ERM exchange rate anchor may not, on its own, produce the desired inflation outcome, and by the importance of this outcome in meeting the inflation criterion for EMU entry. However, the central bank expressly indicated that the reference values would be pursued within the existing policy framework centred on the intermediate

ERM exchange rate target. As it turned out, these two targets did not conflict in practice and EMU entry was comfortably secured.

Furthermore, *Germany* has traditionally (since 1975) publicised the inflation assumption incorporated into its money target, thereby serving as an example of inflation targeting 'avant la lettre'.[16] In this context, it is noteworthy that the absolute deviations under this inflation assumption have on average been half as big as those under the mid-point of its money targets (see Tables 7 and 9). Over the years, this inflation assumption has reflected the Bundesbank's practical interpretation of its ultimate price stability goal. During the first decade of money targeting, the inflation assumption was specified as the 'unavoidable rate of inflation' and varied from year to year, declining in all years except at the time of the second oil supply shock. Subsequently, from 1985 on, the inflation assumption was given a more normative character and was kept at, or close to, 2 per cent – a rate considered broadly consistent with the final objective of maintaining price stability.

7.2 The diversity of inflation targeting frameworks

Similar to the diverse experiences under money targets, the increased role of inflation objectives in European monetary policy frameworks has come in different shapes and sizes. Even the four European countries that adopted full-fledged inflation targeting have varied significantly in their practical implementation of this strategy. These differences have primarily related to choices of (i) the inflation measure being targeted; (ii) the specification of the target as a point, range or ceiling; (iii) the time horizon of the target; (iv) the institutional underpinning of the inflation target; and (v) the communication arrangements supporting the inflation target. While the strategic frameworks have typically maintained significant country-specific idiosyncrasies, there is evidence of some convergence in these practical aspects of inflation targeting.

The choice of inflation measure

The success of an inflation targeting framework depends in part on selecting the right inflation measure. This choice is based on a few prime considerations. In the first place, the choice involves a basic trade-off between controllability, on the one hand, and relevance for the final policy objective, on the other. This is similar to the trade-off governing the choice of money aggregate under a money targeting framework, but then further downstream in the monetary transmission process. Obviously, a monetary authority can enhance its controllability of a targeted inflation measure by stripping the first-round impact of exogenous supply and fiscal shocks to inflation (such as significant changes in terms of trade or indirect taxes). In this respect, price level changes due to monetary policy adjustments (such as mortgage interest payments) may also be excluded from the inflation measure, in order to avoid a perverse short-run circularity between instruments and objectives in the policy framework. At the same time, however, a largely stripped inflation measure will be substantially less relevant for the actual policy objective of containing economy-wide inflation: to a certain extent the problems facing monetary policy are simply defined away. Moreover, a stripped inflation measure is likely to be less visible and familiar, and thus less transparent, than an encompassing inflation measure such as a headline Consumer Price Index (CPI) rate. This consideration will affect the choice of inflation measure, as the communicability of the target importantly determines the influence of the monetary policy framework on economic behaviour – especially in the wage-setting field. In this regard, the trade-off is also one between controllability and communicability. More simply put, there is a choice of either doing a lot of explaining beforehand, or running the risk of having to do so afterwards, under probably less favourable circumstances.[17]

In addition, at a more technical level, the inflation measure needs to meet minimum statistical requirements of promptness, frequency and reliability (i.e., without the risk of major revisions) of new data releases. This may disqualify otherwise appropriate candidates, such as for instance the GDP deflator. Moreover, in order to avoid moral hazard and conflicts of interest, the inflation measure should be computed and published by an independent institution removed from the monetary authority. This requirement is more stringent than under money oriented set-ups, where performance under the target is usually monitored on the basis of monetary statistics produced by the central bank. The difference seems to stem from the greater emphasis on transparency and credibility-building that has been part and parcel of inflation targeting strategies. This basically rules out inflation measures tailored and monitored by the central bank according to the specific needs of its targeting framework.

In practice, European countries have followed both routes in the trade-off between controllability and communicability. In *Finland* and the *United Kingdom*, the inflation target has been defined in terms of an underlying inflation measure. In the former case, the target related to an index (CPIY) that excludes indirect taxes, subsidies and housing-related capital costs. Similarly, in the latter case, the targeting framework is specified in terms of an index (RPIX) that excludes mortgage interest payments, and is complemented by an explicit caveat for the effects of indirect taxes and subsidies and interest costs. In effect, this is comparable to targeting the index (RPIY) that strips these effects.[18] By contrast, *Spain* and *Sweden* have prioritised communicability and have targeted the headline (CPI) inflation rate. The public's familiarity with this measure has been viewed as contributing to the transparency, and thus the credibility, of monetary policy. However, Spain has incorporated broad generic caveats into its framework for such factors as wage developments and fiscal policy, and Sweden initially defined the transitory inflation path towards its first target in terms of underlying inflation. More recently, the Swedish Riksbank has also chosen to highlight its forecasts for underlying inflation alongside those for headline inflation.[19]

In the case of the other European countries that have opted to identify inflation objectives, without however switching to full-fledged inflation targeting, the choice of inflation measure has varied widely, depending on the dominant motive for the announcement. In particular, in *France* and *Italy* the inflation goal has been publicised primarily to provide a clearer guidepost for inflation expectations. Not surprisingly, the announcements have been in terms of headline consumer prices. In the case of *Portugal*, the driving motive was to ensure compliance with the EMU convergence criterion. As a result, the reference inflation rate was explicitly defined in terms of the for this purpose relevant Harmonised Index of Consumer Prices (HICP). And, in the case of *Germany*, the Bundesbank has preferred to emphasise the GDP deflator within its money targeting framework. This has reflected the role of this measure in the conversion of nominal into real production potential as well as its underlying nature, since energy price movements in imports are excluded. Over the last two decades, however, the Bundesbank has not been very explicit about its preferred inflation measure and quite often also referred to the CPI in its analyses.

The specification of the target: a point, range or ceiling?

Of course, the operational definition of the target is closely related to the choice of inflation measure, since the selection of a more communicable, but less controllable, inflation measure can be compensated by a looser target definition. In turn, however, a looser target definition will reduce monetary policy transparency. In this regard, the considerations governing the operational specification of an inflation target in terms of a point, range or ceiling are broadly the same as those for money targets. Specifically, point targets provide firm guidance to expectations and an unequivocal assessment of the inflationary development (in terms of too little or too much) at any moment in time. Their attraction thus lies primarily in the realm of transparency and accountability. However, point targets may also convey a spurious sense of accuracy and target controllability. And, to the extent that point targets elicit an overly tight target pursuit at time horizons shorter than the full duration of monetary policy transmission, they also risk creating interest rate and output instability. This danger is more acute under inflation targets than money targets, as the distance between the policy instrument and the target is much greater. The alternative of target ranges has the advantage of explicitly signalling the limited short-term target controllability and of providing a clear-cut standard for assessing whether monetary policy is, or is not, considered to be on target. In addition, the monetary authority is provided with a dual communication device, as it can adjust not only the mid-point but also the bandwidth of the target. In deciding on bandwidth, the credibility gain of a tight target needs to be balanced against the potential credibility loss of subsequently deviating from this target.[20] Finally, the option of a ceiling may be attractive when policy-makers' preferences are asymmetric, insofar as inflation divergence is strongly disliked above the target, but not below it. However, a ceiling is imprecise and thus ill-suited to establish accountability. This creates difficulty under a contracting approach to inflation targeting, since the central bank is not given an unequivocal objective to pursue. A further drawback is that a ceiling does not set a lower limit to inflation and therefore does not signal a normative aversion to deflation. This makes target definitions in terms of ceilings inherently inappropriate when inflation is near price stability.

In the European experience, the numerical definitions of inflation targets have covered the full spectrum of alternatives, although there does seem to have been a gradual move away from ranges towards point targets. Among the countries with full-fledged inflation targets, the *United Kingdom* started off with a wide target range ('1-4 per cent'), *Sweden* with a mid-point surrounded by a tolerance band ('2 ±1 per cent'), *Finland* with a point target ('about 2 per cent') and *Spain* with a ceiling ('below 3 per cent). These different choices can easily be related to the different starting positions when the new strategy was launched. In the case of the *United Kingdom*, which introduced inflation targeting in Europe in conditions of flux and under time pressure, the target definition was most frequently changed. In particular, the initial decision to adopt a wide range reflected the large uncertainties, but was complemented by the simultaneous announcement of a tighter range (1-2½ per cent) for the more distant future (1997). Later, in 1995, the inflation objective beyond this target was specified as a ceiling ('2½ per cent or less'). But, when the relevant time period actually came, it was replaced by a point target ('2½ per cent at all times'). Thus, the achievement of previous targets and the accumulation of policy credibility finally allowed the adoption of a steady-state target in line with the authorities' medium-term inflation preference. At the same time, it was determined that if the inflation rate were to diverge more than

1 percentage point on either side of the point target, the central bank Governor would send an open letter to the Chancellor explaining the divergence, the envisaged policy reaction and the period within which inflation was expected to return to target.[21] This would allow the central bank to make its case that the divergence had been caused by exogenous shocks and not by policy misjudgements.

In *Sweden* and *Finland*, the targets were directly defined in terms of the preferred steady-state objective and have not been changed since their adoption. The adoption of a tolerance band in Sweden, and not in Finland, reflected the fact that Sweden targeted headline CPI inflation, whereas Finland focused on an underlying inflation measure. Also, inflation was expected initially to rise substantially above target in Sweden, whereas it was projected to remain close to target in Finland. Actually, Finland was the first inflation targeting country to adopt an inflation target in terms of a point figure, predominantly on the assumption that this would provide better guidance to inflation expectations.[22] In the case of *Spain*, the initial choice for a ceiling reflected an upper limit consistent with the country's convergence program, in combination with an unwillingness to set a lower limit that would either lack credibility (if it were set at 1 per cent) or would look bad because it was the putative upper limit in the more stable European countries (if it were set at 2 per cent).[23] In other words, the authorities' inflation preferences were heavily skewed and the inflation target was to be seen more as a staging-post towards the steady-state objective than as an end point in itself. Subsequently, once inflation had been reduced to the medium-term target, Spain also switched to a point target (of 'about 2 per cent').

In the other European countries where central banks have emphasised a quantitative objective for inflation, the chosen format has depended on the message the authorities were seeking to convey. In *Germany*, where the inflation assumption has assumed a normative character and is used to derive a money target, a point or very narrow range has generally been used. By contrast, in *Italy* (until 1998) and *Portugal*, where the central bank has sought to signal a minimum progress in a sustained disinflation effort, the objective has been defined as a ceiling. And in *France*, where the purpose has been to advertise the central bank's determination in maintaining price stability, the inflation objective has been specified as the range considered consistent with price stability (i.e., 'price increases not exceeding 2 per cent'). While this objective at first sight seems to be a ceiling, the reference to *increases* implies a floor of zero, thereby establishing a range of 0-2 per cent. In fact, this specification was a refinement of the earlier agreed European definition of price stability as "a level of inflation close to zero … i.e. a maximum of 2 % in the medium run".[24] Once its disinflationary objectives had been achieved in 1997, *Italy* switched to a similar definition ('a rise in consumer prices of 2 per cent or less'). In these cases, the use of a range has partly reflected the uncertainty that statistical measurement bias implies for any quantified price stability objective; this is a consideration that has not featured explicitly in the target design of inflation targeting countries.

The inflation target time horizon

The third dimension determining the trade-offs in the targeting framework is the time horizon for the realisation of the target. In essence, the longer the time horizon, the greater the target controllability, and therefore the larger the scope to adopt a broader inflation measure or a tighter target definition. But a longer time horizon may also accommodate undue delays in policy adjustments. In itself, the choice of target time horizon can therefore be boiled down to weighing the risk of excessive policy action under short-run targets against that of undue policy inaction under long-run targets. The former implies costs in terms of interest rate and output variability, the latter in terms of deep-seated macroeconomic imbalances. As this makes clear, the optimal target time period is primarily a function of the (varying and unknown) duration of the monetary transmission process. In this respect, the choice of time horizon is more delicate than under money targets, given the longer lags before monetary policy instruments impact price developments.

Besides this, there is the issue of policy precommitment and accountability, which is bound to be looser under longer time horizons that allow greater short-run deviations from target. By the same token, longer time horizons provide weaker guidance to expectations – the communications element of targeting. In practical terms, this means that the optimal target time horizon should also be relevant to the typical length of time for which nominal contracts are fixed. This would apply in particular to the duration of wage contracts and of the budgetary cycle. Since the duration of the monetary transmission process is generally considered to be longer (perhaps 6 to 8 quarters) than the time-span of such (mostly annual) contracts, this can be resolved by defining transitional benchmarks or reference values for inflation. Alternatively, when the inflation rate is at, or near, the desired steady-state rate, the target can be made continuously applicable (perhaps annually reconfirmed).

In practice, most European countries that publicised inflation targets did so to break out of a high inflation environment. By consequence, the initial target has generally been set for two or three years in the future, often complemented by the announcement of a transition path towards this target. For instance, when *Spain* and *Sweden* first adopted inflation targeting, ambitious targets were proclaimed for some three years later, with a transition path specified in terms of a half-way reference range, respectively of not allowing underlying inflation to increase. The *United Kingdom* applied a different technique, initially setting a relatively wide target range (with a ceiling equivalent to prevailing inflation) that was immediately applicable, and simultaneously announcing a much tighter target that would apply some four years in the future. *Finland*, by contrast, only announced an inflation target for three years later, without a transition guidepost. The need for such a guidepost was less evident, since current inflation was subdued and inflationary prospects were in line with the target. Once each of these countries had achieved the target that corresponded to its preferred medium-term inflation rate (generally 2 per cent, except 2½ per cent for the *United Kingdom*), a switch was usually made to time-independent targets (annually reconfirmed in the case of *Sweden*). Only *Spain* never got to announcing an indefinite steady-state target, since the first year under this target was also the last year before the start of EMU.

In the other European countries highlighting numerical inflation objectives, the time horizon has usually been shorter, since these objectives have mainly been announced to guide a downward adjustment in near-term inflation expectations or to signal a normative inflation intolerance. Examples of the former motive are provided by *Italy* and *Portugal*, where the central bank publicised inflation projections or reference values for both the current and the next year in order to provide clear staging-posts in the disinflationary process. *Germany* is an example of the latter motive. In particular, the inflation objective has been linked directly to the time-independent aim of maintaining price stability, but needed to be defined in terms of the price increase over the forthcoming year in order to fit in with the annual money targeting framework. The same holds for *France*, although this country has specified the inflation objective not only for the forthcoming year, but also for the medium term, in line with the medium-term character of its money target.

At a more specific level, this also touches on the question of precisely what *rate* of inflation is actually being targeted at the end of the time period (or on an ongoing basis in the case of time-independent targets) – is this the annual average, the annualised quarterly rate or even the annualised monthly rate? While target announcements have not always spelt out the relevant gauge, common practice has been to focus on the 12-month growth rate. This has the advantage of highlighting the trend development in inflation, rather than short-term fluctuations, and of abstracting from seasonal variation.

Institutional underpinnings of the inflation target

Another area where inflation targeting frameworks have differed markedly is in the institutional underpinning of the target. A first issue is whether the institutional structure provides assurance that the inflation targeting framework will last. This depends primarily on the strength of the central bank's institutional position vis-à-vis other political bodies and on the explicitness of price stability as the paramount goal in its statutory mandate. Confidence in the durability of the target is essential to the success of the policy framework, for instance because the perceived risk of a shift to a more inflationary regime influences a country's financial market premia. A second issue is whether the central bank is free to determine interest rates in pursuit of the targets.[25] Such instrument independence is crucial to avoid the perception that monetary policy may at times be directed at broader policy goals – or, put more bluntly, to rule out the inflationary bias of politicians. Thirdly, there is the question whether the adoption of the inflation target includes an explicit government endorsement. This commitment is important to ensure that governmental policies will be consistent, or at least not inconsistent, with the inflation target. Of course, these issues are linked: the third issue becomes vital when the first and second issues do not support the central bank. In that case, government commitment to an inflation target reduces the risk of political initiatives to adapt the monetary strategy or to overrule the dependent central bank in its operational policy-making.

It is striking that the European inflation targeting countries generally did not complement the introduction of this strategy with supportive institutional changes. This contrasts sharply with the example set by the pioneer of inflation targets, New Zealand. In fact, in the country where inflation targeting was ultimately underpinned by the furthest-reaching (and most highly needed) institutional changes, the new strategy was first adopted without any such support. Specifically, the *United Kingdom*'s October 1992 inflation target announcement did not include any transfer of monetary policy autonomy from the Chancellor to the central bank and only committed monetary policy for the duration of the sitting parliament. By implication, although the new target had the benefit of clear governmental backing, it initially lacked the credibility of a durable and operationally independent targeting framework.

The Bank of England's position was, however, gradually strengthened in a series of incremental steps over the course of the next five years. A first, implicit, strengthening stemmed from the publication of the central bank's views in *Inflation Reports*, which was initiated on a quarterly basis in February 1993 and no longer required Treasury clearance from August 1993. Similarly, starting in April 1994, the minutes of the monthly meetings between the Chancellor and the Governor (the meetings were formalised in February 1993) were made public with a delay of only six weeks. These changes reduced the scope for interest rate adjustments on grounds other than the economic arguments put forward by the central bank. In the same vein, the decision on the timing of interest rate adjustments was transferred from the Chancellor to the Governor in November 1993. From then on, once the Chancellor had determined the need for an adjustment, the central bank was able to pick the date – as long as it was before the next meeting. This further ensured that the timing of policy changes could no longer be calibrated to short-term political considerations. But while these changes all increased the influence and accountability of the central bank, the monetary policy framework remained essentially anomalous: the inflation target and the instruments to achieve it had not been put in the hands of a body that was detached from other objectives. The Rubicon was finally crossed in May 1997, when the new Government granted the Bank of England operational independence in implementing its inflation contract. Underscoring the credibility-enhancing impact of this momentous step, long-term interest rates reacted with a fall of some fifty basis points.

In the other European inflation targeters, the new strategy was similarly introduced without institutional changes. This is perhaps less surprising, since the initiative to announce inflation targets came from the central bank in each of these countries. But, in the face of political headwind, institutional weakness nonetheless translated into low credibility. This was especially the case in *Sweden*, where the Riksbank was dependent on the political cycle (its Board members were appointed by Parliament after each election) and did not have a statutory price stability goal. Since the opposition social democrats were in first instance publicly opposed to inflation targeting and were also expected to win the forthcoming elections (in September 1994), the durability of the framework was originally all but firmly established. This was compounded by a blatant lack of support from the Government – the inflation assumption in the 1995 budget proposal (3 per cent) was actually higher than the (mid-point) inflation target for that year (2 per cent).[26] Thus, the Government not only officially questioned the target's feasibility, but through more generous expenditure appropriations (including for public sector wages) also made it more difficult to achieve. In the event, once the social democrats had won the elections as predicted, they appointed Board members who dismissed a more expansionary policy route and extended the inflation targeting strategy, thus giving it broad political backing. In addition, the Government finally officially accepted the inflation target of the Riksbank, incorporating it into the June 1995 EMU convergence program. More fundamentally, following lengthy debate, a sweeping political majority ultimately emerged to strengthen the institutional structure governing monetary policy. On this basis constitutional amendments and new central bank legislation were passed, effective 1 January 1999, that granted the Riksbank full independence and that stipulated price stability as the foremost objective of monetary policy.

In *Finland*, the institutional structure and political environment were supportive from the outset of inflation targeting in February 1993. Next to the Bank of Finland enjoying a relatively strong institutional position (including policy independence as long as the exchange regime was flexible and a statutory objective that vaguely, although not explicitly, referred to price stability), the inflation target was promptly endorsed by the Government (in April 1993) and was buttressed by the adoption of a comprehensive multi-annual fiscal consolidation programme. Nevertheless, the new strategy initially met with heavy scepticism as it seemed to imply an unduly tight monetary policy stance even before the economy had recovered. The longer-term political viability of the framework was therefore subject to question. In this respect, signs of credibility gains first appeared in the financial markets – particularly in a strengthening of the exchange rate and a decline in the bond market rate – and took much longer to emerge in broad-based household and business surveys of inflation expectations.[27] In fact, only after the inflation targeting framework was reaffirmed by the new Government that entered office in April 1995 did the credibility of the monetary strategy take deep root.

But the interplay between inflation targeting and institutional design also works in the opposite direction. In particular, if a central bank is made independent and is given a paramount price stability objective, it is an almost natural reaction to translate this mandate into a quantitative inflation target considered consistent with that objective. This was the case in *Spain*, where the adoption of an inflation target at the end of 1994 was greatly fostered by the passage of the Law on the Autonomy of the Bank of Spain (in June 1994) and specifically by the identification of price stability as the main aim of monetary policy.[28] Although the central bank's inflation targets were never subsequently given an explicit governmental endorsement, they were directly incorporated into the successive budgets, thereby signalling a consistent policy framework. Amongst the countries that did not go as far as to announce inflation targets, a similar example is provided by *France*, where the central bank adopted the custom of quantitatively defining its ultimate inflation objective within a month of being granted autonomy and assigned a price stability objective.

Communication arrangements supporting the inflation target

Communication arrangements have played a prominent role in direct inflation targeting frameworks – more so than in other monetary policy strategies. This has been driven by several motives. First, the emphasis on communication has reflected the essentially discretionary nature of inflation targeting, owing primarily to the inability to monitor the implicit intermediate policy target (forecast inflation) in an objective manner. Moreover, a weak track record – as was the case in most countries adopting this strategy – adds a premium to transparency, which can help prove the break with the past and advertise a new-born policy commitment. In this context, well-specified communication commitments can also serve to enhance the accountability of the monetary authority to the public at large. However, these motives have weighed differently in the European countries with inflation targets and, accordingly, the evolution of communication arrangements has varied markedly.

In practice, the *United Kingdom* has been the most devout disciple of communication and transparency. The emphasis on communication was evident right from the outset and gained in intensity over the years. Within three weeks of the announced switch to inflation targeting, the Chancellor of the Exchequer had requested the Bank of England to provide an independent public appraisal of progress in achieving the inflation target. Starting in February 1993, this took the form of a quarterly Inflation Report.[29] Since the Chancellor of the Exchequer was then still responsible for monetary policy decisions, these reports were initially essentially a disciplinary device on the Government. This created the curious situation where the central bank was accountable through public scrutiny of its policy analyses long before it was actually granted policy autonomy.

Communication was also enhanced by press notices that accompanied all policy adjustments, setting out the underlying reasons. In this context, since April 1994 the minutes of the monthly monetary policy meetings (initially between the Chancellor and the Governor and, from May 1997 on, between the members of the Monetary Policy Committee (MPC)) have been published with only a short lag. In fact, this publication lag has been steadily reduced: from two weeks after the next meeting, to one week after this meeting (since May 1997), to only two weeks (since the Autumn of 1998). With the transfer of monetary policy responsibility to the MPC, communication arrangements were also stepped up by requiring the Governor to send an open letter to the Chancellor if inflation moves away from the target by more than 1 percentage point in either direction (and, for as long as the deviation remains, a further letter every three months).

The Bank of England further contributed to the communications technology of inflation targeting through the introduction in February 1996 of a fan chart for the inflation forecast.[30] This chart emphasises that the inflation forecast is a (usually skewed) probability distribution, that the final inflation outcome is governed by uncertainty, and that monetary policy decision-making invariably involves a balancing of risks. This powerful illustration of the inflation forecast alleviates the lack of an explicit intermediate variable and facilitates the communication of monetary policy under inflation targeting. It also provides a rigorous analytical framework for the essentially judgmental nature of monetary policy decisions, prompting decision-makers to review a spectrum of possible economic outcomes, rather than just the outcome considered most likely. However, these fan charts have the shortcoming that they are subjectively prepared in a non-transparent manner and do not even reflect the central bank's best forecast (since they necessarily assume an unchanged monetary policy).[31]

The other European inflation targeters similarly expanded their communication channels, even if the arrangements were not always as elaborate and refined as in the United Kingdom. In the case of *Sweden*, the move to inflation targeting was followed after some time (in October 1993) by the introduction of a quarterly Inflation Report. As in the other countries, this has been the prime means of communicating monetary policy to the public. The information content of these Reports has shown a remarkable evolution: while the statements regarding the inflation forecast were quite general in the initial issues, these became increasingly explicit, first in a qualitative sense and then in quantitative terms. In fact, a narrow band for the near-term inflation forecast (much narrower than the inflation target range) was first indicated in the text of the Report in November 1995, an inflation forecast path was first graphically depicted for the coming twenty-four months in December 1997, and a full-blown inflation forecast fan chart like the Bank of England's was first presented in June 1998.[32] In *Spain*, an inflation report was launched on a semi-annual basis concurrent with the adoption of the new strategy (the first issue appeared in March 1995). In addition, customary publications and press statements after policy changes have been upgraded to convey more information on the monetary policy prospects. This latter route was also followed by *Finland*, which has chosen not to issue a separate publication but to beef up its existing bulletins with quarterly articles on the monetary policy and inflation outlook.

But this increased emphasis on communicating inflation and monetary policy prospects has not been restricted to inflation targeting countries. In the other European countries that have signalled explicit inflation objectives, central banks have similarly sought to enhance the transparency of the policy outlook, even if they have not gone as far as to publish an independent Inflation Report. A case in point is *Germany*, where the Bundesbank has traditionally emphasised its explanatory (or, as you will, educational) role. In particular, from 1975 until 1985, the Bundesbank explicitly communicated the 'unavoidable inflation' forecast incorporated in its money targets. Hereafter, following the switch to a normative inflation assumption, the central bank continued to comment on price developments in its Monthly and Annual Reports, especially emphasising the distinction between inflation and discrete jumps in the price level (such as following changes in indirect taxes). In *France*, the quantification of the central bank's inflation objective was accompanied, starting in 1995, by a broad assessment of the inflation outlook for the forthcoming year, at times including explicit messages directed at other parties (such as the government, trade unions and employers) that influence inflation. Similarly, the recent custom of *Italy*'s central bank Governor to publicise an inflation objective has consistently been linked to the broad economic appraisal of the Annual Report and has been further monitored in the bank's Economic Bulletins. In the case of *Portugal*, the announcement of the reference value for inflation in 1997 and 1998 was underpinned by an unusually comprehensive assessment of the main factors influencing inflation. This assessment was not published as a separate inflation report, but was included – and updated – in the central bank's quarterly Economic Bulletin.

7.3 The inflation targeting experiences in perspective

It is, of course, too early to come to definitive judgements on the efficacy of inflation targeting strategies in Europe. The time period that has lapsed since the first European country switched to such a strategy is barely six years, the first two of which can be partly disregarded on account of the transmission lags of monetary policy. Moreover, most countries adopting inflation targets started out with deep-seated credibility problems stemming from poor monetary policy track records and recent exchange rate crises. This makes their initial experiences less relevant for an assessment of the value of inflation targeting under normal circumstances. In addition, these countries' success in controlling inflation occurred in a context of global disinflation, suggesting any achievements on this front may have been largely due to other factors than the monetary policy strategy.

Nonetheless, a comparison of inflation performance between the European countries with inflation targets, and those without, indicates that the former countries have been remarkably successful in maintaining relatively low levels of inflation once the new strategy had been launched (from 1992 onwards; see Chart 7). This achievement is striking since it occurred in the wake of massive currency devaluations in each of these countries and followed a period (in the late 1980s) of significantly weaker inflation performance. Moreover, this relatively favourable inflation performance was sustained through the expansionary phase of the economic cycle, which took off in the second half of the 1990s in most inflation targeting countries. A preliminary appraisal thus suggests inflation targeting frameworks did facilitate a break with past policy behaviour, and did indeed provide a structure – and incentives – for better monetary policy performance.[33]

Chart 7: Inflation in inflation targeting Europe

(CPI inflation, in per cent)

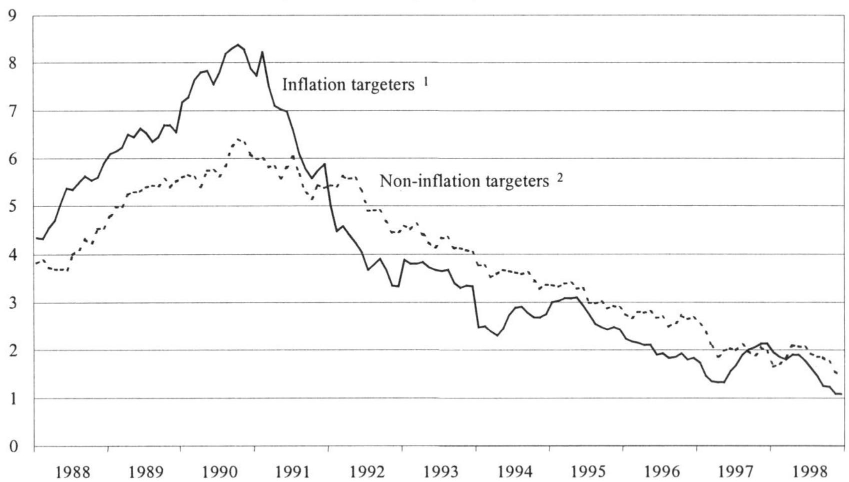

Source: Bank for International Settlements.

1 Finland, Spain, Sweden and the United Kingdom (unweighted average).
2 Austria, Belgium, Denmark, France, Germany, Greece, Ireland, Italy, Luxembourg, the Netherlands and Portugal (unweighted average).

More generally, in the 1990s Europe experienced a broad shift towards emphasising inflation performance in monetary policy frameworks. In line with the institutional requirements of the Maastricht Treaty on European Union, all member countries enshrined price stability as the prime objective of monetary policy and established central bank independence in the pursuit of this objective (the United Kingdom has a derogation and forms an exception to this rule: the Treasury is mandated to specify the Bank of

England's price stability objective). While four counties took the further step of actually pre-committing to an explicitly overriding quantitative inflation target, four others also specified a precise numerical inflation objective as an unequivocal guidepost alongside traditional money or exchange rate targets. And inflation targeting would doubtless have enlisted significantly more European recruits if EMU (and the associated requirement of exchange rate stability) had not beckoned.

At a detailed level, an evaluation of performance against inflation targets should bear in mind that deviations from target only tell part of the story, since some countries will have suffered more exogenous shocks than others. Indeed, under certain circumstances it may even be wrong to bring inflation back to target too quickly. In this regard, outcome data are determined not only by central bank policies, but also by the occurrence of exogenous shocks which monetary policy has not yet had the full opportunity (in terms of policy transmission time) to offset, or which monetary policy has deliberately sought to accommodate (such as the first-round effects of supply shocks). In addition, while performance under inflation targets is more relevant than, for example, under money or exchange rate targets (which are only intermediate goals), a balanced assessment should also consider the contribution of monetary policy to the stabilisation of the real economy. In terms of the accountability for achieving inflation targets, this means that the monetary authority can only be required to: (i) keep forecast inflation on target beyond the relevant time horizon of the monetary transmission process (barring shocks of overwhelming magnitude which may justify a longer adjustment horizon), (ii) provide a thorough explanation every time actual inflation diverges significantly from target, and (iii) meet the target, on average, over a time period that is long enough for outside disturbances to have largely cancelled out. Overall, given the difficulty of objectively determining the inflation forecast (which would also need to allow for future policy adjustments) and of objectively assessing the correctness of any explanation for divergence, a fair assessment of policy effectiveness requires quite a long time horizon – longer than that which has lapsed since most countries embarked on inflation targeting.

Nonetheless, a broad look at the marksmanship record of European inflation targeting countries indicates that performance under this strategy has actually been good (see Table 9). Specifically, the average absolute deviation under inflation targets (0.8 percentage points) has been less than one-third of the average absolute deviation under money targets in Europe (roughly 2.9 percentage points; see Table 7) and also less than one-half of the average absolute deviation under money targets in Germany (1.7 percentage points).[34] This is reflected in a much higher target

Table 9: Inflation targeting marksmanship in Europe, 1993-1998

Country	Period [1]	Average deviation [2]	Average absolute deviation [3]	Average width of target range [4]	Target achieved [5]
Countries with inflation targets:					
United Kingdom [6] (RPIX)	1993-98	0.41	0.44	2.70	100%
Sweden (CPI)	1995-98	-0.78	1.18	2.00	25%
Finland (CPIY)	1995-98	-1.48	1.48	..	25%
Spain (CPI) [7]	1996-98	-0.40	0.40	..	100%
Average	1993-98	-0.46	0.85	2.42	65%
Countries with numerical inflation objective alongside intermediate money and/or exchange rate target:					
Germany [8] (GDP deflator)	1975-98	0.35	0.85	..	75%
France (CPI) [9]	1994-98	0.38	0.62	2.00	80%
Italy (CPI)[10]	1995-98	0.08	0.73	..	75%
Portugal (HICP) [11]	1997-98	-0.08	0.28	..	50%
Average	1975-98	0.30	0.77	2.00	74%

Source: Appendix Tables.

[1] Relates to the period during which inflation targets actually applied. Unless otherwise specified, based on calendar years, except for the United Kingdom where fiscal years apply.

[2] Indicates the average deviation (in percentage points) between the inflation outcome and the point target or target range mid-point.

[3] Indicates the average absolute deviation (in percentage points) between the inflation outcome and the point target or target range mid-point.

[4] Indicates the average width of the target ranges (in percentage points) in those years that target ranges (rather than point targets or ceilings) were announced.

[5] Point targets are assumed to have been met when the outcome was within ± 1 percentage point of target. This corresponds to the target bandwidth in Sweden, to the UK requirement since May 1997 that larger deviations are explained in an open letter, and to the implicit width of the price stability objective specified in France and Italy.

[6] The United Kingdom employed target ranges until May 1997, when a point target was adopted. In the last year of this period, the width of the target range is set at 1.5 percentage points, in line with the originally announced aim of being in the lower half of the 1-4 per cent range by the end of the Parliamentary period (May 1997 at the latest). As RPIX inflation fell to 2.5 per cent in May 1997, the target is assumed to have been met in FY1996/97.

[7] Next to the inflation targets for 1997 and 1998, the reference value for the opening months of 1996 (3½-4 per cent) is assumed to have been a target for the year's first quarter. The target ceiling for 1997 (<3 per cent) is assumed to have corresponded to a mid-point of 2.5, in line with the more precise reference value later specified for this year.

[8] Germany's inflation objectives are based on the (since 1985 normative) inflation assumption explicitly built into its money targets. The GDP deflator has been taken as the inflation measure, reflecting the in recent years preferred measure of the Bundesbank when deriving these targets.

[9] France defined its inflation objective as an overall price *increase* not exceeding 2 per cent, implying a tolerance range for inflation of 0-2 per cent and a 1 per cent mid-point.
[10] Until 1998, the governor of the Banca d'Italia defined the central bank's inflation objectives as ceilings, against which the deviations have been measured. For 1998, as in France, the objective was defined as containing the *rise* in consumer prices to 2 per cent or less, implying a tolerance range for inflation of 0-2 and a 1 per cent mid-point.
[11] Portugal's reference values for inflation were defined as ceilings, against which the deviations have been measured.

achievement ratio in inflation targeting EU countries (65 per cent) than in money targeting EU countries (31 per cent) or, for that matter, than under money targets in Germany (42 per cent). And this more favourable record was attained notwithstanding target ranges that were narrower on average in inflation targeting countries (2.4 percentage points) than in the money targeting countries in general (3.0 percentage points) or Germany in particular (2.5 per cent). The superior marksmanship under inflation targets, even relative to Germany's esteemed performance under money targets, suggests that – other things equal – inflation targets provide more accurate guidance to expectations about monetary policy. By the same token, they also create a stronger basis for policy precommitment and central bank accountability.

It should be recognised, of course, that there is a crucial difference between deviations under an intermediate and a final policy objective. In this context, it is striking to note that the marksmanship record of the European countries with inflation targets has been broadly similar *in terms of inflation* to that of the European countries with numerical inflation objectives alongside money or exchange rate targets. In particular, the average absolute deviation between the outcome data and the preannounced inflation objective has been broadly the same in these two groups of countries (0.8 percentage points). Actually, while the target achievement ratio has been roughly similar in both groups, it has been marginally worse in the inflation targeting countries (65 per cent against 74 per cent, respectively). This provides tentative evidence that the option of targeting inflation directly, rather than pursuing a quantified inflation objective via an intermediate money or exchange rate target, does not improve inflation marksmanship *per se*.

The empirical evidence on the European countries' experiences with inflation targeting further suggests that inflation targets have been pursued in a slightly asymmetric fashion. In particular, EU central banks with inflation targets generally seem to have been happier with outcomes beneath the target (mid-point) than ones above it, since there has been, on average, a significant undershooting of inflation targets (equivalent to almost half a percentage point, see Table 9). This asymmetry may partly reflect the unexpectedly favourable global inflation climate of the 1990s, as well as, in the cases of Finland and Spain, the gravity of meeting the EMU entry criterion on low inflation. At the same time, however, the desire to err on the side of caution for the sake of a rapid build-up of policy credibility also seems to have been at play. In this regard, it is notable that this asymmetry has not been evident in the European countries with numerical inflation objectives alongside money or exchange rate targets. This suggests that the motive of accumulating credibility may have weighed relatively heavily in the monetary policy implementation of countries with inflation targets.

On the real economy, inflation targeting essentially raises two questions, one positive and one negative: does the adoption of inflation targets reduce the sacrifice ratio of disinflation and does the singular focus on inflation performance entail costs in terms of output variability? The first question can also be posed in terms of whether inflation targeting in itself – rather than the policy measures taken within this strategic framework – contributes to policy credibility. On this issue, experiences to date do not allow firm conclusions. Although there are some indications that inflation targeting may have reduced sacrifice ratios, the evidence is thin and ambiguous.[35] In any event, credibility was nowhere gained quickly and disinflation clearly remained painful. As regards the second question, there is ample evidence that central banks have not pursued inflation targets dogmatically at the expense of output considerations. In practice, inflation targeting countries have experienced higher average output growth and lower output variability following the introduction of the new strategy than in the decade preceding this switch. Moreover, performance in terms of output growth and lowering output variability compares favourably with that of similar non-inflation targeting countries – even if output variability has remained somewhat higher in the inflation targeting countries.[36] But these achievements may to a large extent reflect asymmetric cyclical developments that need more time to cancel out. Nonetheless, the broadly similar magnitude of the average absolute deviations from target in countries with explicit inflation targets, on the one hand, and in countries with numerical inflation objectives alongside intermediate money or exchange rate targets, on the other, also testifies that inflation targets have not been followed rigidly. This is further illustrated by the generally gradualist approach to disinflation (usually covering a full two-year horizon) reflected in the inflation forecasts published by Sweden and the United Kingdom when inflation is diverging from target.

All told, the European experience with inflation targetry, while short, is favourable. The inflation performance of countries that switched to this strategy changed from relatively weak to relatively strong and the marksmanship record has been impressive. To the extent there has been a bias in monetary policy, it was, if anything, a disinflationary one. Although inflation targeting may not by itself have reduced the costs of reducing inflation, it seems to have made it easier to sustain the efforts needed to achieve this. In this respect, inflation targeting marked a material change in central bank policy in countries that had a mixed track record and low credibility, as these central banks have subsequently been able to measure up to the best performers in Europe.

The lessons learnt

Beyond these general conclusions, the evolution of inflation targetry in Europe reflects a gradual learning process, as countries have adapted their policy frameworks on the basis of practical experience and improved conceptual insight. This is evident, for instance, in the strengthening of institutional frameworks that eventually took place in most countries with inflation targets. In the United Kingdom, this involved granting the central bank full autonomy to use its policy instruments towards the inflation target – a sea-change that took close to five years to come about. When this adaptation was announced, long-term interest rates fell sharply, vividly illustrating the salutary impact of coherent institutional design on policy credibility. In Sweden the institutional changes took similarly long, although in this case the central bank already enjoyed operational independence and the issue was primarily to confirm the durability of the policy focus on price stability. Besides these legislative alterations, the European inflation targeters generally converged on the practice of having the target supported by both the central bank and the government. This is especially notable in Finland, Spain and Sweden, where the initiative to launch the inflation target came from an operationally autonomous central bank, which strictly speaking did not need governmental endorsement to implement the new framework.

Another field where the countries pursuing inflation targets have made considerable progress during the 1990s is in improving the external communication of monetary policy. This is perhaps the area where the learning curve has been the steepest. The prime vehicle for such communication has been the Inflation Report introduced by each inflation targeting country within a year of adopting the new strategy (except for Finland, which incorporated the elements of an Inflation Report into its existing Bulletin series). These Reports have progressively matured, providing increasingly refined and insightful overviews of the considerations driving monetary policy. A specific challenge was how to epitomise the strategy's wide-ranging orientation in a way that would be easily understood (as with traditional money and exchange rate targets), while also doing justice to the inherent uncertainties and policy transmission lags. This search culminated in the publication, first in the United Kingdom and then also in Sweden, of a visually impressive inflation forecast fan chart in which the central tendency for inflation (the mode), the degree of uncertainty (the variance) and the balance of risks (the skewness of the probability distribution) are jointly projected over the course of time.

In a broader sense, public speeches, press releases after policy changes, hearings before parliamentary committees and – only in the United Kingdom – prompt publication of the minutes of policy meetings, have all been stepped up to enhance the transparency of monetary decision-making. This emphasis on communication has reflected the increasingly popular view (especially so in Anglo-Saxon countries) that transparency is crucial to underpin policy credibility and, by guiding expectations, to enhance policy effectiveness. At the same time, transparency heightens the accountability of monetary authorities, at a minimum vis-à-vis the general public, and thereby provides balance to the institutional autonomy of central banks under inflation targeting. Of course, the trend towards greater transparency has also been apparent in countries implementing strategies other than inflation targeting – Portugal's in-depth public analyses of developments under its reference range for inflation being a case in point. But the inflation targeting countries have been at the forefront. And it looks like this widespread evolution towards greater transparency has some way to go yet.

In terms of operational specifics, European inflation targeting regimes have converged at inflation targets of two per cent. Although the United Kingdom forms an exception – with a steady state RPIX inflation target of 2½ per cent – this level is basically comparable to that in other countries, as the RPIX inflation measure has historically been about one-half of a percentage point higher than the harmonised inflation measure more widely used on the European continent.[37] This common level of two per cent is the highest rate of price increase still consistent with the prevailing European definition of price stability ('inflation close to zero … i.e. a maximum of 2 per cent in the medium run').[38] Thus, the central banks of Finland, Spain, Sweden and the United Kingdom each sought the maximum distance from deflation considered compatible with a legislated price stability mandate. At the same time, this target level had the attraction of tallying with the inflation objective traditionally pursued by the most credible European central bank – the Bundesbank. Actually, this is also the context in which France, Italy and Portugal each opted to announce a numerical inflation objective of 'at most two per cent'. In all, the commonly targeted inflation level of two per cent has therefore essentially reflected a normative verdict against any sustained inflation, rather than a judgement on the optimal rate of inflation. In absence of firm indications that this latter rate lies above two per cent, the common decision (following Germany's footprints) has been to keep the sights on the steady state objective of stable prices, and not to slide on the slippery slope of targets that fall outside the price stability category. The Sirens would not fall silent at, say, three per cent.

As regards the issue of bandwidth, a historical perspective suggests that target ranges of 2 or 3 percentage points are likely to cover most unanticipated shocks to inflation.[39] Specifically, the European track record shows that the average bandwidth was 2.4 percentage points in those years that target ranges (rather than point targets or ceilings) were announced, and that the target range for inflation was observed in 70 per cent of these cases. If point targets are assumed to have corresponded to a bandwidth of 2 percentage points, the overall target observance ratio is still 65 per cent (see Table 9). However, it may be argued that this favourable record primarily reflects the propitious global inflation climate from 1993 on. On this score, Germany's long experience with (since 1985 normative) explicit inflation objectives provides some guidance. Viewed over the 24 years starting in 1975, the standard deviation of the divergence under the inflation objectives amounted to only 1.1 percentage points. Furthermore, the average absolute deviation under these objectives has been similar to the more recent experience of the European inflation targeting countries (in fact, these average deviations have been surprisingly identical: 0.85 percentage points in both cases). In terms of bandwidth, a target range of two (respectively three) percentage points centred around the inflation objective would have covered 75 per cent (respectively 88 per cent) of Germany's inflation outcomes.[40]

In this context, however, there has been a movement towards using point targets rather than ranges, as evidenced by the decisions of Spain and the United Kingdom to join Finland with such a target definition. At the same time, there seems to have been an increased emphasis on underlying inflation, as Spain has highlighted caveats for wage and fiscal developments, Sweden has recently started publishing an inflation forecast for underlying inflation alongside its forecast for headline inflation, and the United Kingdom has stressed the inflation measure (RPIY) excluding indirect taxes and subsidies as well as mortgage interest payments. Overall, while the historical evidence is still scant and the optimal choice may vary from country to country, there would seem to be a case to target a more precise and more controllable inflation measure (implying a point target for underlying inflation) rather than one that is more general and visible (such as a wide target range for headline CPI). The former set-up pins down expectations and highlights the inflation measure on which policy-makers hope economic agents (especially wage setters) will actually base their decisions – even if this is not the inflation measure which these agents, as consumers, are most affected by. In this way, the target definition may help avoid the first round effects of exogenous supply side shocks from becoming ingrained in the economy, while also linking a central bank's credibility and accountability to a measure it can reasonably direct.

Nonetheless, the European experience shows that, whatever the chosen set-up, inflation targets are bound to be missed some of the time. The deviations in Table 9 illustrate this all but perfect controllability of price developments, even if Spain and the United Kingdom have to date shown surprisingly accurate marksmanship. Adjusting the target parameters has not provided much of an escape, since an inflation measure stripped of all variable exogenous elements becomes meaningless, as does an unduly wide target range or a very long target time horizon. The solution, again, has been sought in terms of transparency. In this regard, by acknowledging the uncertainties governing monetary policy, open communication has as it were constituted an insurance premium against the risk of inflation target misses.

NOTES

[1] Berk (1998) provides a comprehensive overview of the learning process – and the remaining uncertainties – on the monetary policy transmission process, and assesses how this incomplete knowledge can nonetheless be put to good use by policy-makers.

[2] Almeida and Goodhart (1998) suggest that raising the accountability of the monetary policy decision-making process was a prime reason for the adoption of direct inflation targeting. It is unclear, however, why a monetary authority in one of the European countries (the Government in the United Kingdom and the central banks in the other countries) would introduce inflation targeting to increase its own accountability, since this accountability generates potentially high costs to that authority. Rather, it seems to have been the underlying quest for policy credibility that drove these countries to this monetary strategy.

[3] For an extensive discussion of this early Swedish experience of inflation targeting, see Jonung (1979) and Berg and Jonung (1999).

[4] The position papers presented to the Swedish Governor in December 1992 after the krona had left the ERM and prior to the decision on the new monetary policy strategy, included a review of Sweden's price level stabilisation policy in the 1930s; see Sveriges Riksbank (1992).

[5] The sustainability of the framework was, as it were, made conditional on the support it could earn from the public and opposition parties; see Mishkin (1997).

[6] The lack of a fall-back scenario is mentioned by Svensson (1995, p. 70). This lack further testifies to the sincerity of the authorities' exchange rate commitment.

[7] In an effort to stimulate an open debate on monetary strategy in the context of a floating exchange rate regime, the articles were promptly published in December 1992 as a Special Issue of the central bank's Quarterly Review; see Sveriges Riksbank (1992).

[8] Åkerholm and Brunila (1995).

[9] Bank of Finland (1996, p. 3). It is noteworthy that the central bank referred to the increasing importance of exchange rate stability in the conduct of economic policy (and not specifically of monetary policy). In this context, Almeida and Goodhart (1998, p. 21) draw a questionable conclusion when they classify Finland as no longer being an inflation targeting

country after it joined the ERM. Although the classification admittedly becomes murky when countries formally pursue multiple policy targets, Finland's position seems to have been very close to that of Spain (which they classify as an inflation targeting country despite its ERM membership).

[10] Vega (1994) and Ortega and Bonilla (1995).

[11] Gutiérrez (1998) and Ayuso and Escrivá (1998).

[12] Visco (1995) discusses the increasing role of inflation objectives in the Italian economy during 1980-94.

[13] An eye-catching proposal was developed at the IMF by Lane, Prati and Griffiths (1995).

[14] The text of the Governor's concluding remarks is customarily reproduced in the central bank's Annual Report.

[15] Next to announcing a prospective inflation path, the Governor indicated that "If price trends over the next few months show a tendency to diverge from the pattern I have just described, we shall not hesitate to tighten credit conditions still further." See Banca d'Italia, Annual Report 1994 (p. 173).

[16] Von Hagen (1995) views the Bundesbank as a covert inflation targeter of sorts and classifies the monetary policy strategy of Germany as a case of combined 'inflation and monetary targeting'. Similarly, Mishkin and Posen (1997) include Germany – next to Canada, New Zealand, and the United Kingdom – in a case study review of inflation targeting experiences.

[17] The arguments for, and against, using a stripped rather than a headline inflation measure are also applicable to the use of caveats for pre-defined events.

[18] In essence, the caveat for indirect taxes, subsidies and interest costs was incorporated – or so it seems – to compensate for initially having chosen the wrong target measure and not wanting to raise suspicions by adjusting this. Consideration was given to switching the targeted inflation measure from RPIX to RPIY in 1995, but the proposal was rejected on the grounds that frequent shifts in the target definition risked undermining the framework's credibility; see Mishkin (1997, p. 73). In fact, to enhance credibility, the calculation and publication of the RPIX index was moved during this year from the Bank of England to the independent UK Office of National Statistics.

[19] Heikestein and Vredin (1998) discuss the complex considerations that governed the Riksbank's initial choice of target variable as well as the gradual change in emphasis that occurred over time.

[20] Goodhart and Viñals (1994). However, a target that is judged to be too tight will not be credible to start with.

[21] As stressed in the Chancellor of the Exchequer's original Remit for the newly created Monetary Policy Committee (printed in the Bank of England's August 1997 Inflation Report, p. 75), the requirement to send an open letter when inflation moves more than 1 percentage point from target is *not* to establish a tolerance range for deviations, but to enhance monetary policy transparency. In line with this instruction, King (1997, p. 441) emphasises that the United Kingdom's inflation target is not a range of 1½ to 3½ per cent, but 2½ per cent on average.

[22] Brunila and Lahdenperä (1995, p. 129).

[23] See the comments by Ortega in Haldane (1995b, p. 77).

[24] The first European definition of price stability was spelt out in a report to the EU central bank governors by the Group of Experts chaired by Raymond (1990).

[25] Along similar lines, Andersson and Berg (1995) draw a distinction between a monetary strategy's political credibility, which reflects investors' confidence that the strategy itself will be maintained (rather than be replaced by a more inflationary alternative), and its operational credibility, which relates to the perceived likelihood that the central bank's policies will actually deliver the announced inflation target.

[26] This can be inferred from Svensson (1995, pp. 73-76).

[27] Brunila and Lahdenperä (1995, p.130).

[28] Ayuso and Escrivá (1998) and Gutiérrez (1998).

[29] The Bank of England's Inflation Report is actually produced in two editions, tailored to different groups of readers: while the standard edition is comprehensive, with considerable detail and analytical depth, there is also a popular version providing a broad-brush and readily accessible overview of developments in (prospective) inflation.

[30] As the Chancellor of the Exchequer was then still in charge of monetary policy-making, his inflation forecast was actually the more relevant. With the transfer of policy autonomy a little more than a year later, this peculiar irregularity was ironed out.

[31] The conditional nature of the inflation forecast in the fan charts leads to a probability distribution that widens as the time horizon is extended. In reality, of course, the controllability of inflation may be assumed to increase beyond the lags of the monetary transmission process, implying a narrowing of the probability distribution. But this requires policy adjustments to keep inflation on track. Moreover, the assumption of unchanged policy raises issues of consistency, since many financial variables that serve as inputs to the forecasts obviously do not assume a static policy. At a technical level it also open to debate whether the fan chart should centre on the mode of the distribution (the outcome considered most likely) as has been the common practice, rather than on the mean (the average outcome). For a discussion of the genesis and technical evolution of the Bank of England's fan chart, see Britton, Fisher and Whitley (1998).

[32] Just as in the United Kingdom, the progress of time has seen the Riksbank's graphical inflation forecasts become fancier and more informative. Remarkable in the case of Sweden is that fan charts are now presented for the targeted CPI inflation measure as well as an underlying inflation measure. Berg and Gröttheim (1997, pp. 169-171) discuss the efforts of the Riksbank to advance market communication.

[33] At a global rather than regional level, Debelle (1997) and McCallum (1996) similarly find evidence of improved central bank performance following the introduction of inflation targeting schemes. However, Almeida and Goodhart (1998) do not find the inflation experiences of countries with inflation targets to be statistically significantly different from those in a variety of control groups (although they do find the fall in inflation on average to have been sharper).

[34] The inflation targeting record is evaluated on the basis of annual figures. While quarterly or monthly (or even higher frequency) figures could also be used, inflation targets have often been cast explicitly in an annual framework (see, for instance, Berg and Gröttheim, p. 170). The impact of inflation targets on inflation assumptions in other sectors (e.g., the budget and wage contracts) also generally follows an annual cycle. As a welcome by-product, an assessment using annual data annual data facilitates comparison with other monetary policy strategies (especially money targeting) where targets are set in annual terms.

[35] Based on a comparison of disinflation costs between seven inflation targeting countries (including the four European ones) and four different control groups, Almeida and Goodhart (1998) find preliminary evidence that the switch to inflation targeting reduced sacrifice

ratios in terms of unemployment and especially foregone output growth. By contrast, Groeneveld, Koedijk and Kool (1998) compare the experiences of New Zealand, Canada and the United Kingdom with those of Australia, the United States and Germany (respectively) and do not find evidence of a structural break in the relationship between inflation and interest rates following the switch to inflation targeting. They conclude that the credibility-enhancing impact of inflation targeting is ambiguous and is in any case not clearly superior to that of other intermediate monetary strategies. Similarly, based on case studies of Germany, New Zealand, Canada and the United Kingdom, Mishkin (1997) concludes that credibility cannot be achieved by adopting an inflation target, but has to be earned the hard way – by consistent policy implementation. This is also the conclusion drawn by Bernanke *et al.* (1999).

[36] Evidence on these two counts is presented in King (1997, p. 436). The control group comprises G7 non-inflation targeting countries.

[37] The estimated differential of one-half of a percentage point between inflation as measured by the Retail Prices Index excluding mortgage interest payments (RPIX) and by the Harmonised Index of Consumer Prices (HICP) has been established as the average for the period 1976-98, although it has varied markedly during this period. The differential can be mainly attributed to different weighting schemes (while the RPIX uses arithmetic averages, the HICP uses geometric means) and to different coverage (especially a larger RPIX coverage of housing costs); see UK Treasury (1998).

[38] According to the definition determined by the group of EU central bank experts chaired by Raymond (1990).

[39] This contrasts sharply with the estimates by Haldane and Salmon (1995). Based on simulations for the United Kingdom (using quarterly data), they find significant inflation uncertainty, suggesting a range as wide as six percentage points may still be missed in about one-third of the time.

[40] Based on the data presented in Appendix VI, where the GDP deflator is used as the measure of inflation.

8 THE MONETARY POLICY STRATEGY OF THE EUROSYSTEM

8.1 The search for a strategy

Once the political decision to go ahead with EMU was unequivocally taken with the signing of the Treaty of Maastricht in December 1991, attention started to focus on what the union's monetary policy would look like. After all, in terms of the targets and traditions governing monetary policy, the potential participants constituted a motley bunch. The need to reach consensus on the strategy for the single monetary policy was thus initially considered a major hurdle in the preparations for EMU. In part, this was because two seemingly irreconcilable views dominated the spectrum of opinions.

On the one hand, there was the view that the prospective Eurosystem (that is, the European Central Bank and the national central banks participating in the monetary union) should basically duplicate the strategy of the theretofore most successful national central bank – money targeting as pursued by the Bundesbank. Such continuity would facilitate the transfer of policy credibility from the Bundesbank to the new-born Eurosystem and would alleviate the system's difficulty of not having a track record with which to instil public confidence. On the other hand, there was the view that money growth was essentially a poor policy compass on account of its limited stability and controllability (other than in the long run), and that the Bundesbank's success actually reflected other factors than its monetary policy strategy. This view was rooted in the unhappy money targeting experiences of other European countries and in the generally wide deviations of money growth from targets, even in Germany. Those favouring this latter view were usually proponents of a broad-based approach such as the then novel strategy of direct inflation targeting.

These views initially seemed irreconcilable because the support for money targeting was evidently not widespread across Europe while, at the same time, it was difficult to imagine Germany compromising on monetary policy strategy. Moreover, the two strategies of money targeting and direct inflation targeting were originally often perceived as diametrical opposites. A further complication lay in the limited experience that had at the time been gathered with direct inflation targeting, allowing its opponents to argue that it was a fad unlikely to survive the test of time. Against this background, the European Monetary Institute (the forerunner of the European Central Bank) asked the EU national central bank experts gathered in its Monetary Policy Sub-Committee to scrutinise the monetary policy strategy options for the third stage of monetary union. Implicitly, the assignment was to find common ground.

In this preparatory stage, the panoply of monetary policy strategy alternatives was duly reviewed.[1] A number of options were readily rejected. In particular, interest rate targeting was ruled out on account of the difficulty of assessing the equilibrium real interest rate that would be consistent with a price stability objective. The alternative of exchange rate targeting was similarly discarded on the grounds that, for a large and relatively closed area like the eurozone, gearing policy to an external target would likely conflict with the internal price stability goal. And nominal income targeting was dismissed because it was not necessarily consistent with the Eurosystem's mandate to prioritise price stability, was vulnerable to data revisions, and did not fit in with the European monetary traditions. On this latter point, domestic credit targeting was not even considered, as it had become all but extinct in the EU. This basically left open the options of money targeting and direct inflation targeting, without, however, excluding a combination of the two.

But the analysis under the aegis of the European Monetary Institute took the strategy discussion a step further by establishing that, although the prime alternatives of money targeting and inflation targeting differ considerably at a theoretical level, their practical application is remarkably similar. The common ground was substantial, as both strategies were ultimately concerned with inflation, were pursued in a forward looking manner, and were typically based on a wide array of indicators of prospective price and output developments. The analysis also identified guiding principles for the eventual strategy decision and recommended five specific elements, regardless of the precise nature of the Eurosystem's future strategy: a publicly quantified definition of price stability; the announcement of specific targets to establish accountability; the monitoring of a broad set of indicators; the establishment of a public target or monitoring range for money growth; and the development of a forecasting ability for inflation and other economic variables. Thus, there was broad agreement on the key elements of the prospective monetary policy strategy, even if the decisions on the weights attached to each of these elements and on the strategy's precise label were still open.

8.2 The initial uncertainties

The final decisions on the choice of monetary policy strategy were heavily influenced by the uncertainties governing the outset of monetary union. Of course, the selection of participating countries also had an impact, since a strategy that provided for continuity with these countries' practices would facilitate the transfer of credibility to the Eurosystem. In this respect, the May 1998 decisions by Sweden and the United Kingdom – two of the chief inflation targeting countries in the EU – not to participate in the third stage of EMU may be expected to have reduced the emphasis on elements of inflation targeting in the final strategy choice. However, the uncertainties stemming from the regime shift to monetary union clearly played a much larger role in the strategy design.

These uncertainties reflected the unpredictable impact of the switch of monetary regime on the structural characteristics and behavioural relationships in the participating economies.[2] Changes were anticipated primarily in the financial sector, as mutual exchange rate risks would disappear and financial markets would become more transparent and more liquid. At an operational level, the adoption of a uniform framework of monetary instruments (notably including a remunerated reserve requirement) would also entail different modifications in participants' financial systems. Depending on the specific use of instruments prior to the third stage of EMU, such modifications could trigger substantive portfolio shifts. Furthermore, at a policy level, participation in the euro would bolster monetary policy credibility in the countries with weak track records, reducing risk premia and evoking further portfolio adjustments. The concurrent activation of the Stability and Growth Pact should similarly contribute to greater fiscal discipline and thus to fiscal credibility – again, especially in countries where this discipline had previously been open to question.

It was clear, however, that the impact of the regime shift would not be limited to the financial sector. In particular, the price transparency created by the adoption of a common unit of account was expected to lead to significantly more intense competition, a development that would be reinforced by the policy changes in the exchange rate, monetary and fiscal sphere. Increased competition would in turn serve to discipline wage and price behaviour, and also to spur innovation – all much to the benefit of the European consumer. As a result, pronounced behavioural changes were to be anticipated throughout the euro-area economy. To paraphrase, uncertainty was a certainty that would make history a poor guide to the future.

Moreover, from a practical perspective, these uncertainties were compounded by the difficulty of actually establishing the historical relationships, as harmonised statistics were scarce and generally only covered short time periods. A case in point was the creation of comprehensive euro area monetary data. Although the framework for such statistics had been available for some time, their compilation effectively had to await the identification of the participating countries in May 1998. Since strenuous efforts were subsequently needed just to achieve a sufficient degree of harmonisation, the time to test the properties of the different monetary aggregates was extremely limited. The rudimentary state of the statistical gauges implied, even more than otherwise, that monetary policy would be an art rather than a science.

The strategy choice of the Eurosystem was directly affected by these uncertainties. In the case of the money targeting option, the regime shift was expected to prompt financial sector changes that could undermine the near-term stability of money demand. This could – at least initially – reduce the reliability of money growth both as an internal policy compass and as a communication device in explaining policy decisions to the general public. Beyond the transition, there were indications that money demand may be stable. In fact, although the construction of hypothetical historical euro area aggregates based on national data raises a host of contentious methodological issues, numerous studies suggested that money demand would be more stable at the European level than at the national (German) level.[3] This greater stability could be explained for instance by the neutralisation of currency substitution within Europe and by the inclusion of cross-border holdings. However, these findings were also overshadowed by uncertainty, as the greater European stability was perhaps nothing more than a statistical artefact stemming from the law of large numbers.[4] Indeed, while desynchronised national shocks would tend to cancel out in aggregation exercises, monetary unification would centralise sources of instability in the financial system, implying that estimates of future stability based on pre-EMU figures were overly sanguine.

Uncertainty about the controllability of the demand for money in the euro area further tarnished the attraction of money targeting. The financial integration and innovation accompanying EMU was expected to lead to more financial products whose short-term expansion could not be readily steered by the central bank. A disconcerting omen was provided by studies suggesting that the controllability of money growth in the euro area would be inferior to that previously enjoyed by Germany.[5] The source of this difference was the prevalence of liquid deposits bearing no or little interest in Germany and the relative scarcity of such deposits in other countries of the euro area. As a result, a monetary policy tightening was relatively effective in reducing money growth in Germany, since it raised the opportunity costs of maintaining liquid deposits. By contrast, in the other EU countries, the remuneration of liquid assets was often linked to the short-term interest rate, creating a perverse effect on money demand when the monetary policy stance changed.

To some extent, similar concerns also clouded the inflation targeting option. In particular, the heightened uncertainties would make it more difficult to project inflation with a sufficient degree of accuracy, thereby weakening the pivotal element of this strategy. Even disregarding the statistical difficulties of estimating economic relationships in the past, the regime shift would make it risky to forecast inflation on the basis of historical behaviour. After all, the changes in the institutional, policy and financial market environment could have a profound impact on these relationships, including for example by changing the way consumers and producers form their expectations and by altering the interest rate sensitivity of domestic expenditure. In addition, from a technical viewpoint, the forecasting ability of the nascent European Central Bank was in many respects still embryonic. Admittedly, this shortcoming could have been mitigated by making common use of modelling capacity elsewhere in the Eurosystem (in fact, the Nederlandsche Bank had a euro-wide model EUROMON that was up and running at the time), but this would have run counter to the aim of creating a strong centre in Frankfurt. Finally, a strategy of inflation targeting would not link up with the monetary traditions of the dominant countries in the euro area, implying that the adoption of this strategy would risk amplifying the uncertainties surrounding the Eurosystem's prospective policy course.

In all, it was evident that the major uncertainties accompanying the transition to monetary union entailed substantive risks for both a money targeting and inflation targeting strategy. The challenge facing the Eurosystem was thus to devise a strategy that provided ample flexibility to react to unforeseen circumstances and that did not overstate the monetary authority's knowledge of the new economic and monetary environment. At the same time, however, the strategy should not be too loose, since it had to structure the internal and external policy debate, guide expectations, and provide for appropriate continuity with previous European monetary experiences. A delicate balance had to be struck.

8.3 The making of a synthesis

Against the background of the prevailing uncertainties, the decision on the precise design of the monetary policy strategy to be pursued starting 1 January 1999 did not come easily. Indeed, although an early announcement would have been a welcome contribution to confidence in the forthcoming euro, it was barely seven weeks before the new currency's launch that the design of the Eurosystem's strategy was finalised and made public. Essentially, the strategy consists of three elements.[6] First, the overriding objective of monetary policy – price stability – has been precisely defined. Second, the development of money growth has been assigned a privileged role in the setting of monetary policy. And, third, the strategic framework has explicitly incorporated a broad-based assessment of indicators of prospective inflationary or deflationary pressures. In figurative speech, money growth may be seen as the Eurosystem's nominal anchor, moored in the bedrock of the price stability definition, and the other indicators are the considerations that determine the length and slack of the anchor cable. These three central elements are elaborated on below.

The definition of price stability

As enshrined in the Treaty on European Union (Article 105), the primary objective of the European System of Central Banks is to maintain price stability. The Eurosystem has opted further to clarify this mandate by precisely specifying what price stability means. Such a clear-cut objective helps avoid any controversy on the monetary policy orientation, while also contributing to a firm anchoring of inflation expectations. Besides this, it offers an objectively measurable and readily monitorable yardstick for central bank accountability. In this context, price stability has been defined as "a year-on-year increase in the Harmonised Index of Consumer Prices (HICP) for the euro area of below 2 per cent." Moreover, this definition has been expressly specified as a medium-term objective. The specification of a non-zero definition of price stability has been explained on the basis of the yet unclear (and varying) magnitude of the measurement bias in the HICP; although concerns about downward nominal rigidities or limited real interest rate flexibility in a context of (near) zero inflation may also have played a role internally, these considerations have not featured in external communications.

This definition is intended to signal important characteristics of the prospective monetary policy orientation of the Eurosystem. By explicitly referring to the development of the harmonised consumer price index for the euro area, the Eurosystem has indicated that it will calibrate its policies on the basis of monetary, economic and financial developments in the euro area as a whole. As a matter of first principle, monetary policy will therefore not react to idiosyncratic regional or national developments. By adding that price stability is to be maintained over the medium term, the Eurosystem has underscored the forward-looking nature of its policy setting. This specification also acknowledges the existence of short-term price movements that are outside the direct reach of monetary policy or that monetary policy may consciously wish to accommodate. For instance, the monetary authority may elect not to offset the first round effects of oil price shocks or fiscal measures (such as adjustments in consumption taxes). As such effects will then only have a temporary impact on inflation, the central bank will avoid unduly destabilising the real economy while maintaining price stability over the medium term (when such random effects will largely cancel out). Furthermore, by justifying the non-zero price stability definition solely on the basis of measurement biases, the Eurosystem has signalled that it will not be lured onto the slippery slope of striving for an optimal inflation rate. To the contrary, it has adopted a normative aversion to any inflation above the price stability definition. Finally, by defining price stability in terms of price increases, sustained declines in the harmonised consumer index for the euro area have been made inconsistent with price stability. By implication, the Eurosystem has precommitted itself not only to combat inflation, but also deflation.

The reference value for money growth

Money has been assigned a central role in the Eurosystem's strategy for maintaining price stability.[7] This reflects the view that inflation is ultimately a monetary phenomenon and that money growth is a precursor to price developments. Given broadly stable money demand, actual money growth then provides a compass for monetary policy decisions, in contrast for example with actual inflation, which is largely determined by monetary policy some six to eight quarters back. In this light, the Eurosystem announced a first reference value of 4½ per cent per year for the money aggregate M3. Although possibly less controllable in the shorter run, this broad aggregate is expected to be more stable than the narrower aggregates because it internalises substitution effects between different liquid assets. In order also to filter out incidental and seasonal influences, performance under the reference value will be measured on the basis of the average year-on-year money growth rate over a three-month period. Furthermore, with the aim of enhancing transparency, the Eurosystem has published the components from which the reference value has been derived. Specifically, the reference value has been constructed on the basis of the norm for price stability (a year-on-year HICP increase of below 2 per cent), the trend growth of real output (projected at 2-2½ per cent per year) and the trend decline in money velocity (estimated at ½-1 per cent per year on the basis of the historic evolution of velocity and of long-run money demand studies). Thus, the chosen reference value corresponds to the minimum of the ranges when the inflation norm is assumed at 2 per cent and to the maximum when it is set at 1 per cent.

The specification of a reference value for money as a strategic gauge provides further insights into the monetary policy orientation of the euro area. On the one hand, the announcement of a reference value for money indicates that monetary developments will play a prominent role in the considerations driving monetary policy – in line with the tradition of the Bundesbank. On the other hand, the money growth norm has been defined as a reference value, and not as a target. This is intended to convey the message that deviations under the reference value will not automatically lead to policy reactions, but in normal circumstances will signal risks to price stability. The role of money growth as a privileged indicator, rather than as an intermediate target, is further expressed by the specification of the reference value as a point and not a range. Thus, the emphasis is not on whether the norm is actually met, but rather on the information provided by significant and sustained deviations from the reference value. In addition, the key role for money underscores the need to base assessments of monetary policy on euro-wide (rather than nationally oriented) analyses. After all, national monetary data lose much of their meaning once the single euro money market is created, in contrast with national inflation figures which will continue to be separately published and which bear the risk of sustaining an undue focus on national rather than euro-wide developments.

The use of other information variables

In view of the uncertainties – especially during the initial phase of monetary union – about the stability and controllability of euro money demand, steering monetary policy tightly on the basis of money growth would be an unduly risky enterprise. This has prompted the Eurosystem to indicate that it will base policy decisions not only on the assessment of money growth relative to the reference value, but also on a host of other indicators for future inflation in the euro area.[8] Examples of these indicators are the euro exchange rate (to the extent this influences the domestic price level and economic activity), labour costs, the output gap and commodity prices, as well as model-based inflation forecasts and implicit price and interest rate expectations incorporated in financial market variables. Put differently, the Eurosystem's monetary policy dashboard consists of one dominant gauge in the middle of the panel (the rate of money growth relative to the reference value) surrounded by lots of further dials (the other information variables). Such a wide-ranging assessment increases insight into price developments over the shorter term and thus serves as an important complement to the more medium-term oriented policy focus on money developments.

8.4 The Eurosystem's strategy in perspective

In assessing the Eurosystem's strategy, a first difficulty lies in classifying what sort of strategy it really is. From a viewpoint of taxonomy, the strategy combines elements typical of inflation targeting (the quantitative definition of the price stability mandate and the broad-based assessment of inflationary pressures) and of money targeting (the reference value for money growth), without however fitting neatly under either of these two headings. Moreover, it is not a combined strategy, since it does not prespecify two potentially incompatible policy bearings, but explicitly prioritises the price stability definition. Overall, while the strategy would perhaps seem somewhat closer to inflation targeting, it essentially constitutes a breed of its own.

An appraisal based on guiding principles

The unique and novel nature of the Eurosystem's strategy means that an appraisal cannot be based on the experiences of others with this strategy, nor on the Eurosystem's track record. A more fruitful approach is therefore to evaluate the strategy according to characteristics that are considered vital to the Eurosystem's success. In this context, the strategy may be assessed on the basis of the guiding principles that the European Monetary Institute preannounced in 1997.[9] At that time, six criteria were identified for the selection of the Eurosystem's monetary policy strategy, of which the first – effectiveness – essentially encompasses the others. The remaining five criteria relate to whether the strategy contributes to the transparency, accountability, medium-term orientation and continuity of monetary policy-making, as well as to whether it is consistent with the given independence of the monetary authority. Together, these criteria may indeed be considered crucial to the establishment of a credible monetary policy strategy that durably fosters the maintenance of price stability in the euro area.

Of these criteria, the requirements of medium-term orientation, consistency with central bank independence and continuity seem to have been most amply met. In particular, the medium-term orientation is reflected in both the time horizon of the price stability definition and in the trend computation of the real growth and velocity assumptions underlying the reference value for money. By implication, the strategy creates scope for the Eurosystem to accommodate some short-term price movements (especially the first-round price effects of supply shocks) and to avoid buying short-term price stability at the cost of heightened output variability. The chosen strategy is also fully consistent with the independent status of the Eurosystem, since the prime element – the price stability definition – corresponds with the prime objective on which the Eurosystem's independence is legally founded. Although this definition circumscribes the system's goal independence, it stresses the statutory instrument independence that has been granted for the achievement of that goal. At a more subtle level, the reference value for money further underpins this independence insofar as it focuses attention on a variable that is considered to lie predominantly in the scope of the monetary policy-makers themselves.

The continuity of the monetary policy strategy may be inferred from each of the three key elements. Specifically, the price stability definition tallies with the normative price stability assumption (usually 2 per cent) that the Bundesbank has incorporated into its money targets since 1985, with the price stability definition that the EU central banks agreed upon in 1990 ('a level of inflation close to zero … i.e. a maximum of 2 per cent in the medium run'), and with the price stability objective that has been expressly enumerated by the Banque de France and the Banca d'Italia in the 1990s (announced in terms of price increases of up to 2 per cent during the coming year). The reference value for money growth is likewise deeply rooted in European monetary tradition. In particular, the emphasis on money developments and the explicit derivation of the reference value have clearly sprouted from the monetary policy strategy that the Bundesbank has pursued with considerable success during the past two-and-one-half decades. At the same time, the selection of an indicative reference point rather than a range dovetails with the objective that the Banque de France, the Banca d'Italia and the Banco de España have each set for money growth in recent years. And the explicit use of other information variables than money reflects the custom of those euro area countries that previously pursued inflation targets (Finland and Spain). Thus, a large degree of continuity has been achieved with the former monetary policy orientation of many EMU participants. The exception is, of course, provided by the countries that had previously targeted the exchange rate, which constitutes an inappropriate strategy for the relatively closed euro area.

An assessment based on the criteria of transparency and accountability is less clear-cut and less favourable. In a sense, the Eurosystem has gone out of its way to enhance transparency, since it has quantified its statutory goal of price stability and has thus clarified its end goal. By providing an explicitly derived reference value for money growth and by simultaneously acknowledging the role of other information variables, the Eurosystem has also indicated how it will set out to achieve that end goal. Moreover, the price stability definition and the reference value for money growth foster accountability, since they provide distinct yardsticks against which the performance of the monetary authority may be assessed.[10]

The vulnerability of the Eurosystem's strategy nevertheless primarily lies with these same two criteria. This reflects the strategy's shortcoming that monetary policy is not precommitted to a well-specified time-bound 'target'. Indeed, although the preparatory work under the aegis of the European Monetary Institute had strongly advocated the announcement of explicit targets, the major uncertainties at the outset of EMU have eventually led the Eurosystem to stop short of such a precommitment.[11] In particular, the quantitative price stability definition has not been stipulated as a direct policy target. And the reference value for money has been expressly identified as an information rather than a target variable. By itself, this noncommittal approach reduces the transparency and accountability of monetary policy-making, which may in turn weaken its consistency and communicability.

However, the distinction between targets and these strategic specifications may in practice amount to little more than a different shade of grey. After all, a target that is regularly missed and that is played down in external communication may be considered less of a precommitment than a quantitative objective or a reference value that features prominently in actual policy-making and publications. Moreover, since the strategy pins down two measurable monitoring points (for money and inflation), it would *a priori* not seem to create any greater scope for wayward policy discretion. On balance, while the absence of a time-bound policy target makes the strategy somewhat opaque, this may be mitigated if sufficient meaning is attached to the price stability definition and the reference value for money when the strategy is actually implemented. Time will tell.

In terms of specifics, questions on transparency may also be raised with respect to the price stability definition. While this definition clarifies the general mandate of the European Central Bank in the Treaty of Maastricht, several aspects nonetheless remain vague. In particular, if price stability is determined as 'price increases below 2 per cent', what is the lower limit of the tolerance range – is this zero, the estimated measurement bias, or something else? Moreover, does the Eurosystem have any preference within this range, or is monetary policy indifferent as long as the limits are not reached? And what is the relevant time horizon if price stability is to be maintained 'over the medium term'?

While these are valid questions, the elements of vagueness in the price stability definition may be partly defended with the argument that the Eurosystem should not overstate the precision (in terms of level or timing) with which it can steer inflation – particularly not considering the initially uncertain conditions. From this viewpoint, a somewhat broad-brush definition helps signal the limitations of what monetary policy can and cannot achieve, and thereby avoids instigating an overly activist, fine-tuning approach to monetary policy. Having said that, however, the Eurosystem would be well-advised actually to pursue the price stability goal asymmetrically, by favouring price developments near the upper limit of the definition and tailoring monetary policy accordingly. This may serve to facilitate adjustments in relative wages and to maintain adequate scope for the establishment of negative real interest rates in times of recession.

Given measurement biases, it would also avoid the deflationary risks associated with zero inflation. In this respect, such a policy would fit in with the decision not to determine the floor of the tolerance range and only to emphasise the ceiling. As regards the issue of time horizon, two requirements may be applied: first, barring identifiable and truly exceptional exogenous shocks, actual inflation should be consistent with the price stability definition on average over a medium-term time period (of, say, five years); second, forecast inflation should generally fall within the definition beyond the estimated monetary policy transmission period (of, say, two years).

Similar questions on transparency may be posed regarding the strategy's broad-based assessment of inflationary pressures. What are the key variables in this assessment? What determines the relative importance attached to these variables and how do these weights shift over the course of time? And, especially, how are these variables brought together in a consistent and comprehensive decision-making framework? In this latter context, why does the Eurosystem's Council not periodically publish its baseline macroeconomic forecast, notably including for price developments? These are relevant questions that could be usefully addressed by the Eurosystem in the near future.

It should be recognised, however, that the Eurosystem has already taken far-reaching steps to enhance the transparency and accountability of its operational policy-making – steps that go significantly further than the previous practices of any of the EU national central banks and than the minimum requirements in the Treaty of Maastricht.[12] The backbone of this communication policy consists of a monthly press conference on the economic outlook, held by the President of the European Central Bank and complemented by the publication of a Monthly Bulletin, Quarterly Reports and an Annual Report.[13] The press conference opens with an introductory statement that assesses the economic situation and the inflation outlook, and that reflects the discussion in the Governing Council. This statement thus fulfils a role akin to the publication of minutes. It is placed directly on the European Central Bank's web-site on the Internet and is supplemented, after a short administrative delay, by a verbatim transcript of the questions and answers during the press conference. Moreover, in addition to possible ad hoc hearings by the European Parliament of members of the Executive Board (and to possible hearings by national parliaments of national central bank governors), the President of the European Central Bank has agreed to testify before the European Parliament at least four times a year on the basis of these Reports.

Further than this, accountability is circumscribed by the Treaty provisions safeguarding the policy independence of the Eurosystem. Conceptually, a strictly limited override mechanism is definitely desirable to establish the ultimately democratic responsibility of monetary policy. However, to be effective and to avoid the risk of abuse, such a mechanism has to be built into a coherent and empowered balance between the (supranational) European executive and legislative branches. Given the lack of such a balance, the creation of an override mechanism needs to await broad-ranging institutional reforms within the Union. Beyond this, the Treaty protects the Governing Council members from outside influence and specifies a confidentiality norm for the proceedings of monetary policy-making meetings.[14] These provisions have been confirmed by the decisions not to publish transcripts nor voting patterns of monetary policy deliberations. In principle, these decisions may be justified by the need to facilitate an open internal discussion, to structure information before it is externally communicated, and to nurture the cohesion and European focus of the new decision-making body. In this latter regard, not publicising individual positions in the Eurosystem's decision-making body reduces the risk that its members may be subjected to nationally oriented or other political influences. This argument is sometimes turned upside-down by claiming that openness on voting behaviour would provide the ultimate check against nationalist or distorted tendencies.[15] However, it is open to debate whether this check would be stronger than any increase in outside pressures. On these issues, the Eurosystem's transparency regime seeks to focus public attention on the substance of the policy decisions, rather than on the personalities and nationalities of those taking the decisions.[16]

The broader policy setting of the monetary strategy

The Eurosystem's strategy raises two broader issues on the role of monetary policy in the economy of the euro area. To what extent does the monetary policy strategy provide scope to support economic objectives besides price stability, notably those related to real economic growth? And what are the implications of the strategy for the relationship between monetary policy and other elements of the policy mix?

On the first issue, the Treaty on European Union stipulates that, without prejudice to the price stability goal, the Eurosystem shall contribute to the achievement of high and stable economic growth.[17] In this context, it is commonly emphasised that monetary policy's prime contribution to high and sustainable output growth lies in maintaining an environment of stable prices, since such an environment is a necessary precondition for the efficient allocation of resources in a market economy. Indeed, this is why price stability is elevated above other goals in the Eurosystem's mandate. Nonetheless, there are inevitably circumstances in which the pursuit of stable prices, particularly in the shorter term, would involve a trade-off in terms of increased output volatility. This is especially the case when the economy experiences supply shocks, as these have an opposite impact on prices and output. Besides this, it may also be appropriate to accept temporary deviations from price stability in the case of transient disturbances or exceptional circumstances (of which German unification is a fine recent example).

The Eurosystem's monetary policy strategy explicitly provides scope to foster the stability of economic growth, even if this entails accepting short-term price variability or transitory deviations from the price stability norm. This is reflected, first, in the definition of price stability as a range encompassing any positive rate of price change below 2 per cent and, second, in the specification of price stability as an objective to be maintained over the medium term. Thus, the Eurosystem may accommodate the price effects of supply-side and temporary shocks within the tolerance range, and even outside this range subject to price stability being maintained over the medium-term. Put differently, the strategy makes clear that the Treaty's blunt hierarchy of monetary policy objectives, whereby the price stability goal stands above all other objectives, does not necessarily apply in the short run. The relevance of real economic considerations is also reflected in the reference value for money growth, which has been established on the basis of the price stability norm and trend developments in output growth and money velocity. Since above-trend production growth is generally associated with above-trend money growth, and vice versa, the reference value thus imparts a countercyclical slant to monetary policy.[18] In the same vein, as long as the economic cycle is primarily driven by developments in demand, the assessment based on other information variables (the third element in the strategy) will also lead to an anti-cyclical monetary policy. This is because the objectives of stabilising prices and output growth then run in parallel. All said, it should surprise no one if the Eurosystem's policy reaction function is later found to resemble a Taylor rule (which takes account of the output gap as well as deviations from the inflation objective) or if, in hindsight, its strategy is reasonably well described as nominal income targeting.

On the second issue, the relationship between monetary policy and the other elements of the policy mix is likely to be a recurrent topic of debate. This is because the objectives of price stability and economic growth involve trade-offs between the different policy instruments. The debate may also be spurred by developments in the euro exchange rate, which partly reflects (prospects for) the overall policy mix in the euro area. On such grounds, one may anticipate calls for the Eurosystem to engage in active policy co-ordination in order to arrive at an optimal euro area policy mix. In fact, the argument may be heard that policy co-ordination is particularly relevant to the Eurosystem, since developments in other policy fields largely determine the economic costs of a monetary strategy aimed primarily at maintaining price stability. More cynically, one may expect political authorities to trumpet the benefits of policy co-ordination in an effort to get a handle on monetary policy setting.

However, the Eurosystem's monetary policy strategy argues against a concept of active policy co-ordination within the euro area. Rather, it elaborates on the separate responsibility of the monetary authority, in line with the objectives spelt out for monetary policy in the Treaty. In this regard, the strategy fulfils a similar role in the realm of monetary policy to that of the Stability and Growth Pact in the realm of fiscal policy. This agnostic view on policy co-ordination reflects the more diverse and shorter term objectives that are likely to dominate the motives of political authorities. In essence, this reverts back to the case for central bank independence as enshrined in the Treaty. Of course, the Eurosystem's strategy does envisage policy co-ordination in the more modest sense of information sharing between different policy authorities, which is incorporated in the strategy's broad-based assessment of other information variables.

Along a similar line of reasoning, the monetary policy strategy implies a non-activist exchange rate policy, according to which exchange rate developments are accepted as the *ex post* outcome of policy mix and cyclical conditions, rather than as an *ex ante* policy target. The arguments against any exchange rate target (or target zone) are the same as those that ruled out an exchange rate targeting strategy in the first place: given the limited openness of the euro area, the monetary policy requirements of an exchange rate target are unlikely to coincide with the monetary policy requirements of the overriding price stability objective. At the same time, however, it should be emphasised that the Eurosystem's exchange rate strategy is not one of neglect, since the exchange rate is an important transmission channel of inflationary pressures. By consequence, while it will not trigger mechanical policy adjustments, the exchange rate is bound to feature prominently amidst the information variables included in the wide-ranging assessment of prospective price developments.

An international comparison

From an international perspective, the Eurosystem's strategy choice may be appraised by drawing a comparison with the key elements of the monetary policy strategy of other major central banks (Table 10). On the basis of such a comparison, the Eurosystem's strategy gives a relatively solid

Table 10: Key elements of the monetary policy strategy of several central banks

	Political independence legally established?	Unequivocal primary end objective?	Price stability objective clearly defined?	Intermediate policy target?	Privileged policy indicator?
Eurosystem	Yes	Yes (price stability)	Yes (HICP price increase below 2% per annum over the medium term)	No	Yes (4½% reference value for money growth, 3-month average year-on-year)
US Federal Reserve	Yes	No (price stability and employment)	No	No	Yes ? (indicative ranges for money growth, M2: 1-5%, M3: 2-6%, and for debt: 3-7%)
Bank of Japan	Yes	Yes (price stability)	No	No	Yes ? (official money growth projection 1999: M2+CDs 4%)
Deutsche Bundesbank[1]	Yes	Yes (maintain value of the currency)	No ? (implicit: money growth target based on 2% inflation per annum)	Yes (1998: M3 growth 3-6%)	No
Bank of England	No (inflation target set by the Treasury)	Yes (price stability)	Yes (2½% RPIX inflation per annum)	No ? (implicit: forecast inflation 2.5% per annum)	No
Swiss National Bank	Yes	No (national interest, interpreted as price stability)	No	Yes (base money growth 1% per annum)	No

[1] Prior to 1999.

impression. In terms of the institutional structure underpinning the strategy, the Eurosystem is one of the most, if not the most, independent central banks in the world.[19] This independence is unequivocally established in Treaty Law and covers not only policy independence from outside instructions or influences, but also financial independence through adequate capital and profit transfers, and personnel independence in terms of qualified procedures for longer-term appointments and strictly demarcated dismissal motives. Furthermore, monetary policy independence is protected from fiscal policy domination through extensive legal provisions that limit the scope for government deficits, that rule out public sector bail-outs, central bank credit facilities for public sector bodies and privileged access to financial institutions by public authorities, and that stipulate budgetary positions in balance or surplus over the cycle. In the same vein, the general orientation of exchange rate policy at other currencies is only legally possible to the extent consistent with monetary policy's primary objective of price stability. Although the political authorities are granted somewhat greater leeway in decisions on the exchange regime of the euro, the statutory scope for such decisions is severely limited.[20] In addition, besides ironclad provisions in a Treaty that has been ratified by fifteen member states and that is most difficult to alter, this independence derives from the absence of an effective supranational political counterweight to the federal Eurosystem. More subtly, the centre of the Eurosystem has been located in a city (Frankfurt) that is a financial and not a political capital, and that harbours a long-standing tradition of central bank rectitude and independence.

The solidity of the Eurosystem's institutional framework further stems from the explicit linkage of this independence to an unequivocal overriding end objective of price stability. In fact, the system's statutory mandate spells out that monetary policy may only support the other objectives of the Community (especially output growth) to the extent consistent with this primary goal. Outside the European Union, this combination of a steadfast independence tied to a clear-cut price stability objective can only be found in Japan (following changes in central bank legislation in 1998). In this respect, the Eurosystem contrasts with the US Federal Reserve, which would be unable to pursue an inflation target or otherwise to specify an overriding price stability objective, since it has an ambiguous legal mandate that stipulates pursuing both price stability and maximum employment.[21]

But the Eurosystem is the only monetary authority that has complemented institutional independence and clarity of mandate with a quantified, objectively measurable definition of what price stability really means. Beyond this, while the major uncertainties during the transition to monetary union have precluded the announcement of an intermediate policy target, the Eurosystem has sought to enhance the transparency of its decision-making by establishing a clearly-founded reference value for money growth as a privileged policy indicator. In all, an international perspective on the Eurosystem's strategy choice thus reveals a relatively robust set-up.

Looking ahead

The past quarter of a century has seen more diversity and experimentation in monetary policy strategy than any other period in history. This is particularly true in Europe, where countries have tried a myriad of different and varying monetary policy recipes. Thanks to this diversity and to major policy mistakes that have been made in almost all of these countries at some time or other during this period, important lessons have been drawn on what central banks should, and should not, be doing. This has allowed considerable consensus to emerge on the key elements of monetary policy success. Rooted in this rich tradition, the Eurosystem has selected a forward-looking strategy centred on maintaining price stability and guided by a broad-based assessment of information variables, foremost amongst which money growth. This policy orientation is underpinned by far-reaching central bank independence, a clear-cut price stability mandate and severe constraints on possibly conflicting actions in the fiscal and exchange rate policy arena. In itself, Europe's long and winding learning process thus seems to have provided a basis on which the Eurosystem's strategy may be expected to endure.

Given the hybrid character of the Eurosystem's strategy, hedged between money targeting and inflation targeting, the question nonetheless arises whether the passage of time will bring an evolution in the direction of either of these polar alternatives. Of these two scenarios, the first – an evolution towards money targeting – seems especially remote. True, money demand may become relatively more stable once the transitional portfolio adjustments associated with the regime shift to monetary union have taken their course. Taken at face value, this will make a money targeting strategy more attractive. But, somewhat ironically, this transitory instability is bound actually to undermine the enthusiasm for money targeting. After all, which central banker would have the courage to move to money targeting in the wake of a period of pronounced swings in velocity? More fundamentally, the launch of the euro will intensify competition in the financial sector, thereby fuelling the ongoing process of financial innovation (notably including the development of electronic money). As a result, the information content and controllability of developments in specific money aggregates may well continue their declining trend.

The scenario of an evolution towards full-fledged inflation targeting is more likely, but still distant. The basic reason is that the adoption of an inflation target is not necessary in terms of credibility, as indicated by the fact that the euro area has inherited the lowest and not the average of participating countries' long-term interest rates. In absence of a track record, this reflects the rock-solid institutional and incentive structure, as well as the appointment of well-qualified and strong-willed individuals to run the European Central Bank. Given this credibility, the Eurosystem will not easily surrender the discretionary scope inherent in its target-less strategy. Nonetheless, it is desirable that some further characteristics of inflation targeting are taken on board, especially a more explicit external communication of the Eurosystem's forecast for inflation and other key macroeconomic variables. Beyond this, a full shift to this strategy may be envisaged if extreme political pressure or substantive policy errors were to demand the greater transparency and accountability that come with the adoption of an explicit, clear-cut and time-bound inflation target.

Looking ahead, the coming years will in any event make clear whether the Eurosystem has a preference within the implicit tolerance range for inflation (0-2 per cent) and whether the system readily accommodates short-term deviations outside this range in the face of supply side disturbances or exceptional factors. On these issues, the Eurosystem would be well-advised to pursue an average inflation rate close to the ceiling of the price stability definition, as well as a pragmatic policy implementation that allows temporary deviations and emphasises the medium-term character of the price stability objective. In the first years of EMU, the system should also provide clarity on key variables in the strategy's broad-based indicators of inflationary pressures. The urgency of shedding light on these variables will be greater if the stability of money demand falls short of expectations – which historical experience in Europe suggests is not unlikely – and leads to a declining emphasis on the reference value for money growth.

Beyond this, it is indeed to be hoped that the Eurosystem's strategy remains broadly unchanged for quite a while, since the continuity of monetary policy strategy runs at a premium and its value is only revealed in the medium term. Of course, it may be argued that judicious monetary policy primarily depends on the wisdom and will of the Eurosystem's decision-makers and that the strategy should evolve together with their thinking. However, the strategy should not be too flexible, since one of its roles is to advance the consistency and continuity of these individuals' policy setting. On this score, the Eurosystem's strategy raises high hopes that its new-born currency will mature in an environment of sustained price stability.

NOTES

[1] See European Monetary Institute (1997). This publication was based on the report by the Monetary Policy Sub-Committee that was endorsed by the Council of the European Monetary Institute in late 1996.

[2] Berk, Houben and Kakes (2000).

[3] Overviews of the numerous empirical studies on EU-wide money demand are provided in Browne, Fagan and Henry (1997) and Van Riet (1993). The methodological intricacies of aggregation are addressed by Monticelli and Strauss-Kahn (1992) and by Winder (1997).

[4] Arnold (1994) forcefully made this point by arguing that money demand instability is primarily caused by factors relating to the financial system and to monetary policy, and that these shocks average out in constructed aggregates. Later, Arnold (1997) reiterated his case

by presenting evidence that the correlation of regional money aggregates in the United States is significantly higher than that of national money aggregates in Europe; this suggests that the greater money demand stability estimated for EMU may only be a diversification effect that disappears once EMU is actually established.

[5] See Vlaar and Schuberth (1998) and Cabrero *et al.* (1998). These studies had a direct influence on the policy discussion within the Eurosystem, as they involved authors from the Dutch, Austrian and Spanish central bank respectively.

[6] European Central Bank (1999a).

[7] For an elaborate discussion of the role of money in the Eurosystem's monetary policy strategy, see European Central Bank (1999b).

[8] An overview of the role of short-term indicators in the analysis of future inflation in the euro area is provided in European Central Bank (1999c).

[9] European Monetary Institute (1997).

[10] On a detailed note, the HICP inflation measure selected in the price stability definition is transparently and independently calculated outside the Eurosystem by EUROSTAT.

[11] In its list of key elements for the monetary policy strategy in Stage Three, the European Monetary Institute highlighted that the Eurosystem "should publicly set *targets* against which its performance can be assessed and explain its policy actions to the public with reference to its targets" (see European Monetary Institute, 1997, p. 12; italics in original text).

[12] For instance, the Treaty (Article 113) only necessitates an annual testimony by the President of the European Central Bank to the European Parliament (on the basis of the Annual Report); the Protocol on the European System of Central Banks (Article 15) requires the publication of at least quarterly reports on the system's activities.

[13] The Monthly Bulletin is produced each month, except in those months that a Quarterly Report is published (implying eight issues a year).

[14] Specifically, Article 10.4 of the Protocol on the European System of Central Banks determines the default setting that "The proceedings of the meetings shall be confidential. The Governing Council may decide to make the outcome of its deliberations public." In the event, the Governing Council has prescribed a 30-year publication lag.

[15] Buiter (1999) further claims that the formal confidentiality of the meetings and votes is likely to be breached through extensive leaks "within five minutes of a vote being taken". This betrays little trust in the integrity of the (continental) European central banking community.

[16] For a staunch defence of the Eurosystem's line on transparency, see Issing (1999a,1999b).

[17] Specifically, Article 105 spells out that "The primary objective of the ESCB shall be to maintain price stability. Without prejudice to the objective of price stability, the ESCB shall support the general economic policies in the Community with a view to contributing to the achievement of the objectives of the Community as laid down in Article 2". This latter Article includes as objectives "to promote throughout the Community a harmonious and balanced development of economic activities, sustainable and non-inflationary growth … a high level of employment …"

[18] See Hoogduin and Sleijpen (1999) who argue that the reference value will imply an anti-cyclical monetary policy as long as money velocity moves a- or anti-cyclically, and even if it moves pro-cyclically as long as the elasticity of velocity with respect to nominal income is less than one (although stabilisation would only be partial in this latter case). They advocate a modest stabilisation approach, whereby ambitions are set realistically and, especially in the uncertain initial years of EMU, monetary policy concentrates on maintaining price stability.

[19] De Haan (1997) and Bini Smaghi (1998).

[20] The Treaty on European Union spells out monetary policy independence in Article 108, financial independence in Articles 28 and 33 of the Protocol on the European System of Central Banks, and personnel independence in Articles 11 and 14 of same Protocol. The Treaty restricts government deficits in Article 104 (as elaborated in the EC Council Regulation 1477/97 on the Excessive Deficit Procedure) and prohibits privileged public sector access to financial institutions in Article 102 and public sector bail-outs in Article 103. As subsequently agreed at the Amsterdam Summit of 1997, the Stability and Growth Pact also includes a commitment to maintain budgets that are balanced or in surplus over the medium term and specifies an early warning procedure for fiscal digressions that put the Treaty limits at risk (stipulated in EC Council Regulation 1466/97). The Treaty establishes that general orientations for exchange rate policy shall be without prejudice to the price stability goal in Article 111.2. Although this Article 111.1 grants the political authorities somewhat greater latitude in decisions on the participation of the euro in formal exchange rate arrangements (including, for instance, Bretton Woods-type arrangements), such a step requires unanimous support within the European Council and may only be taken on a recommendation from the ECB or from the European Commission, after consulting with the ECB in an endeavour to reach a consensus consistent with its price stability goal.

[21] To be precise, the Federal Reserve Act of 1977 requires the US monetary authorities "to maintain long-run monetary and credit aggregates commensurate with the economy's long-run potential to increase production so as to promote effectively goals of maximum employment, stable prices, and moderate long-term interest rates." More succinctly, this is commonly termed the Federal Reserve's 'twin objective', the former of which is readily emphasised by the US Congress.

Appendix I

AUSTRIA

	Monetary Policy Target [1]		
	Exchange Rate		
Year	Date	Target [2]	Outcome [3]
1975		Basket [4]	=
		Snake (± 4.5 %) [5]	=
1976		Basket [4]	=
	13-07 [5]	Snake (± 4.5 %) [5]	ǂ [5]
		Schilling / DM [6]	=
1977		Basket [4]	=
		Schilling / DM [6]	=
1978		Basket [4]	=
	17-10	*Schilling / DM* [7]	-1.0 % [7]
1979		Basket [4]	ǂ [4]
	07-09	*Schilling / DM* [8]	+1.5 % [9]
1980		*Schilling / DM* [8]	=
1981		*Schilling / DM* [8]	=
1982		*Schilling / DM* [8]	=
1983		*Schilling / DM* [8]	=
1984		*Schilling / DM* [8]	=
1985		*Schilling / DM* [8]	=
1986		*Schilling / DM* [8]	=
1987		*Schilling / DM* [8]	=
1988		*Schilling / DM* [8]	=
1989		*Schilling / DM* [8]	=
1990		*Schilling / DM* [8]	=
1991		*Schilling / DM* [8]	=
1992		*Schilling / DM* [8]	=
1993		*Schilling / DM* [8]	=
1994		*Schilling / DM* [8]	=
1995	09-01 [10]	ERM (± 15.0 %) [10]	=
1996		ERM (± 15.0 %)	=
1997		ERM (± 15.0 %)	=
1998		ERM (± 15.0 %)	=

[1] Besides the exchange rate, the central bank also pursued the stability of nominal long-term interest rates until the late 1970s and credit ceilings until the early 1980s. The former objective was frequently communicated by central bank officials, but was never quantitatively defined. The latter ceilings were preannounced, but were frequently adjusted and redefined, and functioned as a policy instrument rather than an intermediate target.

[2] Specifies the exchange rate commitment and the relevant fluctuation margin.

[3] Defined as the percentage devaluation (-), revaluation (+) or unchanged parity (=) relative to the Deutsche mark (DM), or withdrawal (ǂ) of the exchange rate commitment.

[4] From 1971 the schilling was pegged to a currency basket initially comprising the nine most important European trading partners. The weights were not published and were

frequently adjusted, including through a reduction in the number of basket currencies, resulting in a steadily increasing importance of the Deutsche mark. While in practice the basket orientation (called the "indicator") never seriously conflicted with Austria's other exchange rate targets, it was de-emphasised in the late 1970s and lapsed in 1979 (without being formally abandoned) when the Deutsche mark-peg became the only target.

[5] In March 1973 Austria unilaterally pegged the schilling to the Snake with a fluctuation margin of ± 2.25 % that was increased to ± 4.5 % in May 1974. Both the widening of the margin and the subsequent withdrawal from the Snake on 13 July 1976 reflected the appreciation of the Deutsche mark against other Snake currencies in combination with Austria's increasing focus on the Deutsche mark as part of the evolving hard currency strategy.

[6] Austria maintained the Deutsche mark intervention margins (± 4.5 %) of its unilateral peg to the Snake until December 1977.

[7] In the context of the Snake realignment of 17 October 1978 the schilling was devalued by 1 % against the Deutsche mark in what was termed a 'technical correction'.

[8] Starting in late 1978, the schilling/Deutsche mark exchange rate became the dominant, albeit informal and unilateral, monetary policy focus. Since 1982, this exchange rate has only fluctuated minimally (generally within a band of ± 0.1 %).

[9] The schilling was revalued on 7 September 1979 prior to the autumn wage round, and subsequently appreciated by a further 3 % until end-1980, thereby marking the final step in the adoption of the hard currency strategy.

[10] Austria joined the ERM on 9 January 1995. In practice, however, this did not have any substantive implications for the orientation of monetary policy, which remained focused on ensuring the stability of the bilateral schilling/Deutsche mark exchange rate.

Appendix II

BELGIUM / LUXEMBOURG [1]

	Monetary Policy Target [2]		
	Exchange Rate [3]		
Year	Date	Target [4]	Outcome [5]
1975		Snake [6] (± 2.25 %)	=
		Worm [7] (± 1.5%)	=
1976	16-03	Worm [7] (±1.5%)	≠ [7]
	17-10	Snake (± 2.25 %)	-2 %
1977		Snake (± 2.25 %)	=
1978	17-10	Snake (± 2.25 %)	-2 %
1979	13-03 [8]	ERM (± 2.25 %) [8]	=
	24-09	ERM (± 2.25 %)	-2 %
1980		ERM (± 2.25 %)	=
1981	05-10	ERM (± 2.25 %)	-5.5 %
1982	22-02	ERM (± 2.25 %)	-8.5 %
	14-06	ERM (± 2.25 %)	-4.25 %
1983	21-03	ERM (± 2.25 %)	-4 %
1984		ERM (± 2.25 %)	=
1985		ERM (± 2.25 %)	=
1986	07-04	ERM (± 2.25 %)	-2 %
1987	12-01	ERM (± 2.25 %)	-1 %
1988		ERM (± 2.25 %)	=
1989		ERM (± 2.25 %)	=
1990	16-06 [9]	ERM (± 2.25 %) [9]	=
1991		ERM (± 2.25 %)	=
1992		ERM (± 2.25 %)	=
1993	02-08 [10]	ERM (± 15.0 %) [10]	=
1994		ERM (± 15.0 %)	=
1995		ERM (± 15.0 %)	=
1996		ERM (± 15.0 %)	=
1997		ERM (± 15.0 %)	=
1998		ERM (± 15.0 %)	=

[1] In the period under review, Luxembourg did not have its own central bank. For the determination and implementation of both monetary policy and intervention policy in the foreign exchange markets, it made use of the National Bank of Belgium which bore the responsibility in these policy areas for both Belgium and Luxembourg. The exchange rate between the Luxembourg franc and the Belgian franc is fixed at a rate of one-for-one and has been unchanged since 1936, although it was rescaled to parity in 1944. The Belgium-Luxembourg Economic Union (BLEU) that ties the two economies together has been operative since 1922.

[2] During April 1974 until April 1975 and November-December 1978 the central bank used credit ceilings as an instrument to contain liquidity growth respectively to curtail foreign exchange speculation.

[3] Belgium maintained a dual exchange rate regime supported by extensive exchange regulations until 5 March 1990, with a different exchange rate for current and capital transactions. The official exchange rate for current transactions was held within the

fluctuation band of, respectively, the Snake and the ERM; the exchange rate for capital transactions was floating. In practice, deviations in the dual exchange market were large in the mid-1970s and early 1980s (reaching a maximum yearly average of 7.3 % in 1982) and small (generally less than 1 %) after mid-1984.

4 Specifies the exchange rate commitment and the relevant fluctuation margin.

5 Defined as the percentage devaluation (-), revaluation (+) or unchanged parity (=) relative to the Deutsche mark (DM), or withdrawal (⧺) of the exchange rate commitment.

6 Belgium participated in the Snake, without interruption, from the outset on 24 April 1972 until the start of the ERM.

7 The Benelux countries maintained a mutual ± 1.5 % narrow margins agreement (the 'Worm') within the context of the Snake until 16 March 1976.

8 Belgium participated in the ERM, without interruption, from the outset on 13 March 1979 until the start of EMU.

9 Although this policy intention was leaked to the press a few weeks earlier, on 16 June 1990 the central bank formally announced the commitment to peg the franc to the most stable ERM currencies, particularly the Deutsche mark.

10 On 2 August 1993 the general ERM margins were widened from ± 2.25 % to ± 15 %.

Appendix III

DENMARK

	Monetary Policy Target				
	Exchange Rate			Credit [1]	
Year	Date	Target [2]	Outcome [3]	Target	Outcome
1975		Snake (± 2.25 %) [4]	=		
1976	17-10	Snake (± 2.25 %)	-6 %		
1977	01-04	Snake (± 2.25 %)	-3 %		
	28-08	Snake (± 2.25 %)	-5 %		
1978	17-10	Snake (± 2.25 %)	-4 %		
1979	13-03 [5]	ERM (± 2.25 %) [5]	=		
	24-09	ERM (± 2.25 %)	-4.9 %		
	30-11	ERM (± 2.25 %)	-4.8 %		
1980		ERM (± 2.25 %)	=		
1981	05-10	ERM (± 2.25 %)	-5.5 %		
1982	22-02	ERM (± 2.25 %)	-3 %		
	14-06	ERM (± 2.25 %)	-4.25 %		
1983	21-03	ERM (± 2.25 %)	-3 %		
1984		ERM (± 2.25 %)	=		
1985		ERM (± 2.25 %)	=		
1986	07-04	ERM (± 2.25 %)	-2 %		
1987	12-01	ERM (± 2.25 %)	-3 %		
1988		ERM (± 2.25 %)	=		
1989		ERM (± 2.25 %)	=		
1990		ERM (± 2.25 %)	=		
1991		ERM (± 2.25 %)	=	4 - 7 [6]	1
1992		ERM (± 2.25 %)	=	3 - 6 [6]	-9
1993	02-08 [7]	ERM (± 15.0 %) [7]	=		
1994		ERM (± 15.0 %)	=		
1995		ERM (± 15.0 %)	=		
1996		ERM (± 15.0 %)	=		
1997		ERM (± 15.0 %)	=		
1998		ERM (± 15.0 %)	=		

[1] Until the full liberalisation of international capital movements in 1988 various quantitative regulations were imposed on banks, including credit ceilings that served as monetary policy instruments.

[2] Specifies the exchange rate commitment and the relevant fluctuation margin.

[3] Defined as percentage devaluation (-), revaluation (+) or unchanged parity (=) relative to the Deutsche mark.

[4] Denmark joined the Snake on 1 May 1972 and participated until the start of the ERM with a short interruption between 27 June and 10 October 1972, during which the official parity was left unchanged.

[5] Denmark participated in the ERM without interruption from the outset on 13 March 1979 until the start of EMU.

[6] This target was announced in the context of an initiative by the Danmarks Nationalbank to strengthen co-operation between the central banks of the EEC countries by establishing a prior co-ordination of national monetary policy objectives. The target range applied to the

percentage growth in domestic money creation (i.e. the sum of kroner lending to residents and holdings of krone bonds with deduction of tax-privileged deposits, excluding premium saving accounts) and related to the fourth quarter-fourth quarter growth rate.

[7] On 2 August 1993 the general ERM margins were widened from ± 2.25 % to ± 15 %.

Appendix IV

FINLAND

	Monetary Policy Target [1]				
	Inflation		Exchange Rate		
Year	Target	Outcome	Date	Target [2]	Outcome [3]
1975				*Basket* [4]	=
1976				*Basket* [4]	=
1977			03-08	*Basket* [4]	- 3.1 %
			05-04	*Basket* [4]	- 5.7 %
			01-11 [5]	Basket [5] (± 2.25 %) [5]	=
1978			16-02	Basket (± 2.25 %)	- 8.0 %
1979			11-05	Basket (± 2.25 %)	+ 0.8 %
			13-08	Basket (± 2.25 %)	+ 0.5 %
			21-09	Basket (± 3.00 %) [6]	=
1980			25-03	Basket (± 3.00 %)	+ 1.7 %
1981				Basket (± 3.00 %)	=
1982			10-10	Basket (± 2.25 %) [6]	- 5.7 %
1983				Basket (± 2.25 %)	=
1984			01-01 [7]	Basket [7] (± 2.25 %)	=
			27-03	Basket (± 2.25 %)	+ 1.0 %
1985				Basket (± 2.25 %)	=
1986			16-05	Basket (± 2.25 %)	- 1.6 %
1987				Basket (± 2.25 %)	=
1988			30-11	Basket (± 3.00 %) [6]	=
1989			17-03	Basket (± 3.00 %)	+ 4.0 %
1990				Basket (± 3.00 %)	=
1991			07-06 [8]	ECU [8] (± 3.00 %)	=
			15-11	ECU (± 3.00 %)	-12.3 %
1992			08-09 [9]	ECU (± 3.00 %)	╪ [9]
1993	CPIY [10]	0.6			
1994	CPIY [10]	1.3			
1995	CPIY [10] ≈ 2	- 0.1			
1996	CPIY [10] ≈ 2	0.2	14-10 [11]	ERM [11] (± 15.0 %)	=
1997	CPIY [10] ≈ 2	0.7		ERM (± 15.0 %)	=
1998	CPIY [10] ≈ 2	1.3		ERM (± 15.0 %)	=

[1] Next to the listed targets, in February 1989 the central bank agreed with private banks to limit credit growth to 11 % for the year; excess growth triggered an additional interest-free cash reserve requirement (the outcome was 15.2 %). The agreement lapsed in 1990 when credit growth decelerated markedly in the context of economic slowdown.

[2] Specifies the exchange rate commitment and the relevant fluctuation margin.

[3] Defined as the percentage devaluation (-), revaluation (+) or unchanged parity (=) relative to the basket, ECU or Deutsche mark respectively, or withdrawal (╪) of the exchange rate commitment.

[4] From the end of Bretton Woods until 1 November 1977 the markka was officially floating, but was informally tied to a trade-weighted currency basket comprising the currencies of all countries representing at least 1% of Finnish trade.

[5] On 1 November 1977 the new Currency Act was introduced officially pegging the Markka to the currency basket with an unspecified band. The band was subsequently set at ± 2.25 % by the Government.

[6] The fluctuation band was widened from ± 2.25 % to ± 3 % on 21 September 1979; narrowed back to ± 2.25 % on 10 October 1982; and widened again to ± 3 % on 30 November 1988.

[7] Effective 1 January 1984 the Soviet rouble was removed from the currency basket; thereafter the calculation of the currency basket comprised only freely convertible currencies.

[8] On 7 June 1991 the currency basket was replaced by the ECU with an unchanged fluctuation band of ± 3 %.

[9] The Finnish Markka was floated on 8 September 1992.

[10] On 2 February 1993 Finland introduced direct inflation targeting, aiming to stabilise the CPIY inflation rate permanently at 'about 2 %' by 1995. CPIY = Consumer Price Index excluding indirect taxes, subsidies and capital costs for owner occupied housing.

[11] Finland joined the ERM on 14 October 1996.

Appendix V

FRANCE

	Monetary Policy Target[1]						
	Exchange Rate			Money[2]		Inflation	
Year	Date	Target[3]	Outcome[4]	Target	Outcome	Objective	Outcome
1975	10-07[5]	Snake[5] (± 2.25 %)	=	*M2*[6] *13.0*[6]	18.2		
1976	15-03[7]	Snake[7] (± 2.25 %)	ǂ	*M2*[6] *13.0*[6]	12.8		
1977				M2 12.5	14.0		
1978				M2 12.0	12.1		
1979	13-03[8]	ERM[8] (± 2.25 %)	=	M2 11.0	14.4		
	24-09	ERM (± 2.25 %)	-2 %				
1980		ERM (± 2.25 %)	=	M2 11.0	9.8		
1981	05-10	ERM (± 2.25 %)	-8.5 %	M2 12.0[9]	11.4		
1982	14-06	ERM (± 2.25 %)	-10.0 %	M2 12.5 - 13.5	11.5		
1983	21-03	ERM (± 2.25 %)	-8 %	M2 9[10]	10.2		
1984		ERM (± 2.25 %)	=	M2R[11] 5.5 - 6.5	7.6		
1985		ERM (± 2.25 %)	=	M2R[11] 4 - 6	6.9		
1986	07-04	ERM (± 2.25 %)	-6 %	M3 3 - 5	4.6		
1987	12-01	ERM (± 2.25 %)	-3 %	M2 4 - 6	3.8		
				M3 3 - 5	10.8		
1988		ERM (± 2.25 %)	=	M2 4 - 6	4.1		
1989		ERM (± 2.25 %)	=	M2 4 - 6	4.1		
1990		ERM (± 2.25 %)	=	M2 3.5 - 5.5	-0.3		
1991		ERM (± 2.25 %)	=	M3 5 - 7	3.8		
1992		ERM (± 2.25 %)	=	M3 4 - 6	5.5		
1993	02-08[12]	ERM (± 15.0 %)[12]	=	M3 4 - 6.5	-2.3		
1994		ERM (± 15.0 %)	=	M3 ≈ 5[13]	0.8	CPI ≤ 2[14]	1.6
1995		ERM (± 15.0 %)	=	M3 ≈ 5[13]	3.8	CPI ≤ 2[14]	2.1
1996		ERM (± 15.0 %)	=	M3 ≈ 5[13]	-3.7	CPI ≤ 2[14]	1.7
1997		ERM (± 15.0 %)	=	M3[15] ≈ 5[13]	1.7	CPI ≤ 2[14]	1.1
1998		ERM (± 15.0 %)	=	M3[15] ≈ 5[13]	2.7	CPI ≤ 2[14]	0.4

[1] Until 1986 France employed credit ceilings as an instrument towards meeting its intermediate money targets. Since 1994 the central bank has used Total Domestic Debt as a privileged supplementary indicator of domestic liquidity conditions.

[2] Data refer to the percentage growth rate for December-December until 1982 and during 1996-98, the 3-month moving average centred in December during 1983-85, and fourth quarter-fourth quarter during 1986-95.

[3] Specifies the exchange rate commitment and the relevant fluctuation margin.

[4] Defined as the percentage devaluation (-), revaluation (+) or unchanged parity (=) relative to the Deutsche mark, or withdrawal (ǂ) of the exchange rate commitment.

[5] France rejoined the Snake on 10 July 1975 at the same exchange rate parity that had applied when it withdrew from the arrangement on 19 January 1974. Previously it had been a member of the Snake since the arrangement's inception on 24 April 1972.

[6] These targets were not publicly announced at the time, but were used internally by the central bank.

[7] France withdrew from the Snake a second time, but this time definitely, on 15 March 1976.

[8] France participated in the ERM without interruption from the outset on 13 March 1979 until the start of EMU.

[9] The target was raised from 10 to 12 % by the new Government in June 1981.
[10] The target was lowered from 10 to 9 % in March 1983, as part of a disinflationary package.
[11] For 1984-85 the target was set for a new aggregate, M2R, which excluded non-resident bank deposits.
[12] On 2 August 1993 the general ERM margins were widened from ± 2.25 % to ± 15 %.
[13] Following severe money demand instability in 1993, the money targets were explicitly given a medium-term character from 1994 onwards.
[14] On 27 January 1994 the newly created Monetary Policy Council expressly specified the price stability objective as meaning that consumer price increases should not exceed 2 % in 1994 and in the medium term. Such an announcement was repeated at the outset of each year during 1995-98.
[15] Next to M3, developments under the money target in 1997-98 were also explicitly evaluated on the basis of narrower and broader aggregates (M1, M2, M3+P1: 1997 outcomes 6.4, 7.8 respectively 4.7; 1998 outcomes 3.0, 4.3 respectively 3.3).

Appendix VI

GERMANY [1]

	Monetary Policy Target [2]		Memo				
	Money [3]		Money Target Breakdown [4]				
Year	Target [3]	Outcome [3]	Growth of Production Potential	Velocity Adjustment [5]	Inflation Assumption [6]	Inflation Outcome [7]	Inflation Deviation [8]
1975	CBM [9] ≈ 8	10.1	*2* [10]	... [11]	*6* [10]	5.7	-0.3
1976	CBM ≈ 8	9.2	2	... [11]	4 - 5	3.6	-0.9
1977	CBM ≈ 8	9.0	3	*-1*	≈ 3.5	3.7	0.2
1978	CBM ≈ 8	11.5	3	... [11]	≤ 3.5	4.3	0.8
1979	CBM 6 - 9 [12]	6.3	3 [13]	... [11]	4 [14]	3.8	-0.2
1980	CBM 5 - 8 [12]	4.9 [15]	3	≈ *-1*	≈ 4	5.0	1.0
1981	CBM 4 - 7 [12]	3.5 [15]	2.5	*-1*	≈ 3.5 - 4	4.2	0.5
1982	CBM 4 - 7 [12]	6.0	1.5 - 2	... [11]	≈ 3.5	4.4	0.9
1983	CBM 4 - 7 [12]	7.0	1.5 - 2	... [11]	3.5	3.2	-0.3
1984	CBM 4 - 6	4.6	≈ 2	... [11]	≈ 3	2.1	-0.9
1985	CBM 3 - 5	4.5	2	... [11]	2	2.1	0.1
1986	CBM 3.5 - 5.5	7.7	2.5	... [11]	2	3.2	1.2
1987	CBM 3 - 6	8.1	2.5	... [11]	2	1.9	-0.1
1988	M3 3 - 6	6.7	≈ 2	0.5	≤ 2	1.5	-0.5
1989	M3 ≈ 5 [16]	4.7	2 - 2.5	0.5	≈ 2	2.4	0.4
1990	M3 4 - 6	5.6	2.5	0.5	2	3.2	1.2
1991	M3 3 - 5 [17]	5.2 [15]	≈ 2.5	0.5	2	3.9	1.9
1992	M3 3.5 - 5.5	9.4	2.75	0.5	2	5.6	3.6
1993	M3 4.5 - 6.5	7.4	3	1	2	4.0	2.0
1994	M3 4 - 6	5.7	2.5	1	2	2.4	0.4
1995	M3 4 - 6	2.1	2.75	1	≤ 2	2.2	0.2
1996	M3 4 - 7	8.1	2.5	1	≤ 2	1.1	-0.9
1997	M3 3.5 - 6.5 [18]	4.7	2.25 [19]	1	1.5 - 2	0.6	-1.1
1998	M3 3.0 - 6.0 [18]	5.5	2	1	1.5 - 2	0.9	-0.8

1 Data relate to West Germany until 1991 and to unified Germany thereafter.

2 From 1972 until the start of EMU, Germany participated consecutively and without interruption in the Snake and the ERM. Although this formally implied an exchange rate target, in practice the Bundesbank provided the anchor in these systems and pursued an inherently independent monetary policy. In fact, with the exception of Ireland's lone revaluation on the eve of EMU, the Deutsche mark was never devalued against any other currency in the Snake or ERM.

3 Data relate to percentage growth rates and to December-December for 1975, to annual averages for 1976 through 1978, and to fourth quarter-fourth quarter for all subsequent years.

4 The Bundesbank has consistently published its money targets together with an explicit breakdown in terms of the projected growth of production potential (initially including desired changes in capacity utilisation), the trend rate of change in the velocity of circulation of money and the normative rate of inflation that is acceptable in the medium term (until 1984 the inflation that was considered 'unavoidable').

5 A positive velocity adjustment indicates a decline in the velocity of money circulation, and vice versa.

[6] The implicit inflation assumption is derived from the Bundesbank's publicised indications including such qualifications as 'about' or 'around' indicated by '$\approx$' and 'at most' by '$\leq$'.

[7] The inflation outcome refers to the GDP deflator, which in recent years has been the Bundesbank's preferred inflation measure in the context of its money targets. This preference reflects the role of the GDP deflator in the conversion of nominal into real production potential as well as the underlying nature of this inflation measure, since energy price movements in imports are excluded. Over the last two decades, however, the Bundesbank has not been very explicit about its preferred inflation measure and quite often also referred to the CPI in its analyses.

[8] The inflation deviation is defined as the difference between the central assumption and the outcome for the GDP deflator.

[9] CBM = Central Bank Money, comprising currency holdings, plus sight deposits, time deposits, and saving deposits all constantly weighted by the reserve ratios applicable in 1974 (16.6 %, 12.4 %, and 8.1 % respectively).

[10] The Bundesbank did not specify the 1975 target; it did however state that the target was in line with the government forecast which projected GDP growth of 2 % and CPI inflation of 6 %.

[11] For these years, a velocity adjustment was not explicitly quantified.

[12] In the years 1979 through 1983, the Bundesbank specified at mid-year which part of the target range it was aiming for. In 1979 and 1980 this was specified as 'lower limit', in 1981 as 'lower half', and in 1982 and 1983 as 'upper half'. The specification depended mainly on recent developments in prices, economic activity and the exchange rate.

[13] This figure was not explicitly specified, but there was a qualitative statement that growth of production potential should be about the same as before.

[14] This figure was not explicitly specified but can be inferred from the background tables.

[15] On the basis of rounded figures, the Bundesbank considers the money target to have been met in these years.

[16] The Bundesbank defined the 1989 target as 'about 5 %'.

[17] The target range was revised in July 1991 from 4-6 % to 3-5 % with reference to the exceptional circumstances of German unification.

[18] The Bundesbank announced a two-year target of 'about 5 %' for the years 1997-98. At the outset of each of these years, the Bundesbank further specified the targets as 3.5-6.5 % and 3-6 % respectively.

[19] Revised downward to 2 % in December 1997.

Appendix VII

GREECE

	Monetary Policy Target [1]					
	Exchange Rate		Money [2]		Credit [2]	
Year	Target [3]	Outcome [4]	Target	Outcome	Target [5]	Outcome
1975	GRD/$ [6]	ǂ [6]	M1 [7] 20.0	15.6		
1976			M1 12.0	21.9	DCE [5] 18.0	22.8
1977			M1 14.0	18.3	DCE 23.9	24.8
1978			M1 16.6	21.1	DCE 23.8	24.5
1979			M1 15.6	14.2	DCE 22.4	21.7
1980			M1 15.0	14.6	DCE 14.9	25.4
1981			M1 17.2	24.3	DCE 22.5	36.4
1982			M1 24.0	15.2	DCE 30.3	31.7
1983	*GRD/$ [8]*	ǂ [8]	M1 24.0	14.1	DCE 26.4	21.8
			M3 26.1	20.9		
1984			M1 17.2	17.0	DCE 21.6	26.6
			M3 22.0	29.6		
1985			M1 17.0	26.1	DCE 19.7	26.0
			M3 23.4	27.3		
1986			M1 19.8	7.2	DCE 16.4	18.5
			M3 19.8	19.1		
1987			M1 10.5	16.1	DCE 12.1	13.0
			M3 15.4	24.7		
1988			M3 14 - 16	22.9	DCE 10.5 - 11	15.5
1989			M3 18 – 20	24.2	DCE 13 - 14	20.0
1990			M3 19 - 21	15.3	DCE 16.2 - 17.4	15.0
1991			M3 14 - 16	12.3	DCE 12.5 - 13.5	11.2
1992			M3 9 - 12	14.4	DCE 7 - 9	11.6
1993			M3 9 - 12	15.0	DCE 6 - 8	13.5
1994			M3 8 - 11	8.8	DCE 6 - 8	8.9
1995	GRD/ECU (-3.0 %)[9]	-3.0 % [9]	M3 7 - 9	10.3	*DCE 6 - 8* [10]	7.9
			M4 11 - 13 [10]	8.2		
1996	GRD/ECU (-1.0 %)[9]	-1.0 % [9]	M3 6 - 9	9.4	*DCE 5 - 7* [10]	5.9
			M4 9 - 12 [10]	12.0		
1997	GRD/ECU (0.0 %)[9]	-1.7 % [9]	M3 6 – 9	9.5	*DCE 4 - 6* [10]	9.6
			M4 8 - 11 [10]	-1.6		
1998	GRD/ECU (0.0 %)[9]	-12.3 %[11]	*M3 6 - 9* [12]	8.9	*DCE 4 - 6* [10]	9.8
16-03[11]	ERM (± 15.0 %)[11]	=				

[1] Since 1990 increasing attention has been placed on the CPI inflation projection underlying the monetary program without, however, entailing a switch to direct inflation targeting.

[2] Data relate to December-December percentage growth rates.

[3] Specifies the exchange rate commitment, the targeted rate of devaluation under the Drachma/ECU peg, and the relevant fluctuation margin under the ERM.

[4] Defined as the percentage devaluation (-) relative to the ECU, unchanged parity (=) or withdrawal of the exchange rate commitment (ǂ).

[5] DCE = Domestic Credit Expansion; at times targets were also set for domestic credit to the private sector.

[6] The Greek Drachma (GRD) was pegged to the US dollar between the end of 1973 and March 1975.

[7] M1 comprises only currency in circulation, except for 1975 when sight deposits were also included.

[8] The Drachma was pegged to the dollar for 7 months between January and August 1983.

[9] Greece pegged the Drachma to the ECU with a targeted devaluation in 1995 and an objective of 'broadly stable' thereafter; the quantitative targets for 1996-98 are taken from Greece's public convergence program.

[10] With the introduction of the ECU-peg, M4 and DCE became monitoring ranges.

[11] On 16 March 1998 Greece joined the ERM at a parity that implied a 12.3 % devaluation against the ECU-peg.

[12] Subsequent to Greece's entry in the ERM, M3 became a monitoring range.

Appendix VIII

IRELAND

	Monetary Policy Target				
	Exchange Rate			Credit [1]	
Year	Date	Target [2]	Outcome [3]	Target	Outcome
1975		Irish Pound / UK £ [4]	=	17	7
1976		Irish Pound / UK £ [4]	=	15	25
1977		Irish Pound / UK £ [4]	=	18	26
1978		Irish Pound / UK £ [4]	=	20	33
1979	13-03 [5]	ERM [5] (± 2.25 %)	=	18	19
	24-09	ERM (± 2.25 %)	- 2 %		
1980		ERM (± 2.25 %)	=	13	13
1981	05-10	ERM (± 2.25 %)	- 5.5 %	15	15
1982	14-06	ERM (± 2.25 %)	- 4.25%	14	7
1983	21-03	ERM (± 2.25 %)	- 9 %	11	8
1984		ERM (± 2.25 %)	=		
1985		ERM (± 2.25 %)	=		
1986	07-04	ERM (± 2.25 %)	- 3 %		
	04-08	ERM (± 2.25 %)	- 8 %		
1987	12-01	ERM (± 2.25 %)	- 3 %		
1988		ERM (± 2.25 %)	=		
1989		ERM (± 2.25 %)	=		
1990		ERM (± 2.25 %)	=		
1991		ERM (± 2.25 %)	=		
1992		ERM (± 2.25 %)	=		
1993	01-02	ERM (± 2.25 %)	-10 %		
	02-08 [6]	ERM (± 15.0 %) [6]	=		
1994		ERM (± 15.0 %)	=		
1995		ERM (± 15.0 %)	=		
1996		ERM (± 15.0 %)	=		
1997		ERM (± 15.0 %)	=		
1998	16-03	ERM (± 15.0 %)	+ 3 %		

[1] From the mid-1960s, the central bank of Ireland set preannounced credit targets for banks. These targets refer to percentage growth rates and related to private sector credit; target periods did not always correspond with the calendar year. Initially, the targets only served as indicative guidelines, reflecting a lack of instruments in the context of the currency arrangement linking the Irish pound to the British pound. The passage of the Central Bank Act in 1971 granted the bank the power to impose reserve requirements. Following excessive credit growth in the early 1970s, the targets were vigorously pursued through a system of onerous special reserve requirements on excess credit growth. With some fudging, in particular in terms of the statistical coverage, the targets were met 1980-81. In 1983, as the economy moved into recession, the demand for credit fell sharply and the targets became redundant.

[2] Specifies the exchange rate commitment and the relevant fluctuation margin.

[3] Defined as the percentage devaluation (-), revaluation (+) or unchanged parity (=) relative to the British pound and, from 1979 on, to the Deutsche mark.

[4] From 1928 until the inception of the ERM in 1979, the exchange rate of the Irish pound was fixed at a rate of one-for-one, without fluctuation margins, to the British pound.

[5] Ireland participated in the ERM, without interruption, from the outset on 13 March 1979 until the start of EMU.

[6] On 2 August 1993 the general ERM margins were widened from ± 2.25 % to ± 15 %.

Appendix IX

ITALY

	Monetary Policy Target						
	Exchange Rate			Money [1]		Credit [1]	
Year	Date	Target[2]	Outcome[3]	Target	Outcome	Target	Outcome
1975						TDC [4] 17.6 [5]	24.0
1976						TDC [4] 17.5	19.8
1977						TDC [4] 15.2	17.8
1978						TDC [4] 19.3	20.6
	13-03 [6]	ERM (± 6 %)	=			TDC [4] 18.6	18.6
	24-09	ERM (± 6 %)	-2 %				
		ERM (± 6 %)	=			TDC [4] 17.5	18.7
	23-03	ERM (± 6 %)	-6 %			TDC [4] 16.0	18.2
	05-10	ERM (± 6 %)	-8.5 %				
1982	14-06	ERM (± 6 %)	-7 %			TDC [4] 15.1	21.0
1983	21-03	ERM (± 6 %)	-8 %			TDC [4] 18.1	20.6
1984		ERM (± 6 %)	=	M2 10	12.5	CPS [7] 12 [8]	15.3
1985	22-07	ERM (± 6 %)	-8 %	M2 10	11.1	CPS [7] 12	13.0
1986	07-04	ERM (± 6 %)	-3 %	M2 7 - 11	9.4	CPS [7] 7	11.5
1987	12-01	ERM (± 6 %)	-3 %	M2 6 - 9	8.3	CPS [7] 5 - 9	10.3
1988		ERM (± 6 %)	=	M2 6 - 9	8.5	CPS [7] 6 - 10	15.7
1989		ERM (± 6 %)	=	M2 6 - 9	9.5	CPS [7] 7 - 10 [9]	18.1
1990	08-01 [10]	ERM (± 2.25 %)[10]	-3.75 %	M2 6 - 9	9.9		
1991		ERM (± 2.25 %)	=	M2 5 - 8	9.0		
1992	14-09	ERM (± 2.25 %)	-7 %	M2 5 - 7	5.9		
	17-09 [11]	ERM (± 2.25 %)	≠[11]				
1993				M2 5 - 7	7.9	Inflation [12]	
1994				M2 5 - 7	3.1	Objective [12]	Outcome
1995				M2 ≈ 5	1.9	CPI < 4½	5.4
1996	25-11 [13]	ERM (± 15 %)	=	M2 < 5	3.1	CPI < 4	3.9
1997		ERM (± 15 %)	=	M2 < 5 [14]	9.7	CPI < 3	1.8
1998		ERM (± 15 %)	=	M2 ≈ 5	5.8	CPI ≤ 2	1.7

1 Data refer to percentage growth rates for December-December until 1992 and fourth quarter-fourth quarter thereafter. In 1975 the original total domestic credit target referred to the period April-March.

2 Specifies the exchange rate commitment and the relevant fluctuation margin.

3 Defined as the percentage devaluation (-), revaluation (+) or unchanged parity (=) relative to the Deutsche mark, or suspension (≠) of the exchange rate commitment.

4 TDC = Total Domestic Credit; targets were originally expressed in billions of lire.

5 The target was revised to 18.7 % during the course of the year.

6 Italy participated in the wide fluctuation band of the ERM from the outset on 13 March 1979.

7 CPS = Credit to the Private Sector.

8 The target was revised to 14½ % in September 1984.

9 The target was revised to 7-16 % in September 1989.

10 Italy switched from the wide (± 6 %) to the narrow (± 2.25 %) ERM fluctuation band on 8 January 1990, keeping the lower limit unchanged. This implied a devaluation of the central rate of the lira by 3.75 %.

[11] The participation of the lira in the ERM was suspended on 17 September 1992.
[12] Since 1995 the Governor has indicated in May in the concluding remarks of the Annual Report, the inflation objective he considers achievable for the current and next calendar year.
[13] The lira was reinstated in the ERM on 25 November 1996.
[14] The target was revised to "in the order of 10 %" in September 1997.

Appendix X

THE NETHERLANDS

	Monetary Policy Target						
	Exchange Rate			Credit [1]		Money	
Year	Date	Target [2]	Outcome [3]	Target	Outcome	Target	Outcome
1975		Snake [4] (± 2.25 %)	=				
		Worm [5] (± 1.5 %)	=				
1976	16-03	Worm [5] (± 1.5 %)	ǂ [5]				
1977		Snake (± 2.25 %)	=			Liq. ratio -1.0 [6]	-0.3 [7]
1978	17-10	Snake (± 2.25 %)	-2 %			Liq. ratio -1.0 [6]	-0.9 [7]
1979	13-03 [8]	ERM (± 2.25 %)	=			Liq. ratio -1.0 [6]	-0.2 [7]
	24-09	ERM (± 2.25 %)	-2 %				
1980		ERM (± 2.25 %)	=			Liq. ratio -1.0 [6]	-0.8 [7]
1981		ERM (± 2.25 %)	=				
1982		ERM (± 2.25 %)	=				
1983	21-03	ERM (± 2.25 %)	-2 %				
1984		ERM (± 2.25 %)	=				
1985		ERM (± 2.25 %)	=				
1986		ERM (± 2.25 %)	=	5.5-6.0 [9]	10		
1987		ERM (± 2.25 %)	=	1.0-2.0 [10]	4		
1988		ERM (± 2.25 %)	=				
1989		ERM (± 2.25 %)	=	5.0 [11]	5 [11]		
1990		ERM (± 2.25 %)	=				
1991		ERM (± 2.25 %)	=				
1992		ERM (± 2.25 %)	=				
1993	02-08 [12]	ERM (± 2.25 %) [12]	=				
1994		ERM (± 2.25 %) [12]	=				
1995		ERM (± 2.25 %) [12]	=				
1996		ERM (± 2.25 %) [12]	=				
1997		ERM (± 2.25 %) [12]	=				
1998		ERM (± 2.25 %) [12]	=				

[1] During 1977-81 credit ceilings were directly imposed on banks. These primarily served as an instrument to meet the intermediate liquidity ratio targets.

[2] Specifies the exchange rate commitment and the relevant fluctuation margin.

[3] Defined as the percentage devaluation (-), revaluation (+) or unchanged parity (=) relative to the Deutsche mark, or withdrawal (ǂ) of the exchange rate commitment.

[4] The Netherlands participated in the Snake without interruption from the outset on 24 April 1972 until the start of the ERM in 1979.

[5] The Benelux countries maintained a mutual ± 1.5 % narrow margins agreement (the 'Worm') within the context of the Snake until 16 March 1976.

[6] Defined as a minimum reduction in the Liquidity ratio (i.e. M2 as a percentage of nominal income) of on average one percentage point per year during the period 1977-1980.

[7] The outcome corresponds to the decline in the liquidity ratio as reported in the central bank's Annual Report for each respective year. These statistics have been subject to major revisions and definition changes.

[8] The Netherlands participated in the ERM without interruption from the outset on 13 March 1979 until the start of EMU.

[9] Defined as a ceiling for net domestic money creation (i.e. total gross domestic lending adjusted for the share financed through changes in saving deposits).

[10] Following the major target overrun in 1986, the central bank announced a two-year ceiling for 1986-87 of 11-12 %.

[11] Defined as a growth ceiling for the period July 1989 through June 1990 of 6.25 % relative to the average stock in the first quarter of 1989. In light of the outcome over calendar year 1989 of 5 % (effectively 4 % when corrected for specific central bank transactions related to its open market portfolio), the ceiling was suspended as from April 1990.

[12] On 2 August 1993, when the general ERM margins were widened to ± 15 %, Germany and the Netherlands formally agreed (outside the ERM) to maintain a 2.25 % fluctuation margin for their bilateral exchange rate.

Appendix XI

PORTUGAL

	Monetary Policy Target						
	Exchange Rate			Money[1]		Credit[1]	
Year	Date	Target[2]	Outcome[3]	Target	Outcome	Target	Outcome
1975[4]							
1976[4]							
1977	25-08	Crawling peg (-1.00 %)[5]	-4.0 %			TDC 28-29[6]	31.9[6]
1978	05-05	Crawling peg (-1.25 %)[5]	-6.1 %			TDC 21.8[6]	21.4[6]
1979	01-04	Crawling peg (-1.00 %)[5]	=			TDC 20.3[6]	22.1[6]
	01-06	Crawling peg (-0.75 %)[5]	=				
1980	12-02	Crawling peg (-0.75 %)[5]	+6.0 %			*TDC*[6]	
	17-06	Crawling peg (-0.50 %)[5]	=				
1981	02-12	Crawling peg (-0.75 %)[5]	=			*TDC*[6]	
1982	16-06	Crawling peg (-0.75 %)[5]	-9.4 %			*TDC*[6]	
1983	23-03	Crawling peg (-1.00 %)[5]	-2 %			TDC 29.7[6]	22.2
	22-06	Crawling peg (-1.00 %)[5]	-12 %				
1984		Crawling peg (-1.00 %)[5]	=			TDC 22.6[6]	22.1
1985	26-11	Crawl. peg suspended[5]	=			*TDC*[6]	
1986	01-04	Crawling peg (-0.90 %)[5]	=	*L-[7] 18.5[7]*	25.7	*TDC*[6]	
	01-07	Crawling peg (-0.70 %)[5]	=				
	01-10	Crawling peg (-0.60 %)[5]	=				
1987	01-01	Crawling peg (-0.50 %)[5]	=	L-[7] 13.9-17.8	16.8	*TDC*[6]	
1988	01-01	Crawling peg (-0.40 %)[5]	=	L-[7] 10.0-13.0	14.4	*TDC*[6]	
	01-04	Crawling peg (-0.30 %)[5]	=				
	01-07	Crawling peg (-0.25 %)[5]	=				
	01-10	Crawling peg (-0.20 %)[5]	=				
1989	01-01	Crawling peg (-0.25 %)[5]	=	L-[7] 7.5-11.5	8.6	*TDC*[6]	
1990	30-09	Crawling peg (-0.25 %)[8]	‡[8]	*L-[7] 12[7]*	10.9		
	01-10	Basket[8]	=				
1991		Basket[8]	=	*L-[7] 12[7]*	18.1		
1992	05-04	Basket[8]	‡[8]				
	06-04[9]	ERM (± 6.0 %)[9]	=	*L-[7] 12 -16[7]*	13.6		
	23-11	ERM (± 6.0 %)	-6.0 %				
1993	14-05	ERM (± 6.0 %)	-6.5 %				
	02-08[10]	ERM (± 15.0 %)[10]	=				
1994		ERM (± 15.0 %)	=				
1995	06-03	ERM (± 15.0 %)	-3.5 %			**Inflation**	
1996		ERM (± 15.0 %)	=			Reference[11]	Outcome
1997		ERM (± 15.0 %)	=			*HICP <2¼*	1.9
1998		ERM (± 15.0 %)	=			*HICP <2*	2.2

1 The data on money and credit targets refer to year-on-year percentage rates of change in December except for the credit target in 1979 which relates to the final end-March target under the IMF-supported program and the internal money targets in 1990-92 which are annual averages.

2 Specifies the exchange rate commitment, the monthly rate of devaluation (-) under the crawling-peg, and the relevant fluctuation margin (±) under the ERM.

[3] Defined as the percentage devaluation (-), revaluation (+) or unchanged parity (=) relative to the crawling-peg, respectively the ERM central rate or withdrawal (╪) of the exchange rate commitment.

[4] In light of considerable political unrest and institutional changes following the revolution, no explicit targets were pursued in 1975 and 1976. During this period, monetary policy was broadly directed at supporting economic activity, with exchange rate policy being generally orientated at stability vis-à-vis the Snake currencies in 1975 and at compensating the loss of external competitiveness in 1976.

[5] Portugal adopted a crawling peg devaluation regime on 25 August 1977. The monthly rate of crawl was preannounced in terms of the central bank's nominal effective exchange rate (essentially a trade-weighted currency basket) and was frequently adjusted as indicated in parentheses. Initially, the objective was to maintain external competitiveness. In November 1985, the orientation of the exchange regime became counter-inflationary. This was reflected in a suspension of the crawl between November 1985 and April 1986 and, hereafter, in a declining rate of crawl that no longer fully accommodated inflation differentials.

[6] In the period 1977 to 1989, targets for Total Domestic Credit (TDC) were pursued on the basis of individual bank credit ceilings. The targets were primarily geared at objectives for the external position and were not made public, except for those in the three IMF-supported programs covering April 1977-April 1978, June 1978-June 1979 and October 1983-February 1985, the last two of which were upper credit tranche arrangements. These programs included quarterly ceilings. The figures for 1977-78 and 1983-84 relate to the end-December targets and outcomes; the figures for 1979 relate to end-March after which the second program ended and the publication of the targets was discontinued. The use of credit ceilings as instruments of monetary control was suspended in March 1990 (and replaced by recommendations on credit growth) and abandoned altogether in January 1991.

[7] The 1986 and 1990-92 money targets were not announced but were used internally. L- is a broad money aggregate comprising the liquid assets (including Treasury bills) held by the resident non-financial sector.

[8] At end September 1990, amid massive net capital inflows, Portugal abandoned the crawling peg and switched to a more flexible exchange rate regime, according to which the exchange rate was loosely targeted at a trade-weighted basket comprising the ERM's five main currencies (i.e. the Deutsche mark, Spanish peseta, French franc, Pound sterling and the Italian lira) with the weight of the Deutsche mark adjusted to reflect also the relative importance of trade with the Benelux countries. At the same time, however, no fluctuation range was announced and considerable deviations were allowed in short-term exchange rate developments. The basket orientation of exchange rate policy was pursued until the escudo joined the ERM.

[9] On 6 April 1992 Portugal joined the ERM with wide fluctuation margins (± 6 %).

[10] On 2 August 1993 the general ERM margins were widened to ± 15 %.

[11] In March 1997 the central bank announced reference values for inflation for the conduct of monetary policy: average inflation as measured by the EU Harmonised Index of Consumer Prices (HICP) of at most 2¼ per cent in 1997 and at most 2 % in 1998. These targets sought to anchor wages and prices more firmly, and thereby to ensure observation of the low inflation criterion for EMU entry.

Appendix XII

SPAIN

	Monetary Policy Target [1]						
	Inflation [2]		Exchange Rate			Money [2]	
Year	Target	Outcome	Date	Target [3]	Outcome [4]	Target	Outcome
1975						*M3* *18* [5]	19.1
1976						*M3* *16 - 17* [5]	18.6
1977						*M3* *20 - 21* [5]	19.2
1978						M3 14.5 - 19.5	19.8
1979						M3 15.5 - 19.5	19.1
1980						M3 16.0 - 20.0	16.1
1981						M3 14.5 - 18.5	15.9
1982						M3 13.5 - 17.5	16.2
1983						M3 11.0 - 15.0	13.8
1984				*Basket (OECD)* [6]		ALP [7] 10.5 - 14.5	15.1
1985				*Basket (OECD)* [6]		ALP 11.5 - 14.5	13.8
1986				*Basket (EC)* [6]		ALP 9.5 - 12.5	12.5
1987				*Basket (EC)* [6]		ALP 6.5 - 9.5	15.8
1988				*Peseta / DM* [6]		ALP 8.0 - 11.0	13.9
1989			19-06 [8]	ERM [8] (± 6 %)	=	ALP 6.5 - 9.5	13.4
1990				ERM (± 6 %)	=	ALP 6.5 - 9.5	12.6
1991				ERM (± 6 %)	=	ALP 7.0 - 11.0	10.9
1992			17-09	ERM (± 6 %)	-5 %	ALP 8.0 - 11.0	5.2
			23-11	ERM (± 6 %)	-6 %		
1993			14-05	ERM (± 6 %)	-8 %	ALP 4.5 - 7.5	8.7
			02-08 [9]	ERM (± 15 %) [9]	=		
1994				ERM (± 15 %)	=	ALP 3.0 - 7.0	8.2
1995	CPI [10]	4.3	06-03	*ERM (± 15 %)* [11]	-7 %	*ALP* *< 8* [12]	9.2
1996	CPI *3½ - 4* [10]	3.2		*ERM (± 15 %)* [11]	=	*ALP* *< 8* [12]	6.5
1997	CPI < 3 [10]	2.0		*ERM (± 15 %)* [11]	=	*ALP* *< 7* [12]	3.7
1998	CPI ≈ 2 [10]	1.4		*ERM (± 15 %)* [11]	=		

1 From August 1989 through 1990, credit ceilings were used as a policy instrument towards the intermediate money targets.

2 Data relate to the 12-month rate of change in December, unless otherwise indicated.

3 Specifies the exchange rate commitment and the relevant fluctuation margin.

4 Defined as the percentage devaluation (-), revaluation (+) or unchanged parity (=) relative to the Deutsche mark (DM).

5 During 1975-77, the money targets were used for internal policy-making purposes and were not publicly announced. The targets did not cover the full year: in 1975 the 18 % target applied to January-June and was complemented by a 14 % target for July-December. In 1976 the 16-17 % target was complemented by a 20 % target for August and a 21 % target for September-December. In 1977 the target was complemented by a 17-20 % target for August-December.

6 In 1984 a reference index of a trade-weighted currency basket, comprising a group of OECD countries, was adopted internally by the central bank as a prime indicator for monetary policy. When Spain joined the EC in 1986 this index was adapted to cover only the effective exchange rate against the EC countries, excluding Greece and Portugal. In 1988 the central bank switched to using the bilateral exchange rate against the Deutsche mark as a privileged policy indicator.

[7] ALP is the broad money aggregate comprising private sector liquidity.

[8] Spain joined the ERM on 19 June 1989 and participated until the start of EMU.

[9] On 2 August 1993 the general ERM margins were widened to ± 15 %.

[10] In 1995, Spain switched to direct inflation targeting in terms of the 12-month rate of increase of the Consumer Price Index (CPI). At end-1994 when the target was announced for 1997 ('below 3 %') a reference range of '3½-4 %' was set for the opening months of 1996. Similarly, when the target was later announced for 1998 ('about 2 %'), a reference rate of 'about 2½ %' was set for 1997.

[11] From 1995 on, the central bank indicated that the inflation target was the only monetary policy goal. Achievement of this goal was expected to foster the stability of the peseta in the ERM and to ensure observance of the ERM exchange rate stability criterion for EMU entry.

[12] Together with the adoption of direct inflation targeting, the money targets were downgraded to reference ranges defined as ceilings with a medium-term character. These preannounced ranges lapsed at end 1997.

Appendix XIII

SWEDEN

	Monetary Policy Target [1]				
	Inflation		**Exchange rate**		
Year	Target	Outcome	Date	Target [2]	Outcome [3]
1975				Snake [4] (± 2.25 %)	=
1976			17-10	Snake [4] (± 2.25 %)	-3 %
1977			01-04	Snake [4] (± 2.25 %)	-6 %
			28-08 [5]	Snake [4] (± 2.25 %)	ǂ
			29-08	Basket (unspecified) [6]	-10 % [5]
1978				Basket (unspecified) [6]	=
1979				Basket (unspecified) [6]	=
1980				Basket (unspecified) [6]	=
1981			14-09	Basket (unspecified) [6]	-10 %
1982			08-10	Basket (unspecified) [6]	-16 %
1983				Basket (unspecified) [6]	=
1984				Basket (unspecified) [6]	=
1985			27-06	Basket (± 1.50 %) [7]	=
1986				Basket (± 1.50 %)	=
1987				Basket (± 1.50 %)	=
1988				Basket (± 1.50 %)	=
1989				Basket (± 1.50 %)	=
1990				Basket (± 1.50 %)	=
1991			17-05 [8]	ECU [8] (± 1.50 %)	=
1992			19-11 [9]	ECU (± 1.50 %)	ǂ [9]
1993	CPI [10]	4.7			
1994	CPI [10]	2.3			
1995	CPI 2 ± 1 [11]	2.8			
1996	CPI 2 ± 1 [11]	0.8			
1997	CPI 2 ± 1 [11]	0.9			
1998	CPI 2 ± 1 [11]	0.4			

1 Sweden used credit ceilings and other restrictive instruments within a general framework of regulated credit markets until the mid-1980s. However, these credit regulations did not constitute intermediate policy targets, but were instruments towards wider policy objectives, including for the housing market.

2 Specifies the exchange rate commitment and the relevant fluctuation margin.

3 Defined as the percentage devaluation (-), revaluation (+) or unchanged parity (=) relative to the Deutsche mark, the basket or the ECU, respectively, or withdrawal (ǂ) of exchange rate commitment.

4 Sweden was an associated member of the European currency Snake from 19 March 1973 until 28 August 1977.

5 When Sweden withdrew from the Snake on 28 August 1977, the krona was devalued by 10 % relative to the new benchmark, a trade-weighted currency basket.

6 The fixed exchange rate was based on a target value relative to a trade-weighted currency basket comprising Sweden's 15 main trading partners. The relevant fluctuation margin was not publicly specified, but the Riksbank later disclosed that it had been working with a margin of ± 2.25 %.

[7] On 27 June 1985 the Riksbank announced an official fluctuation margin of ± 1.5 % around the target value for the basket.

[8] On 17 May 1991 Sweden announced a shift to a unilateral ECU peg with a central rate that kept the overall exchange rate unchanged. To indicate that this decision was more than a change of currency basket, the Riksbank also announced that Sweden would seek formal association with the EMS, the ultimate goal being participation in the ERM.

[9] The krona was floated on 19 November 1992.

[10] On 15 January 1993 Sweden switched to direct inflation targeting, announcing targets for the inflation outcome two years later. The inflation objective for 1993 and 1994 was to keep the underlying inflation from increasing.

[11] The target was to limit the twelve-month increase in the Consumer Price Index (CPI) to 2 %, with a tolerance interval of plus or minus one percentage point.

Appendix XIVa

UNITED KINGDOM

	Monetary Policy Target[1]						
	Inflation		**Money**		**Exchange Rate**		
Period	Target	Outcome	Target[2]	Outcome	Date	Target[3]	Outcome[4]
04/76-04/77			M3 9-13[5]	8.0			
04/77-04/78			£ M3 9-13	15.1			
04/78-04/79			£ M3 8-12[6]	11.4			
10/78-10/79			£ M3 8-12[7]	13.7			
06/79-10/80			£ M3 7-11[8]	17.2			
02/80-04/81			£ M3 7-11	19.4			
02/81-04/82			£ M3 6-10	12.8[9]			
02/82-04/83			M1 8-12	12.4			
			£ M3 8-12	11.2[9]			
			PSL2[10] 8-12	11.6			
02/83-04/84			M1 7-11	14.0			
			£ M3 7-11	9.5[9]			
			PSL2[10] 7-11	12.6			
02/84-04/85			M0 4-8	5.6			
			£ M3 6-10	11.9[9]			
03/85-03/86			M0 3-7	3.9			
			£ M3 5-9[11]	16.7			
03/86-03/87			M0 2-6	4.0			
			£ M3 11-15[12]	19.0		*£/DM*[13]	⧧[13]
03/87-03/88			M0 2-6	5.5			
03/88-03/89			M0 1-5	6.8			
03/89-03/90			M0 1-5	6.5			
03/90-03/91			M0 1-5	2.7	08-10	ERM (± 6.0 %)[14]	=
03/91-03/92			M0 0-4	1.9		ERM (± 6.0 %)	=
03/92-03/93	RPIX[15] 1-4[16]	3.5	*M0*[17] *0-4*	*4.6*	17-09	ERM (± 6.0 %)	⧧[18]
			M4[17] *4-8*	*3.3*			
03/93-03/94	RPIX[15] 1-4[16]	2.4	*M0*[17] *0-4*	*5.5*			
			M4[17] *3-9*	*5.4*			
03/94-03/95	RPIX[15] 1-4[16]	2.8	*M0*[17] *0-4*	*6.3*			
			M4[17] *3-9*	*4.8*			
03/95-03/96	RPIX[15] 1-4[16]	2.9	*M0*[17] *0-4*	*6.3*			
			M4[17] *3-9*	*10.0*			
03/96-05/97	RPIX[15] 1-2½[16]	2.5[19]	*M0*[20] *0-4*	*6.4*			
			M4[20] *3-9*	*11.2*			
05/97-03/98	RPIX[15] 2½[21]	2.6					

1 The United Kingdom employed the instrument of credit ceilings towards meeting its intermediate money targets until 1979.

2 In the context of the Medium-Term Financial Strategy (MTFS) introduced in 1980, multi-annual targets (for up to five years) were set for each targeted money aggregate. Although these medium-term targets were downgraded to indicator status in 1981, they were maintained until 1991. Specific information on the monetary MTFS objectives is provided in Appendix XIVb.

3 Specifies the exchange rate commitment and the relevant fluctuation margin.

4 Defined as the percentage devaluation (-), revaluation (+) or unchanged parity (=) relative to the Deutsche mark (DM), or withdrawal (⧧) of the exchange rate commitment.

5 The target of 12 % growth for £M3 was superseded by a 9-13 % target in the December 1976 IMF supported program.

6 New target after 6 months.

[7] New target after 8 months.

[8] The original target to April 1980 was extended for one year in October 1979; this was overtaken by a new target set for the period beginning in February 1980.

[9] During the four years 1981/82 to 1984/85 actual £M3 was massaged down on average by nearly 4 % a year through overfunding. With this technique, the Treasury sold more gilt-edged securities than needed to finance the public deficit in order to attract money that would otherwise have been left with banks.

[10] PSL2 is a broad money aggregate compromising private sector liquidity; it was later rechristened M4.

[11] The target was suspended in October 1985.

[12] The target was suspended in October 1986.

[13] The Deutsche mark was informally shadowed at 3 DM per pound for nearly a year until the spring of 1988.

[14] The United Kingdom joined the ERM with wide fluctuation margins (± 6 %) on 8 October 1990.

[15] RPIX = Retail Price Index excluding mortgage interest payments.

[16] On 8 October 1992, the inflation target range was announced together with the further objective of being in the lower part of the range (i.e. 1-2½ %) by the end of the parliamentary period (i.e. by May 1997 at the latest). On 8 June 1995 the inflation target was updated to 2½ % or less beyond the end of the parliamentary period (by which time the earlier target would have expired).

[17] With the adoption of direct inflation targeting in October 1992, money targets were downgraded to monitoring ranges.

[18] The United Kingdom left the ERM on 17 September 1992 and switched to a floating exchange rate regime.

[19] Equivalent to the RPIX inflation rate in May 1997 for which the inflation target of 1-2½ % applied (see note 16).

[20] The monitoring ranges lapsed in May 1997. As part of the decision to make the Bank operationally independent, the Government gave the Bank's Monetary Policy Committee (MPC) discretion over whether or not to employ intermediate targets or monitoring ranges. The MPC subsequently decided not to reinstate the monitoring ranges.

[21] The inflation target is 2½ % at all times. If the inflation rate is more than 1 percentage point from the target, an open letter will be sent by the Governor to the Chancellor explaining the divergence, the policy reaction and the period within which inflation is expected to return to target.

Appendix XIVb

UNITED KINGDOM

Medium-Term Financial Strategy [1]

(Annual percentage increases for March)

£ M3	Year of Publication								Memo
Year Targeted	1979	1980	1981	1982	1983	1984	1985	1986	Outcome
1978/79	8-12								11.4
1979/80	7-11								17.2
1980/81		7-11							19.4
1981/82		6-10	6-10						12.8
1982/83		5-9	5-9	8-12					11.2
1983/84		4-8	4-8	7-11	7-11				9.5
1984/85				6-10	6-10	6-10			11.9
1985/86				5-9	5-9	5-9	5-9		16.7
1986/87						4-8	4-8	‡ [2]	19.0
1987/88						3-7	3-7		20.7
1988/89						2-6	2-6		21.3

M1	Year of Publication						Memo
Year Targeted	1979	1980	1981	1982	1983	1984	Outcome
1982/83				8-12			12.4
1983/84				7-11	7-11		14.0
1984/85				6-10	6-10	‡ [2]	13.5
1985/86					5-9		20.8

PSL2	Year of Publication						Memo
Year Targeted	1979	1980	1981	1982	1983	1984	Outcome
1982/83				8-12			11.6
1983/84				7-11	7-11		12.6
1984/85				6-10	6-10	‡ [2]	14.9
1985/86					5-9		13.4

M0	Year of Publication								Memo
Year Targeted	1984	1985	1986	1987	1988	1989	1990	1991	Outcome
1984/85	4-8								5.6
1985/86	3-7	3-7							3.9
1986/87	2-6	2-6	2-6						4.0
1987/88	1-5	1-5	2-6	2-6					5.5
1988/89	0-4	0-4	1-5	1-5	1-5				6.8
1989/90			1-5	1-5	1-5	1-5			6.5
1990/91				0-4	0-4	0-4	1-5		2.7
1991/92					0-4	0-4	0-4	‡ [2]	1.9
1992/93						-1-3	0-4		4.6
1993/94							-1-3		5.5

[1] The medium-term money growth objectives (beyond one year) were announced as targets in the first (1980) Medium-Term Financial Strategy (MTFS); subsequent MTFS's identified these as indicative ranges. After published medium-term targets were discontinued in 1991, these were reinstated for M0 and M4 during 1993-97, but only as monitoring ranges considered consistent with the overriding inflation target.

[2] Publication of medium-term range discontinued ('ǂ').

Bibliography

Aaltonen, Ari, Esko Aurikko and Jarmo Kontulainen (1994), *Monetary Policy in Finland*, Bank of Finland, No. A:92, Helsinki.

Adams, Charles, and Daniel Gros (1986), 'The Consequences of Real Exchange Rate Rules for Inflation: Some Illustrative Examples', *IMF Staff Papers*, Vol. 33, pp. 439-476.

Aghevli, Bijan, Moshin Khan and Peter Montiel (1991), 'Exchange Rate Policy Issues in Developing Countries: Some Analytical Issues', *IMF Occasional Paper*, No. 78, International Monetary Fund, Washington, DC.

Åkerholm, Johnny, and Anne Brunila (1995), 'Inflation Targeting: The Finnish Experience', in: Leonardo Leiderman and Lars E.O. Svensson (eds.), *Inflation Targets*, CEPR, London.

Akerlof, George A., William T. Dickens and George L. Perry (1996), 'The Macroeconomics of Low Inflation', *Brookings Papers on Economic Activity*, No. 1, pp. 1-59.

Alberola, Enrique, and Timo Tyrväinen (1998), 'Is There Scope for Inflation Differentials in EMU? – An Empirical Evaluation of the Balassa-Samuelson Model in EMU Countries', *Bank of Finland Discussion Papers*, No. 15/98, Bank of Finland, Helsinki.

Alchian, Armen A., and Benjamin Klein (1973), 'On a Correct Measure of Inflation', *Journal of Money, Credit and Banking*, Vol. 5, No. 1, pp. 183-191.

Alesina, Alberto, and Lawrence H. Summers (1993), 'Central Bank Independence and Macroeconomic Performance: Some Comparative Evidence', *Journal of Money, Credit and Banking*, Vol. 25, pp. 151-162.

Alesina, Alberto, Gerald D. Cohen and Nouriel Roubini (1992), 'Macroeconomic Policy and Elections in OECD Democracies', in: Alex Cukierman, Zvi Hercowitz and Leonardo Leiderman (eds.), *Political Economy, Growth, and Business Cycles*, MIT Press, Cambridge, Mass.

Alexander, William E., and Francesco Caramazza (1994), 'Money versus Credit: The Role of Banks in the Monetary Transmission Process', in: Tomás J.T. Baliño and Carlo Cottarelli (eds.), *Frameworks for Monetary Stability – Policy Issues and Country Experiences*, International Monetary Fund, Washington, DC.

Almeida, Alvaro, and Charles Goodhart (1998), 'Does the Adoption of Inflation Targets Affect Central Bank Behaviour?', *Banca Nazionale del Lavoro Quarterly Review*, Special Issue, March, pp. 19-107.

Andersson, Krister, and Claes Berg (1995), 'The Inflation Target in Sweden', in: Andrew G. Haldane (ed.), *Targeting Inflation*, Bank of England, London, pp. 207-223.

Angeloni, Ignazio, and Franco Passacantando (1991), 'Monetary Policy in Italy: Institutional and Economic Aspects', in: *The Orientation of Monetary Policy and the Monetary Decision-Making Process*, BIS Conference Proceedings, No. CB390, Basle, pp. 87-111.

Argy, Victor (1990), 'Choice of Exchange Rate Regime for a Smaller Economy: A Survey of Some Key Issues', in: Victor Argy and Paul De Grauwe (eds.), *Choosing an Exchange Rate Regime: The Challenge for Smaller Industrial Countries*, International Monetary Fund, Washington, DC, pp. 6-81.

Argy, Victor (1983), 'France's Experience with Monetary and Exchange Rate Management: March 1973 to end-1981', *Banca Nazionale del Lavoro Quarterly Review*, pp. 387-411.

Argy, Victor, Anthony Brennan and Glenn Stevens (1990), 'Monetary Targeting: The International Experience', *The Economic Record*, pp. 37-62.

Argy, Victor, and Paul De Grauwe (eds.) (1990), *Choosing an Exchange Rate Regime: The Challenge for Smaller Industrial Countries*, International Monetary Fund, Washington, DC.

Arnold, Ivo J.M. (1997), 'Monetary Targeting in the EMU: Lessons from the United States', *Kredit und Kapital*, No. 3, pp. 348-368.

Arnold, Ivo J.M. (1994), 'The Myth of a Stable European Money Demand', *Open Economies Review*, No. 5, pp. 249-259.

Artis, Michael (1990), 'The United Kingdom and the EMS', in: Paul De Grauwe and Lucas Papademos (eds.), *The European Monetary System in the 1990s*, Longman, London, pp. 286-301.

Artis, Michael J., and Mark P. Taylor (1988), 'Exchange Rates, Interest Rates, Capital Controls and the European Monetary System: Assessing the Track Record', in: Francesco Giavazzi, Stefano Micossi and Marcus Miller (eds.), *The European Monetary System*, Cambridge University Press, Cambridge.

Atkinson, Paul, Adrian Blundell-Wignall, Manuela Rondoni and Helmut Ziegelschmidt (1984), 'The Efficacy of Monetary Targeting: The Stability of Demand for Money in Major OECD Countries', *OECD Economic Studies*, No. 3, Paris.

Ayuso, Juan, and José Luis Escrivá (1998), 'Trends in the Monetary Policy Strategy in Spain', in: José Luis Malo de Molina, José Viñals and Fernando Gutiérrez (eds.), *Monetary Policy and Inflation in Spain*, Macmillan, London.

Bakker, Age F.P. (1996), *The Liberalization of Capital Movements in Europe: The Monetary Committee and Financial Integration, 1958-1994*, Financial and Monetary Policy Studies No. 29, Kluwer Academic Publishers, Dordrecht.

Balassa, Bela (1964), 'The Purchasing Power Parity Doctrine: A Reappraisal', *The Journal of Political Economy*, Vol. 72, No. 6, pp. 584-596.

Banca d'Italia, *Annual Report*, Rome, various issues.

Banca d'Italia, *Economic Bulletin*, Rome, various issues.

Banco de Portugal, *Economic Bulletin*, Lisbon, various issues.

Bank of England, *Inflation Report*, London, various issues.

Bank of England (1972), *Quarterly Bulletin*, Vol. 12, No. 3, London.

Bank of Finland (1996), 'Inflation, Monetary Policy and Economic Performance', *Bank of Finland Bulletin*, Vol. 70, No. 12, pp. 3-8.

Barran, Fernando, Virginie Coudert and Benoît Mojon (1996), 'The Transmission of Monetary Policy in the European Countries', *Document de Travail*, No. 96-03, Centre D'Etudes Prospectives et D'Informations Internationales, Paris.

Barro, Robert J. (1989), 'Interest-Rate Targeting', *Journal of Monetary Economics*, Vol. 23, pp. 3-30.

Barro, Robert J. (1986), 'Rules versus Discretion', in: Colin D. Campbell and William R. Dougan (eds.), *Alternative Monetary Regimes*, The John Hopkins University Press, Baltimore, pp. 16-29.

Barro, Robert J., and David B. Gordon (1983a), 'Rules, Discretion and Reputation in a Model of Monetary Policy', *Journal of Monetary Economics*, Vol. 12, No. 1, pp. 101-121.

Barro, Robert J., and David B. Gordon (1983b), 'A Positive Theory of Monetary Policy in a Natural Rate Model', *Journal of Political Economy*, Vol. 91, No. 4, pp. 589-609.

Bayoumi, Tamim, and Paul R. Masson (1998), 'Liability-Creating versus Non-Liability-Creating Fiscal Stabilization Policies: Ricardian Equivalence, Fiscal Stabilization, and EMU', *Economic Journal*, Vol. 108, pp. 1-20.

Bayoumi, Tamim, and Barry Eichengreen (1996), 'Operationalizing the Theory of Optimum Currency Areas', *CEPR Discussion Paper*, No. 1484, CEPR, London.

Bayoumi, Tamim, and Eswar Prasad (1997), 'Currency Unions, Economic Fluctuations, and Adjustment: Some New Empirical Evidence', *IMF Staff Papers*, Vol. 44, No. 1.

Berg, Claes, and Richard Gröttheim (1997), 'Monetary Policy in Sweden since 1992', in: *Monetary Policy in the Nordic Countries: Experiences since 1992*, BIS Policy Papers, No. 2, Basle.

Berg, Claes, and Lars Jonung (1999), 'Pioneering Price Level Targeting: The Swedish Experience 1931-1937', *Journal of Monetary Economics*, Vol. 43, No. 3, pp. 525-551.

Berger, Helge, and Jakob De Haan (1999), 'A State within a State? – An Event Study on the Bundesbank', *Scottish Journal of Political Economy*, Vol. 46, No. 1, pp. 17-39.

Berk, Jan Marc (1998), 'Monetary Transmission: What Do We Know and How Can We Use It?', *Banca Nazionale del Lavoro Quarterly Review*, No. 205, pp. 145-170.

Berk, Jan Marc, and Carlo C.A. Winder (1994), 'Price Movements in the Netherlands and Germany and the Guilder-Dmark Peg', *De Economist*, Vol. 142, No. 1, pp. 63-74.

Berk, Jan Marc, Aerdt Houben and Jan Kakes (2000), 'The Monetary Policy Strategy of the Eurosystem', in: Peter van Bergeijk, Ron Berndsen and Jos Jansen (eds.), 'Economics of the Euro Area', Edward Elgar, Cheltenham.

Bernanke, Ben, and Ilian Mihov (1997), 'What Does the Bundesbank Target?', *European Economic Review*, No. 41, pp. 1025-1053.

Bernanke, Ben, and Frederic Mishkin (1992), 'Central Bank Behavior and the Strategy of Monetary Policy: Observations from Six Industrialized Countries', in: Olivier J. Blanchard and Stanley Fischer (eds.), *NBER Macroeconomics Annual 1992*, The MIT Press, Cambridge, Mass.

Bernanke, Ben, and Michael Woodford (1997), 'Inflation Forecasts and Monetary Policy', *Journal of Money, Credit and Banking*, Vol. 29, No. 4, pp. 653-684.

Bernanke, Ben, Thomas Laubach, Frederic S. Mishkin, Adam S. Posen (1999), *Inflation Targeting*, Princeton University Press, New Jersey.

Bertola, Giuseppe (1989), 'Factor Mobility, Uncertainty and Exchange Rate Regimes', in: Marcello De Cecco and Alberto Giovannini (eds.), *A European Central Bank? Perspectives on Monetary Unification After Ten Years of the EMS*, Cambridge University Press, Cambridge, pp. 95-119.

Bhandari, Jagdeep S., and Thomas H. Mayer (1990), 'A Note on Saving-Investment Correlations in the EMS', *IMF Working Paper*, WP/90/97.

Bini Smaghi, Lorenzo (1998), 'The Democratic Accountability of the European Central Bank', *Banca Nazionale del Lavoro Quarterly Review*, No. 205, pp. 119-143.

Bini Smaghi, Lorenzo, and Silvia Vori (1993), 'Rating the EC as an Optimal Currency Area: Is it Worse than the US?', *Temi de Discussione*, No. 187, Banca d'Italia, Roma.

Blinder, Alan S. (1998), *Central Banking in Theory and Practice*, The MIT Press, Cambridge, Mass.

Blinder, Alan S. (1997), 'What Central Bankers Could Learn from Academics – and Vice Versa', *Journal of Economic Perspectives*, Vol. 11, No. 2, pp. 3-19.

Blinder, Alan S., and Joseph E. Stiglitz (1983), 'Money, Credit Constraints, and Economic Activity', *American Economic Review*, Papers and Proceedings, pp. 297-302.

Boonstra, Wim W., and Sylvester C.W. Eijffinger (eds.) (1997), *Banks, Financial Markets and Monetary Policy*, NIBE, Amsterdam.

Bordo, Michael D., and Lars Jonung (1997), 'The History of Monetary Regimes – Some Lessons for Sweden and the EMU', *Swedish Economic Policy Review*, Vol. 4, No. 2, pp. 285-358.

Bordo, Michael D., and Anna J. Schwartz (1997), 'Monetary Policy Regimes and Economic Performance: The Historical Record', *NBER Working Paper*, No. 6201, Cambridge, Mass.

Borio, Claudio E.V. (1995), 'The Structure of Credit to the Non-Government Sector and the Transmission Mechanism of Monetary Policy: A Cross-Country Comparison', *BIS Working Paper*, No. 24, Basel.

Boskin, Michael J., Ellen R. Dulberger, Robert J. Gordon, Zvi Griliches and Dale Jorgenson (1996), *Towards a More Accurate Measure for the Cost of Living*, Final Report to the Senate Finance Committee, Washington, DC.

Briault, Clive, Andrew Haldane and Mervyn King (1996), 'Independence and Accountability', *Bank of England Working Paper Series*, No. 49, London.

Britton, Erik, Paul Fisher and John Whitley (1998), 'The Inflation Report Projections: Understanding the Fan Chart', *Bank of England Quarterly Bulletin*, Vol. 38, No. 1, pp. 30-37.

Brown, Francis, Gabriel Fagan and Jerome Henry (1997), 'Money Demand in EU Countries: A Survey', *Staff Paper*, No. 7, European Monetary Institute, Frankfurt.

Brown, W.W., and G.J. Santoni (1981), 'Unreal Estimates of the Real Rate of Interest', *Review*, Federal Reserve Bank of St. Louis, Vol. 63, pp. 18-26.

Brunila, Anne, and Harri Lahdenperä (1995), 'Inflation Targets: Principal Issues and Practical Implementation', in: Andrew G. Haldane (ed.), *Targeting Inflation*, Bank of England, London, pp. 119-134.

Budd, Alan (1998), 'The Role and Operations of the Bank of England Monetary Policy Committee', *The Economic Journal*, Vol. 108, pp. 1783-1794.

Buiter, Willem H. (1999), 'Alice in Euroland', *Journal of Common Market Studies*, Vol. 37, No. 2.

Buiter, Willem H., Giancarlo M. Corsetti and Paolo A. Pensenti (1998), 'Interpreting the ERM Crisis: Country-Specific and Systemic Issues', *Princeton Studies in International Finance*, No. 84, Princeton, New Jersey.

Buiter, Willem H. and Marcus Miller (1981), 'Monetary Policy and International Competitiveness: The Problems of Adjustment', *Oxford Economic Papers*, Vol. 33, pp. 143-175.

Buttiglione, Luigi, Paola Del Giovane and Oreste Tristani (1997), 'Monetary Policy Actions and the Term Structure of Interest Rates: A Cross-Country Analysis', *Temi di Discussione*, No. 306, Banca d'Italia, Roma.

Cabrero, Alberto, José Luis Escrivá, Emilio Muñoz, Juan Peñalosa (1998), 'The Controllability of a Monetary Aggregate in EMU', *Servicio de Estudios*, No. 9817, Banco de España, Madrid.

Calmfors, Lars, and John Drifill (1988), 'Bargaining Structure, Corporatism and Macroeconomic Performance', *Economic Policy*, No. 6, pp. 14-61.

Capel, Jeannette, and Aerdt Houben (1998), 'Asset Inflation in the Netherlands: Assessment, Economic Risks and Monetary Policy Implications', *BIS Conference Proceedings*, Basle.

Caranza, Cesare, and Antonio Fazio (1983), 'Methods of Monetary Control in Italy: 1974-1983', in: Donald R. Hodgman (ed.), *The Political Economy of Monetary Policy: National and International Aspects*, Conference Series, No. 26, Federal Reserve Bank of Boston, pp. 65-87.

Cecchetti, Stephen G. (1997), 'Central Bank Policy Rules: Conceptual Issues and Practical Considerations', *NBER Working Paper*, No. 6306, Cambridge, Mass.

Chadha, Jagjit S., and Norbert G.J. Janssen (1997), 'What Monetary Authorities Do – An Examination of Reaction Functions for Germany, Japan, the UK and the US', *Swiss Journal of Economics and Statistics*, Vol. 133 (3), pp. 455-476.

Chowdhury, Abdur R. (1991), 'The Relationship between the Inflation Rate and its Variability: The Issues Reconsidered', *Applied Economics*, Vol. 23, pp. 993-1003.

Christensen, Anders Møller, and Jacob Topp (1997), 'Monetary Policy in Denmark since 1992', in: *Monetary Policy in the Nordic Countries: Experiences since 1992*, BIS Policy Papers, No. 2, Basle.

Clarida, Richard, Jordi Galí and Mark Gertler (1997), 'Monetary Policy Rules in Practice: Some International Evidence', *CEPR Discussion Paper*, No. 1750, CEPR, London.

Clark, Todd E. (1994), 'Nominal GDP Targeting Rules: Can They Stabilize the Economy?', *Economic Review*, Federal Reserve Bank of Kansas, pp. 11-25.

Cobham, David, and Jean-Marin Serre (1986), 'Monetary Targeting: A Comparison of French and UK Experience', *Royal Bank of Scotland Review*, No. 149, pp. 24-42.

Collins, Susan M. (1988), 'Inflation and the European Monetary System', in: Francesco Giavazzi, Stefano Micossi and Marcus Miller (eds.), *The European Monetary System*, Cambridge University Press, Cambridge.

Committee for the Study of Economic and Monetary Union (The Delors Committee) (1989), *Report on Economic and Monetary Union in the European Community*, Office for Official Publications of the European Communities, Luxembourg.

Cottarelli, Carlo, and Curzio Giannini (1997), 'Credibility Without Rules? – Monetary Frameworks in the Post-Bretton Woods Era', *IMF Occasional Paper*, No. 154, International Monetary Fund, Washington, DC.

Crockett, Andrew (1994a), 'Monetary Implications of Increased Capital Flows', in: *Changing Capital Markets: Implications for Monetary Policy*, Federal Reserve Bank of Kansas City, pp. 331-363.

Crockett, Andrew (1994b), 'Rules versus Discretion in Monetary Policy', in: J. Onno De Beaufort Wijnholds, Sylvester C.W. Eijffinger and Lex H. Hoogduin (eds.), *A Framework for Monetary Stability*, Kluwer Academic Publishers, Dordrecht, pp. 165-184.

Cukierman, Alex (1995), 'Towards a Systematic Comparison Between Inflation Targets and Monetary Targets', in: Leonardo Leiderman and Lars E.O. Svensson (eds.), *Inflation Targets*, CEPR, London.

Cukierman, Alex (1992), *Central Bank Strategy, Credibility, and Independence: Theory and Evidence*, MIT Press, Cambridge, Mass.

Cukierman, Alex, Pantelis Kalaitsidakis, Lawrence H. Summers and Steven B. Webb (1993), 'Central Bank Independence, Growth, Investment, and Real Rates', *Carnegie-Rochester Conference Series on Public Policy*, Vol. 39, pp. 95-140.

Cukierman, Alex, and Allan H. Meltzer (1986), 'A Theory of Ambiguity, Credibility, and Inflation Under Discretion and Asymmetric Information', *Econometrica*, Vol. 54, No. 5, pp. 1099-1128.

Danmarks Nationalbank, *Annual Report*, Copenhagen, various issues.

Danmarks Nationalbank, *Monetary Review*, Copenhagen, various issues.

Debelle, Guy (1997), 'Inflation Targeting in Practice', *IMF Working Paper*, WP/97/35.

De Bondt (1999), 'Banks and Monetary Transmission in Europe: Empirical Evidence', *Banca Nazionale del Lavoro Quarterly Review*, No. 209, pp. 149-168.

De Grauwe, Paul (1997), *The Economics of Monetary Integration*, Oxford University Press, Third Edition, Oxford.

De Grauwe, Paul (1990), 'The Cost of Disinflation and the European Monetary System', *Open Economies Review*, No. 1, pp. 147-173.

De Grauwe, Paul, and Wim Vanhaverbeke (1990), 'Exchange Rate Experiences of Small EMS Countries: Belgium, Denmark and the Netherlands', in: Victor Argy and Paul De Grauwe (eds.), *Choosing an Exchange Rate Regime: The Challenge for Smaller Industrial Countries*, International Monetary Fund, Washington, DC.

De Greef, Irene, Paul Hilbers and Lex Hoogduin (1998), 'Moderate Monetarism: A Brief Survey of Dutch Monetary Policy in the Post-War Period', *DNB Staff Reports*, No. 28, De Nederlandsche Bank, Amsterdam.

De Haan, Jakob (1997), 'The European Central Bank: Independence, Accountability and

De Haan, Jakob, Fabian Amtenbrink and Sylvester C.W. Eijffinger (1998), 'Accountability of Central Banks: Aspects and Quantification', *Center for Economic Research*, No. 9854, Tilburg.

De Haan, Jakob, and Willem Kooi (1997), 'What Really Matters: Conservativeness or Independence?', *Banca Nazionale del Lavoro Quarterly Review*, No. 200, pp. 23-38.

De Haan, Jakob, Klaas Knot and Jan E. Sturm (1993), 'On the Reduction of Disinflation Costs: Fixed Exchange Rates or Central Bank Independence?', *Banca Nazionale del Lavoro Quarterly Review*, No. 187, pp. 429-443.

De Haan, Jakob, and Jan E. Sturm (1992), 'The Case for Central Bank Independence', *Banca Nazionale del Lavoro Quarterly Review*, No. 182, pp. 305-327.

Deutsche Bundesbank (1995), 'The Monetary Policy of the Deutsche Bundesbank', Frankfurt.

Dornbusch, Rudi, Carlo Favero and Francesco Giavazzi (1998), 'Immediate Challenges for the ECB – Issues in Formulating a Single Monetary Policy', *Economic Policy*, Vol. 26, pp. 15-64.

Dornbusch, Rudiger (1989), 'Credibility, Debt and Unemployment: Ireland's Failed Stabilization', *Economic Policy*, No. 8, pp. 174-201.

Drazen, Allan, and Paul R. Masson (1994), 'Credibility of Policies versus Credibility of Policymakers', *Quarterly Journal of Economics*, Vol. 109, pp. 735-754.

Egebo, Thomas, and A. Steven Englander (1992), 'Institutional Commitments and Policy Credibility: A Critical Survey and Empirical Evidence from the ERM', *OECD Economic Studies*, No. 18, Paris.

Eichengreen, Barry (1993), 'Labor Markets and European Monetary Unification', in: Paul R. Masson and Mark P. Taylor (eds.), *Policy Issues in the Operation of Currency Unions*, Cambridge University Press, pp. 130-162.

Eichengreen, Barry, and Charles Wyplosz (1993), 'The Unstable EMS', *Brookings Papers on Economic Activity*, No. 1, pp. 51-143.

Eijffinger, Sylvester (1996), 'Future European Monetary Policy', *Inaugural Lecture*, Humboldt University, Berlin.

Eijffinger, Sylvester (1993), 'Convergence of Monetary Policies in Europe – Concepts, Targets and Instruments', in: Klaus Gretchmann (ed.), *Economic and Monetary Union: Implications for National Policy-Makers*, Martinus Nijhoff Publishers, Dordrecht.

Eijffinger, Sylvester, and Jakob De Haan (1996), 'The Political Economy of Central Bank Independence', *Princeton Special Papers in International Economics*, No. 19, Princeton.

Eijffinger, Sylvester, and Eric Schaling (1993), 'Central Bank Independence: Criteria and Indices', *Kredit und Kapital*, Supplements to Heft 13, Berlin.

Escrivá, José Luis, and José Luis Malo de Molina (1991), 'Implementation of Spanish Monetary Policy in the Framework of European Integration', in: *The Orientation of Monetary Policy and the Monetary Decision-Making Process*, BIS Conference Proceedings, No. CB390, Basle, pp. 150-171.

Escrivá, José Luis, and Román Santos (1991), 'A Study of the Change in the Instrumental Variable of the Monetary Control Outline in Spain', *Economic Bulletin*, Banco de España, October, pp. 45-47.

European Central Bank (1999a), 'The Stability-Oriented Monetary Policy Strategy of the Eurosystem', *ECB Monthly Bulletin*, Frankfurt, January, pp. 39-50.

European Central Bank (1999b), 'Euro Area Monetary Aggregates and Their Role in the Eurosystem's Monetary Policy Strategy', *ECB Monthly Bulletin*, Frankfurt, February, pp. 29-40.

European Central Bank (1999c), 'The Role of Short-Term Economic Indicators in the Analysis of Price Developments in the Euro Area, *ECB Monthly Bulletin*, Frankfurt, April, pp. 27-39.

European Commission (1996), 'Economic Evaluation of the Internal Market', *European Economy*, No. 4, Brussels.

European Commission (1995), 'The Commission Services' Method for the Cyclical Adjustment of Government Budget Balances', *European Economy*, No. 60, Brussels.

European Commission (1990), 'One Market, One Money', *European Economy*, No. 44, Brussels.

European Commission (1989), *The EMS: Ten Years of Progress in European Monetary Co-operation*, Brussels.

European Monetary Institute (1997), *The Single Monetary Policy in Stage Three – Elements of the Monetary Policy Strategy of the ESCB*, Frankfurt am Main.

Fackler, James, and Andrew Silver (1983), 'Credit Aggregates as Policy Targets', *Quarterly Review*, Federal Reserve Bank of New York, pp. 2-9.

Fase, Martin M.G. (1987), 'Dutch Monetarism in Retrospect', in: Donald A. Walker (ed.), *Perspectives on the History of Economic Thought*, Vol. 2, pp. 187-198.

Fase, Martin M.G. (1985), 'Monetary Control: The Dutch Experience – Some Reflections on the Liquidity Ratio', in: C. Van Ewijk and J.J. Klant (eds.), *Monetary Conditions for Economic Recovery*, Martinus Nijhoff Publishers, Dordrecht, pp. 95-125.

Fase, Martin M.G. and Carlo C.H. Winder (1993), 'The Demand for Money in the Netherlands and the Other EC Countries', *De Economist*, Vol. 141, No. 4, pp. 471-496.

Fforde, John (1983), 'The United Kingdom – Setting Monetary Objectives', in: Paul Meek (ed.), *Central Bank Views on Monetary Targeting*, Federal Reserve Bank of New York, New York, pp. 51-59.

Fischer, Stanley (1996), 'Why are Central Banks Pursuing Long-Run Price Stability?', in: *Achieving Price Stability*, Symposium Proceedings, Federal Reserve Bank of Kansas City, pp. 7-34.

Fischer, Stanley (1994), 'Modern Central Banking', in: Forrest Capie, Charles Goodhart, Stanley Fischer and Norbert Schnadt (eds.), *The Future of Central Banking*, Cambridge University Press, pp. 262-308.

Fischer, Stanley (1990), 'Rules versus Discretion in Monetary Policy', in: Benjamin M. Friedman and Frank H. Hahn (eds.), *Handbook of Monetary Economics*, Volume II, pp. 1155-1184.

Flood, Robert P., and Peter Isard (1989), 'Monetary Policy Strategies', *IMF Staff Papers*, Vol. 36, No. 3, pp. 612-632.

Flood, Robert P., and Michael Mussa (1994), 'Issues Concerning Nominal Anchors for Monetary Policy', *NBER Working Paper*, No. 4850, Cambridge, Mass.

Folkerts-Landau, David, and Donald J. Mathieson (1989), 'The European Monetary System in the Context of the Integration of European Financial Markets', *IMF Occasional Paper*, No. 66, International Monetary Fund, Washington, DC.

Foot, Michael D.K.W. (1981), 'Monetary Targets: Their Nature and Record in the Major Economies', in: Brian Griffiths and Geoffrey E. Wood (eds.), *Monetary Targets*, St. Martin's Press, New York.

Forder, James (1998), 'The Case for an Independent European Central Bank: A Reassessment of Evidence and Sources', *European Journal of Political Economy*, No. 14, pp. 53-71.

Forder, James (1996), 'On the Assessment and Implementation of "Institutional" Remedies', *Oxford Economic Papers*, No. 48, pp. 39-51.

Fournier, Pierre-Etienne, and Monique Alleron (1991), 'The Monetary Policy Decision-Making Process', in: *The Orientation of Monetary Policy and the Monetary Decision-Making Process*, BIS Conference Proceedings, No. CB390, Basle, pp. 58-68.

Frankel, Jeffrey A. (1990), 'International Nominal Targeting: A Proposal for Monetary Policy Coordination in the 1990s', *The World Economy*, Vol. 13, No. 2, pp. 263-273.

Frankel, Jeffrey A., and With Menzie Chinn (1995), 'The Stabilizing Properties of a Nominal GNP Rule', *Journal of Money, Credit and Banking*, Vol. 27, pp. 318-334.

Frankel, Jeffrey A., and Andrew K. Rose (1996), 'The Endogeneity of the Optimum Currency Area Criteria', *CEPR Discussion Paper*, No. 1473, CEPR, London.

Frankel, Jeffrey A., and Shang-Jin Wei (1995), 'European Integration and the Regionalization of World Trade and Currencies: The Economics and the Politics', in: Barry Eichengreen, Jeffry Frieden and Jürgen von Hagen (eds.), *Monetary and Fiscal Policy in an Integrated Europe*, Springer-Verlag Press, New York, pp. 202-231.

Friedman, Benjamin M. (1994), 'Intermediate Targets versus Information Variables as Operating Guides for Monetary Policy', in: J. Onno De Beaufort Wijnholds, Sylvester C.W. Eijffinger and Lex H. Hoogduin (eds.), *A Framework for Monetary Stability*, Kluwer Academic Publishers, Dordrecht, pp. 165-184.

Friedman, Benjamin M. (1990), 'Targets and Instruments of Monetary Policy', in: Benjamin M. Friedman and Frank H. Hahn (eds.), *Handbook of Monetary Economics*, Volume II, pp. 1185-1230.

Friedman, Benjamin M. (1983), 'Monetary Policy with a Credit Aggregate Target', *Carnegie-Rochester Conference Series on Public Policy*, Vol. 18, pp. 117-48.

Friedman, Milton (1968), 'The Role of Monetary Policy', *The American Economic Review*, Vol. 58, No. 1, pp. 1-17.

Friedman, Milton (1953), 'The Case for Flexible Exchange Rates', in: Milton Friedman (ed.) (1970), *Essays in Positive Economics*, University of Chicago Press, pp. 157-203.

Fuhrer, Jeffrey C., and Brian F. Madigan (1997), 'Monetary Policy When Interest Rates are Bounded at Zero', *The Review of Economics and Statistics*, Vol. 79, No. 4, pp. 573-585.

Gagnon, Joseph (1993), 'Exchange Rate Variability and the Level of International Trade', *Journal of International Economics*, No. 34, pp. 269-287.

Garrett, Geoffrey, and Christopher Way (1995), 'The Sectoral Composition of Trade Unions, Corporatism, and Economic Performance', in: Barry Eichengreen, Jeffry Frieden and Jürgen von Hagen (eds.), *Monetary and Fiscal Policy in an Integrated Europe*, Springer-Verlag Press, New York, pp. 38-61.

George, Eddie (1998), 'Exchange Rates: An Intractable Aspect of Monetary Policy', *Quarterly Bulletin*, Bank of England, London, pp. 178-181, May.

Ghosh, Atish, and Steven Phillips (1998), 'Inflation, Disinflation, and Growth', *IMF Working Paper*, WP/98/68.

Ghosh, Atish R., Anne-Marie Gulde, Jonathan D. Ostry and Holger C. Wolf (1995), 'Does the Nominal Exchange Regime Matter?', *IMF Working Paper*, WP/95/121.

Giavazzi, Francesco, and Alberto Giovannini (1989), *Limiting Exchange Rate Flexibility – The European Monetary System*, The MIT Press, Cambridge, Mass.

Giavazzi, Francesco, and Alberto Giovannini (1988), 'The Role of the Exchange Rate Regime in a Disinflation: Empirical Evidence on the European Monetary System', in: Francesco Giavazzi, Stefano Micossi and Marcus Miller (eds.), *The European Monetary System*, Cambridge University Press, Cambridge.

Giavazzi, Francesco, Stefano Micossi and Marcus Miller (eds.) (1988), *The European Monetary System*, Cambridge University Press, Cambridge.

Giavazzi, Francesco, and Marco Pagano (1988), 'The Advantage of Tying One's Hands: EMS Discipline and Central Bank Credibility', *European Economic Review*, No. 32, pp. 1055-1082.

Giavazzi, Francesco, and Luigi Spaventa (1990), 'The "New" EMS', in: Paul De Grauwe and Lucas Papademos (eds.), *The European Monetary System in the 1990s*, Longman, London, pp. 65-85.

Glück, Heinz, Dieter Proske and John A. Tatom (1992), 'Monetary and Exchange Rate Policy in Austria: An Early Example of Policy Coordination', in: Homa Motamen-Scobie and Christian Starck (eds.), *Economic Policy Coordination in an Integrating Europe*, Bank of Finland, Helsinki.

Gnan, Ernest (1994), 'Austria's Hard Currency Policy and European Monetary Integration', in: Eduard Hochreiter (ed.), 'Austrian Exchange Rate Policy and European Monetary Integration – Selected Issues', *Working Paper*, No. 19, Oesterreichische Nationalbank.

Goodfriend, Marvin (1986), 'Monetary Mystique: Secrecy and Central Banking', *Journal of Monetary Economics*, Vol. 17, pp. 63-92.

Goodhart, Charles A.E. (1999), 'Central bankers and uncertainty', *Bank of England Quarterly Bulletin*, Vol. 39, No. 1, pp. 102-121.

Goodhart, Charles A.E. (1997), 'Whither Now?', *Banca Nazionale del Lavoro Quarterly Review*, No. 203, pp. 383-430.

Goodhart, Charles A.E. (1995), 'Price Stability and Financial Fragility', in: *Financial Stability in a Changing Environment*, Proceedings of the 1993 Bank of Japan Conference, Macmillan, London.

Goodhart, Charles A.E. (1989), *Money, Information and Uncertainty*, 2nd ed., MIT Press, Cambridge, Mass.

Goodhart, Charles A.E. (1984), *Monetary Theory and Practice: The UK Experience*, Macmillan, London.

Goodhart, Charles A.E., and José Viñals (1994), 'Strategy and Tactics of Monetary Policy: Examples from Europe and the Antipodes', in: J.C. Fuhrer (ed.), *Goals, Guidelines and Constraints Facing Monetary Policymakers*, Federal Reserve Bank of Boston, pp. 139-187.

Green, John H. (1996), 'Inflation Targeting: Theory and Policy Implications', *IMF Working Paper*, WP/96/65.

Grilli, Vittorio, Donato Masciandaro and Guido Tabellini (1991), 'Political and Monetary Institutions and Public Financial Policies in the Industrial Countries', *Economic Policy*, No. 13, pp. 342-392.

Groeneveld, Johannes M., Kees G. Koedijk and Clemens J.M. Kool (1998), 'Inflation Dynamics and Monetary Strategies: Evidence from Six Industrialized Countries', *Open Economies Review*, No. 9, pp. 21-38.

Gros, Daniel, and Alfred Steinherr (1997), 'Openness and the Cost of Fixing Exchange Rates in a Mundell-Fleming World', in: Mario Blejer, Jacob A. Frenkel, Leonardo Leiderman and Assaf Razin (eds.), *Optimum Currency Areas: New Analytical and Policy Developments*, International Monetary Fund, Washington, DC.

Gros, Daniel, and Niels Thygesen (1992), *European Monetary Integration: From the European Monetary System to European Monetary Union*, St. Martin's Press, New York.

Guitián, Manuel (1994), 'The Choice of an Exchange Rate Regime', in: Richard Barth and Chorng-Huey Wong (eds.), *Approaches to Exchange Rate Policy*, IMF Institute, International Monetary Fund, Washington, DC, pp. 13-36.

Guitián, Manuel (1994a), 'The Role of Monetary Policy in IMF Programs', in: J. Onno De Beaufort Wijnholds, Sylvester C.W. Eijffinger and Lex H. Hoogduin (eds.), *A Framework for Monetary Stability*, Kluwer Academic Publishers, Dordrecht, pp. 185-209.

Guitián, Manuel (1994b), 'Rules or Discretion in Monetary Policy: National and International Perspectives', in: Tomás J.T. Baliño and Carlo Cottarelli (eds.), *Frameworks for Monetary Stability – Policy Issues and Country Experiences*, International Monetary Fund, Washington, DC.

Guitián, Manuel (1972), 'Credit Versus Money as an Instrument of Control', reprinted in: *The Monetary Approach to the Balance of Payments* (1977), International Monetary Fund, Washington, DC, pp. 227-242.

Guitián, Manuel, Massimo Russo and Giuseppe Tulio (1988), 'Policy Coordination in the European Monetary System', *IMF Occasional Paper*, No. 61, International Monetary Fund, Washington, DC.

Gutiérrez, Fernando (1998), 'Monetary Policy Following the Law on the Autonomy of the Bank of Spain', in: José Luis Malo de Molina, José Viñals and Fernando Gutiérrez (eds.), *Monetary Policy and Inflation in Spain*, Macmillan, London.

Gylfason, Thorvaldur (1990), 'Exchange Rate Policy, Inflation and Unemployment: The Nordic EFTA Countries', in: Victor Argy and Paul De Grauwe (eds.), *Choosing an Exchange Rate Regime: The Challenge for Smaller Industrial Countries*, International Monetary Fund, Washington, DC, pp. 163-192.

Hacche, Graham, and John Townend (1981), 'Exchange Rates and Monetary Policy: Modelling Sterling's Effective Exchange Rate, 1972-80', in W.A. Eltis and P.J.N. Sinclair (eds.), *The Money Supply and the Exchange Rate*', Oxford University Press, Oxford, pp. 201-47.

Haldane, Andrew G. (1995a), 'Inflation Targets', *Bank of England Quarterly Bulletin*, Vol. 35, No. 3, pp. 250-259.

Haldane, Andrew G. (ed.) (1995b), *Targeting Inflation*, Bank of England, London.

Haldane, Andrew G., and Nicoletta Batini (1998), 'Forward-Looking Rules for Monetary Policy', *NBER Working Paper*, No. 6543, Cambridge, Mass.

Haldane, Andrew G., and Christopher K. Salmon (1995), 'Three Issues on Inflation Targets', in: Andrew G. Haldane (ed.), *Targeting Inflation*, Bank of England, London, pp. 170-201.

Hall, Robert E. (1985), 'Monetary Strategy with an Elastic Price Standard', in: *Price Stability and Public Policy*, Symposium Proceedings, Federal Reserve Bank of Kansas City, p. 137-159.

Halttunen, Hannu, and Sixten Korkman (1983), 'External Shocks and Adjustment Policies in Finland, 1973-80', in: Marcello De Ceccho (ed.), *International Economic Adjustment – Small Countries and the European Monetary System*, Basil Blackwell, Oxford.

Heikensten, Lars, and Anders Vredin (1998), 'Inflation Targeting and Swedish Monetary Policy – Experience and Problems', *Sveriges Riksbank Quarterly Review*, No. 4, Stockholm.

Helg, Rodolfo, Paolo Manasse, Tommaso Monacelli and Riccardo Rovelli (1994), 'How much (A)symmetry in Europe? Evidence from Industrial Sectors', *IGIER Working Paper*, No. 70.

Hilbers, Paul (1998), 'Financial Sector Reform and Monetary Policy in the Netherlands', *IMF Working Paper*, WP/98/19.

Hilton, Spence, and Vivek Moorthy (1990), 'Targeting Nominal GNP', in: *Intermediate Targets and Indicators for Monetary Policy – A Critical Survey*, Federal Reserve Bank of New York, New York, pp. 232-273.

Hochreiter, Eduard, and Georg Winckler (1995), 'The Advantages of Tying Austria's Hands: The Success of the Hard Currency Strategy', *European Journal of Political Economy*, Vol. 11, pp. 83-111.

Hoffmann, Johannes (1998), 'Problems of Inflation Measurement in Germany', *Discussion Paper*, No. 1/98, Economic Research Group of the Deutsche Bundesbank, Frankfurt.

Honohan, Patrick (1997), 'Currency Board or Central Bank? Lessons from the Irish Pound's Link with Sterling, 1928-79', *Banca Nazionale del Lavoro Quarterly Review*, No. 200, pp. 39-67.

Hoogduin, Lex, and Olaf Sleijpen (1999), 'The Role of Stabilisation Policies in EMU', Paper prepared for a Workshop on Tools for Regional Stabilisation organised by the Dutch Ministry of Economic Affairs, The Hague.

Hörngren, Lars, and Hans Lindberg (1993), 'The Struggle to Turn the Swedish Krona into a Hard Currency', *Arbetsrapport*, No. 8, Sveriges Riksbank.

Hörngren, Lars, and Ann Westman-Mårtensson (1991), 'Swedish Monetary Policy: Institutions, Targets and Instruments', in: *The Orientation of Monetary Policy and the Monetary Decision-Making Process*, BIS Conference Proceedings, No. CB390, Basle, pp. 172-190.

Houben, Aerdt (1997), 'Exchange Rate Policy and Monetary Strategy Options in the Philippines: The Search for Stability and Sustainability', *IMF Paper on Policy Analysis and Assessment*, PPAA/97/4.

Icard, André (1994a), 'The Transmission of Monetary Policy in an Environment of Deregulation and Exchange Rate Stability: The French Experience', *Journal of Monetary Economics*, Vol. 33, pp. 87-103.

Icard, André (1994b), 'Monetary Policy and Exchange Rates: The French Experience', in: J. Onno De Beaufort Wijnholds, Sylvester C.W. Eijffinger and Lex H. Hoogduin (eds.), *A Framework for Monetary Stability*, Kluwer Academic Publishers, Dordrecht, pp. 239-255.

International Monetary Fund (1984), 'Exchange Rate Volatility and the Level of International Trade', *IMF Occasional Paper*, No. 28, International Monetary Fund, Washington, DC.

Isard, Peter, and Liliana Rojas-Suarez (1986), 'Velocity of Money and the Practice of Monetary Targeting: Experience, Theory and the Policy Debate', *Staff Studies for the World Economic Outlook*, International Monetary Fund, Washington, DC.

Issing, Otmar (1999a), 'The Euro – Four Weeks After the Start', Speech delivered to the European-Atlantic Group on January 28, House of Commons, London.

Issing, Otmar (1999b), 'The Eurosystem: Transparent and Accountable or "Willem in Euroland" ', *Journal of Common Market Studies*, Vol. 37, No. 3.

Issing, Otmar (1997), 'Monetary Targeting in Germany: The Stability of Monetary Policy and of the Monetary System', *Journal of Monetary Economics*, Vol. 39, pp. 67-79.

Issing, Otmar (1992), 'Theoretical and Empirical Foundations of the Deutsche Bundesbank's Monetary Targeting', *Intereconomics*, HWWA-Institut für Wirtschaftsforschung, Vol. 27, No. 6, pp. 289-300.

James, Harold (1996), *International Monetary Cooperation Since Bretton Woods*, Oxford University Press, Oxford.

Jonung, Lars (1979), 'Knut Wicksell's Norm of Price Stabilization and Swedish Monetary Policy in the 1930's', *Journal of Monetary Economics*, Vol. 5, pp. 459-496.

Judson, Ruth, and Athanosios Orphanides (1996), 'Inflation, Volatility and Growth', *Finance and Economics Discussion Series*, No. 96-19, Board of Governors of the Federal Reserve System, Washington, DC.

Jurgensen, Philippe (1983), 'Report of the Working Group on Exchange Market Intervention', US Treasury, Washington, DC.

Kahn, George A. (1988), 'Nominal GNP: An Anchor for Monetary Policy?', *Economic Review*, Federal Reserve Bank of Kansas, pp. 18-35.

Kakes, Jan (2000), *Monetary Transmission: The Credit View*, Edward Elgar, Cheltenham.

Kenen, Peter B. (1969), 'The Theory of Optimum Currency Areas: An Eclectic View', in: Robert A. Mundell and Alexander K. Swoboda (eds.), *Monetary Problems of the International Economy*, University of Chicago Press, Chicago, pp. 41-60.

Kessler, G.A. (1958), 'Statement Concerning the Method of Monetary Analysis Used by the Netherlands Bank', in: J. Onno De Beaufort Wijnholds, Jakob De Haan, Lex Hoogduin, Piet Mallekoote and Sandra Wesseling (eds.) (1990), *Monetaire Diagnose en Therapie*, De Nederlandsche Bank, Amsterdam, pp. 63-70.

Keynes, John Maynard (1936), *The General Theory of Employment, Interest, and Money*, First Harvest Harcourt Brace Edition 1964, Florida.

Kieler, Mads, and Tuomas Saarenheimo (1998), 'Differences in Monetary Policy Transmission? – A Case not Closed', *EC Economic Papers*, No. 12, Brussels.

King, Mervyn (1997), 'The Inflation Target Five Years On', *Bank of England Quarterly Bulletin*, Vol. 37, No. 4, pp. 434-442.

King, Mervyn (1994), 'The Transmission Mechanism of Monetary Policy', *Bank of England Quarterly Bulletin*, Vol. 34, No. 3, pp. 261-267.

Kloten, Norbert (1992), 'The Control of Monetary Aggregates in the Federal Republic of Germany under Changing Conditions', in: Stephen F. Frowen and Dietman Kath (eds.), *Monetary Policy and Financial Innovations in Five Industrial Countries*, Macmillan, London.

Knot, Klaas, Jan-Egbert Sturm and Jakob De Haan (1998), 'The Credibility of the European Exchange Rate Mechanism', *Oxford Economic Papers*, Vol. 50, pp. 186-200.

Kole, Linda S., and Ellen E. Meade (1995), 'German Monetary Targeting: A Retrospective View', *Federal Reserve Bulletin*, Vol. 81, No. 10, Board of Governors of the Federal Reserve System, Washington, DC, pp. 917-931.

König, Reiner (1996), 'The Bundesbank's Experience of Monetary Targeting', in: Deutsche Bundesbank (ed.), *Monetary Policy Strategies in Europe: A Symposium at the Deutsche Bundesbank*, Verlag Vahlen, München.

Kool, Clemens J.M. (1995), 'Monetary Policy Under Fixed Exchange Rates: Lessons From the Netherlands, Belgium and Austria, 1973-1992', *De Economist*, No. 143, pp. 329-351.

Korkman, Sixten (1978), "The Devaluation Cycle', *Oxford Economic Papers*, Vol. 30.

Kremers, Jeroen J.M. (1990), 'Gaining Policy Credibility for a Disinflation – Ireland's Experience in the EMS', *IMF Staff Papers*, Vol. 37, No. 1, pp. 116-145.

Krugman, Paul (1979), 'A Model of Balance-of-Payments Crises', *Journal of Money, Credit and Banking*, Vol. 11, No. 3, pp. 311-325.

Kruse, D.C. (1980), *Monetary Integration in Western Europe: EMU, EMS and Beyond*, Butterworths European Studies, London.

Kydland, Finn E., and Edward E. Prescott (1977), 'Rules Rather than Discretion: The Inconsistency of Optimal Plans', *Journal of Political Economy*, Vol. 85, No. 3, pp. 473-91.

Lane, Timothy D., Alessandro Prati and Mark E.L. Griffiths (1995), 'An Inflation Targeting Framework for Italy', *IMF Paper on Policy Analysis and Assessment*, PPAA/95/4.

Lawson, Nigel (1993), *The View from No. 11 – Memoirs of a Tory Radical*, Transworld Publishers, London.

Leddin, Anthony, and Brendan Walsh (1995), 'The Economy of Ireland – Fiscal, Monetary and Exchange Rate Policy', in: J.W. O'Hagan (ed.), *The Economy of Ireland: Policy and Performance of a Small Open Economy*, Gill and Macmillan, Dublin.

Lehmussaari, Olli-Pekka, Antti Suvanto and Laura Vajanne (1992), 'The Currency Band and Credibility: The Finnish Experience', *Bank of Finland Discussion Papers*, No. 37/92.

Leiderman, Leonardo, and Lars E.O. Svensson (eds.) (1995), *Inflation Targets*, CEPR, London.

Ludlow, Peter (1982), *The Making of the European Monetary System*, Butterworths European Studies, Butterworth Scientific, London.

Marston, Richard C. (1982), 'Wages, Relative Prices and the Choice Between Fixed and Flexible Exchange Rates', *Canadian Journal of Economics*, pp. 87-103.

Masson, Paul R. (1995), 'Gaining and Losing ERM Credibility: The Case of the United Kingdom', *Economic Journal*, Vol. 105, pp. 571-582.

Masson, Paul R., Miguel Savastano and Sunil Sharma (1997), 'The Scope for Inflation Targeting in Developing Countries', *IMF Working Paper*, WP/97/130.

Masson, Paul R., and Mark P. Taylor (1993), 'Currency Unions: A Survey of the Issues', in: *Policy Issues in the Operation of Currency Unions*, Cambridge University Press, pp. 3-51

Masson, Paul R., and Mark P. Taylor (1992), 'Issues in the Operation of Monetary Unions and Common Currency Areas', in: Morris Goldstein, Peter Isard, Paul R. Masson and Mark P. Taylor (eds.), 'Policy Issues in the Evolving International Monetary System', *IMF Occasional Paper*, No. 96, International Monetary Fund, Washington, DC.

Mastropasqua, Cristina, Stefano Micossi and Roberto Rinaldi (1988), 'Interventions, Sterilisation and Monetary Policy in European Monetary System Countries, 1979-87', in: Giavazzi, Micossi and Miller (eds.), *The European Monetary System*, Cambridge University Press, Cambridge.

McCallum, Bennett T. (1996), 'Inflation Targeting in Canada, New Zealand, Sweden, and the United Kingdom, and in General', *NBER Working Paper*, No. 5579, Cambridge, Mass.

McCallum, Bennett T. (1995), 'Two Fallacies Concerning Central-Bank Independence', *American Economic Review*, Vol. 85, No. 2, pp. 205-211.

McCallum, Bennett T. (1987), 'The Case for Rules in the Conduct of Monetary Policy: A Concrete Example', *Economic Review*, Federal Reserve Bank of Richmond, pp. 10-18.

McCallum, Bennett T. (1985), 'On Consequences and Criticisms of Monetary Targeting', *Journal of Money, Credit and Banking*, Vol. 17, No. 4, pp. 570-597.

McCallum, Bennett T. (1981), 'Price Level Determinacy with an Interest Rate Policy Rule and Rational Expectations', *Journal of Monetary Economics*, Vol. 8, pp. 319-329.

McClam, Warren D. (1978), 'Targets and Techniques of Monetary Policy in Western Europe', *Banca Nazionale del Lavoro Quarterly Review*, pp. 3-27.

McKinnon, Robert I. (1963), 'Optimum Currency Areas', *The American Economic Review*, Vol. 53, No. 4, pp. 717-725.

Meltzer, Allan H. (1987), 'Limits of Short-Run Stabilization Policy', *Economic Inquiry*, Vol. 25, pp. 1-14.

Michielsen, Jan (1994), 'Credibility of Exchange Rate Policies: The Belgian Experience', in: H.M. Scobie (ed.), *The European Single Market – Monetary and Fiscal Policy Harmonization*, Chapman & Hall, London.

Mishkin, Frederic S. (1997), 'Strategies for Controlling Inflation', *NBER Working Paper*, No. 6122, Cambridge, Mass.

Mishkin, Frederic S., and Adam Posen (1997), 'Inflation Targeting: Lessons from Four Countries', Federal Reserve Bank of New York, *Economic Policy Review*, pp. 9-110.

Monticelli, Carlo, and Luca Papi (1996), *European Integration, Monetary Co-ordination, and the Demand for Money*, Clarendon Press, Oxford.

Monticelli, Carlo, and Marc-Olivier Strauss-Kahn (1992), 'Broad Monetary Aggregates and National Money Demand in Europe', *Economies et Sociétés*, No. 9, pp. 147-197.

Mote, Larry R. (1988), 'Looking Back: The Use of Interest Rates in Monetary Policy', *Economic Perspectives*, Federal Reserve Bank of Chicago, Vol. 12, pp. 15-29.

Mundell, Robert A. (1961), 'A Theory of Optimum Currency Areas', *The American Economic Review*, Vol. 51, No. 4, pp. 657-665.

Nederlandsche Bank, De, *Annual Report*, Amsterdam, various issues.

Obstfeld, Maurice (1995), 'The Logic of Currency Crises', in: Barry Eichengreen, Jeffry Frieden and Jürgen von Hagen (eds.), *Monetary and Fiscal Policy in an Integrated Europe*, Springer-Verlag Press, New York, pp. 62-90.

Obstfeld, Maurice, and Kenneth Rogoff (1995), 'The Mirage of Fixed Exchange Rates', *NBER Working Paper*, No. 5191, Cambridge, Mass.

Oort, Coen J. (1979), 'Managed Floating in the European Community', in: Samuel I. Katz (ed.), *US-European Monetary Relations*, American Enterprise Institute for Public Policy Research, Washington, DC, pp. 194-219.

Organisation for Economic Co-operation and Development (1979), *Monetary Targets and Inflation Control*, OECD Monetary Studies Series, Paris.

Orphanides, Athanasios, and Volker Wieland (1998), 'Price Stability and Monetary Policy Effectiveness when Nominal Interest Rates are Bounded at Zero', *Finance and Economics Discussion Series Papers*, No. 1998-35, US Federal Reserve Board.

Ortega, Eloisa, and José-Maria Bonilla (1995), 'Reasons for Adopting an Inflation Target', in: Andrew G. Haldane (ed.), *Targeting Inflation*, Bank of England, London, pp. 49-58.

Padoa-Schioppa, Tommaso (1988), 'The EMS: A Long-Term View', in: Francesco Giavazzi, Stefano Micossi and Marcus Miller (eds.), *The European Monetary System*, Cambridge University Press, Cambridge.

Padoa-Schioppa, Tommaso (1985), 'Policy Cooperation and the EMS Experience', in: Willem H. Buiter and Richard C. Marston (eds.), *International Economic Policy Coordination*, Cambridge University Press, Cambridge.

Papademos, Lucas (1990), 'Greece and the EMS: Issues, Prospects and a Framework for Analysis', in: Paul De Grauwe and Lucas Papademos (eds.), *The European Monetary System in the 1990s*, Longman, London, pp. 251-285.

Papademos, Lucas, and Franco Modigliani (1990), 'The Supply of Money and the Control of Nominal Income', in: Benjamin M. Friedman and Frank H. Hahn (eds.), *Handbook of Monetary Economics*, Vol. I, pp. 399-494b.

Passacantando, Franco (1996), 'Building an Institutional Framework for Monetary Stability: The Case of Italy (1979-1994)', *Banca Nazionale del Lavoro Quarterly Review*, No. 196, pp. 83-132.

Persson, Torsten, and Guido Tabellini (1993), 'Designing Institutions for Monetary Stability', *Carnegie-Rochester Conference Series on Public Policy*, Vol. 39, pp. 53-84.

Pikkarainen, Pentti, Antti Suvanto, Juhana Hukkinen and Ilmo Pyyhtiä (1997), 'Monetary Policy in Finland: Experiences since 1992', in: *Monetary Policy in the Nordic Countries: Experiences since 1992*, BIS Policy Papers, No. 2, Basle.

Polak, Jacques J. (1997), 'The IMF Monetary Model at Forty', *IMF Working Paper*, WP/97/49.

Polak, Jacques J. (1991), 'The Changing Nature of IMF Conditionality', *Essays in International Finance*, No. 184, Princeton University Press, New Jersey.

Polak, Jacques J. (1988), 'Economic Policy Objectives and Policymaking in the Major Industrial Countries', in: Wilfried Guth (moderator), *Economic Policy Coordination*, International Monetary Fund, Washington, DC, pp. 1-25.

Polak, Jacques J. and Victor Argy (1971), 'Credit Policy and the Balance of Payments', reprinted in: *The Monetary Approach to the Balance of Payments*, International Monetary Fund, Washington, DC, pp. 205-225.

Poole, William (1970), 'Optimal Choice of Monetary Policy Instruments in a Simple Stochastic Macro Model', *Quarterly Journal of Economics*, Vol. 84, pp. 197-216.

Posen, Adam S. (1993), 'Why Central Bank Independence Does Not Cause Low Inflation: There Is No Institutional Fix for Politics', *Amex Bank Review*, pp. 40-65.

Pringle, Robert (ed.) (1995), 'The Bank of Greece', *Central Banking*, Vol. 6, No. 3, pp. 54-85.

Puro, Ilkka (1984), 'Finland's Currency Index System and Its Development', *Bank of Finland Monthly Bulletin*, Vol. 58, No. 2, pp 26-30.

Quintyn, Marc, and Jef Vuchelen (1992), 'Monetary Policy', in: M.A.G. Van Meerhaeghe (ed.), *Belgium and EC Membership Evaluated*, St. Martin's Press, New York.

Radecki, Lawrence J. (1990), 'A Review of Credit Measures as a Policy Variable', in: *Intermediate Targets and Indicators for Monetary Policy – A Critical Survey*, Federal Reserve Bank of New York, New York, pp. 183-231.

Ramaswamy, Ramana, and Torsten Sloek (1997), 'The Real Effects of Monetary Policy in the European Union: What are the Differences?', *IMF Working Paper*, WP/97/160.

Raymond, Robert (chairman) (1990), 'Special Report on a Common Framework for the Monitoring of Monetary Policies', Report by the Group of Experts under the Chairmanship of Mr. Raymond, *Committee of Governors of the Central Banks of the Member States of the European Economic Community*, Basle.

Raymond, Robert (1983), 'The Formulation and Implementation of Monetary Policy in France', in: Paul Meek (ed.), *Central Bank Views on Monetary Targeting*, Federal Reserve Bank of New York, New York, pp. 105-117.

Richardson, G. (1978), 'Reflections on the Conduct of Monetary Policy', *Bank of England Quarterly Bulletin*, Vol. 18, No. 1, pp. 31-37.

Rogoff, Kenneth (1998), 'The Risks of Unilateral Exchange Rate Pegs', Paper prepared for a Conference on Implications of Globalisation for Macroeconomic organised by the Bank of Korea, Seoul.

Rogoff, Kenneth (1985), 'The Optimal Degree of Commitment to an Intermediate Monetary Target', *Quarterly Journal of Economics*, Vol. 100, pp. 1169-1189.

Rojo, Luis A., and J. Aríztegui (1984), 'Financial Innovation and Monetary Policy in Spain', in: *Financial Innovation and Monetary Policy*, BIS, Basle.

Sardelis, Christopher (1993), 'Targeting a European Monetary Aggregate', *Economic Papers*, No. 102, European Commission, Brussels.

Sarel, Michael (1996), 'Nonlinear Effects of Inflation on Economic Growth', *IMF Staff Papers*, Vol. 43, No. 1, pp. 199-215.

Sargent, T.J., and N. Wallace (1981), 'Some Unpleasant Monetarist Arithmetic', *Federal Reserve Bank of Minneapolis Quarterly Review*, No. 5, pp. 1-17.

Sargent, T.J., and N. Wallace (1975), '"Rational" Expectations, the Optimal Monetary Instrument, and the Optimal Money Supply Rule', *Journal of Political Economy*, Vol. 83, pp. 241-254.

Schlesinger, Helmut (1983), 'The Setting of Monetary Objectives in Germany', in: Paul Meek (ed.), *Central Bank Views on Monetary Targeting*, Federal Reserve Bank of New York, New York, pp. 6-17.

Schlesinger, Helmut (1979), 'Recent Experience with Monetary Policy in the Federal Republic of Germany', in: Karl Brunner and Manfred J. M. Neumann (eds.), *Inflation, Unemployment and Monetary Control*, Berlin, pp. 303-320.

Shigehara, Kumiharu (1996), 'The Options Regarding the Concept of a Monetary Policy Strategy', in: Deutsche Bundesbank (ed.), *Monetary Policy Strategies in Europe: A Symposium at the Deutsche Bundesbank*, Verlag Vahlen, München.

Solomon, Robert (1982), *The International Monetary System: 1945-1981*, Harper and Row, New York.

Soskice, David (1990), 'Wage Determination: The Changing Role of Institutions in Advanced Industrialized Countries', *Oxford Review of Economic Policy*, Vol. 6, No. 4, pp. 36-61.

Steindel, Charles (1990), 'Interest Rates as Targets and Indicators for Monetary Policy', in: *Intermediate Targets and Indicators for Monetary Policy – A Critical Survey*, Federal Reserve Bank of New York, New York, pp. 274-305.

Stella, Peter (1997), 'Do Central Banks Need Capital?', *IMF Working Paper*, WP/97/83.

Stokman, Ad C.J. (1995), 'Effect of Exchange Rate Risk on Intra-EC Trade', *De Economist*, Vol. 143, No. 1, pp. 41-54.

Summers, Lawrence (1991), 'How Should Long-Term Monetary Policy Be Determined?', *Journal of Money, Credit and Banking*, Vol. 23, No. 3, pp. 625-631.

Svensson, Lars E.O. (1997), 'Inflation Forecast Targeting: Implementing and Monitoring Inflation Targets', *European Economic Review*, No. 41, pp. 1111-1146.

Svensson, Lars E.O. (1995), 'The Swedish Experience of an Inflation Target', in: Leonardo Leiderman and Lars E.O. Svensson (eds.), *Inflation Targets*, CEPR, London, pp. 69-89.

Sveriges Riksbank (1992), *Monetary Policy with a Flexible Exchange Rate*, Stockholm.

Swank, Job, and Lidwin van Velden (1997), 'Instruments, Procedures and Strategies of Monetary Policy: An Assessment of Possible Relationships for 21 OECD Countries', *BIS Conference Proceedings*, Vol. 6, pp. 1-13.

Szász, André (1999), *The Road to European Monetary Union*, St. Martin's Press, New York.

Tavlas, George A. (1994), 'The Theory of Monetary Integration', *Open Economies Review*, Vol. 5, No. 2, pp. 211-230.

Tavlas, George A. (1993), 'The 'New' Theory of Optimum Currency Areas', *The World Economy*, Vol. 16, No. 6, pp. 663-685.

Taylor, John B. (1996), 'How Should Monetary Policy Respond to Shocks While Maintaining Long-Run Price Stability?', in: *Achieving Price Stability*, Symposium Proceedings, Federal Reserve Bank of Kansas, Kansas City, Miss., pp. 181-196.

Taylor, John B. (1993), 'Discretion versus Policy Rules in Practice', *Carnegie-Rochester Conference Series on Public Policy*, Vol. 39, pp. 195-214.

Taylor, John B. (1985), 'What Would Nominal GNP Targeting do to the Business Cycle?', *Carnegie-Rochester Conference Series on Public Policy*, Vol. 22, pp. 61-84.

Taylor, John B. (1981), 'On the Relation between the Variability of Inflation and the Average Inflation Level', in: Karl Brunner and Allan H. Meltzer (eds.), *The Costs and Consequences of Inflation*, Carnegie-Rochester Conference Series on Public Policy, Vol. 15, pp. 57-85.

Thatcher, Margaret (1993), *The Downing Street Years*, HarperCollins Publishers, New York.

Thomas, Alun H. (1994), 'Expected Devaluation and Economic Fundamentals', *IMF Staff Papers*, Vol. 41, No. 2, pp. 262-285.

Thomas, Alun H. (1994a), 'The Response of Wages and Labor Supply Movements to Employment Shocks Across Europe and the United States', *IMF Working Paper*, WP/94/158.

Thygesen, Niels (1979), 'The European Monetary System: Precursors, First Steps and Policy Options', *Bulletin de la Banque Nationale de Belgique*, Vol. 54, pp. 57-125.

Tobin, James (1983), 'Monetary Policy: Rules, Targets, and Shocks', *The Journal of Money, Credit and Banking*, Vol. 15, No. 4, pp. 506-518.

Torres, Francisco S. (1990). 'Portugal, the EMS and 1992: Stabilization and Liberalization', in: Paul De Grauwe and Lucas Papademos (eds.), *The European Monetary System in the 1990s*, Longman, London, pp. 227-250.

Townend, John C. (1991), 'The Orientation of Monetary Policy and the Monetary Policy Decision-Making Process in the United Kingdom', in: *The Orientation of Monetary Policy and the Monetary Decision-Making Process*, BIS Conference Proceedings, No. CB390, Basle, pp. 201-214.

Triffin, Robert (1960), *Gold and the Dollar Crisis – The Future of Convertibility*, Yale University Press, New Haven.

Turnovsky, Stephen J. (1976), 'The Relative Stability of Alternative Exchange Rate Systems in the Presence of Random Disturbances', *Journal of Money, Credit and Banking*, Vol. 8, pp. 29-50.

UK Treasury (1998), 'The Harmonised Index of Consumer Prices: Some Factual Information', Pre-Budget Report.

Ungerer, Horst (1997), *A Concise History of European Monetary Integration: From EPU to EMU*, Quorum Books, London.

Ungerer, Horst, Owen Evans and Peter Nyberg (1983), 'The European Monetary System: The Experience, 1979-82', *IMF Occasional Paper*, No. 19, International Monetary Fund, Washington, DC.

Ungerer, Horst, Owen Evans, Thomas Mayer and Philip Young (1986), 'The European Monetary System: Recent Developments', *IMF Occasional Paper*, No. 48, International Monetary Fund, Washington, DC.

Ungerer, Horst, Jouko J. Hauvonen, Augusto Lopez-Claros and Thomas Mayer (1990), 'The European Monetary System: Developments and Perspectives', *IMF Occasional Paper*, No. 73, International Monetary Fund, Washington, DC.

Vaciago, Giacomo (1985), 'Monetary Policy with Credit Targets: The Italian Experience', *Greek Economic Review*, Vol. 7, No. 1, pp. 1-33.

Van Bergeijk, Peter, Ron Berndsen and Jos Jansen (eds.) (2000), *The Economics of the Euro Area*, Edward Elgar, Cheltenham.

Van Riet, Ad G. (1993), 'Studies of EC Money Demand: Survey and Assessment', *Quarterly Bulletin*, 1992/4, De Nederlandsche Bank, pp. 63-75.

Vega, Juan L. (1994), 'Is the ALP Long-Run Demand Function Stable?', *Documento de Trabajo*, No. 9422, Banco de España.

Viñals, José (1990), 'The EMS, Spain and Macroeconomic Policy', in: Paul de Grauwe and Lucas Papademos (eds.), *The European Monetary System in the 1990s*, Longman, London, pp. 201-226.

Visco, Ignazio (1995), 'Inflation, Inflation Targeting and Monetary Policy: Notes for Discussion on the Italian Experience', in: Leonardo Leiderman and Lars E.O. Svensson (eds.), *Inflation Targets*, CEPR, London, pp. 142-168.

Vlaar, Peter J.G., and Helene Schuberth (1998), 'Monetary Transmission and Controllability of Money in Europe: A Structural Vector Error Correction Approach', *Research Memorandum WO&E*, No. 544, De Nederlandsche Bank, Amsterdam.

Volcker, Paul, and Toyoo Gyohten (1992), *Changing Fortunes – The World's Money and the Threat to American Leadership*, Random House, New York.

Von Hagen, Jürgen (1999), 'Money Growth Targeting by the Bundesbank', *Journal of Monetary Economics*, Vol. 43, No. 3, pp. 681-701.

Von Hagen, Jürgen (1995), 'Inflation and Monetary Targeting in Germany', in: Leonardo Leiderman and Lars E.O. Svensson (eds.), *Inflation Targets*, CEPR, London.

Von Hagen, Jürgen (1989), 'Money Targeting with Exchange Rate Constraints: The Bundesbank in the 1980s', *Working Paper*, Federal Reserve Bank of St. Louis.

Wallich, Henry C., and Peter M. Keir (1978), 'The Role of Operating Guides in U.S. Monetary Policy: A Historical Review', *Kredit und Kapital*, No. 1, pp. 30-51.

Walsh, Brendan M. (1983), 'Ireland in the European Monetary System: The Effects of a Change in Exchange Regime', in: Marcello De Ceccho (ed.), *International Economic Adjustment – Small Countries and the European Monetary System*, Basil Blackwell, Oxford.

Walsh, Carl E. (1995), 'Optimal Contracts for Central Bankers', *American Economic Review*, No. 85, pp. 150-167.

Walters, Alan (1986), *Britain's Economic Renaissance*, Oxford University Press, Oxford.

Wellink, Arnout (1994), 'The Economic and Monetary Relation between Germany and the Netherlands', in: Age Bakker, Henk Boot, Olaf Sleijpen and Wim Vanthoor (eds.), *Monetary Stability through International Cooperation – Essays in Honour of André Szász*, De Nederlandsche Bank, Amsterdam, pp. 67-84.

Wellink, Arnout (1989), 'Dutch Monetary Policy in an Integrating Europe', in: Bub Von Norbert, Dieter Duwendag and Rudolf Richter (eds.), *Geldwertsicherung und Wirtschaftsstabilität*, Frankfurt am Main.

Wenninger, John (1990), 'Monetary Aggregates as Intermediate Targets', in: *Intermediate Targets and Indicators for Monetary Policy: A Critical Survey*, Federal Reserve Bank of New York, New York, pp. 67-108.

Williamson, John, and Marcus H. Miller (1987), *Targets and Indicators: A Blueprint for the International Coordination of Economic Policy*, Institute for International Economics, Washington, DC.

Winder, Carlo C.A. (1997), 'On the Construction of European Area-Wide Aggregates – A Review of the Issues and Empirical Evidence', *Irving Fisher Committee Bulletin*, No. 1, pp. 15-23.

Woodford, Michael (1994), 'Nonstandard Indicators for Monetary Policy: Can Their Usefulness Be Judged from Forecasting Regressions?', in: N. Gregory Mankiw (ed.), *Monetary Policy*, University of Chicago Press, Chicago.

Yates, Anthony (1998), 'Downward Nominal Rigidity and Monetary Policy', *Bank of England Working Paper Series*, No. 82, London.

Zijlstra, Jelle (1985), 'Monetary Theory and Monetary Policy: A Central Banker's View', in: C. Goedhart, G.A. Kessler, J. Kymmell and F. De Roos (eds.), *Jelle Zijlstra, A Central Banker's View*, Financial and Monetary Policy Studies, No. 10, Martinus Nijhoff Publishers, Dordrecht.

Author index

Subject Index

FINANCIAL AND MONETARY POLICY STUDIES

* 1. J.S.G. Wilson and C.F. Scheffer (eds.): *Multinational Enterprises.* Financial and Monitary Aspects. 1974 ISBN 90-286-0124-4

* 2. H. Fournier and J.E. Wadsworth (eds.): *Floating Exchange Rates.* The Lessons of Recent Experience. 1976 ISBN 90-286-0565-7

* 3. J.E. Wadsworth, J.S.G. Wilson and H. Fournier (eds.): *The Development of Financial Institutions in Europe, 1956–1976.* 1977 ISBN 90-286-0337-9

* 4. J.E. Wadsworth and F.L. de Juvigny (eds.): *New Approaches in Monetary Policy.* 1979 ISBN 90-286-0848-6

* 5. J.R. Sargent (ed.), R. Bertrand, J.S.G. Wilson and T.M. Rybczynski (ass. eds.): *Europe and the Dollar in the World-Wide Disequilibrium.* 1981 ISBN 90-286-0700-5

* 6. D.E. Fair and F.L. de Juvigny (eds.): *Bank Management in a Changing Domestic and International Environment.* The Challenges of the Eighties. 1982 ISBN 90-247-2606-9

* 7. D.E. Fair (ed.) in cooperation with R. Bertrand: *International Lending in a Fragile World Economy.* 1983 ISBN 90-247-2809-6

8. P. Salin (ed.): *Currency Competition and Monetary Union.* 1984 ISBN 90-247-2817-7

* 9. D.E. Fair (ed.) in cooperation with F.L. de Juvigny: *Government Policies and the Working of Financial Systems in Industrialized Countries.* 1984 ISBN 90-247-3076-7

10. C. Goedhart, G.A. Kessler, J. Kymmell and F. de Roos (eds.): *Jelle Zijlstra, A Central Banker's View.* Selected Speeches and Articles. 1985 ISBN 90-247-3184-4

11. C. van Ewijk and J.J. Klant (eds.): *Monetary Conditions for Economic Recovery.* 1985 ISBN 90-247-3219-0

*12. D.E. Fair (ed.): *Shifting Frontiers in Financial Markets.* 1986 ISBN 90-247-3225-5

13. E.F. Toma and M. Toma (eds.): *Central Bankers, Bureaucratic Incentives, and Monetary Policy.* 1986 ISBN 90-247-3366-9

*14. D.E. Fair and C. de Boissieu (eds.): *International Monetary and Financial Integration.* The European Dimension. 1988 ISBN 90-247-3563-7

15. J. Cohen: *The Flow of Funds in Theory and Practice.* A Flow-Constrained Approach to Monetary Theory and Policy. 1987 ISBN 90-247-3601-3

16. W. Eizenga, E.F. Limburg and J.J. Polak (eds.): *The Quest for National and Global Economic Stability.* In Honor of Hendrikus Johannes Witteveen. 1988 ISBN 90-247-3653-6

*17. D.E. Fair and C. de Boissieu (eds.): *The International Adjustment Process.* New Perspectives, Recent Experience and Future Challenges for the Financial System. 1989 ISBN 0-7923-0013-0

18. J.J. Sijben (ed.): *Financing the World Economy in the Nineties.* 1989 ISBN 0-7923-0090-4

19. I. Rizzo: *The 'Hidden' Debt.* With a Foreword by A.T. Peacock. 1990 ISBN 0-7923-0610-4

*20. D.E. Fair and C. de Boissieu (eds.): *Financial Institutions in Europe under New Competitive Conditions.* 1990 ISBN 0-7923-0673-2

21. R. Yazdipour (ed.): *Advances in Small Business Finance.* 1991 ISBN 0-7923-1135-3

FINANCIAL AND MONETARY POLICY STUDIES

22. D.E. Fair and C. de Boissieu (eds.): *Fiscal Policy, Taxation and the Financial System in an Increasingly Integrated Europe.* 1992 ISBN 0-7923-1451-4
23. W.C. Boeschoten: *Currency Use and Payment Patterns.* 1992 ISBN 0-7923-1710-6
24. H.A. Benink: *Financial Integration in Europe.* 1993 ISBN 0-7923-1849-8
25. G. Galeotti and M. Marrelli (eds.): *Design and Reform of Taxation Policy.* 1992 ISBN 0-7923-2016-6

*26. D.E. Fair and R. Raymond (eds.): *The New Europe: Evolving Economic and Financial Systems in East and West.* 1993 ISBN 0-7923-2159-6

27. J.O. de Beaufort Wijnholds, S.C.W. Eijffinger and L.H. Hoogduin (eds.): *A Framework for Monetary Stability.* Papers and Proceedings of an International Conference (Amsterdam, The Netherlands, 1993). 1994 ISBN 0-7923-2667-9

*28. D.E. Fair and R. Raymond (eds.): *The Competitiveness of Financial Institutions and Centres in Europe.* 1994 ISBN 0-7923-3131-1

29. A.F.P. Bakker: *The Liberalization of Capital Movements in Europe.* The Monetary Committee and Financial Integration, 1958–1994. 1996 ISBN 0-7923-3591-0
30. H.A. Benink: *Coping with Financial Fragility and Systemic Risk.* 1995 ISBN 0-7923-9612-X
31. K. Alders, K. Koedijk, C. Kool and C. Winder (eds.): *Monetary Policy in a Converging Europe.* Papers and Proceeding of an International Workshop. 1996 ISBN 0-7923-3746-8

*32. F. Bruni, D.E. Fair, R. O'Brien (eds.): *Risk Management in Volatile Financial Markets.* 1996 ISBN 0-7923-4053-1

33. M. Balling, E. Hennesey, R. O'Brien (eds.): *Corporate Governance, Financial Markets and Global Convergence.* 1997 ISBN 0-7923-4825-7
34. A.C.F.J. Houben: *The Evolution of Monetary Policy Strategies in Europe.* 2000 ISBN 0-7923-7869-5

*Published on behalf of the *Société Universitaire Européenne de Recherches Financières* (SUERF), consisting the lectures given at Colloquia, organized and directed by SUERF.

Kluwer Academic Publishers – Dordrecht / Boston / London